SunSoft™ Solaris® 2.* for Managers and Administrators

Kent Parkinson, Curt Freeland, and Dwight McKay

ONWORD® PRESS

SunSoft™ Solaris® 2.*
for Managers and Administrators

By Kent Parkinson, Curt Freeland, and Dwight McKay

Published by:
OnWord Press
2530 Camino Entrada
Santa Fe, NM 87505-4835 USA

Copyright © 1995 Kent Parkinson, Curt Freeland, and Dwight McKay
SAN 694-0269
First Edition, 1995
10 9 8 7 6 5 4
Printed in the United States of America

Cataloging-in-Publication Data

```
Parkinson, Kent, Freeland, Curt, and McKay, Dwight
SunSoft Solaris 2.* for Managers and Administrators / by Kent
Parkinson, Curt Freeland, and Dwight McKay -- 1st ed.

p.   cm.

Includes index.

SunSoft Solaris (computer software) I. Title

92-060076

ISBN 0-934605-75-0
```

Trademark Acknowledgments

SunSoft™, Solaris®, DeskSet®, and OpenWindows™ are trademarks of Sun Microsystems, Inc. OnWord Press is a registered trademark of High Mountain Press, Inc. Many other products and services are mentioned in this book that are either trademarks or registered trademarks of their respective corporations. OnWord Press and the authors make no claim to these marks.

Warning and Disclaimer

This book is designed to provide information about SunSoft Solaris. Every effort has been made to make the book as complete, accurate, and up to date as possible; however, no warranty or fitness is implied.

The information is provided on an "as-is" basis. The authors and OnWord Press shall have neither liability nor responsibility to any person or entity with respect to any loss or damages in connection with or arising from the information contained in this book.

About the Authors

Kent Parkinson is a principal of Parkinson and Associates, a UNIX systems consulting and training firm located in West Lafayette, Indiana. A former faculty member of Purdue University, Kent has worked with UNIX systems for over 20 years, and with Sun/Solaris operating environments since their respective introductions.

Curt Freeland, manager of Systems Engineering at Purdue University's engineering computer network, earned a bachelor's degree in systems engineering from the same university. He has worked with various UNIX operating systems since 1979, and with SunSoft Solaris 2 since its introduction in 1992. Curt has contributed articles to trade publications such as *Advanced Systems* (formerly *SunWorld*), the *SuperUser* systems administration newsletter, and *Hardcopy*.

Dwight McKay is a system manager with over 10 years of experience managing Sun systems and integrating them with a variety of other UNIX, VMS, and Macintosh systems. He has a bachelor's degree in psychology from Princeton University.

Acknowledgments

We would like to thank the following people for reviewing our manuscript for technical accuracy: Mike Oshry, systems engineer at Sun Microsystems in Indianapolis; Ed Gamble, systems engineer at Sun Microsystems in Indianapolis; Sally Goldberg, site specialist for the Schools of Electrical and Materials Engineering at Purdue University; and John Theobald and the staff at JMP & Associates in Atlanta, GA. Their comments and critiques gave us the courage and patience to see this project through to completion.

Thanks also to Harry Elston and the rest of the staff at Sun Microsystems in Indianapolis for their assistance, and to the editors and production staff of High Mountain Press for their contributions and encouragement on this project.

I am grateful to Curt Freeland and Dwight McKay for sharing their knowledge, time, and experience. I would also like to thank my wife Susan, and children Heidi, Alex, and Nick for their patience, support and endurance during the production of this book.

Kent Parkinson

I would like to extend thanks to Dr. Janet Smith and to the members of the Structural Studies Group at Purdue for encouraging me to participate in developing this book. Thanks to Curt and Kent for the friendship, the good humor, and the pizza. Thanks to my daughter, Catherine, and to my wife, Mary, for her tireless proofreading, love and support.

Dwight McKay

To Kent Parkinson and Dwight McKay I extend my thanks for the opportunity to contribute to this publication. I would also like to thank my wife Sally, and my children Shaun and Erin for their support and sacrifices during the production of the book. In addition I would like to thank my staff and co-workers at Purdue University, and Mindy Canada and her staff at Computer Aided Tools and Service in Indianapolis. Without their support and generosity, my contributions would not have been possible.

Curt Freeland

OnWord Press Credits

President: Dan Raker
Publisher: Kate Hayward
Associate Publisher: Gary Lange
Acquisitions Editor: David Talbott
Marketing Director: Janet Leigh Dick
Project Editor: Frank Conforti
Project Editor: Barbara Kohl
Production Manager: Carol Leyba
Production Editor: Michelle Mann
Production Assistant: Robert Leyba
Cover Designer: Lynn Egensteiner
Indexer: Kate Bemis

Introduction

Welcome to *SunSoft Solaris 2.* for Managers and Administrators*. This book was written by system administration professionals with over 40 years of combined experience in managing corporate-sized computer installations. Our intent was to approach the topics we cover from a practitioner's perspective. In the following we discuss who should read this book, how the book is organized, and the typographical conventions we use.

Who Should Read This Book

SunSoft Solaris 2.* for Managers and Administrators was written for beginning Solaris systems administrators and managers who have general UNIX knowledge but little or no Sun systems administration experience. The purpose of this book is to deliver practical information regarding the installation and maintenance of Solaris 2 systems situated in local area networks.

Throughout the book, we endeavor to provide helpful tips and examples to explain and illustrate important concepts. Many of the examples used in this book come from our experiences as system administrators. Other examples were derived by polling experienced and inexperienced system administrators to identify the tools they used, and how they approach daily system administration tasks.

We hope that this text becomes a handy reference for beginning and experienced Solaris system administrators. It is also our wish that readers enjoy learning about the topic of Solaris system administration as much as we enjoyed producing this reference. If you have any comments, questions, or recommendations about the book, we encourage you to contact us at OnWord Press, 2530 Camino Entrada, Santa Fe, NM 87505-4835 USA, or e-mail us at readers@hmp.com.

Book Organization

Part 1 covers the concepts of the Solaris distributed environment, the planning and installation of Solaris, and general administration information. In the first six chapters of the book, we explore the terminology of distributed computing as well as Solaris terminology. We also examine the issues we must contend with before beginning conversion from the SunOS to the Solaris operating system.

Once we have covered selected background information, we walk through a typical Solaris installation while exploring the multitude of options provided by Solaris. Having successfully installed Solaris, we learn how to perform basic systems administration tasks such as installing accounts, using the windowing environment, and editing files. We also examine how an administrator installs and manages user accounts, how to boot the system, and (sometimes more importantly) how to shut the system down.

Part 2 accounts for the next ten chapters and is focused on system security maintenance, device naming, and disk and file system management. We also explore peripheral device administration and diverse ways of managing system software. Separate chapters are devoted to the administration of the disk subsystem, terminals and modems, and printers.

In Part 3 of the book, or the final six chapters, we cover the basics of network hardware, the use of network utilities such as the Network File System (NFS), the Network Information System (NIS+), diskless and dataless client administration, and system backups. In the final chapter, we delve briefly into automating a few of the more mundane system administration tasks. The *cron* command, the *find* command, and some of the built-in functions of the Bourne and C shells are discussed, and we examine several examples of ways to cascade these constructs in developing useful administration tools.

The book concludes with a detailed index.

Typographical Conventions

✗   *TIP: Tips on command usage, shortcuts, and other information aimed at saving you time appear like this.*

✔   *NOTE: Information on features and tasks that is not immediately obvious or intuitive appears in notes.*

❗   *WARNING: The warnings appearing in this book are intended to help you avoid committing yourself to results that you may not have intended.*

The following monospaced font is used for examples of prompts and computer responses:

```
id:run level:action:process
```

The same monospaced font in boldface is used for examples of user input:

```
ln /etc/init.d/lmf etc/rc0.d/K211lmf
```

A boldface font in regular text is used to highlight command names and options appearing for the first time in a section. Examples appear below.

Another approach for securing sensitive files is to encrypt them using the Solaris **crypt** command.

The **chmod** command makes the changes. It has an **-r** option like **chown** for handling entire directories, and accepts two different methods of specifying the permission changes to be made.

The boldface font is also used to highlight options, parameters, and the like which appear in lists. An example follows:

❑ **ncyl** is the number of data cylinders the operating system thinks the drive has.

❑ **acyl** is the number of alternate cylinders to be used for bad block remapping.

❑ **pcyl** is the actual physical number of cylinders on the drive (usually derived from the drive technical manual).

Italics are used to indicate new terms, file names, directory and path names, and general emphasis in regular text. Examples appear below.

These logical drives became known as *partitions*.

The init process reads in its own configuration file called */etc/inittab*. The */etc/inittab* file contains a series of directives.

The files are located in the */sbin* directory, and script directories are located in the */etc* directory.

Since the daemon needs to communicate over the network, it should be started *after* the network utilities are started.

First letter capitalization is used for menu names, selections, and button names. See the example below.

The Modify Service menu of the admintool's Serial Port Manager allows you to set parameters such as the baud rate, terminal type, and port enable or disable, among others.

Named keys on the keyboard are enclosed in angle brackets. Examples appear below.

<Shift>

<Esc>

<Ctrl>

<Enter>

Key sequences, or instructions to press a key immediately followed by another key, are linked with a plus sign. Examples follow:

<Ctrl>+s

<Shift>+<Tab>

Table of Contents

An Introduction to Distributed Computing

Many UNIX fluent system administrators have never dealt with a System V operating system. The primary goal of this book is to deliver practical information regarding the installation and maintenance of Solaris 2 systems. In this chapter, we will examine some of the advantages and disadvantages of the mainframe and workstation computing models. Subsequent chapters will explore the Solaris operating system in detail.

An Abbreviated History of the Microcomputer

In the past decade corporate computing has undergone many drastic changes. (In this chapter, "corporation" and "corporate" are interchangeable with "organizational" and "organization," or any public or private sector entity using computing power in daily operations.) While the complexity of data processing jobs increased, typical corporate mainframe computers could not keep up with computing demands. These older *mainframe* computers employed discrete logic circuits (chips) to implement the computer hardware. Many computer manufacturers were having problems making these discrete components operate at the speeds required to produce faster computers.

At about the same time, chip manufacturers were developing single chip computers which could outperform many of the discrete logic mainframes on the market. These single chip computers were dubbed *microprocessors* or *microcomputers*. Upon taking advantage of these new chips, many computer manufacturers began developing a new type of system, the *personal* or *desktop* computer. The higher performance systems soon became known as *workstations*.

A Short History of Sun Microsystems and the Workstation

Sun Microsystems Computer Corporation was one of the manufacturers at the forefront of the workstation computing revolution. The first workstations produced by Sun employed microprocessors from the Motorola MC68000 chip family. These systems ran an operating system called SunOS (Sun Operating System). SunOS was based on the University of California at Berkeley software distribution UNIX, also referred to as Berkeley UNIX, or BSD UNIX.

The UNIX operating system was originally developed at the American Telephone and Telegraph corporation's Bell laboratories in the late 1960s and early 1970s. Due to the flexibility of the UNIX operating system, UNIX quickly became the software of choice in many research and educational institutions. The founders of Sun Microsystems believed that a UNIX operating system would be the most desirable option for their new line of workstations.

Enter the SPARC

While the systems based on these chips were faster than many mainframes, there was still room for improvement. Sun promptly began developing its own microprocessor. In the 1980s Sun introduced a Reduced Instruction Set Computer (RISC) chip called the Scalable Processor ARChitecture (SPARC) processor. The first implementation of the SPARC chip ran at twice the speed of the fastest MC68000-based systems that Sun was producing at the time.

The SPARC processor chip allowed Sun to produce very powerful, inexpensive, desktop workstations. These systems also ran the SunOS operating system. Many other workstation manufacturers were delivering operating systems based on the American Telephone and Telegraph (AT&T) System V (five) release 3 operating system standard (also referred to as the System V Interface Description or SVID).

Sun Develops a New Operating System

For the purpose of standardization, Sun announced plans to develop a new operating system based on the AT&T System V release 4 UNIX operating system. The new operating system was called the *Solaris 2* operating system. Because Solaris is a System V based operating system, it is quite different from the previous BSD based SunOS operating system.

While most of the user-level commands are similar under SunOS and Solaris, the system administration commands are very different. Many of the "old reliable" commands from BSD-based UNIX are missing from Solaris. New commands with more functionality have replaced these BSD commands. The architecture of the operating system is also very different under Solaris. Access to and management of system devices under Solaris is foreign to BSD system administrators. Throughout the book we will point out the differences similarities between these two variants of UNIX operating systems.

A Look At Traditional Mainframe Computing

The workstation computing revolution presented business computing with quite a quandary: Should the corporation rely on one large computer system which was not keeping up with computing demands, or should it "downsize" to the new workstations and distribute computing power to mainframe users?

The corporation had to examine computing needs, and how these needs could be addressed by the systems available on the market. Decisions were often reduced to a choice between the mainframe computing model and the distributed computing model.

The Mainframe Model

What is the mainframe computing model? In brief, the corporation employs one large (mainframe) computer system. This system provides computing power for everything from payroll to materials management and production management.

A typical corporate mainframe computing environment.

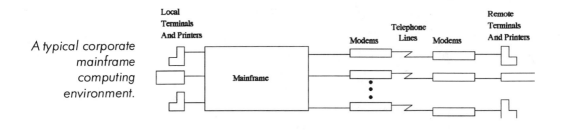

Access to the mainframe is typically via an ASCII terminal. These terminal connections may be local (in the same building or complex as the mainframe) or remote (via telephone lines and modems). Regardless of the type of connection, the data rate between the mainframe and the terminal is usually slow. Viewing a large document or accessing information from a database may take several minutes via ASCII terminal connections.

The Hybrid Mainframe Model

A typical extension of the mainframe computing environment produced a so-called tree-shaped computing environment. In this model, the corporation still relied on a mainframe computer (at the root of the tree). Smaller minicomputers were distributed throughout branch offices. These systems were tightly coupled to the mainframe, and in many cases were completely controlled by the mainframe.

Even smaller microcomputers were connected to the branch minicomputers. These microcomputers were used to control machinery and collect data. This information was shipped to the minicomputer for processing. The results of these computations were shipped off to the corporate mainframe for storage and/or further processing.

This version of mainframe computing typically used telephone lines and modems for the interconnecting system elements. As in the traditional mainframe computing model, this led to low data rates and lengthy delays in data access.

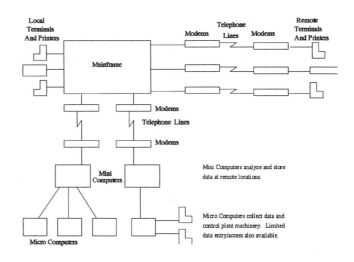

A hybrid mainframe computing environment.

The Distributed Computing Environment

The distributed computing environment was originally an offshoot of the modified mainframe computing environment. As the minicomputers and micro-computers positioned upon the leaves of the tree became more powerful, they assumed some of the data storage and processing responsibilities. If the mainframe needed access to the information on these leaves, it had to request that information from the workstations.

In addition to more powerful processing elements, interconnection technology underwent significant advances. In the distributed computing model, the processing elements are typically tied together via *local area* or *wide area* networks. These connections are an order of magnitude faster than the mainframe's ASCII terminal connections. Documents which once required several minutes to access could now be accessed in less than a minute.

Eventually, these developments led to the distribution of corporate data among the multitude of processing elements owned by the corporation. No one processor accessed all corporate data, but each processor had access to the data required to maintain relevant activities of a particular portion of the company. This data became almost instantly available to the other processing elements via local and wide area data networks.

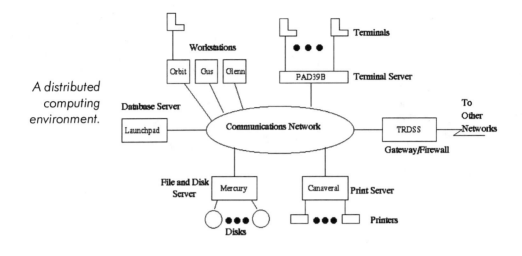

A distributed computing environment.

Each of the above computing models presented advantages and disadvantages to be evaluated by corporate management.

Advantages of Mainframe Computing

The mainframe computing model presents certain advantages over alternative models. One of its major advantages is the centralization of corporate data. In some instances it is desirable to store all of the corporate data in one place. In other instances, the reliance on one central repository of information became a liability to the corporation.

Consider the credit card division of a large banking operation. If all customer data is maintained on one system, corporate headquarters can easily determine the "value" and status of any and all customers.

Another advantage of mainframe computing is that the corporation does not have to worry about maintaining large numbers of geographically separated computers. Finally, certain applications simply require enormous computing power to accomplish basic objectives, and thus are best served with a mainframe system. Examples here might include the operation of international airlines and stock exchanges.

Disadvantages of Mainframe Computing

While the centralization of data allows corporate offices to more closely monitor everyday operations, it could also cause unreasonable operating expenses, and delays in distribution to branch offices or other entities requiring data access.

Revisiting the credit card division of the bank mentioned above, what happens if customers are serviced by geographically distributed branch offices? If one of the branch offices requires information pertaining to customers serviced by that particular branch, we may be dealing with several tens of gigabytes of information. Using a typical ASCII terminal connection over a phone line, it would take the branch office days to access the information required to conduct daily business. In most instances, this would not be an acceptable situation.

One possible solution would be to ship magnetic tapes to branch offices at regular intervals. In this scenario, tape loss or destruction in transit becomes a factor.

Another disadvantage of mainframe computing is the "single point of failure" problem. If the corporation owns one large computer system and the system fails, all corporate data processing capability is off-line. While many manufacturers provide 24-hour service contracts, these service policies may not cover occurrences such as natural disasters.

A typical mainframe computer is a very large, very expensive system. As the mainframe becomes obsolete, the corporation must plan well in advance to provide the capital for upgrading the system. Because mainframe computers from different manufacturers rarely run the same operating systems or the same versions of language compilers, the corporation must also plan for the crossover between the old and new systems.

The Distributed Computing Model

In the distributed computing model, the data processing chores are distributed among many systems. These systems are typically high-speed workstations which are linked via a local area or wide area network. Each of these processing elements has a specific task assigned as its primary function. But each of these workstations is typically a general purpose computer which can also provide processing capabilities beyond its primary task.

Advantages of Distributed Computing

One of the principal advantages of the distributed computing model is geographic distribution. Systems can now be distributed to the geographic region as required to best serve corporate needs. By linking these systems via high-speed networks, the branch offices have instant access to the data required for their everyday operations. In addition, the corporate office computers can still access the branch office data via high-speed networks with minimal delays.

Another advantage of the distributed computing model is that each component of the system is typically less expensive than its equivalent in the mainframe computer model. Consequently, the corporation can often purchase several computer systems for the same capital investment required to purchase one mainframe computer.

As the workstations in the distributed computing model become obsolete, the capital burden of upgrading to new systems can be spread over a longer period of time by upgrading the critical systems first, and the less critical systems at a later date. In addition, because many of the workstations run the same operating system, the corporation should not have as many problems porting software to the new systems.

Another major advantage of the distributed computing model is the "many points of failure" feature. Because no single computer stores all corporate data, no single system failure should be able to shut down corporate data processing. Instead, if one system fails, it is often possible to have another system automatically assume the computing responsibilities of the failed system. This feature allows the corporation to maintain operations and provide maximum access to critical corporate data at all times.

Disadvantages of Distributed Computing

While distributed computing offers many advantages, it also offers a few disadvantages to the corporate data processing center. Because workstations are widely distributed over a broad geographic area, maintenance can become a problem for the corporation. Spatial dispersion of computing equipment may force the corporation to add personnel in order to maintain these systems.

File system backups, installation of new software, system security, and installation of user accounts can also become complicated. When the corporation operates only one computer, the tasks of monitoring the system, allowing access, and installing software are simple when compared to the distributed computing model.

In the event of a network failure, corporate office computer systems may not be able to access certain essential data for indeterminate periods of time. This is not an acceptable mode of operation in some applications (e.g., stock trading, control of the space shuttle, or banking transactions).

Summary

In the past decade, business computing has seen vast changes. The introduction of high-end workstations and high-speed data networks has enabled many corporations to take advantage of distributed computing. One of the premier players in the distributed computing revolution is Sun Microsystems. With the SPARC-based workstations and the Solaris operating system, Sun has helped to revolutionize the computing industry.

This book strives to deliver practical information for beginning Solaris system administrators. In this chapter, we have examined some of the advantages and disadvantages of the mainframe and workstation computing models. Subsequent chapters will explore the installation, maintenance, and customization of the Solaris 2 operating system.

Solaris Concepts and Terminology

In this chapter the Solaris concepts and terminology presented are essential to understanding the many ways in which Solaris can be installed and configured. The configuration and role of servers, clients, diskless clients, dataless clients and diskfull clients are defined. A solid understanding of such terms and concepts provides the foundation on which a distributed environment is built. In Chapter 3, we step through a Solaris 2.4 installation.

The Solaris Operating Environment

Thus far, we have discussed the differences between a mainframe and distributed computing environment. For the remainder of this book, we will focus on the Solaris 2 distributed computing environment. But what is Solaris? Many people think it is an operating system. This is partially correct. Solaris is an operating environment consisting of three components: SunOS (Sun's Operating System), OpenWindows (Sun's Graphical User Interface), and the OpenWindows Desk-Set, a collection of standard OpenWindows applications.

SunOS

SunOS is the heart of the Solaris operating environment. Like all operating systems, SunOS is a collection of software that manages system resources and schedules system operations. In brief, system resources include system hard-ware, memory and I/O.

OpenWindows

OpenWindows, often referred to as Openwin, is Sun's Graphical User Interface (GUI). OpenWindows is based on AT&T's OPEN LOOK Graphical User Interface Functional Specification. Applications adhering to the OPEN LOOK specification assure users that they can expect these applications to have a standard look and feel. In much the same way that the automobile industry adheres to standards that assure drivers of U.S.-made cars that they will always find the turn signal lever on the left side of the steering column, the OPEN LOOK specification assures OpenWindows applications users a standard arrangement of window controls regardless of the application's third party developer. The advantages of standardization are less time required to learn new applications and improved communications between applications.

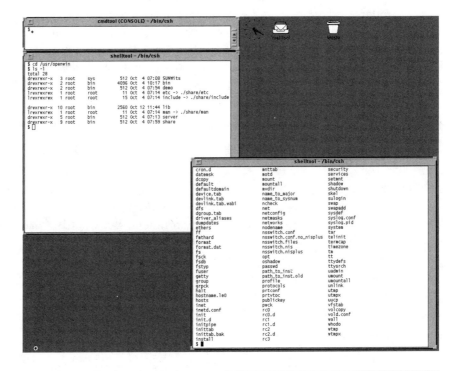

The OpenWindows graphical user interface.

DeskSet

The OpenWindows DeskSet is a collection of about a dozen standard end-user productivity applications. Examples are the Mail Tool, which is used to compose, send, and receive electronic mail, and the Calendar Manager, which can be used as an appointment and resource scheduling tool.

The OpenWindows DeskSet tools.

Solaris Versions

At present, there are two major versions of Solaris: Solaris 1 and Solaris 2. In Solaris 1, SunOS is based on the Berkeley Software Distribution (BSD)—commonly known as Berkeley UNIX—, and OpenWindows Version 2 or Version 3. With Solaris 2, SunOS is based on System V Release 4 (SVR4)—known as AT&T UNIX—, and OpenWindows Version 3. If you are currently running SunOS 4.1.2 or SunOS 4.1.3, you are, in fact, running Solaris 1.0.1 or Solaris 1.1, respectively.

Differences Between Solaris 1 and Solaris 2

Solaris 1	Solaris 2
OpenWindows Version 3 (SunOS 4.1.3, 4.1.4)	
SunOS 4 Berkeley UNIX (BSD)	SunOS 5 AT&T UNIX (SVR4)
OpenWindows Version 2 (SunOS 4.1.1, 4.1.2)	OpenWindows Version 3 (SunOS 4.1.3, 4.1.4)
DeskSet	DeskSet

Working with Hosts

Hosts are computers. The term *host* derives from the notion that computer hardware hosts the operating system and applications. Think of the hardware as the house in which the "guests" or programs live.

In order to distinguish one computer from another, hosts are assigned names, or *hostnames*. In keeping with the house metaphor, the hostname would be the system's address. In the Solaris operating environment, hostnames are assigned by the system administrator.

Assigning the Host a Name

In many organizations, hostnames follow a uniform naming convention. That does not mean such names have to be stuffy or boring. In fact, many systems have very interesting names. For example, the rocket motor division of an aerospace company may decide to name its hosts after astronauts, while the aircraft division would name its hosts after famous test pilots. The advantage of a naming convention is one of convenience. It makes keeping track of the hosts belonging to particular organizations easier. Furthermore, system users are more accepting of environments with organized hostnames because the system appears more personable.

> ✖ *TIP: The* ***uname*** *command returns system information about the current host. For example, when you enter* ***uname -n*** *at the system prompt, the system returns the hostname.*

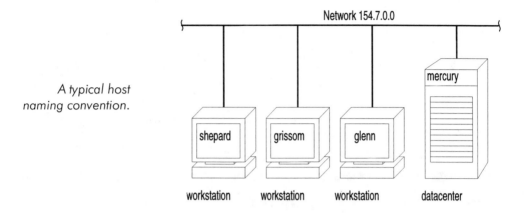

*A typical host
naming convention.*

The previous figure illustrates four hosts connected to a network. The host named *mercury* is a large capacity computer that provides network services to other computers connected to the network. Hosts such as *mercury* are frequently referred to as *datacenters* or *servers*. The hosts named *cooper, grissom,* and *glenn* are desktop workstations that utilize network services provided by *mercury.* Desktop workstations are often referred to as *clients.* The role of clients and servers in a network is covered in a later section of this chapter.

Assigning a Network Address to a Host

Hosts are also assigned Internet addresses by the system administrator. The Internet address is one of two addresses which enable hosts to communicate with one another. The Internet address is similar to a phone number. For example, when you make a long distance telephone call, you dial the area code, exchange number, and line number in order to communicate with a specific telephone network location. Similar to a telephone number, a host's Internet address describes "where" a host is located in the Internet. In the network example appearing in the previous illustration, the hosts are connected to the Internet network number 154.7.0.0. Detailed discussion of Internet addressing is presented in a later chapter.

The Host Ethernet Address

Hosts are also assigned Ethernet addresses. An Ethernet address is a unique and permanent hardware address (assigned by the hardware manufacture) that enables hosts to communicate via Ethernet. An Ethernet address is similar to a social security number in that it identifies the host in the Ethernet world.

 NOTE: *Hostnames are similar to the names of people. Ethernet addresses are similar to social security numbers. An Ethernet address uniquely identifies hosts on a network regardless of the hostnames. Internet addresses are similar to telephone numbers in that they identify a host's location in the Internet.*

The UNIX Operating System

Like all UNIX systems, Solaris utilizes a hierarchical operating system design. Each layer in the hierarchy is responsible for specific system functions and is capable of communicating with adjacent layers.

The UNIX hierarchical operating system.

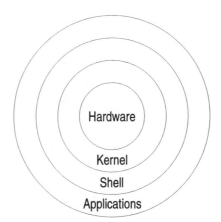

The Hardware Core

As illustrated, the core of all computers is hardware. But CPUs, disks, monitors and other hardware require management in order for hardware components to work as a team. The layer that manages the hardware on a UNIX system is called the *kernel*. The kernel is a collection of software whose primary functions are control and management of the system's hardware. When information is written to a disk drive, the kernel manages the system's hardware components to make the write occur. The kernel directs hardware components through programs called *systems calls*.

> ✔ **NOTE:** *The term "kernel" is used to indicate a part of the operating system found at the core of the UNIX environment.*

The Shell Layer

Although systems calls are very efficient for managing hardware, they are not convenient for humans. That is one of the reasons for the *shell layer*, the primary user interface with the computer. The shell layer processes command line instructions issued by a system user and passes them to the kernel for further processing.

> ✔ **NOTE:** *Solaris 2 provides three versions of the shell: Bourne shell (sh), C-shell (csh), and Korn shell (ksh). The Bourne shell is the default shell for the root user.*

The Applications Layer

The *applications layer* is where end user applications reside, such as word processors, spreadsheets and databases. These applications are invoked by the user issuing commands to the shell which causes the kernel to start the application. The applications interact with both the user (via the shell) and the system hardware (via the kernel) to accomplish the desired task.

UNIX Modularity

One of the major advantages of the modularity design of the UNIX operating system is portability. In order to port a UNIX operating system to a new hardware platform, only the kernel needs to be changed. The shell and applications layers remain unaffected. This greatly reduces system development time as new hardware technology becomes available. More important, however, is that end users are essentially unaffected by changes in hardware. The applications they run on one hardware platform will function the same on another.

System Architectures

Architecture describes the design and interaction of the various components of a computer system. There are two types of architecture that administrators must be aware of when configuring and maintaining Solaris systems: application architecture and kernel architecture.

Application Architecture

Application architecture defines the version of applications and commands that run on a CPU. In the mid-1980s, Sun's dominant architecture was the Sun3, based on the Motorola 68000 CPU chip set. In the late 1980s, the dominant architecture became Sun4, based on Sun's SPARC chip set. SPARC is an acronym for Scalable Processor ARchitecture. It is important to note that applications ported to the Sun3 architecture are not compatible with Sun4 architecture (see the following table).

Kernel Architecture

Kernel architecture defines the kernel (Operating System) version and kernel-specific binaries that run on a CPU. The following table lists several Sun systems, CPU models, kernel architectures, and applications architectures.

Differences Between Sun3 and Sun4 Application Architecture

Application Architecture	CPU Architecture
sun3	Motorola 68xxx
sun4	SPARC

Sun Systems Supporting Solaris 2

System Name	CPU Model	Kernel Architecture	Application Arch
SPARCstation SLC	4/20	sun4c	sun4
SPARCstation ELC	4/25	sun4c	sun4
SPARCstation IPC	4/40	sun4c	sun4

Sun Systems Supporting Solaris 2

System Name	CPU Model	Kernel Architecture	Application Arch
SPARCstation IPX	4/50	sun4c	sun4
SPARCstation 1	4/60	sun4c	sun4
SPARCstation 1+	4/65	sun4c	sun4
SPARCstation 2	4/75	sun4c	sun4
SPARCclassic	4/15	sun4m	sun4
SPARCstation LX	4/30	sun4m	sun4
SPARCstation 10	SS10	sun4m	sun4
Sun-4/100	4/110	sun4	sun4
Sun-4/200	4/2xx	sun4	sun4
SPARCserver 300	4/3xx	sun4	sun4
SPARCserver 400	4/4xx	sun4	sun4
SPARCserver 600MP	SS6xxMP	sun4m	sun4
SPARCserver 1000	SS1000	sun4d	sun4
SPARCserver 2000	SS2000	sun4d	sun4
SPARCengin 1E	4/E	sun4e	sun4

When purchasing applications for a Sun system, check the host's application architecture. When configuring the host's kernel (O/S), check the host's kernel architecture type.

✗ TIP: *Use the **uname** command to obtain information on the host's kernel architecture.*

```
# uname -m
sun4c
```

✗ TIP: *Similar to the **uname** command, the **showrev** command can also be used to display system information.*

```
# showrev
Hostname: mercury
Hostid: 240015cf
Release: 5.3
```

```
Kernel architecture: sun4m
Application architecture: sparc
Hardware provider: Sun_Microsystems
Domain:
Kernel version: SunOS 5.3 Generic September 1993
```

The Role of Servers and Clients

In a distributed computing environment, there are two basic types of hosts: servers and clients. A *server* is a process or program that provides services to hosts on a network. Hosts running a server process or multiple processes are often referred to as servers. A *client* is a process that uses services provided by the server. Hosts running a client process are also referred to as clients. For the moment, a process is a program that is part of the kernel.

There are a wide variety of server processes and respective client processes that may be operating in a network environment. *File servers* share disk storage with hosts on a network. *Application servers* share applications. *Client servers* provide boot services to clients on a network. *Print servers* share attached printers and provide network printing services.

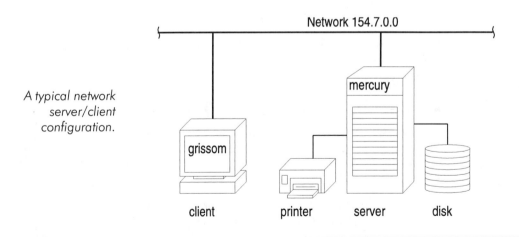

A typical network server/client configuration.

The above figure illustrates that the host named *grissom* (a network client) is able to utilize the resources (i.e., printer and disk) attached to the host named *mercury* (a network server). *Mercury* is said to be "sharing" its resources with *grissom.* A more detailed discussion of resource sharing is covered in the chapter on the network file system (NFS).

Host Configurations

There are three standard host configurations in the Solaris environment: stand-alone, dataless and diskless. While these terms seem straightforward, they can be confusing. For example, did you know that a diskless client can have a local disk? The important point to remember is that the host's configuration refers to how it boots.

In order for a host to boot to the multi-user state, it must be able to locate three areas on the disk: *root* (/), *swap* and *usr* (pronounced user). The *root* area contains the boot code, system files, and directories that are necessary for host operations. The *usr* area contains the system software, executable commands, and system libraries. The *swap* area is used for virtual memory. Virtual memory and the swap mechanism are discussed in Chapter 3. For the moment, think of virtual memory as an extension of RAM to the disk.

✔ **NOTE**: *If the system cannot locate the /usr file system, it will still boot to the single-user state.*

The Stand-alone Host Configuration

Stand-alone hosts boot up independent of network services. When booted, they obtain their root, swap and usr areas from a local disk. The term *stand-alone* refers to a host that is not connected to a network, while *networked stand-alone* refers to a standalone host that is connected to a network. One advantage of networked stand-alone hosts is that in the event of a network shutdown, they can continue to operate (although the utilization of network services may not be possible).

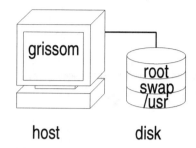

A stand-alone host configuration.

The Dataless Client Configuration

Unlike stand-alone hosts, *dataless clients* depend on network services provided by a client server. With a dataless client, only the root and swap areas are located on the host's local disk. The usr area is maintained on a client server.

The advantage of the dataless configuration over a stand-alone configuration is disk space economy. For example, the */usr* area of a typical end-user Solaris 2 system requires approximately 120 Mb of disk space. If there are 10 stand-alone hosts on a network, and each host requires 120 Mb of */usr* area, then 1200 Mb of */usr* disk space would be required on the network. If the ten stand-alone systems were converted to dataless clients, only 120 Mb of total */usr* disk space would be required on the network. This is because the dataless client server maintains a copy of the usr area and shares that resource with the dataless clients.

> **! WARNING:** *It is imperative that each host maintains its own unique root and swap areas. Sharing the root and swap areas among hosts can cause severe operating system damage.*

Another advantage of the dataless client configuration is ease of administration. If a change is required in the */usr* area, the change is made in the */usr* area of the server because the */usr* is a shared resource. All hosts sharing the server */usr* will see the change. Unlike stand-alone hosts, there is no need to copy files to hosts or to be physically located at the hosts when changes are made.

One disadvantage of the dataless client configuration is increased network load. However, the increased load is generally insignificant and usually does not outweigh the conservation of disk space and administrative advantages.

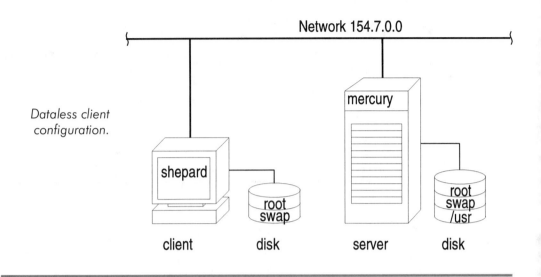

Dataless client configuration.

The Diskless Client Configuration

Diskless clients are wholly dependent on network services to boot and operate. A diskless client's root, swap and usr are supplied by a client server on the network. Two advantages of the diskless client configuration are reduced equipment cost (since no local disk is required) and centralized services. The major disadvantage is network load. When a diskless client boots, pages (writes) to the swap area or executes a library routine, all of the I/O must go through the network.

As mentioned previously, every host must have both a unique root and swap area in order to function properly. A host configured as a diskless boot server has two areas (file systems) on its disk used to store the root and swap areas for diskless clients (see previous figure).

Under the */export* area (file system) on the server is a directory named *root*. The */export/root* directory contains a subdirectory for each diskless client supported by the diskless client server. For example, the */export/root/glenn* directory located on *mercury's* disk holds the root area for the diskless client named *glenn*.

The diskless client swap areas are handled in a fashion similar to the root area. Under the */export/swap* area (file system) are special files called *swap files*, one for each diskless client being supported. For example, the */export/swap/ glenn* file is the swap area for the diskless client named *glenn*.

✘ **TIP:** *A quick way to determine if a host is supporting diskless clients, and to discover their host names, is to change directories (cd) to /export/swap (if it exists) and list (ls) the files.*

```
# cd /export/swap
# ls -l
-rw-----T 1 root   285036 Jan 6 1992 glenn
```

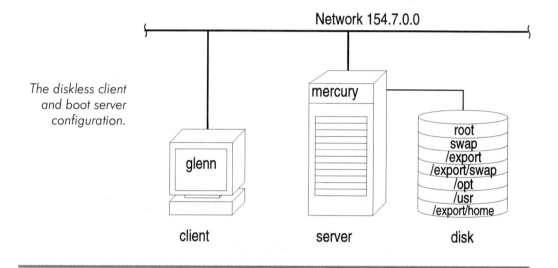

The diskless client and boot server configuration.

_____

Software Terminology

Solaris 2 bundled and unbundled software is distributed as software packages, that is, a collection of files that perform a function such as the on-line manual pages or the OpenWindows demonstrations. There are over 80 software packages in Solaris 2. The format of software package names is SUNWxxx. For example, the package name for the on-line manual pages is SUNWman and the package name for the OpenWindows demos is SUNWowdem.

The software packages in Solaris 2 conform to a software standard known as the *Applications Binary Interface* (ABI). ABI compliant software can be easily managed (i.e., installed and/or removed) with standard systems administration utilities. The package administration utilities will be discussed in Chapter 14, "Managing System Software."

Related software packages are grouped into software clusters. Cluster names use the SUNWC prefix. For example, the OpenWindows Version 3 cluster contains 13 software packages related to OpenWindows version 3.

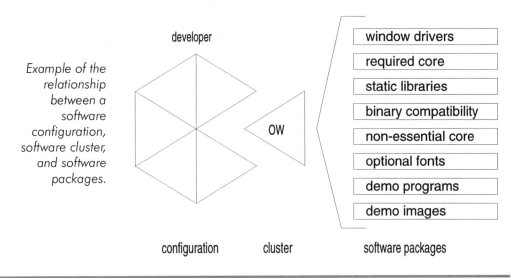

Example of the relationship between a software configuration, software cluster, and software packages.

Working with Software Configurations

The SunInstall utility further groups software packages and clusters into categories known as *software configurations*. There are four software configurations in Solaris 2. Each configuration supports different levels of system sophistication. The four configurations are *core, end user, developer,* and *entire.*

Core Software

The *core* software configuration contains the minimum required software to boot and operate a stand-alone host. It does not include the OpenWindows software or the on-line manual pages. It does, however, include sufficient networking software and OpenWindows drivers to run OpenWindows from a server sharing the OpenWindows software. A server would not be built from the core configuration. The core software configuration requires approximately 70 Mb of disk space.

End User Software

The *end user* software configuration contains the core configuration software and additional software typically used by end users. It includes OpenWindows version 3 and the end user version of AnswerBook. It does not, however, contain the on-line manual pages. The end user software configuration requires approximately 180 Mb of disk space.

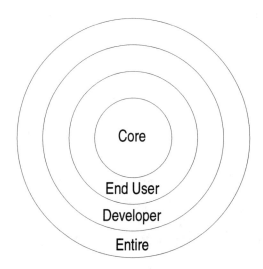

The relationship of the four software configurations.

Core

End User

Developer

Entire

Developer Software

The developer software configuration contains the core and end user configuration software and additional software typically used by systems and software developers. This configuration includes the on-line manual pages, the full implementation of OpenWindows and compiler tools. It does not include compilers or debugging tools. In Solaris 1 and earlier releases of Sun operating systems, compilers were bundled with the release media. Compilers and debuggers are unbundled product in Solaris 2. The developer's software configuration requires approximately 270 Mb of disk space.

The entire software configuration contains the entire Solaris 2.x release. It requires approximately 360 Mb of disk space. It is important to note that the software configurations can be modified. For example, the on-line manual pages cluster could be added to the end user configuration. Likewise, the on-line manual pages could be removed from the developer's configuration. These modifications can be made when the system is being constructed or afterwards.

Disk Space Required for Different Software Configurations

Software Configuration	Size
Core	70 Mbytes
End User	180 Mbytes
Developer	270 Mbytes
Entire Distribution	360 Mbytes

Obtaining System Access

People who use the UNIX system are known as *users*. On a Solaris system, every person who wants to use the system must gain access to it through a *login* procedure. The login process is a security mechanism which helps ensure that only authorized users gain access to the system resources and information.

The User Account

Before a user can log in, the system administrator must create a user account. The account contains a variety of information about the user such as which areas of the system s/he can access. The creation of user accounts is discussed in Chapter 7. In order for users to log in to a system, they must possess a login name and a password.

The login name is a lower case alphabetic string up to eight characters in length that identifies the user to the system. Many sites make the users' last names their login names. For example, Kathy Smith's login name would be *smith*. In cases where more than one person has the same last name, the last name and first initial would be used as the login name. For example, Mark Smith would be assigned the login name *smithm*.

A simple login naming convention makes it easier for system administrators to track and manage system users. It also makes it easier for users to communicate with each other through utilities like electronic mail. If you wanted to send electronic mail to co-workers, would you like having to remember cryptic login names such as "zastpuxl"?

✔ *NOTE: Experience has shown that a simple login naming convention will reduce the amount of user account management and security problems. This is especially true in large or changing system environments.*

Assigning Passwords

System users must also possess a password. The login name identifies a user to the system, and the password is used to assure that the user logging in is who s/he claims to be. By default, passwords must be at least six characters in length. Passwords should never use the proper spelling of words nor should they have anything to do with the user that could be easily guessed.

Special Systems Accounts

There are several special systems accounts that are used for system management. The one most often used by system administrators is named *root*. The root user account must be carefully guarded because it has virtually unlimited access privileges. In the wrong hands, root access can allow the user to cause extensive system damage or corrupted data.

Logging in to Your System

To log in to your system (in this case as root) type the login name at the login prompt, then press the <Return> key (see the following figure). You will then be prompted for a password. Type in your password and press <Return>. Note that the password is not echoed to the terminal screen. This prevents anyone who is watching you from seeing your password. If the information you provide the system is correct, you will see a command prompt. The command prompt is the shell interpreter that passes commands for execution to the kernel.

To log off the system, enter the exit command at the shell prompt and press <Return>.

! *WARNING: Never leave a root login unattended! A clever system cracker could take advantage of the unattended root login to alter critical system files, thus allowing the cracker undetected root access. The integrity of entire corporate computer system can be compromised due to lax root security.*

*Example of login
and logoff.*

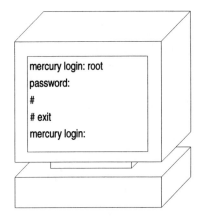

Summary

In this chapter we covered fundamental concepts and terminology used in the Solaris operating environment. We defined the role of servers and clients in a distributed computing environment, and the server, standalone, diskless and dataless host configurations. In addition, software management under Solaris was discussed.

Preparing for a Solaris Installation

One of your principal tasks as a systems administrator is planning for company software needs under Solaris 2 and identifying a hardware configuration required to support the software. In this chapter we look at basic pre-installation considerations to bear in mind about your software applications. Requirements may differ depending on whether you are working with a new system installation versus an upgrade from the Solaris 1.X (SunOS) to the Solaris 2 operating system. Next, we will take a look at what your application and operating system demands mean in terms of hardware configurations. Finally, we show you how to plan your system configuration.

Evaluating Your Applications

If you are planning on upgrading a SunOS system to a Solaris 2 system, you should be aware that there are several important differences between these operating systems. Some of the differences involve changing the names of commands or function calls which perform certain operations. Other changes involve portability issues such as how the compiler links or includes the library calls into the binaries. Because of these differences, you will need to examine the software currently in use on your system to determine which applications are mission-critical, and which applications are not.

While many of the applications that you have been using under SunOS are available under Solaris 2, it is also possible that some of the applications will not be available to run under Solaris 2. This is the time to evaluate the packages to determine if you need to replace this or that functionality, and if so, how replacement should be accomplished. In some cases, it may be possible to use existing SunOS binaries under Solaris 2. You will need to understand some of the internals of the applications before they can be used under Solaris 2.

If you are planning a new installation, some of the same compatibility and portability concerns may come into play. Even in this case, it is best for system administrators to understand the differences between the two operating systems so that the differences can be explained to users who have used SunOS or other Berkeley-derived UNIX operating systems in the past.

Program Linking

Two types of binaries are found in SunOS applications: dynamically linked, and statically linked. Linking is the process performed by the linking loader (ld) to resolve references to variables within the program binaries. In early versions of SunOS, all binaries were statically linked. Under Solaris 2, the preferred method of linking binaries is dynamic. What are the differences between the two methods of linking a program binary?

A statically linked program links (or includes) all of the library functions at compile time. If changes are made to a library routine, the program must be re-compiled to take advantage of those changes. A statically linked program will usually be quite large because it includes all library functions.

A dynamically linked program is one that loads the library functions at run time. This allows the program to include the latest version of all library functions upon invocation. No recompilation is required to enjoy the advantages of the updated library routines. Dynamically linked programs are usually smaller than their statically linked counterparts, because the library functions are not included in the on-disk binary image.

Native Mode Applications

In Solaris, applications run under native mode or binary compatibility mode. There are benefits and costs to both operating modes. For instance, because Solaris is based on industry standards, native mode applications enjoy application portability across all System V Release 4 platforms. Applications which contain native mode binaries will operate on Solaris systems, but will not operate on SunOS 4.x systems.

To be considered a native mode application, a program must be compiled under the Solaris environment. This typically means that the binaries are dynamically linked programs.

✔ **NOTE:** *As noted in Chapter 2, compilers are not included in the core Solaris operating system. The compilers must be purchased and installed separately. You need to keep this in mind for cataloging applications software later.*

✘ **TIP:** *Developers can save significant time porting applications to Solaris if the applications are developed under SunOS 4.1 using the System V environment, OpenWindows, and dynamic linking.*

Binary Compatibility Mode Applications

What happens if you do not have source code for the application, or if a critical application is not available for Solaris? Would such a situation prevent you from converting to Solaris? Fortunately, in many cases, the answer is no.

Solaris provides a binary compatibility mode package (BCP) for existing SunOS 4.x programs, including SunView applications. It might be possible to run your mission-critical application in binary compatibility mode until Solaris versions are available.

✔ **NOTE:** *The binary compatibility package is intended as a short-term transition aid, and should not be used as a long term solution.*

In order to operate in compatibility mode, the application must strictly adhere to some simple guidelines. The following table summarizes the restrictions on running an application in compatibility mode.

Binary Compatibility Mode Restrictions

Feature	Must use	Cannot use
Dynamic Linking	X	
Traps to O.S.		X
Application Specific IOCTLs		X
Read/Write directly to system files		X
Access /dev/kmem or libkvm		X
Use of undocumented SunOS interfaces		X

Any application run in compatibility mode must dynamically link the C library, and other system library routines. Any application that is statically linked *will not* work in binary compatibility mode.

Another condition for proper operation in binary compatibility mode includes the absence of traps directly to the operating system, application specific IOCTLs or drivers, and direct read or write access to the system files. Further conditions require that the application not attempt to access and interpret kernel data structures through the */dev/kmem* or *libkvm* facilities, nor should applications attempt to use any undocumented SunOS interface.

In the case of locally developed software or applications which include source code, it is relatively easy to determine if the code follows the rules of the table. In order to determine if third-party or binary-only applications will work in binary compatibility mode, it may be necessary to contact the original software supplier.

Cataloging Current Applications

Planning for application availability under Solaris involves cataloging existing and planned applications, and determining the availability date of these applications under Solaris.

The cataloging process requires that you examine your current systems to determine the software you have in use. Once you develop a catalog of the required applications, you need to determine when these applications will be available for use under Solaris, and how this will affect your corporate computing plans.

In order to facilitate the cataloging process you should develop a form to tabulate your findings. This form should allow you to collect as much information as possible about the applications. Some of the more important information about applications includes package size in megabytes (Mb), package developer, the number of users who will require this application, and whether the application runs in native or binary compatibility mode. Appearing below is a sample of such a form.

General Information

System Model: _____

System Configuration Type: Server, Standalone, Diskless, Dataless

Hostname: _____

IP Address: ___.___.___.___

Subnet Mask: ___.___.___.___

Name Service: NIS, NIS+, None

    Name Server Hostname: _____

    Name Server IP Address: ___.___.___.___

Time Zone: _____

Domain Name: _____

Disk Layout

Device	Size	Mount Point
sd0a	32M	/
sd0b	128M	swap
sd0d	200M	/usr
sd0e	_____	_____
sd0f	_____	_____
sd0g	_____	_____
sd0h	_____	_____

A sample software inventory form.

Locally Developed Software

Application	Author	Language	#users	Native/ BCP	Size Mb	When Available
_____	_____	_____	_____	_____	____	_____
_____	_____	_____	_____	_____	____	_____

Third Party Software

Application	Author	Language	#users	Native/ BCP	Size Mb	When Available
_____	_____	_____	_____	_____	____	_____
_____	_____	_____	_____	_____	____	_____

Sun Software Products

Application	Author	Language	#users	Native/ BCP	Size Mb	When Available
_____	_____	_____	_____	_____	____	_____
_____	_____	_____	_____	_____	____	_____

Evaluating Hardware Requirements

Once you have identified your software requirements, you need to determine hardware dependencies. For instance, do you have enough disk space to support the operating system, users' files, and the necessary application software?

You also need to consider any special hardware requirements as the Solaris installation plan is developed. Do you rely on third-party or other special hardware to operate your enterprise? If so, is a special device driver required for the operation of this hardware? Which systems have this hardware? Do you know if software is available to allow the operation of this hardware under Solaris 2?

Cataloging Hardware Requirements

When you consider hardware requirements, you need to pay close attention to any non-standard hardware on your system. As with the software, this requires that all hardware found on the system is cataloged. Again, you could develop a form to facilitate the cataloging process. Appearing next is an example of such a form.

General Information

System Memory Size: _____ Mb
Disk 1 Size: _____
Disk 2 Size: _____
Disk 3 Size: _____
Disk 4 Size: _____

Locally Developed Hardware

Product	Supplier	System(s)	Driver Req'd	Date Available
_____	_____	_____	_____	_____
_____	_____	_____	_____	_____

A sample hardware inventory form.

Network Sketch

Sketch your current network layout

Minimal Hardware Requirements

Once you have determined your specific software and hardware requirements, you need to determine if your system(s) meet the minimal Solaris requirements. To install and run Solaris 2, systems must have a SPARC or Intel 386/486/Pentium processor with a minimum 150 Mb of disk space. The following systems manufactured by Sun Microsystems Computer Corporation are examples of the SPARC based systems that are capable of running Solaris 2.

SPARC Processor Based Systems

System Name	CPU Model	Kernel Architecture	Application Architecture
SPARCstation Classic	4/15	sun4m	sun4
SPARCstation SLC	4/20	sun4c	sun4
SPARCstation ELC	4/25	sun4c	sun4
SPARCstation LX	4/30	sun4m	sun4
SPARCstation IPC	4/40	sun4c	sun4
SPARCstation IPX	4/50	sun4c	sun4
SPARCstation 1	4/60	sun4c	sun4
SPARCstation 1+	4/65	sun4c	sun4
SPARCstation 2	4/75	sun4c	sun4
SPARCstation 5	SS5	sun4m	sun4
SPARCstation 10	SS10	sun4m	sun4
SPARCstation 20	SS20	sun4m	sun4
Sun-4/100	4/110	sun4	sun4
Sun-4/200	4/2xx	sun4	sun4
SPARCserver 300	4/3xx	sun4	sun4
SPARCserver 400	4/4xx	sun4	sun4
SPARCserver 600MP	SS6xxMP	sun4m	sun4
SPARCserver 1000	SS1000	sun4d	sun4
SPARCserver 2000	SS2000	sun4d	sun4
SPARCengine 1E	4/E	sun4e	sun4

In addition to the SPARC/Intel processor requirements to run Solaris, other minimum hardware requirements must be met. These requirements include the availability of certain amounts of disk space which will be used to hold the Solaris 2 binaries.

Disk Space Requirements

Software Configuration	Size	Comments
Core	70 Mb	Minimal configuration
End User	180 Mb	Adequate for canned application clusters

Software Configuration	Size	Comments
Developer	270 Mb	Typical for Stand-alone and Servers
Entire Distribution	360 Mb	Only if you have LOTS of disk space!

The Solaris 2 binaries are contained in predefined file systems on the disk drives. These file systems, or disk partitions, must meet certain minimum size requirements. The requirements are summarized in the following table.

Contents of Important Components under Solaris

File System	Minimum Space Required	Comment
/	15 Mb	32 Mb typical
swap	32 Mb	Usually 2x memory size
/usr	30 Mb	140 Mb typical for end-user
/opt	varies	varies based on applications installed
/export/root	10 Mb	10 Mb base + 20 Mb per diskless client
/export/swap	0 Mb	24 Mb per 16 Mb diskless client is recommended (minimum)
/export/exec	15 Mb	15 Mb per unique client architecture.

 NOTE: When installing a server system, it is often desirable to provide a separate partition for the /var directory. This directory stores log files and mailboxes, provides temporary storage for print jobs as well as space for the NIS+ database and user accounting. At a typical large site, this partition may be 128 MB, and at smaller sites, 32 MB.

Other Important Hardware Considerations

Another requirement which must be met before running Solaris 2 includes the availability of particular hardware to be used as the software "load" media when performing the initial Solaris 2 system installation. Unlike its SunOS predecessors which were available on several distribution media, Solaris 2 is only distributed on CD-ROM media.

In order to provide reasonable performance on systems running Solaris 2 these systems must contain (at least) a specified amount of main memory. The developers of the Solaris operating system determined that systems must contain a minimum of 16 megabytes of RAM in order to load and run the operating system.

In order to load and run the Solaris 2 operating system your system must include:

❑ A CD-ROM drive (either on the system, or the network).

✔ **NOTE:** *A local or network accessible CD-ROM drive is required to load a Solaris 2 system.*

❑ The system must have a minimum of 16 megabytes of RAM memory,

✔ **NOTE:** *Solaris 2 will not boot on systems with less than 16 Mb of main memory.*

Type of Installation

Each of the following basic types of Solaris systems is designed for a specific function:

❑ Stand-alone
❑ Dataless
❑ Diskless
❑ Heterogeneous and homogeneous servers

Stand-alone

A stand-alone system typically requires a minimum of 210 Mb of disk. Stand-alone systems run entirely from a local disk. They do not rely upon other network service providers. Some stand-alone systems are also servers.

Dataless

These systems require a minimum 45 Mb of disk space, and depend on network services provided by a server. Dataless systems obtain their root and swap space from an internal disk, but rely on servers to provide the other essential file systems.

Diskless

These systems typically require 64 Mb of disk space on the server. Diskless systems are totally dependent on network services. The root, swap, and other file systems are provided by one of the servers on the network.

Heterogeneous and Homogeneous Servers

Servers usually have disk requirements in excess of 250 Mb. Servers are a special class of stand-alone systems. The servers boot from local disks and provide other network hosts with the file systems that they require. Because servers provide boot and applications services to clients, they require additional available software on the local disks than non-server stand-alone configurations.

A homogeneous server is a system which serves only one client kernel architecture. For instance, a Sun4m server with all Sun4m clients is considered a homogeneous installation.

A heterogeneous server, on the other hand, is a system which serves at least one client with a different kernel application than that of the server. An installation which includes a Sun4m server with Sun 3, Sun4c, and 386i clients would be considered a heterogeneous installation.

An Example of Installation Evaluation

Now that the terms used in the Solaris installation process are understood, you need to determine the specifics of your installation. For illustration purposes, we have chosen a SPARCcenter 2000 server installation (hostname:mercury), with one diskless client (hostname:glenn), and one dataless client (hostname: grissom). For illustration purposes, *mercury* will also be our master Network Information System (NIS) NIS+ nameserver. NIS+ is the replacement for the original NIS nameserver distributed under SunOS operating systems. The NIS+ package manages network-wide information such as passwords, file system availability, and names of hosts on the network. NIS+ is discussed in greater detail in chapter 20 in this book.

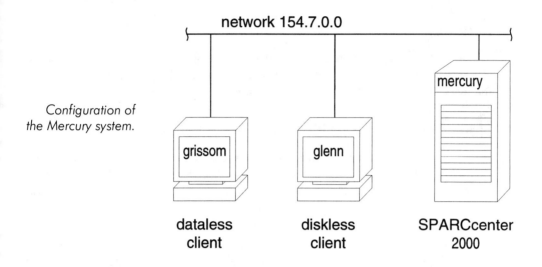

Configuration of the Mercury system.

In the example installation, we will install the server as a "full install" Solaris cluster. For the purpose of simplicity, we do not have any locally developed or non-Sun hardware. We will have two applications installed: one requires 50 Mb of disk space and runs in binary compatibility mode, and the other requires 75 Mb of disk space and runs in native mode. The inventory forms for the *mercury* system Solaris installation might resemble the following illustrations.

```
General Information
    System Model: SPARCServer 2000
    System Configuration Type: Server
    Hostname: Mercury
    IP Address: 154.7.0.1
    Subnet Mask: 255.255.255.0
    Name Service:  NIS+
        Name Server Hostname: Mercury
        Name Server IP Address: 154.7.0.1
    Time Zone: US/East-Indiana
    Domain Name: _____
    Disk Layout
        Device          Size          Mount Point
        sd0a            32M        /
        sd0b            128M       swap
        sd0d            200M       /usr
        sd0e            _____      _____
        sd0f            _____      _____
        sd0g            _____      _____
        sd0h            _____      _____
```

```
Locally Developed Software
    Application Author   Language   #users   Native/   Size   When
                                             BCP       Mb     Available

    Package-2  Jim S.    C          17       Native    75     Now
    _____  _____    _____   _____   _____  ____   _____
```

```
Third Party Software
    Application Author   Language   #users   Native/   Size   When
                                             BCP       Mb     Available

    Package-1  XYZ Corp  Binary     21       BCP       50     Now
    _____  _____    _____   _____   _____  ____   _____
```

```
Sun Software Products
    Application Author   Language   #users   Native/   Size   When
                                             BCP       Mb     Available

    _____  _____    _____   _____   _____  ____   _____
    _____  _____    _____   _____   _____  ____   _____
```

Mercury system software inventory form.

General Information

System Memory Size: 64 Mb
  Disk 1 Size: _1Gb_____
  Disk 2 Size: _____
  Disk 3 Size: _____
  Disk 4 Size: _____

Locally Developed Hardware

Product	Supplier	System(s)	Driver Req'd	Date Available
_____	_____	_____	_____	_____
_____	_____	_____	_____	_____

Mercury system hardware inventory form.

Network Sketch

154.7.0.

Mercury
  glenn   grissom

154.8.0.

Sketch your current network layout

Because the *mercury* system is to be the server for a number of client systems, we need to include inventory information for these clients in our planning as well.

Mercury system client inventory information.

```
General Information
    System Model: SPARCStation ELC
    System Configuration Type: Diskless
    Hostname: Glenn
    IP Address: 154.7.0.2
    Subnet Mask: 255.255.255.0
    Name Service:  NIS+
        Name Server Hostname: Mercury
        Name Server IP Address: 154.7.0.1
    Time Zone: US/East-Indiana
    Memory size: 16 MB

General Information
    System Model: SPARCStation LX
    System Configuration Type: Dataless
    Hostname: Grissom
    IP Address: 154.7.0.3
    Subnet Mask: 255.255.255.0
    Name Service:  NIS+
        Name Server Hostname: Mercury
        Name Server IP Address: 154.7.0.1
    Time Zone: US/East-Indiana
    Memory size: 24 MB
    Disk 1 size: 424 MB
```

From the inventory forms, we can calculate that we will need a minimum of 605 Mb of disk space on the *mercury* system. The disk space breakdown appears below.

- ❏ 32 Mb for /
- ❏ 128 Mb for swap
- ❏ 140 Mb for /usr
- ❏ 125 Mb for /opt (applications)
- ❏ 32 Mb for /export/root
- ❏ 32 Mb for /export/swap
- ❏ 16 Mb for /export/exec
- ❏ 100 Mb for /home/mercury (users' files)

Determining Disk Partitions

Now that we have determined the type of installation and the amount of disk space required for our installation, we must decide how to partition (or segment) our disks to provide for these needs. This requires a rudimentary understanding of disk terminology. In a later chapter we will take a closer look at disk geometry.

At a very simple level, the figure below shows a disk drive divided into many sectors. Each Solaris data sector is capable of storing 512 bytes of data. A UNIX file system is comprised of numerous sectors bound together by the **newfs** command. A disk drive may be partitioned into eight file systems.

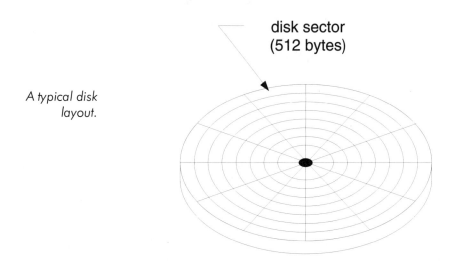

disk sector
(512 bytes)

A typical disk layout.

From this information we can calculate that in order to provide a 100 Mb file system we will need a disk partition with at least 200,000 data sectors, or 200,000 * 512 = 102,400,000 bytes. In reality, the file system structure requires extra sectors in order to provide a file system that will hold 100 Mb of data.

A typical rule of thumb when partitioning disks is to allow for ten percent of the sectors in a file system to be consumed by overhead. It is also a good idea to allow for future growth for each file system.

For our installation, we already determined that we would require eight file systems: /, /usr, swap, /opt, /export/root, /export/swap, /export/exec, and /home/ mercury. These file systems require a minimum of 605 Mb disk space.

Under Solaris 2 a disk can be divided into eight partitions. Our server has two 1.05 gigabyte (Gb) disk drives which may be used to contain the operating system binaries. We expect our users to accumulate more files as time goes by, so we will set one disk drive aside for /home/mercury.

This leaves us with one 1.05 Gb disk to contain the other seven file systems for our server. For the purpose of simplicity, we will use file system sizes which are multiples of powers of two. Disk partitioning appears in the following table.

Example File System Sizes

File system mount point	Minimum Size (in Mb)	Mercury's Size (in Mb)	Amount of growth allowed
/	15	32	100%
swap	32	128	0%
/usr	30	164	20%
/opt	0	256	100%
/export/root	30	32	7%
/export/swap	24	32	33%
/export/exec	15	32	100%

At this point we have determined how to organize Solaris 2 on our file server disks. If this is a new installation, you can proceed to the next chapter, and begin the installation process. If this is an upgrade installation, you need to perform a few other tasks before you can begin the installation of Solaris 2.

Saving Critical Data

Before SunOS is shut down for the last time, there are several files you may wish to save. For instance, because you may not have to change the partitioning to load Solaris 2, it would help to know how the disks on the system are currently partitioned. You may also wish to save the password file, NIS name server maps, and other critical information before you begin the SunOS shutdown procedure.

Saving the SunOS Disk Configuration

There are two ways to determine the current disk configuration information on a system. First, the **dmesg** command will display output from a recent reboot, or the **format** command will display all of the currently available disks. Since the dmesg information will not be available if the system has been up and running for several days, we will use the format command:

```
 ▽                                    xterm
# format
Searching for disks...done

AVAILABLE DISK SELECTIONS:
      0. c0t0d0 <SUN0535 cyl 1866 alt 2 hd 7 sec 80>
         /io-unit@f,e0200000/sbi@0,0/dma@0,81000/esp@0,80000/sd@0,0
      1. c0t1d0 <SUN0535 cyl 1866 alt 2 hd 7 sec 80>
         /io-unit@f,e0200000/sbi@0,0/dma@0,81000/esp@0,80000/sd@1,0
      2. c1t1d0 <SUN2.1G cyl 2733 alt 2 hd 19 sec 80>
         /io-unit@f,e1200000/sbi@0,0/dma@1,81000/esp@1,80000/sd@1,0
      3. c1t3d0 <SUN2.1G cyl 2733 alt 2 hd 19 sec 80>
         /io-unit@f,e1200000/sbi@0,0/dma@1,81000/esp@1,80000/sd@3,0
Specify disk (enter its number): █
```

Using format to determine available disks under SunOS.

Once we know the device names of all disk drives on the system, we can obtain a hardcopy of the current partitioning information by using the **dkinfo** command:

```
# /etc/dkinfo sd0 sd1 | lpr
```

Another bit of information that may prove useful is a copy of our current *fstab* file. This will allow us to avoid damaging users' file systems during the conversion process. We can obtain a hardcopy of the current file system information by keying in the following string:

```
# lpr /etc/fstab
```

Saving Critical SunOS System Information

It is always wise to have a copy of all critical system information prior to installing a new version of an operating system. The most critical files to be saved are listed below.

- ❑ ./etc
- ❑ ./.cshrc
- ❑ ./.login
- ❑ ./.logout
- ❑ ./.profile
- ❑ ./.rhosts
- ❑ ./var/spool/mail
- ❑ ./var/spool/calendar

❑ ./var/spool/cron

❑ ./var/spool/uucp

❑ ./var/nis

If we create a file containing the above list of files we can use the **tar** command to make a tape for these critical system configuration files.

```
# cd /
# tar cvf tape_drive `cat filename`
```

In the above example, *tape_drive* refers to the device name of the drive we wish to write on (e.g., */dev/rst0*). Next, *filename* is the name of the file containing the list of files and directories we wish to save.

✔   **NOTE:** *The list of critical files to save is only a suggested list. The actual list is highly dependent on your installation.*

Summary

In this chapter, we examined the prerequisites for installing Solaris 2 on your system. In Chapter 4, we will use the information collected in this chapter to walk through a server installation of Solaris 2.4

Installing Solaris with SunInstall

Overview of the Installation Process

In the previous chapter we examined Solaris pre-installation requirements. We made several decisions that will affect your Solaris 2 installation. In this chapter we will walk through a typical installation of Solaris 2.4.

In order to install Solaris on your system, you will need the hardware and software inventory forms which were completed in the previous chapter. You will also need access to a CD-ROM drive on the local workstation or the network, the Solaris 2.4 distribution media, and a fair amount of patience.

Preparing for the Installation Process

Prior to actually installing the Solaris software you need to shut down the system. This means that anyone presently using the system or planning to use the system must be logged out. To do this you must perform an orderly shutdown of the entire system.

Performing the System Shutdown

As installation day nears, you need to warn users of the impending down-time, and then stop all system activities. One way to accomplish this is to use the SunOS shutdown command:

```
# shutdown +10 "System going down for Solaris 2.4 installation"
```

When used as shown, the shutdown command will send the message "System going down for Solaris 2.4 installation" to each user logged into the system. The message will also tell the users that the shutdown time is 10 minutes from receipt of the first shutdown message. When the shutdown time arrives the system will transition to single-user mode operation.

Immediately before you shut down the SunOS operating system for the last time, you need to perform a final file system backup of all files on your systems. This will allow you to back out of the Solaris installation in case problems develop.

Once you have completed the file system backup, you need to shut down the system. Halting the system can be accomplished with the halt command:

```
# /etc/halt
```

You are now ready to begin the installation of Solaris 2.4!

The System Identification Phase

Once your system is halted, you need to place the Solaris 2.4 distribution CD in the CD-ROM drive and boot Solaris 2.4. The following table gives the system type to boot device mapping for a local CD-ROM drive.

System Type to Solaris Boot Device Correspondence

System Type	Boot Command
4/110	
4/2XX	b sd(0,30,1)
4/3XX	
4/4XX	
SPARCstation 1 (4/60)	
SPARCstation 1+ (4/65)	boot sd(0,6,2)
SPARCstation SLC (4/20)	
SPARCstation IPC (4/40)	
SPARCengine 1E	boot sd(0,6,5)
SPARCstation ELC (4/25)	
SPARCstation IPX (4/50)	
SPARCstation 2 (4/75)	boot cdrom

System Type	**Boot Command**
SPARCstation 10	
SPARCstation LX (4/30)	
SPARCserver 6XXMP and newer	
SPARCcenter 1000	
SPARCcenter 2000	
SPARCcenter LX	
SPARCclassic	

Example of Booting From CD-ROM

For the Mercury SPARCServer 2000 system, the boot command would be the following:

```
ok boot cdrom
```

This will load the SunInstall program from the CD-ROM, and the SunInstall program will be invoked.

The SunInstall Phase

The SunInstall program is the user interface to the Solaris installation process. SunInstall will prompt you for vital system information such as hardware configurations, types of clients, software to load, and network information. The SunInstall program will checkpoint its operation at various steps along the way and allow you to correct any information which was entered incorrectly. The following sections present a walk-through of the Solaris 2.4 installation.

Running SunInstall

When the SunInstall program starts, it will display general information about the installation process.

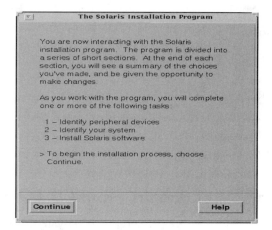

The Solaris installation program.

Select Continue to begin the installation process.

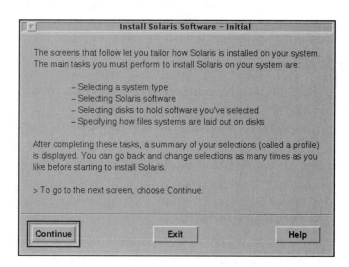

Solaris initial software installation.

The installation program displays more general information about the Solaris installation process. Select Continue to proceed to the next screen.

At this point, SunInstall will prompt you for the host name of your system.

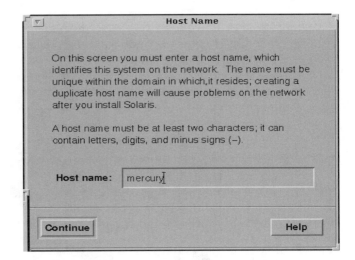

Setting the host name.

Type the name *mercury* and select Continue. Host names can include alphanumeric characters and minus signs. The first and last characters of a host name *cannot* be minus signs.

Next you are asked whether your system is connected to a network. Because the *mercury* system is connected to a network, you should answer Yes, and then select Continue.

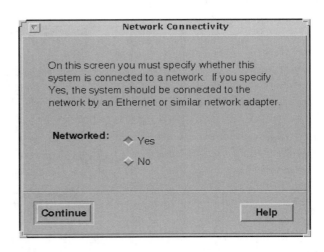

Network information under SunInstall.

Since you answered that *mercury* is on a network, SunInstall prompts you for the Internet Protocol (IP) address of your system. This is a unique address for your system as assigned by the Network Operations Center, or your network manager. See the chapter on Understanding Basic Local Area Networking for more information on IP addresses.

Setting the IP address.

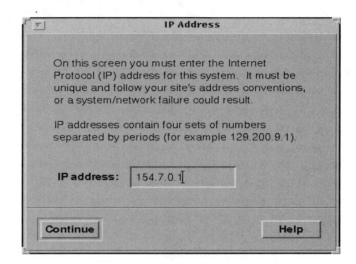

Enter *154.7.0.1* and select Continue. SunInstall will then display a page of information and ask whether this information is correct.

SunInstall system identification confirmation.

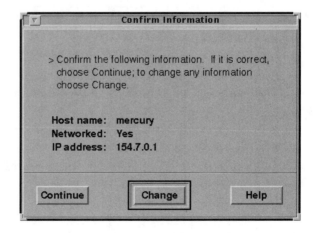

If the information contains errors, you would select Change which would send you back to the host name prompt. Since there are no errors, select

Continue. The system will pause momentarily, and display messages about what it is doing.

SunInstall informs you that there is more to come.

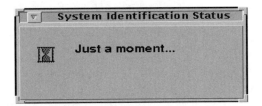

The next thing the system will display is a form which allows you to select the network name service. *Mercury* will be our network NIS+ name server; select *none* and then Continue.

✔ **NOTE:** *If you are installing name server clients, you will need to answer several additional setup questions at this point.*

Selecting the name service for the system.

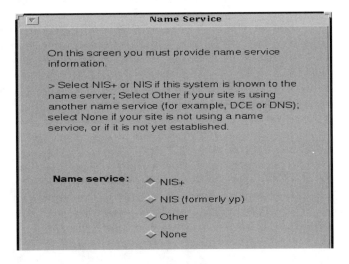

By selecting the NIS or NIS+ option, SunInstall will ask a few specialized questions which provide information required for this system, such as the current network domain.

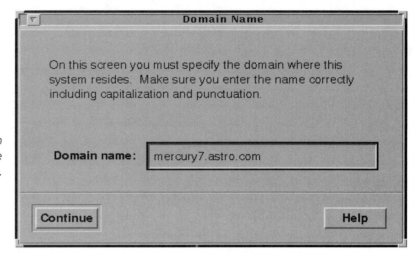

Setting the domain name for the system.

Once the domain name for this system is set, SunInstall will ask if you would like it to locate the name server. Specify the name server, and select Continue.

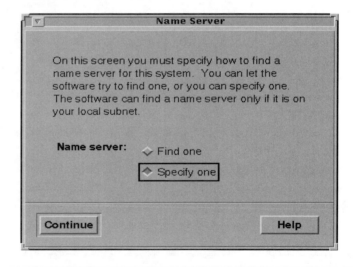

Informing SunInstall how it should locate the name server.

Because SunInstall was told not to look for name servers, it will ask for the name server address and host name for our domain. Once you enter the required information, select Continue.

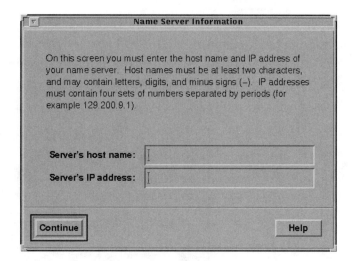

Setting the name server name and address.

The system responds by asking whether this system has subnetworks. Because we have a subnetwork with our client machines connected to it, select Yes and then Continue.

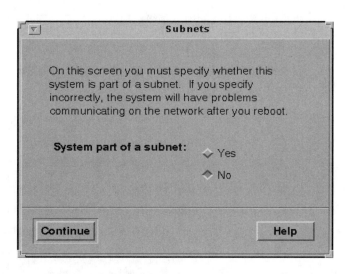

Informing SunInstall about the local area network.

At this point, you are asked to enter the subnet mask in use at your installation. Enter *255.255.255.0* and select Continue. The subnet mask is a value which is used by the system to determine if a packet is destined for this network. By performing a simple logical AND operation, the system can determine if this packet requires any system actions be taken.

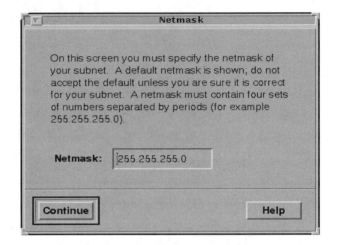

Setting the subnet mask for our system.

The system will again display a page of information, and ask us whether the information is correct before we continue.

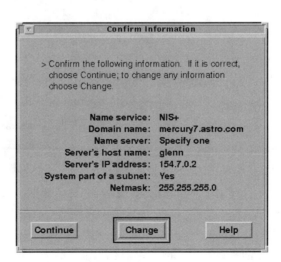

SunInstall confirms the name server information.

If errors are noticed in the information and you select Change, the system will return to the screen that prompts for a network name service. Since there are no errors, select Continue. The system pauses and displays some informational messages before responding with a screen asking us to select the geographic region of our installation.

SunInstall uses the information entered about the name server, and builds a set of internal "maps" that will allow this system to communicate on the network. Once this is complete, SunInstall will request information about your geographic location, and how to set the time zone for the system clock.

Selecting the geographic location of your system.

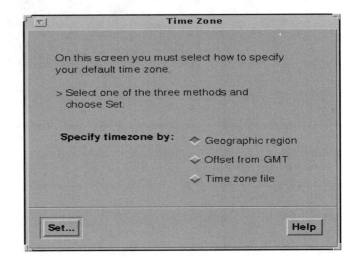

Select the *United States* and a time zone in the United States.

Setting the time zone information for the system.

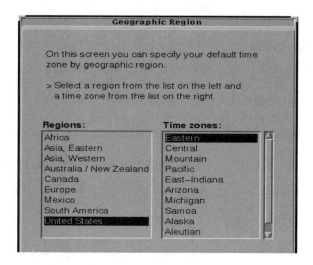

Select the appropriate time zone, and select Continue. This time zone information is used by the system so that the current date and time will be displayed in a format which users will recognize. Time zone acronyms such as EDT (Eastern Daylight Time) correspond to the international time zone standards. Once you have entered the time zone information, the system responds by displaying the current date and time for the chosen time zone. You have the option of resetting these parameters, or continuing on. Select Continue to proceed with the SunInstall process.

Setting the date and time for the system.

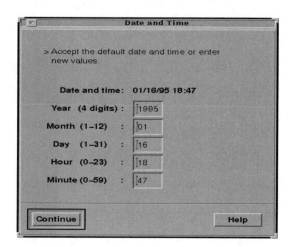

The system responds by asking you to confirm the information you just entered.

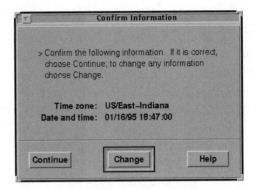

SunInstall asks you to confirm the location and time zone information.

If you detect an error and select Change, the system returns to the screen which prompts you for a specific geographic area. Since there are no errors, select Continue.

The software installation process is now ready to begin! The next screen provides basic information about software installation. Select Continue to proceed.

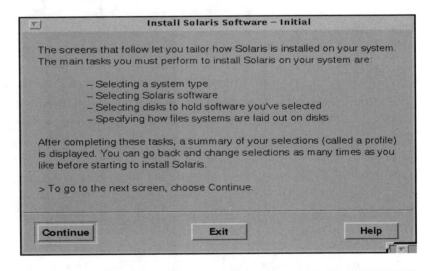

Information on the software installation process.

At this point the system identification phase of SunInstall is complete. You are now ready to move on to the software selection phase of the installation.

Software Selection Phase

We are ready to begin with the selection of software and hardware specific to your installation. The system prompts you with a screen asking the type of installation you desire. For the *mercury* system, you must choose Initial Install so that you can load the proper software for the server installation.

Server installation consists of the following steps:

Setting the system type to server.

❑ Setting up the client parameters.

❑ Selecting the software we wish to install.

❑ Selecting one or more localizations (optional).

❑ Configuring the disks.

❑ Setting up remote file systems (optional).

❑ Starting the installation.

Selecting the type of installation to perform.

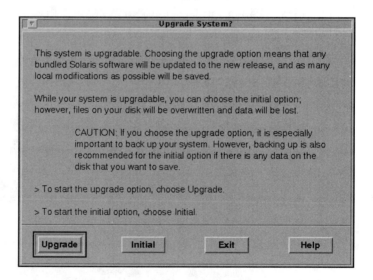

The next screen displayed allows you to select the System Type for your installation.

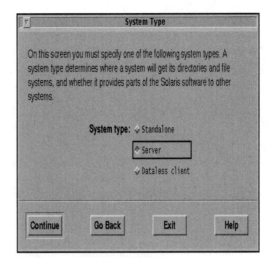

*Selecting the
system type.*

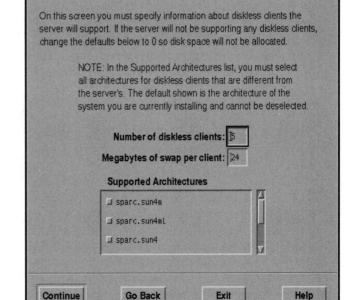

*Selecting the client
configurations.*

SunInstall will prompt you to select the type of system you are installing. Click on Server and then select Continue.

At this point, you need to select the architecture of each client of your server. In this case, we have one Sun4c and one Sun4m client. You need to select each of these architectures, and fill in the client count, the number of diskless clients, and the swap space required by the client before you continue.

When you finish selecting the appropriate client configurations, select Continue. The installation process next asks you to choose the Software Selection parameters.

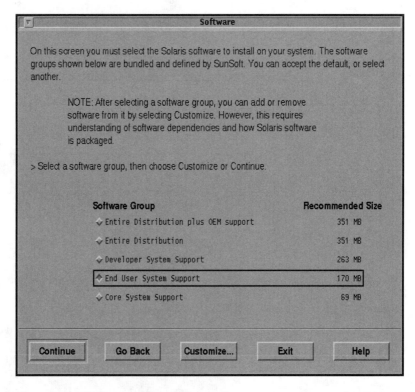

The software selection menu.

Select the Entire Distribution option for your server installation. Once you make this selection, select Continue to proceed with your installation.

The default software configuration screen shows the available configuration clusters. A dark square marks the currently selected cluster. If you want to edit the software configuration, select the Edit button.

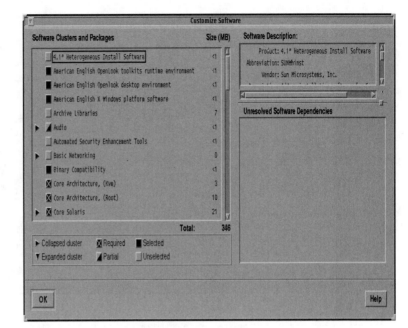

Customizing the software configuration.

You can step through each component of the End User System Configuration and determine whether you would like to load that package.

Once you finish editing your installation, dismiss the pop-up menu, and select OK to continue the system configuration. At this point Solaris informs you of how much disk space you have consumed with your selections.

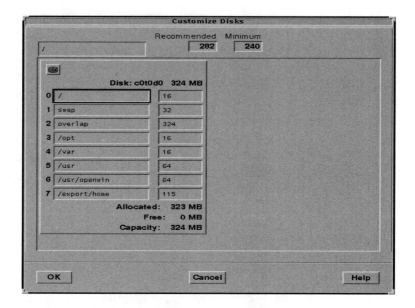

Displaying the file system size requirements.

This information can be compared to your inventory forms to determine if you have reasonable estimates for your space requirements. You can now dismiss this screen by selecting OK, and continue with the server setup.

The Disks screen allows you to select which disks will be used to hold the system binaries.

Select Continue to allow setting up your system disk drive as it was laid out earlier in this chapter.

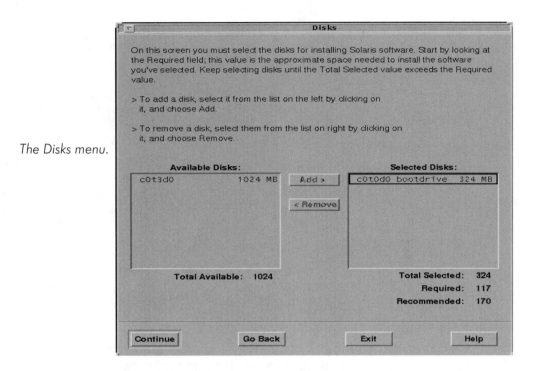

The Disks menu.

Disks

On this screen you must select the disks for installing Solaris software. Start by looking at the Required field; this value is the approximate space needed to install the software you've selected. Keep selecting disks until the Total Selected value exceeds the Required value.

> To add a disk, select it from the list on the left by clicking on it, and choose Add.

> To remove a disk, select them from the list on right by clicking on it, and choose Remove.

Available Disks: **Selected Disks:**

c0t3d0   1024 MB   Add >   c0t0d0 bootdrive   324 MB

                                       < Remove

Total Available: 1024   **Total Selected:**   324
                                             Required: 117
                                       Recommended: 170

Continue   Go Back   Exit   Help

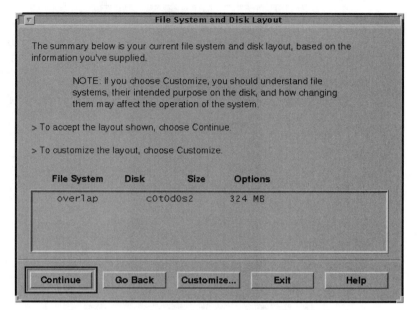

Configuring the disk drives.

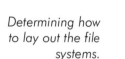

Determining how to lay out the file systems.

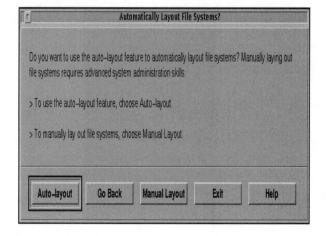

A new feature to Solaris 2.4 is the "auto layout" selection for file system setup. Alternately, you may choose to manually lay out the file systems.

The next screen allows you to set the size and mount point of each file system. You can now enter the appropriate file system sizes and mount points as determined earlier.

Once you are happy with your disk layout, select the Apply item and type <Enter> to continue. At this point the system checks your layout for errors. If the system finds an error, it displays an appropriate warning screen, and allows you to make changes to the configuration. If you have not allowed enough space for the installation, you will get a screen that allows you the option to make changes to your layout, or continue with the layout as selected.

Editing the disk configurations.

Beginning the installation process.

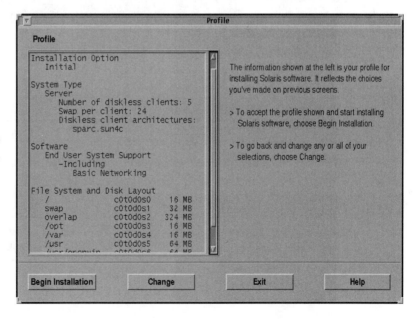

Once you have completed the disk layout phase of software selection, select the Begin Installation item, and the system will begin the installation process.

The system will now ask if a reboot is acceptable after the software is installed on the disks. Select Reboot to continue with the installation process.

System query on reboot.

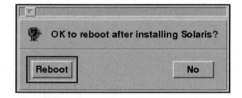

After the system makes the required file systems, a screen will appear that allows you to follow the installation procedure.

Graphic display of the progress of the installation process.

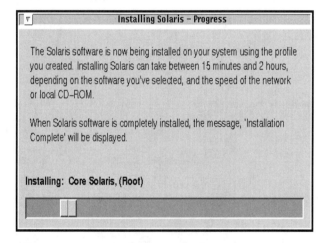

When the installation is complete the system will reboot.

The Post-installation Phase

Once Solaris is loaded and running, you need to integrate critical SunOS 4.1 data into the system. This restoration is divided into the following five sections:

Restoration Steps and Chapter Discussion

Step	Chapter
Setting up the NIS+ master name service	Managing Network Data with NIS+
Restoring SunOS 4.1.X user data	System Backups and Disaster Recovery
Restoring SunOS 4.1.X system data	System Backups and Disaster Recovery
Setting up users, printers, and mail	Everyday System Administration Commands and Practices / Adding Terminals and Modems
Removing a remote install client (discussed below)	

To remove an install client once the remote Solaris installation is complete, you need to use the following two commands:

```
# cd /cdrom
# ./rm_install_client client_name
```

The shell script removes the */etc/export* entry, the */tftpboot* entry, and the */etc/bootparams* entry for the client.

Using the sys-unconfig Command

What happens if you notice a setup error once the installation is complete? You can use the **sys-unconfig** command to unconfigure the system. This command will remove much of the system configuration information, and halt the system. When the system is rebooted, you will be prompted for this information as part of the system boot process. This method allows you to build several systems in a production line environment with one procedure, and then customize the system upon delivery to its final resting place.

The system will prompt you for information such as the system name, network address, time zone, and the name service. As you enter this information, the system will update the pertinent files such that this information becomes the current system information.

Results after using sys-unconfig upon reboot.

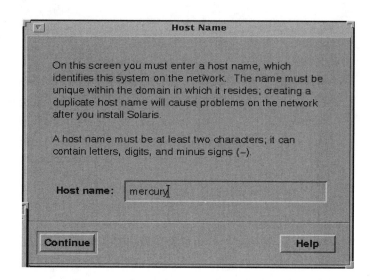

Summary

In this chapter the SunInstall program was used to install a Solaris 2.4 server with two clients. In addition, the chapter included information on how to use the **sys-unconfig** script file to correct any errors made during the installation process. In Chapter 5, you will learn simple system administration commands that can be used to complete the setup of Solaris systems. In the chapter on system administration with OpenWindows, you will learn how to use OpenWindows to perform simple system administration and complete the setup of your Solaris system.

5

System Administration with OpenWindows

Now that Solaris is loaded on your computer, you need to begin setting up the system for your users. In this chapter, we will review some simple UNIX commands, and how to use the OpenWindows package to perform simple administration tasks. The basics you learn in this chapter will allow you to set up the system, and monitor system performance for your users.

Most modern operating systems provide some type of window management software. Under Solaris, the standard windowing software package is called OpenWindows. This and other graphic user interface products allow the user to have multiple screens, or windows available at the same time. This makes the task of switching between operations much easier, because you can open a window for each operation you wish to work with.

An Overview of OpenWindows

Most personal computer (PC) based systems are single-user/single-tasking systems. These systems usually have a window based operating mode, but they still only allow one program to run at a time. Conversely, Solaris is a multi-user/multi-tasking operating system. Under the Solaris windowing system, a user may have many programs running at the same time. This allows the system administrator the flexibility to have several windows open at a time. Each of these windows may be dedicated to a separate task.

OpenWindows is a successor to the SunView windowing system in earlier releases of the SunOS operating system. SunView (also known as SunTools) was a closed architecture windowing system. It was only available on Sun workstations, and it could not interoperate with other popular windowing packages. OpenWindows is an open architecture windowing system. The specifications of OpenWindows are available to window system implementors so that OpenWindows can be implemented by other system designers. OpenWindows also allows the user to include features from the popular X11 window package. Most X11 applications will run in the OpenWindows environment.

The default OpenWindows window manager is the *olwm* or Open Look Window Manager. This is the program that manages the resources of the system display. The user may choose to have certain windows and utilities appear on startup. These windows may be open, or iconified as specified by the user. The window manager keeps track of the location of the mouse pointer, and causes the windows to "pop to the top" of the display stack as soon as the mouse enters the borders of a particular window. If the user prefers, the window manager will wait for the user to select the desired window with a click of the mouse button.

OpenWindows includes several helpful utility programs in the default desktop environment. Some of these utilities are the Calendar Manager (to keep track of appointments and dates), the File Manager (to provide a graphical interface to the file system), the Mail Tool (to provide a point and click based mail interface), the Text Editor (to provide mouse driven editing capabilities), and Calc Tool (to provide a simple graphical calculator).

Combined with a multi-user/multi-tasking workstation, the OpenWindows windowing system provides the system administrator with a very flexible tool kit for overseeing daily systems operations. Through the use of multiple windows and built-in Solaris utilities, the system administrator's task of system management can be automated to some degree, allowing the system administrator more time to deal with more important issues.

A Review of Important UNIX Commands

Before opening multiple windows to administer a system, you need to master some of the basic UNIX commands that you will be using.

cp (Copy Files)

The command **cp file_a file_b** will copy file_a to file_b. Two useful command line options to the **cp** command are **-p** (preserve file modes), and **-r** (recursively copy files in a directory). For example, **cp -p /etc/motd mymotd** will copy the /etc/motd file to file *mymotd* in your current directory.

cat (Concatenate and Display Files)

The **cat** command provides a way to concatenate a file onto standard output (display the file), or to concatenate multiple files into a single file. An example follows:

```
$ cat mymotd
Sun Microsystems Inc. SunOS 5.3 Generic September 1993
```

Typing in *cat mymotd /etc/passwd > /tmp/xxx* will create a file named */tmp/xxx* containing the contents of the file *mymotd*, followed by the contents of the file */etc/passwd*.

more (Browse or Page Through a Text File)

The **more** command provides a way for the user to page through long files. Its operation is very similar to **cat**. To see the next screen of text, type a space. To move forward in the text one line at a time, you can type <Enter>. To see the previous screen of text, type <Ctrl>+b (^b).

Output of the command more /etc/services.

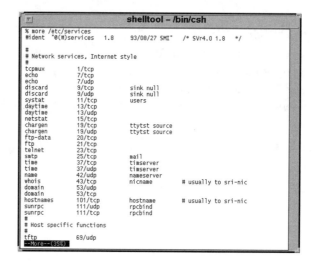

```
                         shelltool – /bin/csh
% more /etc/services
#ident  "@(#)services   1.8     93/08/27 SMI"   /* SVr4.0 1.8  */

#
# Network services, Internet style
#
tcpmux          1/tcp
echo            7/tcp
echo            7/udp
discard         9/tcp                   sink null
discard         9/udp                   sink null
systat          11/tcp                  users
daytime         13/tcp
daytime         13/udp
netstat         15/tcp
chargen         19/tcp                  ttytst source
chargen         19/udp                  ttytst source
ftp-data        20/tcp
ftp             21/tcp
telnet          23/tcp
smtp            25/tcp                  mail
time            37/tcp                  timserver
time            37/udp                  timserver
name            42/udp                  nameserver
whois           43/tcp                  nicname         # usually to sri-nic
domain          53/udp
domain          53/tcp
hostnames       101/tcp                 hostname        # usually to sri-nic
sunrpc          111/udp                 rpcbind
sunrpc          111/tcp                 rpcbind
#
# Host specific functions
#
tftp            69/udp
--More--(35%)
```

ls (List Contents of Directories)

The **ls** command comes complete with a plethora of command line options. The most useful of these are **-l** (long listing), **-a** (all files), **-s** (give size of file in blocks), and **-i** (list inode number for the file). The command **ls -lasi mymotd** will give you information on the file you just created with the **cp** command. An example follows.

```
33 8 -rw-r--r-- 2 curt root 55 Jun 29 16:07 mymotd
```

ln (Make Hard or Symbolic Links to Files)

Sometimes it is desirable to "point" a file at another file in order to avoid duplication of information and wasted disk space. It is possible to carry out such file linking under Solaris with the **ln** command.

Solaris allows two types of links: hard links, and symbolic links. A hard link, created with the **ln file_a file_b** comand, is indistinguishable from the original directory entry, but cannot span file systems. A symbolic link, created with the **ln -s file_a file_b** command, contains the name of the file to which it is linked. Symbolic links may cross file system boundaries. For example, **ln mymotd b** will create a hard link from file *b* to file *mymotd*, while **ln -s mymotd c** will create a symbolic link from file *c* to file *mymotd*.

Using the **ls -lasi** command to examine *mymotd*, *b*, and *c*, you will see the following:

```
33 8 -rw-r--r-- 2 curt root 55 Jun 29 16:07 mymotd
33 8 -rw-r--r-- 2 curt root 55 Jun 29 16:07 b
34 8 lrwxrwxrwx 1 curt root 1 Jun 29 16:07 c -> mymotd
```

By using the **-i** flag on the **ls** command, the output lists not only the name, creation date, and size of the file, but also two numbers at the beginning of the output. These numbers are the inode number, and the number of links to the file.

Note that files *mymotd* and *b* have the same inode number. File *c* has a different inode number.

mv (Move Files)

The **mv** command moves files from one file name to another file name. If you look at the current directory listing, you see that we have the files *b*, *c*, and *mymotd*.

```
33 8 -rw-r--r-- 2 curt root 55 Jun 29 16:07 mymotd
33 8 -rw-r--r-- 2 curt root 55 Jun 29 16:07 b
34 8 lrwxrwxrwx 1 curt root 1 Jun 29 16:07 c -> mymotd
```

The **mv mymotd d** command will move the *mymotd* file to a file named *d*. An example follows:

```
$ ls -lasi mymotd b c d
mymotd: No such file or directory
33 8 -rw-r--r-- 2 curt root 55 Jun 29 16:07 b
34 8 lrwxrwxrwx 1 curt root 1 Jun 29 16:07 c -> mymotd
33 8 -rw-r--r-- 2 curt root 55 Jun 29 16:07 d
```

Note that the symbolically linked file points to something that no longer exists, while the hard linked file still contains the correct information. If you use **mv d mymotd**, all links will be back to normal.

rm (Remove Files)

When dealing with plain files, **rm** removes the file name you give it. When used with links, funny things happen. As seen in the following, in the current directory listing you can see files *b*, *c*, and *mymotd*.

```
$ ls -lasi
33 8 -rw-r--r-- 2 curt root 55 Jun 29 16:07 b
34 8 lrwxrwxrwx 1 curt root 1 Jun 29 16:07 c -> mymotd
33 8 -rw-r--r-- 2 curt root 55 Jun 29 16:07 mymotd
```

For example, **rm mymotd** will remove the file mymotd, leaving a copy in the hard linked file, but the symbolically linked file c now points to nowhere:

```
$ ls -lasi
33 8 -rw-r--r-- 2 curt root 55 Jun 29 16:07 b
34 8 lrwxrwxrwx 1 curt root 1 Jun 29 16:07 c -> mymotd
$ ls -lasi mymotd b c
mymotd: No such file or directory
33 8 -rw-r--r-- 2 curt root 55 Jun 29 16:07 b
34 8 lrwxrwxrwx 1 curt root 1 Jun 29 16:07 c -> mymotd
```

Two of the most commonly used flags to **rm** include **-i** (interactive, or a prompt to make sure the user really wants to do this), and **-r** (recursively remove files from a directory).

> **!** **WARNING:** *The **rm** command does not make a backup copy of the file before removing it. Care must be taken to avoid removing important files. Typically, a better route is to **mv** the file to another file name until you are sure you can operate the system without that file.*

mkdir (Make Directory)

The **mkdir** command makes a directory with a name you specify in the current directory. If you wish to make a directory somewhere other than in the current directory, you need to specify the full path to the target directory, such as **mkdir /tmp/foo**. This command will not overwrite an existing file or directory.

```
# ls -lsa /tmp/xyz
/tmp/xyz not found
# mkdir /tmp/xyz
# ls -lsa /tmp/xyz
/tmp/xyz:
Total 2
1 drwx--S--- 4 root 512 Oct 12 13:12 .
1 drwxrwxrwx 6 root 1024 Oct 12 13:12 ..
# mkdir /tmp/xyz
/tmp/xyz: file exists
```

rmdir (Remove Directories)

Rmdir will only remove a directory which is empty. If you attempt to remove a non-empty directory, **rmdir** will inform you that the directory is not empty. The **rm -r directory_name** command will recursively remove the directory and all contents of the directory. Examples follow:

```
# mkdir /tmp/xyz
# mkdir /tmp/xyz/abc
# mkdir /tmp/xyz/def
# ls -lsa /tmp/xyz /tmp/xyz/abc /tmp/xyz/def
/tmp/xyz:
Total 4
1 drwx--S--- 4 root 512 Oct 12 13:12 .
1 drwxrwxrwx 6 root 1024 Oct 12 13:12 ..
1 drwx--S--- 4 root 512 abc
1 drwx--S--- 4 root 512 def
# rmdir /tmp/xyz
rmdir: /tmp/xyz: Directory not empty
# rmdir /tmp/xyz/abc
# ls -lsa /tmp/xyz /tmp/xyz/abc /tmp/xyz/def
/tmp/xyz/abc not found
/tmp/xyz:
Total 4
1 drwx--S--- 4 root 512 Oct 12 13:12 .
1 drwxrwxrwx 6 root 1024 Oct 12 13:12 ..
1 drwx--S--- 4 root 512 def
# rm -r /tmp/xyz
# ls -lsa /tmp/xyz /tmp/xyz/abc /tmp/xyz/def
/tmp/xyz not found
/tmp/xyz/abc not found
/tmp/xyz/def not found
```

passwd (Change User Password)

The **passwd** command may be used to change user passwords, or other information fields in the password file. Examples appear below.

To change the super-user password:

```
# passwd
```

Changing the password for root:

```
Old password:
New password:
Retype new password:
```

> ✔ **NOTE:** *The password will not echo on the screen. This is done to prevent bystanders from obtaining the password as it is typed.*

To change the password of user "jim":

```
# passwd jim
Changing password for jim
New password:
Retype new password:
```

pwd (Print Working Directory)

The **pwd** command gives you a way to determine which directory you are currently working in. An example follows:

```
pwd
/tmp
```

cd (Change Working Directory)

The **cd** command allows you to traverse the file system tree. The following command lines will set the current directory to the *foo* directory which you just created:

```
$ cd foo
$ pwd
/tmp/foo
```

chown (Change Ownership of a File)

The **chown** command allows the super-user to change any file ownership to any valid user ID on the system. As demonstrated below, users are only allowed to change ownership on files for which they have write permission.

```
# ls -lsa /tmp/foo
rwxr-xr-o 2 curt root 37 Jun 29 16:54 foo
# chown root /tmp/foo
# ls -lsa /tmp/foo
rwxr-xr-o 2 root root 37 Jun 29 16:54 foo
```

> ✔ **NOTE:** *You must be the super-user or have write access on the target directory to **chown** a file from one user to another. This prevents users from changing ownership of their files to another user ID without the permission of both users.*

chmod (Change the Permissions Mode of a File)

The **chmod** command allows the user to change a file mode from read only to read+write+execute, read+write, read+execute, write only, write+execute, or execute only. These permissions can be allowed for the user, the group that the user belongs to, or to all system users. The super-user is allowed to select other modes for files. An example follows:

```
# ls -lsa /tmp/foo
rwxr-xr-o 2 root root 37 Jun 29 16:54 foo
# chmod 710 /tmp/foo
# ls -lsa /tmp/foo
rwx--x--- 2 root root 37 Jun 29 16:54 foo
```

> ✔ **NOTE:** *You must have write permission on the file before you can **chmod** it to another mode. This prevents a user from changing modes on another user's files.*

ps (Report Process Status)

The **ps** command, which provides a simple method of monitoring system performance, also comes with a plethora of command line options. A couple of the most useful options are **-e**, which reports all processes, and **-f**, which gives a full listing for each process.

grep (Search a File for a Pattern)

As illustrated below, the **grep** command can be used to look for the occurrence of a string in a file. When combined with other commands, it allows you to look for occurrences of particular events.

The following example shows how to find all processes being run by the user *curt*:

```
$ ps -e |grep curt
curt 178 1 80 19:41:28 console 0:01 -csh
curt 218 206 51 20:12:07 console 0:00 /bin/csh -c ps -e |grep curt
curt 222 218 19 20:12:07 console 0:00 ps -e
curt 223 218 6 20:12:07 console 0:00 grep curt
```

> ✔ **NOTE:** *Under UNIX, the vertical bar (|) is called a "pipe." It allows the user to pipe (or feed) the output of a command into the input stream of another command. This allows the user to construct complex operations by piping the output from one utility to another until the desired result is obtained.*

man (Manual Pages)

The **man** command allows you to view the on-line manual page on a specific topic or command. For example, **man ls** will display the on-line manual page for the **ls** command. The manual pages explain the use of all command line options, and any peculiarities of the command.

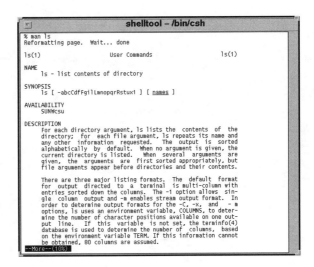

Output of the man ls command.

find (Find Files)

The **find** command allows the user to search the file system tree for the occurrence of a pattern. The find command allows the use of Boolean operations to structure the search fields, and also has many "actions" which can be taken once the pattern is found. The **find** command options are far too numerous to list here. For more information on the find command, consult the appropriate on-line manual page. A simple example of using the **find** command to remove all files in the home directory named *a.out* or **.o* that have not been accessed for seven days or more appears in the following command line and illustrations.

```
find $HOME \( -name a.out -o -name '*.o' \) -atime +7 -exec rm {} \;
```

```
% date
Sat Oct 15 10:00:12 EST 1994
% ls -lsa
total 634
   2 drwxr-xr-x   3 jim    root      512 Aug  8 11:15 .
   2 drwxr-xr-x   3 jim    root      512 Sep 19 16:32 ..
   2 -rw-------   1 jim    root      911 Aug  8 11:12 COPYRIGHT
   2 -rw-------   1 jim    root      493 Aug  8 11:12 MANIFEST
   4 -rw-------   1 jim    root     1881 Aug  8 11:13 Makefile
  12 -rw-------   1 jim    root     5155 Aug  8 11:13 README
  12 -rw-------   1 jim    root     5905 Aug  8 11:13 format.c
   2 -rw-------   1 jim    root      281 Aug  8 11:13 format.h
  38 -rw-r--r--   1 jim    root    19024 Aug  8 11:15 format.o
   2 -rw-------   1 jim    root      125 Aug  8 11:13 patchlevel.h
  60 -rwxr-xr-x   1 jim    root    30340 Aug  8 11:15 a.out
 118 -rw-r--r--   1 jim    root    59530 Aug  3 13:05 scsiinfo-3.3.shar
  10 -rw-------   1 jim    root     5083 Aug  8 11:13 scsiinfo.1
  24 -rw-------   1 jim    root    11382 Aug  8 11:13 scsiinfo.c
 224 -rw-r--r--   1 jim    root   101292 Aug  8 11:17 scsiinfo.o
   2 drwx------   2 jim    root      512 Aug  8 11:13 sundev
   8 -rw-------   1 jim    root     3173 Aug  8 11:13 sunos4.h
   8 -rw-------   1 jim    root     4060 Aug  8 11:13 sunos5.h
  14 -rw-------   1 jim    root     6268 Aug  8 11:13 uscsi.c
   2 -rw-------   1 jim    root      445 Aug  8 11:13 uscsi.h
  52 -rw-r--r--   1 jim    root    25792 Aug  8 11:15 uscsi.o
  10 -rw-------   1 jim    root     4163 Aug  8 11:13 utils.c
   4 -rw-------   1 jim    root     1848 Aug  8 11:13 utils.h
  20 -rw-r--r--   1 jim    root    10012 Aug  8 11:14 utils.o
```

Directory listing before using find to remove a.out and .o files.

```
% date
Sat Oct 15 10:10:08 EST 1994
% ls -lsa
total 240
   2 drwxr-xr-x   3 jim    root      512 Aug  8 11:15 .
   2 drwxr-xr-x   3 jim    root      512 Sep 19 16:32 ..
   2 -rw-------   1 jim    root      911 Aug  8 11:12 COPYRIGHT
   2 -rw-------   1 jim    root      493 Aug  8 11:12 MANIFEST
   4 -rw-------   1 jim    root     1881 Aug  8 11:13 Makefile
  12 -rw-------   1 jim    root     5155 Aug  8 11:13 README
  12 -rw-------   1 jim    root     5905 Aug  8 11:13 format.c
   2 -rw-------   1 jim    root      281 Aug  8 11:13 format.h
   2 -rw-------   1 jim    root      125 Aug  8 11:13 patchlevel.h
 118 -rw-r--r--   1 jim    root    59530 Aug  3 13:05 scsiinfo-3.3.shar
  10 -rw-------   1 jim    root     5083 Aug  8 11:13 scsiinfo.1
  24 -rw-------   1 jim    root    11382 Aug  8 11:13 scsiinfo.c
   2 drwx------   2 jim    root      512 Aug  8 11:13 sundev
   8 -rw-------   1 jim    root     3173 Aug  8 11:13 sunos4.h
   8 -rw-------   1 jim    root     4060 Aug  8 11:13 sunos5.h
  14 -rw-------   1 jim    root     6268 Aug  8 11:13 uscsi.c
   2 -rw-------   1 jim    root      445 Aug  8 11:13 uscsi.h
  10 -rw-------   1 jim    root     4163 Aug  8 11:13 utils.c
   4 -rw-------   1 jim    root     1848 Aug  8 11:13 utils.h
```

Directory listing after using find to remove a.out and .o files.

 TIP: *One way to prevent a file system from running out of space is to periodically run a **find** process to remove typical temporary or trash files which accumulate in the directory. For example, removal of .o files and core files will often free much needed space in oversubscribed file systems.*

Starting OpenWindows

Now that you have seen some of the simple UNIX commands available, you need to apply them to system administration chores. But first you will want to open up some windows to allow additional flexibility.

In a typical installation, the OpenWindows package will reside in the */usr/openwin* directory. Under this directory are several subdirectories which contain the libraries, binaries, include files, demo packages, manual pages, and several other applications. To start OpenWindows, you need to log in on the system console, and type the following command:

```
# /usr/openwin/bin/openwin
```

✔ **NOTE**: *Copying the /etc/skel/local.profile file to the / directory may be helpful. This will cause the system to set up the path variable such that OpenWindows will know where to find all of its libraries and associated binaries.*

The system will load the OpenWindows package and display the greeting window as it locates and loads the rest of the binary.

Sample of the OpenWindows greeting window.

Välkommen till

ようこそ

Bienvenue à

歡 迎

Welcome to

Benvenuti a

환 영

Willkommen zu

欢 迎

Solaris

Once the binary is loaded, OpenWindows will bring up several windows, including the system console window. This window will receive copies of system error messages.

*OpenWindows
console window.*

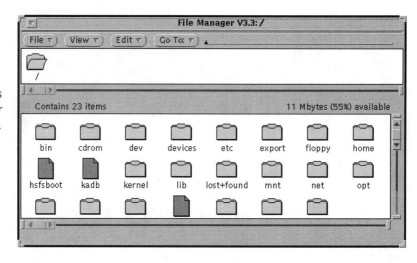

✔ **NOTE:** *While you may be tempted to iconify or close the console window, it is recommended that you keep it open at all times. By closing or iconizing the console window, you are no longer able to see important system error and informational messages.*

*The OpenWindows
file manager
window.*

Another window which will be opened upon start-up is the File Manager window. The File Manager window provides the ability to graphically peruse the file system.

Running Multiple Utilities

OpenWindows employs pop-up menus to select and start applications. If you move the cursor to a location which is not contained in an already open window, and hold down the right mouse button, a pop-up menu will appear. This menu will allow you the flexibility to open more windows; start system monitoring tools, text editors, and mail handlers; set screen preferences; and ultimately, exit the windowing system.

✔ **NOTE:** *The system default menu templates for the pop-up windows are contained in the /usr/openwin/lib directory. By changing these files, the administrator can change the default settings for all system users.*

✘ **TIP:** *Users may customize their own pop-up menus through the use of setup files in their home directories. The .openwin-menu file allows for the customization of the pop-up workspace menus. The .openwin-init file allows for customization of the windows which are opened at start-up.*

Example OpenWindows control menu.

*Example
OpenWindows
pop-up menu.*

Cmdtool Versus Shelltool

There are two basic types of windows under OpenWindows: *cmdtool* windows, and *shelltool* windows. The choice of the type of window you use is strictly personal. The differences between these two window types follow:

❑ The shelltool windows run a shell or other programs which use a standard tty based interface within the window.

❑ The cmdtool windows use mouse-based editing, logging functions, and scrolling. Cmdtool windows may also execute shell commands.

If you want to open a few windows, select the Programs menu, and select Shell Tool to open a *shelltool* window. Once the shelltool window appears, you have a window to use for system administration commands on your local system. You may also find it useful to open separate windows for each of your client systems so that you can easily access them. Once these windows are opened, use the **rlogin machine_name** command to activate a remote log-in to another machine.

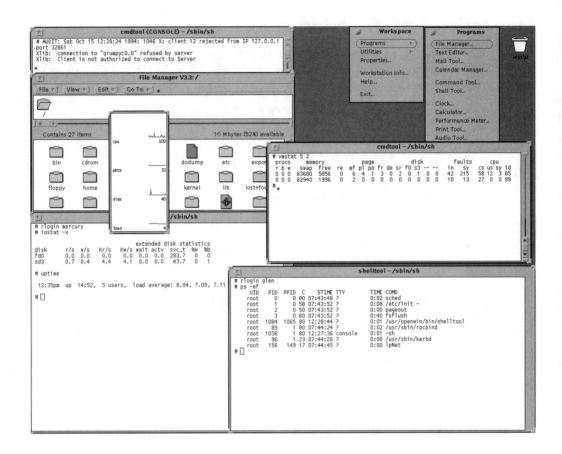

Opening multiple windows enables effective administration of the system.

One nice feature of owning a multi-tasking workstation is that you can start several concurrent applications at a time and let them run. Now that you have opened several windows on your system, you have the freedom to move between these applications at will. You can open a window on the *glenn* system, and use the **ps** command to look at the process table. Concurrently, you can use a window on the *gus* system to run the **cp** command to copy files. Also concurrently, you can use a window on the *mercury* server to monitor system performance.

Monitoring System Performance

One of the most common applications for multiple windows is monitoring system performance. Several applications available under Solaris that allow you to monitor various portions of system performance are listed below:

❏ **sar** The System Activity Reporter.

❏ **iostat** Reports I/O statistics.

❏ **netstat** Reports network statistics.

❏ **snoop** Captures and displays network packets.

❏ **vmstat** Reports virtual memory statistics.

❏ **mpstat** Reports per-processor activity on multi-cpu systems.

❏ **sag** The System Activity Graph.

❏ **perfmeter** Provides graphical displays of system performance.

Identifying a System Performance Problem

As an example of how these tools may be used, suppose the *glenn* machine is not performing up to expectations. You would like to determine the cause of its poor performance. The first thing you should do is move to the window you previously opened on the *glenn* machine, and use the **ps -ef** command to see which processes are currently running on *glenn*.

From the output of the **ps -e** command, you can see that the normal system daemons are running. You can also see that a couple of long-running user jobs are currently active on the *glenn* system. But you do not have enough information from the **ps** command to determine why the system is slow. Is the problem lack of memory? Is the problem lack of swap space? Is the problem a network or I/O bandwidth bottleneck? Further examination is necessary to determine the cause of poor performance.

```
# ps -ef
    UID   PID  PPID  C   STIME TTY       TIME COMD
   root     0     0 80 07:43:48 ?        0:02 sched
   root     1     0  8 07:43:52 ?        0:06 /etc/init -
   root     2     0 46 07:43:52 ?        0:00 pageout
   root     3     0 80 07:43:52 ?        0:32 fsflush
   root    89     1 80 07:44:24 ?        0:02 /usr/sbin/rpcbind
   curt   539  1161 10:28:05 console     0:01 -csh
   root    96     1 23 07:44:26 ?        0:00 /usr/sbin/kerbd
   root   156   149 17 07:44:45 ?        0:00 lpNet
   root    84     1  7 07:44:23 ?        0:00 /usr/sbin/in.routed -q
   root    91     1  5 07:44:25 ?        0:00 /usr/sbin/keyserv
   root   105     1 80 07:44:32 ?        0:01 /usr/sbin/inetd -s
   root   112     1 19 07:44:33 ?        0:00 /usr/lib/autofs/automountd
   root   149     1 80 07:44:45 ?        0:01 /usr/lib/lpsched
   root   139     1 19 07:44:43 ?        0:00 /usr/sbin/cron
   root   185     1 46 07:44:50 ?        0:00 /usr/lib/saf/sac -t 300
   root   158     1 54 07:44:47 ?        0:00 /usr/lib/sendmail -bd -q1h
   root   161     1 65 07:44:47 ?        0:02 /usr/sbin/vold
   curt   842   833 54 11:26:09 console  0:01 olwmslave
   root   193   185 44 07:44:51 ?        0:00 /usr/lib/saf/ttymon
   curt   816   539 80 11:25:56 console  0:00 /bin/sh /usr/openwin/bin/openwin
   curt   822   820160 11:26:04 console  0:00 sh /home/curt/.xinitrc
   curt   881   833 80 11:28:32 ?        0:02 /usr/openwin/bin/xview/shelltool
   curt   820   816 20 11:25:58 console  0:00 /usr/openwin/bin/xinit -- /usr/c
penwin/bin/X :0 -auth /home/curt/.xsun.glenn:0
   curt   884   881 80 11:28:33 pts/1    0:01 /bin/csh
   curt   826     1 33 11:26:04 console  0:00 fbconsole
   curt   844     1 51 11:26:10 console  0:01 vkbd -nopopup
   curt   847     1 80 11:26:12 console  0:01 ttsession -s
   curt   927   884 24 11:47:29 pts/1    0:00 ps -ef
   curt   833   822 80 11:26:06 console  0:04 olwm -3
 marvin   910   884 80 11:39:01 pts/1    8:02 mailtool
```

Using the ps command to obtain a listing of processes currently active on the system.

Using the vmstat command to help determine the cause of system performance problems.

```
# vmstat ; sleep 5 ; vmstat

 procs     memory            page            disk          faults      cpu
 r b w   swap  free  re  mf pi po fr de sr f0 s3 -- --   in   sy  cs us sy id
 0 0 0  84112  6224   0   6  4  1  3  0  2  0  1  0  0   45  236  54 14  4 83

 procs     memory            page            disk          faults      cpu
 r b w   swap  free  re  mf pi po fr de sr f0 s3 -- --   in   sy  cs us sy id
 0 0 0  83001  7394   0   8 14  1  5  0  2  0  1  0  0   54  362  44 24  4 73
```

✘ **TIP:** *By running **vmstat**, waiting five seconds, and then running another **vmstat**, you can get a rough idea of how much memory traffic a system has experienced during a five-second interval. If the memory usage statistics are increasing very rapidly, it is a good sign that this host is running in a memory starved environment.*

Using the iostat command to help determine the cause of system performance problems.

```
# iostat -x ; sleep 5 ; iostat -x

                           extended disk statistics
disk      r/s  w/s   Kr/s   Kw/s wait actv  svc_t  %w  %b
sd3      27.2  9.9   39.1    9.1  0.0  0.0   31.7   0   1

                           extended disk statistics
disk      r/s  w/s   Kr/s   Kw/s wait actv  svc_t  %w  %b
sd3      45.7  7.4   49.5    4.0  0.0  0.0   42.9   0   1
```

✖ **TIP:** *By running **iostat**, waiting five seconds, and then running another **iostat**, you can get a rough idea of how much disk traffic a system has read/written to disk during a five-second interval. If the transfer counts are increasing very rapidly, it is a good sign that this host is performing a lot of disk I/O.*

By using the **vmstat** and **iostat** commands, you find that *glenn* has sufficient free memory, and that the disk I/O is not excessive. If you look back at the output of the **ps -ef** command, you notice that one of the long running jobs is a *mailtool* process. It does not seem reasonable that one user spends so much time trying to read his/her mail. Something does not look right with this process. Let's take a closer look.

Using ps to obtain more information on a process.

```
# ps -p 910
  PID TTY         TIME COMD
  910 pts/1      10:33 mailtool
```

When you input **ps -p 910**, you see that the *mailtool* process with process ID 910 is indeed accumulating quite a large amount of cpu time. Upon using the **who** command, you notice that this user is not logged in at the current time.

Using the who command to determine which users are currently logged into the system.

```
# who
curt        console       Oct 13 10:28
curt        pts/0         Oct 15 08:20
varmint     pts/1         Sep 10 11:08
sally       pts/2         Oct 14 09:18
erin        pts/5         Oct 15 13:48
```

It appears that somehow a *mailtool* process has become an orphan. An orphan process is one which has no controlling terminal, and/or the input file has been removed. The process is in a spin loop trying to perform a function, but cannot do so because of lack of input. Further, the process cannot report its condition, as there is no controlling terminal. But just what is the orphan process doing?

If you look at the network activity with **netstat**, you notice that the *glenn* system seems to be sending and receiving quite a few packets over the network.

Using the netstat command to look for a runaway process.

```
# netstat –i –n ; sleep 5 ; netstat –i –n
Name  Mtu   Net/Dest      Address       Ipkts   Ierrs Opkts  Oerrs Collis Queue
lo0   8232  127.0.0.1     127.0.0.1     371     0     371    0     0      0
le0   1500  154.8.0.2     154.8.0.2     118660  2     21174  0     303    0

Name  Mtu   Net/Dest      Address       Ipkts   Ierrs Opkts  Oerrs Collis Queue
lo0   8232  127.0.0.1     127.0.0.1     371     0     371    0     0      0
le0   1500  154.8.0.2     154.8.0.2     119030  2     21833  0     303    0
```

✘ *TIP: By running **netstat**, waiting five seconds, and then running another **netstat**, you can get a rough idea of how much network traffic a system has sent/received during a five-second interval. If the packet counts are increasing very rapidly, it is a good sign that this host is performing a lot of network I/O.*

Now that you know the *glenn* system is using excessive network bandwidth, maybe you can determine the reason why. Upon using the **snoop** command, you can see that the *glenn* machine is sending and receiving many User Datagram Protocol (udp) packets every second. Upon checking the */etc/inet/services* file, you determine that the port number being used is the Network File Service (nfs) udp service port. The *glenn* machine appears to be asking the file server for a lot of nfs service.

If you think about it, this scenario makes sense: a user is reading mail; the mail resides on the server (*mercury*). The MailTool application is attempting to read the user's mail file on *mercury*, and display it on *glenn*. But didn't you determine that the user was not logged in? When you input another **who** command, your earlier findings are confirmed. The user is not presently logged in.

Using the snoop command to look for a runaway process.

```
# snoop -d le0 -c 20
Using device le0 (promiscuous mode)
glen -> mercury UDP
mercury -> glen UDP
glen -> mercury UDP
glen -> mercury UDP
mercury -> glen UDP
glen -> mercury UDP
mercury -> glen UDP
glen -> mercury UDP
mercury -> glen UDP
mercury -> glen UDP
glen -> mercury UDP
glen -> mercury UDP
mercury -> glen UDP
glen -> mercury UDP
glen -> mercury UDP
mercury -> glen UDP
glen -> mercury UDP
mercury -> glen UDP
glen -> mercury UDP
snoop: 20 packets captured
```

When you use your *mercury* window and examine the */var/mail* directory, you notice there is no file for this user! Now you are suspicious. When you use the **kill -STOP** command on the *mailtool* process on *glenn*, you notice that the system becomes much more responsive, and the network traffic drops to normal levels. You seem to have found the reason for your poor system performance. To confirm your suspicions, you use the **kill -CONT** command to restart the process and determine whether your problems return. Indeed, the *glenn* system performance drops, and the network traffic increases when you restart the process.

Using the kill command to stop and restart processes.

```
% ps -p 910
   PID TTY        TIME COMD
   910 pts/1     11:10 mailtool

% kill -STOP 910

% /bin/ps -p 910
   PID TTY        TIME COMD
   910 pts/1     11:10 mailtool

% kill -CONT 910

% ps -p 910
   PID TTY        TIME COMD
   910 pts/1     10:24 mailtool
```

✘ *TIP: If you suspect a particular process is causing system performance problems, you can temporarily stop it from executing with the **kill -STOP*** *command. Processes stopped in this manner can be continued by using the kill -CONT command.*

Killing a runaway process with the kill command.

```
% ps -p 910
     PID TTY          TIME COMD
     910 pts/1     10:24 mailtool

% kill -TERM 910

% ps -p 910
     PID TTY          TIME COMD

%
```

✔ **NOTE:** *The kill command allows several levels of severity in its attempt to terminate a process. It is best to start with a low priority, and work up to higher priorities. A list of severity levels may be found in the /usr/include/sys/signal.h file. Some of the most frequently used signals appear in the next table.*

Kill Process Command Options

Signal name	Signal Number	Description
HUP	1	Hang up
INT	2	Interrupt
QUIT	3	Quit
KILL	9	Kill
TERM	15	Terminate
STOP	23	Stop
CONT	25	Continue

✔ **NOTE:** *You can use either the signal number or the signal name character-string value with this command.*

At this point you decide to terminate the process with the **kill** command. Your system performance returns to acceptable levels, and the users are happy.

The Possible Cause of the Problem

Why did this problem develop in the first place? One possible explanation is related to erroneous log-ins by the user. First, the user logged in to the *glenn* machine and read his mail. Without logging out, the user happened to log in to the *glenn* machine again from another window or a different workstation, and once again read his mail. From the second login, he discarded all of the messages in his mail file.

When the user exited the second mail process, the mail process from the first login was left looking for a mail file to read. The *glenn* machine asked the server for some portion of the mail file. The server responded that it did not have such a file. The *glenn* machine's mail process still had a file descriptor for the mail file that once existed, so it again asked the server for a copy of the file. This cycle continues until the mail process is forced to terminate!

✔   *NOTE: While the **kill** command allows for several levels of severity in processing the signals, the use of the **kill -9** command should be reserved for situations where nothing else will work. Halting a process with **kill -9** does not allow the process to exit gracefully, and may cause other more serious problems to appear.*

Editing Files With the Text Editor

One of the built-in applications under OpenWindows is a simple text editor. For many UNIX novices the standard text editors can be very intimidating. The OpenWindows Text Editor is an easy-to-use window and mouse based editor. The Text Editor is very similar to the X11 text editor program and several popular word processing programs available for PC users.

To start the Text Editor, you simply click on the icon on the File Manager window. The system responds by loading and invoking the Text Editor. Once the editor starts up, the user can use the mouse to open and close files, change setup parameters for the editor, search for regular expressions in files, or edit text. For on-line help with the Text Editor, click on the Help button.

For more detailed information on the Text Editor, consult the *Solaris 2.* User's Guide* by the OnWord Press Development Team with Sam Kimery (OnWord Press, 1994).

Text Editor window with control panel.

Using the Mail Tool

Another of the built-in applications under OpenWindows is the Mail Tool. Mail Tool provides a simple OpenWindows interface for the user to send and read electronic mail. Mail Tool uses the Text Editor for editing and composition of mail messages.

To start the Mail Tool, you simply select it under the FileManager. Once Mail Tool has started, the user can use the mouse to open and close files, change setup parameters, and compose or read electronic mail. For on-line help with the Mail Tool, simply click on the Help button.

For more detailed information on the Mail Tool, consult the *Solaris 2.* User's Guide* by the OnWord Press Development Team with Sam Kimery (OnWord Press, 1994).

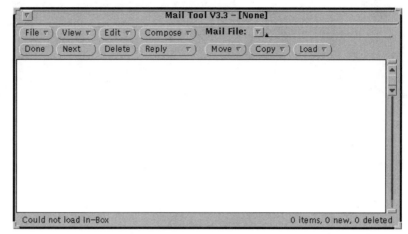

*Mail Tool window
with control panel.*

Summary

In this chapter we reviewed the use of certain everyday UNIX and Solaris commands. We also covered some of the basics of operating in the OpenWindows environment. We walked through a sample system problem, and saw how using several open windows simultaneously simplified the troubleshooting process.

In the following chapters we will be using these simple commands to perform tasks such as adding user accounts, creating file systems, and tuning system performance. By using multiple windows, these tasks will be simplified, and allow you more flexibility in your daily system administration practices.

Everyday System Administrator Commands and Practices

Over the past four chapters, your Solaris systems were configured, and are up and running. Now begins the daily task of keeping them running.

Day-to-day survival as a system administrator means that you must spend some time planning, learning, and practicing basic tasks. These include tasks such as installing new systems and peripherals, maintaining a set of systems backups, installing user accounts, allocating disk space, monitoring system performance, and updating system and application software. Each of these tasks is covered elsewhere in this book in more detail. Here we will discuss an overall strategy for system management.

Planning day-to-day operations occurs at two levels. At one level, you will need to work with your organization to find procedures for setting aside time and other resources to perform tasks such as system backups or the installation of new hardware or software. At another level, you will need to develop procedures for doing such tasks, learn about basic tools required to perform certain tasks and even create some simple tools to assist you in daily chores.

Learning occurs not only by reading books such as this one, but also by reading the documentation that comes with your system and by keeping notes on what works and does not work, and how you accomplished various tasks.

If you have the Solaris AnswerBook software, take a few moments now to read up on how to use it. There is nothing more frustrating than trying to remember how you did something weeks or months later when you need to do it again. Get a laboratory style notebook and jot down the procedures you use when performing tasks such as installing new hardware or software. This builds a library of procedures specific to your situation.

Learning also means understanding a few very basic UNIX tools that all system administrators should know just in case they need them. This is rather like knowing how to change a flat tire. You might not use these tools daily, but when you need them, you *really* need them.

Practice refers not to the drilling or repetition you may have done in school. Here it means the discipline of tasks carried out daily, weekly, or monthly that help to maintain your systems' functioning, to prepare you for unexpected problems, and to preserve system performance. These tasks might include a schedule of system backups, routine audits of user accounts to find and remove expired accounts, checks to find capacity problems such as full disks, and trimming system log files. Practice also refers to the way basic tasks are performed. A cautious, safe way of working saves a lot of headaches. The extra time spent developing a conservative methodology is well compensated in ease of recovery from problems or missteps.

Rules of thumb for performing system maintenance and administration tasks follow:

❑ Avoid using *root* as much as possible. Use a less privileged account where mistakes will be less drastic.

❑ Avoid using magic characters such as the asterisk (*) when using *root*. Accidents do happen, and nearly everyone has at one time done something like, **rm -r /usr/***, by mistake.

❑ Make a backup copy of any file you edit. Make it a habit to use something like the following command: **cp file file.orig ; vi file**. This will give you an easy out if you make errors while editing.

❑ System administration tasks can be time-consuming. Allow plenty of time for your first experience with installing a software package or any other new task. Schedule more down-time than you need. The users of your systems will appreciate it if you happen to finish early much more than if you run late.

The Basic Tools

vi

A fundamental system task is editing files. There are numerous files on a Solaris system which control its functioning, such as the password and group files for user accounts, the hosts and networks files for networking, configuration files for daemons such as inetd and init, and so on.

You might be accustomed to using Text Edit to modify files. However, there are a surprising number of situations where you do not have OpenWindows and tools like Text Edit available to you, such as working on a server that does not have OpenWindows installed or working over a modem from a PC. At these times it helps to know how to use **vi**, a terminal oriented editor which is common on most UNIX systems, including Solaris.

While not as simple to use as Text Edit, vi is widely available. Consequently, vi will most likely be available on any system you need to work on. The vi editor works on almost any terminal with cursor positioning capability, which includes common PC terminals that emulate VT100 or ANSI terminals. The discussion here is not intended to be a complete introduction to vi, but rather a description of selected basic functions so that you can use vi to make changes to files when needed.

Starting vi

To start vi, simply type **vi filename**, where *filename* is the name of a file you wish to edit. For example, to edit the file */tmp/test*, you would type **vi /tmp/test**. If this is a new file, vi will present you with a screen which resembles the following illustration.

Starting up vi.

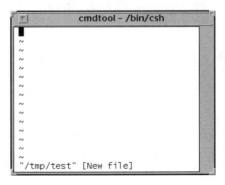

✔ *NOTE: A very small window is used to make it easy to see the cursor position in the current and following examples. The **vi** editor adapts to the window size.*

The name of the file is shown at the bottom of the screen. The "tilde" characters along the left edge of the screen are vi markers indicating the empty region at the end of the file. The markers are not part of the file you are creating; they are shown to you by vi to help you see the boundaries of the screen and the file you are working on.

Entering Text in vi

When you enter vi you are placed in the command mode. The vi editor has two modes: command and input. To switch to the input mode, you type either an **A** to append input to the line the cursor is on, or an **i** to insert input at the current cursor position. To see how this works you might want to follow along using vi on your workstation for the remainder of this section.

✔ *NOTE 1: There are actually several commands which will place vi in the input mode. We use the A and ; (semi-colon) as examples.*

✔ *NOTE 2: The vi editor is modal. It has an input mode and a command mode. Keeping track of the mode is the key to using vi.*

Editing */tmp/test* and typing **A** will put vi into input mode. Type in the following text. Be sure to press <Return> at the end of each line. Unlike Text Edit and some text processor editors you may be accustomed to, vi does not handle text wrapping from one line to another—unless you type **:set wm=#** while in command mode. If you type in a paragraph without hard returns at the end of each line, vi will create one very long line. When you finish the last line, switch from input mode back to command mode by pressing the <Esc> key.

✘ *TIP: If you have forgotten which mode you are in, press the <Esc> key. The vi editor will switch to command mode if you were in input mode, or cause the terminal bell to beep if you were already in command mode. Either way, you end up in command mode.*

In command mode, there are two basic functions you can perform: editing using the edit keys, and issuing commands which start with a colon (:).

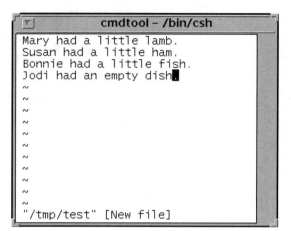

Entering text in vi.

Moving the Cursor

Moving the cursor is a basic function of the editing keys. The vi editor uses a set of keys to the right side of the home row on the keyboard.

vi Cursor Movement Keys

key	cursor action
H	left
J	down
K	up
L	right

Try moving around the text you just typed in. Finish your motion with the cursor on the "l" in "little" on the second line.

✔ **NOTE:** *On many terminals, the arrow keys can also be used to move the cursor.*

```
┌─────────────────────────────────────────┐
│  ▽  │           cmdtool - /bin/csh        │
├─────────────────────────────────────────┤
│ Mary had a little lamb.                   │
│ Susan had a █ittle ham.                   │
│ Bonnie had a little fish.                 │
│ Jodi had an empty dish.                   │
│ ~                                         │
│ ~                                         │
│ ~                                         │
│ ~                                         │
│ ~                                         │
│ ~                                         │
│ ~                                         │
│ ~                                         │
│ ~                                         │
│ ~                                         │
│ "/tmp/test" [New file]                    │
└─────────────────────────────────────────┘
```

Moving the cursor.

✗   TIP: *Tired of moving around one character at a time? The vi editor has motion accelerator keys. The **b** key moves you left one word, and **w** moves you right one word.*

Checking Your Terminal Type

A common problem for vi users is improper cursor motion. This usually occurs because Solaris does not know what type of terminal or terminal emulator you are using. The vi editor depends on this information to emit the proper sequences of escape and control characters needed to move the cursor around the screen. These sequences vary from terminal to terminal. The vi program determines the type of terminal you are using by consulting an environment variable set in your command interpreter or shell.

To check the TERM environment variable type, use the following command:

```
echo $TERM
```

If you see your terminal type listed, you are all set. If not, you will need to set it to the correct terminal type. For example, if you are using a VT100 or terminal emulator which emulates a VT100, and you use the C-shell (/bin/csh), you would type **setenv TERM vt100** to set the TERM environment variable.

Be sure to check the TERM environment variable if vi does not draw the screen correctly, refuses to work (i.e., asserts that your terminal does not have the needed cursor functions), or moves your cursor incorrectly in response to the motion keys.

Changing Text

Changing text can be accomplished either with a substitution command, or the **c** edit key. The c key is followed by an argument to indicate which objects are to be changed, and optionally how many objects are to be changed. Two command usages are **cw** to change the word, and **c** (that's c followed by the space bar) to change a single character. The change word command changes the characters from the cursor position to the right until a space or punctuation mark is encountered. To change the entire remainder of a line, from the cursor position to the right end of the line, type **c$**. The vi program marks the characters to be changed by placing a **$** at the right end of the group of characters to be changed and then enters input mode. Try typing **cw** with the cursor positioned on the "l" in "little" on the second line of the example file.

The change command before entering new text.

```
┌────────────────────────────────────────────┐
│  ▽         cmdtool – /bin/csh                │
├────────────────────────────────────────────┤
│ Mary had a little lamb.                      │
│ Susan had a █ittl$ ham.                      │
│ Bonnie had a little fish.                    │
│ Jodi had an empty dish.                      │
│ ~                                            │
│ ~                                            │
│ ~                                            │
│ ~                                            │
│ ~                                            │
│ ~                                            │
│ ~                                            │
│ ~                                            │
│ ~                                            │
│ ~                                            │
│ "/tmp/test" [New file]                       │
└────────────────────────────────────────────┘
```

Type the string, *lot of.* The vi editor inserts the characters in the space where "little" used to be. You can insert as many characters as you need to. As usual, press the <Esc> key to exit input mode and return to command mode.

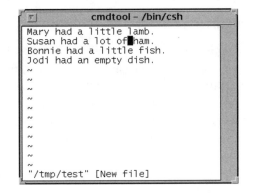

The change command after entering new text.

Undoing an Action

Oops! Suppose you did not intend to make that change. No problem. The vi editor has a one-command "oops" buffer. Type **u** to undo the change. You can type **u** again to "redo" the change if you like. For the example presented here, we will keep the change as made.

Deleting Text

The **d** or delete edit key works in a similar manner to the **c** key. It takes an argument to specify what is to be deleted. Try positioning the cursor in the "S" in "Susan." Type **dw** for delete word. Type **u** to undo the change. Type **x**. The **x** key deletes a single character and is the equivalent of typing **d** (d, space bar). To delete the whole line, type **dd**. The following sequence of pictures shows the screen changes as each of these editing key combinations is used.

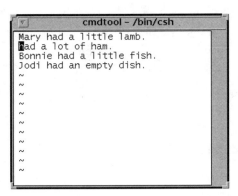

Using dw to delete a word.

The **dw** key sequence deletes the first word and the space following it. This neatly cleans up a misplaced word without an additional delete command.

Using u to undo.

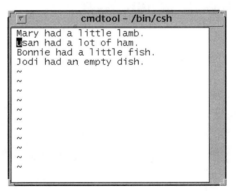

The undo command, **u**, pops the deleted text right back into place.

✔ **NOTE:** *Remember that vi only has a one-item undo buffer. If you make a mistake two or more commands ago, you won't be able to recover from it using the u command.*

Using x to delete a single character.

The single character delete command, **x**, deletes the character at the current cursor position. In this case the character deleted is "S" in "Susan."

✘ **TIP:** *A handy way to fix transposed characters is to place the cursor on the first letter, and then use xp. This deletes the character under the* *cursor, and places the same character after the letter which ends up under the cursor.*

Using dd to delete an entire line.

A Review of vi Features

The following table summarizes the basic vi key sequence commands including commands used in the preceding examples.

Common vi Editing Keys

Character	vi Action
H	Move left one character.
J	Move down one line.
K	Move up one line.
L	Move right one character.
c or r	Change character.
cw	Change word.
c$ or C	Change remainder of line.
x	Delete character.
dw	Delete word.
d$ or D	Delete remainder of line.
dd	Delete entire line.

✗   TIP: *The dot or period (.) editing key repeats the last edit function. If you just inserted a word, or deleted the remainder of a line, you can move to* *a new cursor location and type a period (.) to repeat the insertion or deletion.*

vi's Line Commands

Moving the cursor and making changes with the editing keys is great for small changes, but what about wholesale changes across a large file? For that you need to use vi line commands entered by typing a colon (:).

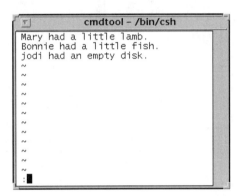

The vi editor is ready to accept a command.

The colon drops the cursor down to the bottom of the screen to allow you to enter a line command. Once a line command is entered, you press the <Return> key to execute it and vi will automatically return to command mode at the location in the file where the line command you entered finished working. In most instances, line command changes result in your cursor positioned on the last line in the file.

Substituting Text Using a Regular Expression

The most common editing command is a string substitution. The substitution takes the form of a "regular expression." This is a specialized string substitution and pattern matching language found in several UNIX commands, including the **grep** family and **sed**, the stream editor. Regular expressions are a rich language with many features. The most commonly used feature is their ability to match arbitrary strings when carrying out substitutions.

Let's use a regular expression to change our test file into the present tense. Type the following expression:

```
:1,$ s/had/has/
```

The expression you just typed is read from left to right. In English it reads: "Starting with the first line and going to the last line, substitute the exact string, *had* with the string *has*, once per line."

Using a regular expression to substitute has for had.

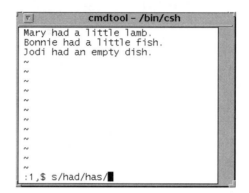

A regular expression is divided into two parts. The first half (1,$) is an address range. The second half is the expression (s/had/has/). The address range specifies the line numbers over which the expression will be applied. In the case of this example, we specify the entire file by giving the range (1,$). The *$* stands for the last line of the file when used in the address range portion of a regular expression.

You can restrict a regular expression to the line the cursor was on before you typed the colon by omitting the address range section altogether (e.g., *:s/had/has/*). You can specify the range as an offset from the position of the cursor before you typed the colon by using the plus sign (+) and minus sign (-) as well as line numbers. An example follows:

```
:-1,+2 s/foo/bar/
```

This instructs vi to substitute *bar* for the first occurrence of *foo* starting on the line before the cursor position (-1), through two lines below the cursor position (+2).

✔ **NOTE:** *Regular expressions "overload" characters. In other words, characters have several different meanings depending on the context in which they are used. Be careful to note the meanings of characters like $ in different parts of a regular expression.*

Now let's try something more exotic. Try typing the substitution command below exactly as shown:

```
:1,$ s/^.* h/Bob h/
```

Now our little file is all about Bob. How did that work?

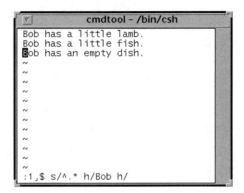

Substituting Bob for the first word in each line.

Reading this command from left to right we find the address portion which indicates the substitution should be done on every line of the file. Next, we see the substitution string. The carat symbol (^) indicates the beginning of the line. The dot or period (.) matches any character. The asterisk (*) means any number of whatever precedes it, so that taken together .* means any number of characters. The space and the letter *h* after the .* matches the first space and letter *h* encountered in the line. Taken all together, the first half of the substitution matches the first word on each line.

✔ **NOTE:** *If you need to substitute for a period (.) or an asterisk (*), you will need to prevent those characters from being interpreted as special matching characters. This is done by placing a backslash (\) before each character. For example, s/./,/ would change the first character encountered into a comma (,) in the current line, while s/\./,/ would change the first period (.) to a comma (,).*

❗ **WARNING:** *The .* construct can lead to unexpected results if not used carefully! Consider the results if the example had been "Mary had a hairy little lamb." You might be very surprised when the line becomes "Bob hairy little lamb"!*

The use of magic characters such as the dot (.), and especially the asterisk (*), requires special care. It's easy to create a matching string which matches more than you intended. Remember that you have a one-command oops buffer.

If you execute a substitution which changes more than you intended, you can type **u** and try again.

Exiting vi

With the file editing completed, it's time to save our work and exit from vi. Like many editors, vi allows you to exit in several different ways. You may wish to save your changes as you exit, save your changes into a different file or disregard your changes. To meet this variety of exit methods, vi has a variety of commands described in the table below. The most common way to exit is to type **ZZ** in the command mode which tells vi to save your changes and exit.

Exiting vi

characters typed	vi action
:w	Write the current file out.
:w!	Write the current file out even if it is marked as "read only."
:w foo	Write the current editor contents to the file "foo."
:q	Quit the editor.
:q!	Quit even if unsaved changes are present.

Some Final Comments on vi

Confused? You are not alone. The vi program is a difficult editor to learn. However, its wide use and general availability on all types of UNIX platforms makes it worth the effort to learn, and not only for Solaris systems. Use vi to edit some practice files and focus in on these key points:

❑ Which mode are you in? If you don't know, press the <Esc> key to be sure you are in command mode.

❑ What is the context of the character you are typing? A $ can mean move to the end of the line in command mode, the last line of a file in the address part of a regular expression, or simply the $ character in input mode. Practice using overloaded characters such as the $ in each context.

❑ Think of using vi like playing a card game. Much as you would need to think about what cards another player may have, you need to keep a picture in your mind of what vi is doing with the characters you type. It takes concentration and practice.

In general, editing system files needs to be done carefully. It is easy to make mistakes in vi, especially if you are new to using vi. A good approach to editing any system file is to make yourself a backup copy of any file *before you begin editing it.* Suppose you needed to make changes to the */etc/hosts* file which contains system host names and their IP addresses. A good habit to get into is to do something like the following:

```
# cp /etc/hosts /etc/hosts.940530

# vi /etc/hosts
```

Preceding vi with the **cp** command gives you a backup copy you can use as a quick way out should your changes to the file not work as expected, or should you run into problems editing and need to start over. This is much preferred to having to go to a recent system backup to recover from a typo when editing a file.

If you are worried about leaving lots of old files lying around, don't be. They are actually pretty easy to clean up if you use a naming convention such as the numerical form of the date used above. For example, you could clean out any of these backup files from last year by typing the following:

```
# rm -i /etc/*.93????
```

The above string will match any file name that contains a *93* date code on the end and will ask you if you want to remove it. You should do this *after* you do a system backup so that these files will be on a backup tape, just in case you need the old copies.

 ✖   *TIP: The -i option on rm is a good one to use when using magic characters such as the asterisk (*) and working as root. As root you have privileges to remove anything, including things you really do not want to remove such as critical system files, device entries, even the system kernel itself. The -i option gives you a chance to avoid unwanted results from a magic character which has matched more than you expected it to.*

grep

Sometimes finding the information you want or figuring out which file contains the item you need to change is more difficult than the change itself. That's where the **grep** family of commands comes in. There are three grep commands: **grep**, **egrep** and **fgrep**. The first two are frequently used to find things in files and as filters to process the output of commands such as **ps**.

The **grep** command takes two arguments: a regular expression to be searched for and a list of files to search in. A common usage might be to locate a specific piece of data in a file. For example, what was the IP address of the machine named *grissom?*

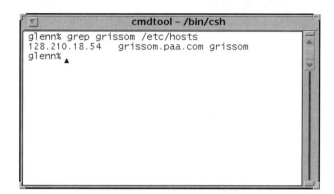

Using grep to find a line in a file.

The grep command can accept regular expressions, but typing those expressions in so that the magic characters are not acted upon by the shell before they are passed on to grep can be difficult.

The file */etc/inet/hosts* contains the names and IP addresses of the systems on your network. On a large network, it can be quite lengthy. Suppose we had a long */etc/inet/hosts* file and we wanted to find all the hosts which had a *.54* as the last part of their IP address. A regular expression makes this easy, although the expression looks pretty complicated after the magic characters are hidden from the shell.

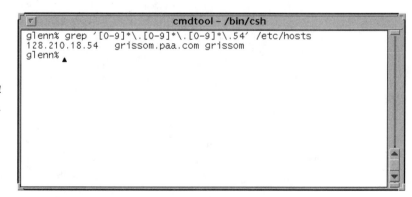

Searching for .54 using grep.

Reading across the **grep** command we first see a single quote. Look carefully: this is a *quote* ('), not a back quote ('). This tells the shell to pass the characters between this quote and the next quote along to the **grep** command without trying to interpret the magic characters. Using quotes like this is an important aspect of effectively using the shell. Double quotes, single quotes, and back quotes have different meanings to the shell.

Inside the single quotes, there's a regular expression. It's a bit more complex than the ones used in the discussion of vi. The *[0-9]* phrase means any number. The square brackets can be used to hold other lists such as *[a-z]*, which means any lower-case letter, or *[p-t]*, which means any of the letters from *p* to *t*. A match occurs if a character is in the range of characters in the list.

Following the bracketed list is an asterisk, meaning one or more of the preceding items. In the phrase *[0-9]**, it means one or more numbers. After matching the first few numbers, you need to match the period between the parts of the IP address. This is done by using a backslash (\) which translates to "do not apply any special meanings to the next character," followed by a period (.). The phrase \. matches a period.

✔ **NOTE:** *Be careful to notice the difference between the phrase containing a period (.) alone, which matches any single character, and \. which matches a period only.*

To match the first three parts of the IP address, the phrase *[0-9]*\.* is repeated three times. At the end, add the *.54* you are looking for and then give **grep** the name of the file to search in.

By building up regular expressions such as this one, you can use **grep** to perform sophisticated searches on files. But suppose you don't know where to look. In that case, try giving **grep** a list of files as shown in the next illustration.

Searching a list of files using grep.

```
                          cmdtool – /bin/csh
 glenn% grep cernan /etc/*
 /etc/hosts:128.210.18.55            cernan.paa.com cernan
 grep: can't open /etc/initpipe
 grep: can't open /etc/killall
 grep: can't open /etc/link
 grep: can't open /etc/oshadow
 grep: can't open /etc/shadow
 grep: can't open /etc/unlink
 glenn%
```

The asterisk (*) in this case is handled by the shell. The asterisk is replaced with a list of all the files in the */etc* directory. In this case only one of the files contained the match, and **grep** lists the name of the file and the line it found which matches the search request. grep also notes files which this account does not have permission to read. Combining regular expressions and lists of files can help you figure out which file contains the information you need or which file you may need to edit to make changes to your system.

grep: Summary of Options

If you are unsure if the string you are looking for is upper-case or lower-case, use the **-i** option to **grep** which matches strings without regard to case.

If you are looking for more than one string, use **egrep** instead. Egrep can accept expressions which may match for several different strings. A common usage for egrep is as a filter for the output of the **ps** command. As you may have already seen, the command **ps -ef** produces a listing of all the processes on a system. If the system is a busy server, this listing can be quite long. Combining **ps** and **egrep** allows you to filter out the things you are not interested in seeing in the list.

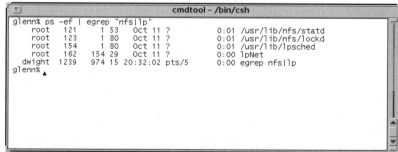

Filtering the output of ps with egrep.

In the above example, **egrep** is used to find any commands containing the strings *lp* or *nfs*. Although the strings are separated by a pipe (|), they are part of the expression. The pipe character is also used to connect the output of the ps command to the input of the egrep command. The pipe is an extremely handy way to combine commands.

The other member of the grep family, **fgrep**, is a limited form of grep. It uses a special fast algorithm to search for strings and strings only. Fgrep does not accept regular expressions.

tar

Files frequently need to be saved onto tape or moved as a group from directory to directory. While you could use the **mv** or the **cp** command, a better way is to use the **tar** command. This command is among the oldest UNIX commands, and while it does not follow all the conventions for option flags, it has survived because it is very handy.

In the early days of the development of the UNIX operating system, command option flags were given without a preceding hyphen (-). The tar command is one of the few commands which maintains this heritage instead of using the now conventional hyphen or dash before option flags. The name tar comes from a shortening of "tape archive" which was the original usage of tar. Thankfully, the designers of tar and much of the UNIX environment made each command flexible enough to allow a wide variety of uses.

The conventional usage for tar is to use it to copy files and directories to tape. A common tar command follows:

```
                        cmdtool – /bin/csh
# cd /usr
# tar cvf /dev/rst0 ./local
a ./local/ 0 tape blocks
a ./local/bin/ 0 tape blocks
a ./local/bin/prog 1 tape blocks
a ./local/lib/ 0 tape blocks
a ./local/lib/locallib.a 13 tape blocks
a ./local/lib/proglib.a 13 tape blocks
#
```

Writing files to tape using tar.

The command shown above would copy files from */usr/local* onto the tape device, */dev/rst0*. The tar option **c** is used to create an archive called **v** to be verbose and print out the path of each item as it is written to the archive file, **f**, to specify what device or file to put the archive in, followed by the archive device, and finally the list of directories or files to be archived. The important thing to note is in what directory the **tar** command was issued and how the file list given to tar was formed.

Using a Relative Path Name with tar

When **tar** writes an archive file, it includes the path name of the files it is given from the file list in the archive file. It is good practice to make this file list a relative path. "Relative" refers to a path that starts from the current or dot (.) directory rather than from the root directory (/). When you read a tar archive, tar will extract the files in the archive into the locations stored in the archive. If you gave an absolute path, such as */usr/local*, you could only extract files back into that same location. This is not always possible or even what you intend to do.

If you use a relative path, tar will extract the files relative to your current directory when you invoked the command. As a result you can extract files into a different location if needed. On the other hand, if you do want to extract the files into their original places, you can easily do so by changing your active directory to the original location. For example, if you needed to check one of the files in */usr/local* against a copy saved by the **tar** command in the previous example, you could do the following:

```
cmdtool – /bin/csh
# cd /tmp
# tar xvf /dev/rst0
x ./local/, 0 bytes, 0 tape blocks
x ./local/bin/, 0 bytes, 0 tape blocks
x ./local/bin/prog, 27 bytes, 1 tape blocks
x ./local/lib/, 0 bytes, 0 tape blocks
x ./local/lib/locallib.a, 6176 bytes, 13 tape blocks
x ./local/lib/proglib.a, 6176 bytes, 13 tape blocks
# diff /tmp/local/bin/prog /usr/local/bin/prog
#
```

Extracting files from tape using tar.

First, move into the */tmp* directory. Then extract the files from the tape device. You can use the **x** option to tar which means "extract"; the **v** option for a verbose list of each file as it is extracted from the archive file; and the **f** option to specify which device or file to read from. Finally, you can compare the files in question with those in */usr/local* using the **diff** command.

Moving Directories with tar

Another more powerful usage of **tar** is to move whole directories from place to place in the UNIX file system. Suppose you decided to move your directory of local software from */usr/local* to */usr/share/local*. You could do so by using a number of **cp** commands, and creating the directories you need as you go within */usr/local*. You would also need to be careful to preserve special file ownerships and permissions. With the combination of shell and tar illustrated below you can do all that with a single but complex command.

Moving a directory using tar.

```
                            cmdtool – /bin/csh
# cd /usr
# tar cf - ./local | ( cd /usr/share ; tar xpvBf - )
x ./local/, 0 bytes, 0 tape blocks
x ./local/bin/, 0 bytes, 0 tape blocks
x ./local/bin/prog, 27 bytes, 1 tape blocks
x ./local/lib/, 0 bytes, 0 tape blocks
x ./local/lib/locallib.a, 6176 bytes, 13 tape blocks
x ./local/lib/proglib.a, 6176 bytes, 13 tape blocks
#
```

This looks like alphabet soup, but it's really several simple commands being used together. First, we moved into the */usr* directory. Then things get complex. Reading the command from left to right, you start **tar** writing an archive of *./local* to the standard output; that's what the hyphen (-) means in the place of an archive device or file name. The output from the first tar command is given as input via a pipe (|) to the remainder of the line.

This combination of commands, pipes, and shells gives you an idea of how a complex procedure can be carried out by piecing together simple UNIX commands. To help you follow the flow of commands and data, a block diagram of the procedure appears below. The basic flow of data is from the portion of the UNIX file tree the first **tar** command is given to read from, to a new section of the UNIX file tree written by the second **tar** command. The second shell serves as a container to hold the **cd** command needed to move to a different directory before the second tar begins writing files.

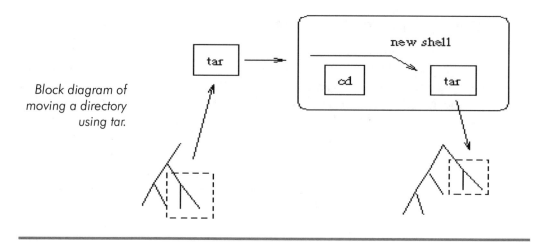

Block diagram of moving a directory using tar.

The commands in the parentheses are executed by the second shell. It is as if you created a new command which moves to a new location in the UNIX file tree and extracts a **tar** archive file presented to it as input. As far as the first tar command and the pipe are concerned, they are just something which accepts their output. This second shell does two things: it moves to the */usr/share* directory (cd /usr/share) and then it reads the standard input for a tar archive which it extracts (tar xpvBf -). The extra option flags to tar preserve the file ownerships and protection modes (p), and inform tar to specially handle reading from a pipe (B).

Moving Files From One Machine to Another Using tar

Another example appears in the following illustration. This moves the files from our machine to the machine called *grissom,* preserves their ownership and protection information, and avoids using any temporary files or tapes.

Notice the lack of parentheses and the \;. Since the **rsh** command will run a shell for us on another machine, we do not need to locally start a second shell by using the parentheses. However, we want the remote shell to do two things, so we need to make sure the local shell does not interpret the semicolon (;), but rather passes it to the other machine. To do that we use the backslash (\) character much as it is used in a regular expression. It prevents the shell from applying a special interpretation to the semicolon character (;), so that it will be passed through the **rsh** command and on to the remote machine, *glenn.*

```
┌────────────────────── cmdtool – /bin/csh ──────────────────────┐
│ ▼                                                              □ │
├────────────────────────────────────────────────────────────────┤
│ # cd /usr                                                        │
│ # tar cf - ./local | rsh glenn cd /usr \; tar xvBpf -            │
│ x ./local/, 0 bytes, 0 tape blocks                               │
│ x ./local/bin/, 0 bytes, 0 tape blocks                           │
│ x ./local/bin/prog, 27 bytes, 1 tape blocks                      │
│ x ./local/lib/, 0 bytes, 0 tape blocks                           │
│ x ./local/lib/locallib.a, 6176 bytes, 13 tape blocks            │
│ x ./local/lib/proglib.a, 6176 bytes, 13 tape blocks             │
│ # ▲                                                              │
│                                                                  │
│                                                                  │
└──────────────────────────────────────────────────────────────┘
```

Moving a directory between machines using tar and rsh.

tar: Summary of Options

A table of the commonly used **tar** option flags and their meanings appears below. Be sure to note that not all flags are used when reading or writing tar archives.

Commonly Used tar Options

Option	Description
c	Create a tar archive.
x	Extract files from a tar archive.
B	Handle the special case of reading a tar archive from a pipe or across the network.
p	Preserve the ownership.
f	Specify where to read or write the archive. Use dash (-) to specify standard input or output.

rdist

While **tar** can be used to move files between machines, copying all the files in a directory to another machine is time-consuming. This is especially true when only a few files have changed, which is often the case. Fortunately, there is another tool specifically designed for this task: **rdist**.

The rdist command is the short form for "remote distribution." It is designed to aid in the automated distribution and maintenance of collections of files between machines on a network. It automatically compares and updates collections of files, saving hours of work and making duplication of changes between machines almost effortless.

A common usage of **rdist** is to compare and optionally copy files between machines. For example, if you made some changes to */usr/local* and wanted to be sure those changes were made on the *glenn* machine, you could do the following:

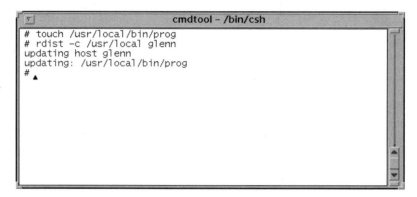

```
cmdtool – /bin/csh
# touch /usr/local/bin/prog
# rdist -c /usr/local glenn
updating host glenn
updating: /usr/local/bin/prog
#
```

Using rdist to update a directory on a remote machine.

✔ *NOTE: The* **touch** *command updates the modification time on the file without changing the file itself. It is used here to make the copy of /usr/local/bin/prog on the local machine have a different modifcation time than the copy on the glenn machine.*

The **-c** option tells **rdist** to expect a file or directory list and the name of a remote machine to go to. The rdist command will compare the sizes and dates of the files in the file or directory list on the remote machine with those on the local machine. If they are different, **rdist** will copy the file from the local machine to the remote machine.

Scripting with rdist

The **rdist** command has a scripting language which allows you to build lists of machines and files and directories to be compared. A complete discussion of the language is more than we have time for here, but a simple example will give you an idea of how helpful **rdist** can be in maintaining and installing software on multiple machines. A sample script follows:

```
#
# check and update directories on grissom and shepard
#

REMOTE = ( grissom shepard )

FILES = (
    /usr/local
    /etc/hosts
    /etc/group
    )
${FILES} - ${REMOTE}
    install;
```

The above script specifies two files and a directory to be checked and updated if needed on two remote hosts, *grissom* and *shepard*. The script is run by giving it as the argument to the **-f** option to **rdist** (e.g., rdist -f script). Scripts like this can be a big time-saver at large sites where local applications need to be distributed and maintained on numerous machines.

 NOTE: *The **rdist** command is part of the SunOS/BSD Source Compatibility Package. In order to use **rdist**, you will need to have the package loaded on your system.*

rdist: Summary of Options

The following table lists common **rdist** options.

rdist Command Options

Option	Description
-c file host	Distribute the file or directory listed after the -c to the host listed after the file or directory.
-f script	Read the script file listed after the -f flag and follow the commands therein.

Option	Description
-n	List actions to be taken but do not do anything. Handy for testing scripts.
-m machine	Limits scripts to acting on only the listed machine even if more machines are specified in the script.

df and du

Another common chore for the system administrator is monitoring disk space usage. The two most common tools are **df** and **du**. The df command lists the mounted file systems and their current size and total usage statistics. For example, on the *glenn* machine, typing **df** gives the following output:

Looking at disk space usage with df.

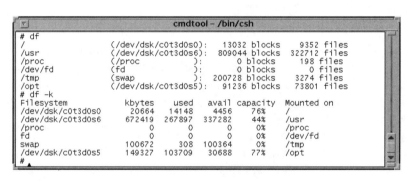

```
                                cmdtool – /bin/csh
# df
/                       (/dev/dsk/c0t3d0s0):     13032 blocks     9352 files
/usr                    (/dev/dsk/c0t3d0s6):    809044 blocks   322712 files
/proc                   (/proc         ):         0 blocks      198 files
/dev/fd                 (fd            ):         0 blocks        0 files
/tmp                    (swap          ):    200728 blocks     3274 files
/opt                    (/dev/dsk/c0t3d0s5):     91236 blocks    73801 files
# df -k
Filesystem              kbytes      used    avail capacity  Mounted on
/dev/dsk/c0t3d0s0        20664     14148     4456    76%    /
/dev/dsk/c0t3d0s6       672419    267897   337282    44%    /usr
/proc                        0         0        0     0%    /proc
fd                           0         0        0     0%    /dev/fd
swap                    100672       308   100364     0%    /tmp
/dev/dsk/c0t3d0s5       149327    103709    30688    77%    /opt
#
```

The **df** command without option flags gives you the current usage on each disk device in 512 byte blocks. By using the **-k** option, you can switch to units of 1024 bytes or kilobytes, and obtain information on maximum, used and available space, and percentage used for each device and slice.

In contrast, **du** gives you the usage for a particular sub-tree of the UNIX directory tree. If you think of the UNIX file system as a tree which grows downward, a sub-tree is a part of the larger tree starting at a particular node or branching point and proceeding down from that point. The following illustration shows the view of part of the UNIX directory tree which is shown by the file manager.

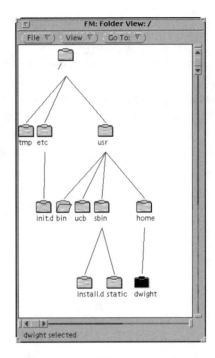

*Part of the UNIX
file tree as seen in
the File Manager.*

In this picture, some sub-trees would be the part of the graph from */usr* downward, or from */etc* downward, or from */usr/sbin* downward. The **du** command walks down the sub-tree and all its branches. Typing *du /usr/sbin* would result in output similar to that shown in the next illustration.

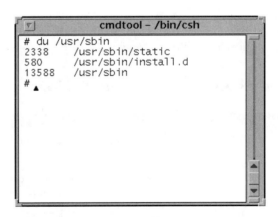

*Disk space used by
/usr/bin.*

By default the values listed for each file and subdirectory are in 512-byte blocks. To see them in kilobytes, use the **-k** option. The **du** command reports the total space used in each directory in the sub-tree.

A common usage of du is to see which users of a given disk are using the most space. You can get this information easily by combining **du** and **sort**, as shown in the next illustration.

Disk space usage summarized by user.

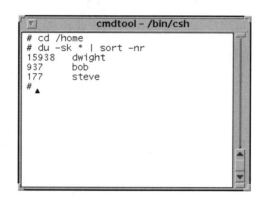

```
           cmdtool - /bin/csh
# cd /home
# du -sk * | sort -nr
15938    dwight
937      bob
177      steve
#
```

The **-s** option to **du** lists the total amount of space in each of the sub-trees, without listing all the sub-trees inside each sub-tree. Because each sub-tree is a user's home directory in */home* on this system, this command totals up each user's disk usage and then sorts usages in descending order with the largest listed first.

Summary of Options

The following table presents a list of common **df** and **du** command options.

The df and du Command Options

Command	Option	Description
df	-k	The -k flag causes df to display file system space in kilobyte units instead of 512 byte block units.
du	-s	The -s flag causes du to print only the total space used by the sub-tree given to it.
du	-k	The -k flag causes du to display size information in kilobyte units rather than 512 byte block units.

ps

With the files on your system under control and the disk space usage being monitored, the remaining tool you need to keep at hand is **ps**. This command lets you list information concerning the status of the processes which are currently executing or waiting to execute on your system.

Before we begin, let's review a little UNIX terminology. A *program* is a binary image stored in secondary storage, such as disk. A *process* is an instance of a program which has been loaded into primary storage or is temporarily stored in backing storage (i.e., swap or paging areas). It has been allocated storage for variables, and may be awaiting some event or is actively executing.

The **ps** command lists the status of processes (instances of programs) on a system. An example of typical **ps** output appears below.

The ps command lists processes.

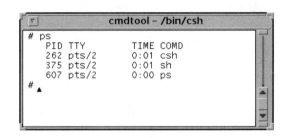

The listing is broken into three columns. The first lists a process identification number or PID. The second column lists the terminal or window the process is running from. If you were to use the **-e** option to **ps** to list all of the processes on a system, some of the processes listed would have a question mark in the terminal column. These processes are not associated with any terminal and are referred to as background or daemon processes. The term "daemon" is usually reserved for processes that are not associated with a terminal and which perform system functions such as sending electronic mail or providing remote file access or printing services. The last column lists the first part of the command that was typed to start the process.

To see all the processes running on a system, you would use the **-e** option to ps. However, a long list of processes is not always the most helpful way to view system activity. Fortunately, **ps** includes options to filter the output to be more specific. For example, as shown in the following illustration, the **-t** option lists only those processes associated with a specific terminal or window.

Listing processes belonging to a specific terminal or window.

```
┌─────────────────────────────────────────┐
│ ▽ │           cmdtool – /bin/csh          │
├─────────────────────────────────────────┤
│ # tty                                     │
│ /dev/pts/2                                │
│ # ps -t pts/2                             │
│    PID TTY         TIME COMD              │
│    262 pts/2       0:01 csh               │
│    375 pts/2       0:01 sh                │
│    617 pts/2       0:00 ps                │
│ #                                         │
│   ▲                                       │
└─────────────────────────────────────────┘
```

✔ **NOTE:** *The* **tty** *command shown above will print the path of the terminal device executing it.*

As shown earlier, another approach to filtering the output of **ps** is to use **grep**. A common task is to try to find the ID of a process you wish to stop, or to send a signal to use the **kill** command. Many daemons will accept certain signals and perform actions such as rereading their configuration files upon receiving a signal. An example of what you could do to find the PID for the *inetd* process appears in the next illustration.

Using grep to filter the output of ps.

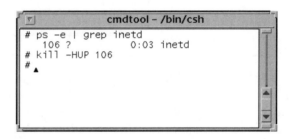

The **ps** command gives you a view of the processes or instances of programs which are running on your system. You can use the **-e** option flag to get a complete list of all the processes, or the **-t** option to view only those processes which are associated with a specific terminal or window.

ps Command Options

Option	Description
-e	List all the processes on the system.
-t terminal	List only those processes associated with the terminal device given after the -t flag.
-f	Produce a more detailed listing of process status information.

Summary

This chapter covered a number of basic UNIX tools found on Solaris systems. These tools give you the ability to manage your system and determine certain aspects of its performance. As you manage your systems, take time to practice using these basic tools and study the options which are not covered here. System management involves continual learning of the capabilities and features of the systems you manage.

Creating, Deleting, and Managing User Accounts

Solaris is a multi-user operating environment. Not only can multiple windows and processes be running on a Solaris system, but many people can use such a system. Unlike a single-user system, such as a PC or Macintosh, Solaris needs to keep track of each user's preferences, the location of their files and electronic mail. Each user must also have some way of identifying and authenticating him/herself to Solaris.

A user account is the name given to the collection of information that defines a user on a Solaris system. This information is used when a user logs into the system, sends and receives electronic mail, starts up OpenWindows, and so on. The maintenance of user account information is a continuing task of the system manager. Solaris provides numerous tools to make user account maintenance easier.

The User Account

A user account is a collection of information which defines a user on a Solaris system. The definition starts with the user's ID or user name which is used when logging in, and sending or receiving electronic mail. This definition also contains various pieces of information used to control access to files as well as a password used for authenticating the user.

The component parts of a user account follow:

❏ A name by which the user is known to the system.

❏ A password by which the user authenticates him/herself to the system.

❏ A set of credentials consisting of a user identification number, group identification(s), and access lists which control ownership and access to directories, files, and devices such as printers and tape drives.

❏ A home directory, where basic user files such as .*login* and .*cshrc* are stored.

❏ A command interpreter, or shell as it is called in UNIX terminology.

❏ An optional disk space usage limit or quota.

You can think of an account as analogous to the collection of items in your wallet or purse. The user name is like the name on your driver's license. The picture on your license is like the password in that it allows others to verify who you are in the same way your password is used by the system to verify who you are. The license number grants you certain privileges, much like your user identification number does. An account's group identification(s) are similar to club or other membership cards that grant access to shared resources. Your credit cards resemble the disk quota, giving you certain resource usage limits.

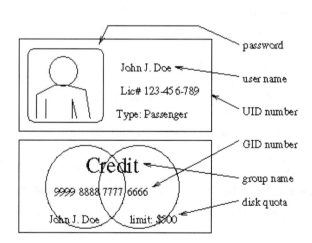

License and credit card analogs to user account items.

The Admintool

Managing this collection of account information on earlier UNIX systems required editing several files and using a couple of different commands. Under Solaris, account management is brought together under one tool, the **admintool**.

An Overview of Admintool

The **admintool** is a jumping-off station for accessing a collection of administrative functions. These functions include user account management, editing and updating various system databases, setting up printers, modems, terminals and other devices, and managing host names. Throughout this book we will return to the admintool by way of addressing each of these functions. Here we will concentrate on editing a system database file and using the user account management functions.

Using Admintool to Manage User Accounts

You will need to log in as *root* and start OpenWindows, or use the **su** command to gain root privileges from a window if you are logged in as yourself and are already running OpenWindows. Once you have done either of these things and have the root prompt, type **admintool &** to start the admintool and put the process in the background. You should see the base admintool window as shown in the next illustration.

The base admintool window allows you to open up several different "managers" which in turn allow you to create, delete and edit various data files to control various functions. In this chapter, we will focus on the User Account Manager and the Database Manager as they relate to the management of user account information.

Before diving into setting up an account, there are a number of housekeeping items that need to be taken care of and policy decisions that need to be made. Accomplishing these tasks now will speed up the actual account creation and lay the foundation for easier management of accounts in the future.

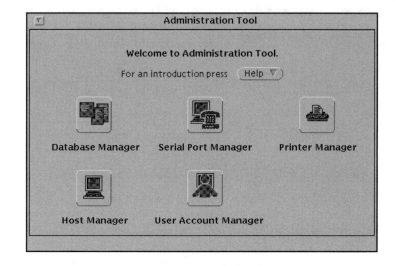

The admintool opening screen.

Names, UIDs, and GIDs

Each user account will need to be assigned a name. This name is used to identify the account for purposes such as electronic mail and for logging into a machine. While you can use just about any string of two to eight characters for an account name, many sites prefer to use a naming convention, such as the initials of the person who owns the account (e.g., ddm), the owner's last name (e.g., mckay) or first name (e.g., dwight), or a combination of initials and names (e.g., ddmckay, or dwightm). A number can be added if there is more than one user with the same name or initials (e.g., ddm2). This sort of naming scheme makes it easy for people to guess at a user's account name which is very handy for sending electronic mail, transferring files, etc.

For example, for a person whose name is John Doe, you can construct account names such as: doej, johnd, jd, jdoe, doe, john, jd1, etc.

User IDs

Along with a name, each account is assigned a user identification number or UID. Solaris uses the UID number to tag files owned by the account and to control access permissions to files and devices. The first 100 UID numbers (1 through 100) are reserved by the Solaris system to be assigned to system accounts such as *root* and *uucp*. Likewise, UIDs above 60000 are assigned to special purposes. However, assigning a UID is a bit more complicated than simply picking a number between 100 and 60000.

❏ UID numbers *must* be unique for each user account. File ownership is recorded and controlled by the UID number. Accounts with the same UID number are effectively the same as far as file ownership and other owned items such as processes and accounting records are concerned.

❏ In order for NFS file sharing to work correctly UID Numbers *must* be consistent between machines on a network. NFS uses the UID number when determining if a given user has access to a given file.

✔ **NOTE:** *Avoid reusing UID numbers whenever possible. The UID number is kept in several data files, all of which must be carefully checked and cleaned up before a UID can be reused. Reuse occurs when an account is deleted and then a new account is created which uses the same UID number.*

✘ **TIP:** *Consistency in UID and GID numbering can be easily maintained by using NIS+ to manage the various account database files. See Chapter 18.*

Group IDs

A second number, called a "group identification number" or GID, is also assigned to each account. Unlike UID numbers, multiple users can share GID numbers. Groups and their GID numbers are used to provide shared file access. Like UID numbers, Solaris also tags files with a GID number to control access for other users which share the same GID number. In addition, the first 100 GID numbers (1 through 100) are reserved by the Solaris system to be assigned to special uses. GIDs must also be consistent between machines which share files systems via NFS. GIDs are an important and powerful mechanism in Solaris for controlling sharing of files.

If you look at a long file listing produced by **ls -l**, you will see that each file listed has both an owner and a group associated with it. There are separate permission bits for reading, writing, and execution associated with the file's owner, group, and everyone else. By setting these bits you can create files which are readable or writeable by collections of user accounts who are members of a group, but not everyone who may use your systems. The GID given to a user's account specifies the primary group that user is in, but that user can be a member of up to 15 other groups by using the database manager to add that user's account name to a group listed in the group file.

Devising a scheme for grouping accounts together before creating new accounts is recommended. Consider the ways in which the various user accounts on your systems need to be able to work together. Do you need groups for each project? What about functional groupings such as accounting, engineering, or clerical? Creating groups first and then assigning accounts to groups makes file sharing and resource management easier later on.

Keep in mind the following guidelines which are similar to those for UID numbers:

❑ GID numbers *must* be unique for each group.

❑ GID numbers *must* be consistent between machines on a network in order for NFS file sharing to work correctly.

✔ *NOTE: Avoid reuse of GID numbers as well. While the GID number is kept in fewer data files than the UID number, you will still need to carefully check for potential problems before reusing a GID number.*

Creating a Group

To create a group, click on the Database Manager icon in the base admintool window.

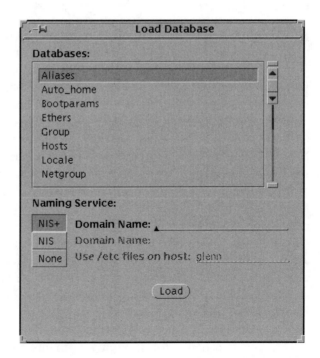

The Load Database window.

The Load Database window offers a selection of various databases from various naming services. For the discussion of account management, we will use the None choice which acts on the database files on the local workstation only. In a network of workstations, you might use NIS or better still, NIS+, to manage databases shared by many workstations. Procedures for setting up and working with these services are discussed later in the book.

Selecting None for the naming service, Group for the database, and clicking on the load button brings up the Group Database window.

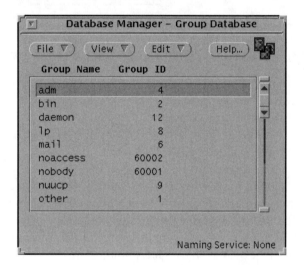

The Group Database window.

As an example, let's assume we have a group of users who will be using an accounting package. They need to have permission to access the package's data, but that data needs to be protected from access by other users. To meet this need, create a group called *account*. This is done by selecting "add entry" from the edit menu. A small window appears with a form that is filled in to specify the group name and identification number.

If more groups are needed, the process can be repeated. One of the nice things about the **admintool** is that you can add groups and user accounts in any order at any time, so that you need not have your entire grouping and account naming and numbering scheme organized at the outset. You can set up some of your accounts now and others later, adding groups and accounts as needed.

The Add Entry form.

```
┌─────────────────────────────────────────────────┐
│  🖳          Database Manager: Add Entry          │
│  ═══════════════════════════════════════════════  │
│                                                   │
│   Group Name:  accounting                         │
│                                                   │
│      Group ID:  1000       △ ▽                     │
│   Members List: _____  │
│                                                   │
│          ( Add )  ( Reset )   ( Help... )          │
│                                                   │
│                        Naming Service: None       │
└─────────────────────────────────────────────────┘
```

Preconfiguring with Skeleton Files

When a user logs into his or her account, a command interpreter or shell is started. The setup of the shell, how it behaves, where it looks for programs and so forth can be modified to fit your environment. Similar to account naming and UID and GID numbering, planning and preparation before setting up new accounts will save time later on.

Solaris gives you two levels of shell customization: a system-wide set of files which are read by every shell started by every user, and a set of files which can be copied into the user's home directory when an account is created. The global files are */etc/.login* for the C shell, and */etc/profile* for the Bourne and Korn shells. The global files should contain only the settings you wish *all* shells to have when they start. These global initialization files have the advantage of not being modifiable by individual users. However, any initialization files the user creates can make changes to the shell settings given by the global files.

In */etc/skel*, you can create directories for each shell and place the initialization files you want copied into a user account's home directory when the user's account is created. The copying of files takes all the files in a directory, so you will need to make subdirectories for each shell, such as */etc/skel/c-shell*, */etc/skel/bourne*, and */etc/skel/korn*. In */etc/skel/c-shell*, you might have a *.cshrc* and a *.login* file to specify settings such as the command search path and any procedures to be taken when the user logs into the account. One possible setup is shown in the following table.

An Example Search Path

Directory	Description
/etc/skel/c-shell	Contains a .cshrc, and .login to be copied into the home directory of a user who uses /bin/csh as his or her command shell.
/etc/skel/bourne	Contains a .profile and .login to be copied into the home directory of a user who uses /bin/sh as his or her command shell.
/etc/skel/korn	Contains a .profile to be copied into the home directory of a user who uses /bin/ksh as his or her command shell.

The advantage of these skeleton files over the global initialization files is that they are given to the user and can be modified by the user if needed. The advantage to you as system manager is that you can give each of the new users of your system a predefined set of shell initialization files to ensure that things like their search path set correctly, without requiring them to create initialization files from scratch.

Sun provides some sample initialization files for Bourne, Korn and C shells in */etc/skel* which serve as a basis for your own files. In version 2.3 of Solaris, these initialization files include handy start-up procedures for OpenWindows as well as search path settings for commonly used Solaris programs and tools.

Creating an Account

With the preparatory work in place, you can open the User Account Manager by clicking on its icon in the base **admintool** window. Similar to the Database Manager, the first thing you need to do is select a naming service and the users you wish to view. For this example, we will select None for the naming service and All Users for viewing. Limited lists of users are handy when you need to find and modify user accounts.

After clicking on Apply, the User Account Manager window appears. It is similar in appearance to the Database Manager window we just worked with to create a group. To create a new user account, select Add User from the Edit menu.

The Add User form that appears is divided into four sections, each dealing with a different aspect of the account to be created. We will discuss each section in turn as we fill in the form to create an account.

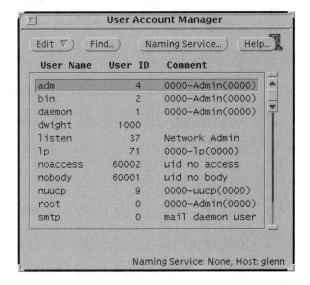

*The User Account
Manager window.*

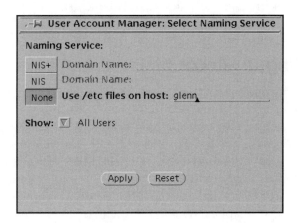

*Selecting a naming
service for the
User Account
Manager.*

```
┌─────────────────────────────────────────────────┐
│ ▣         User Account Manager: Add User          │
│  USER IDENTITY                                     │
│         User Name: ▲_____                        │
│            User ID: _____                      │
│     Primary Group: nobody___                       │
│   Secondary Groups: _____          │
│           Comment: _____         │
│        Login Shell: ▽  Bourne  /bin/sh             │
│  ACCOUNT SECURITY                                  │
│          Password: ▽  Cleared until first login    │
│        Min Change: 0____  days                     │
│        Max Change: ____  days                      │
│       Max Inactive: ____  days                     │
│    Expiration Date:▽ None  ▽ None  ▽ None          │
│           Warning: ____ days                       │
│  HOME DIRECTORY                                    │
│    Create Home Dir: ☐  Yes if checked              │
│               Path: _____        │
│             Server: _____        │
│      Skeleton Path: _____        │
│     AutoHome Setup: ☐  Yes if checked              │
│       Permissions  Read Write Execute              │
│             Owner:  ✔    ✔    ✔                     │
│             Group:  ✔    ☐    ✔                     │
│             World:  ✔    ☐    ✔                     │
│  MISCELLANEOUS                                     │
│        Mail Server: _____        │
│                                                    │
│         ( Add )  ( Reset )  ( Help... )            │
│                                                    │
└─────────────────────────────────────────────────┘
```

The Add User form.

User Identity

The User Identity section contains the basic name and number information for the account. The User Name field is limited to eight characters, as well as the name the user will use when logging into a workstation, and the name other users will use when sending this user electronic mail. The User ID is the number we discussed earlier that identifies this user. The primary group is the group ownership given by default to files created by this user. In this example, we will use *account*, the group created earlier using the Database Manager. The

Secondary Groups are other groups in which this account is a member. Under Solaris, a user can be a member of as many as 16 groups.

The comment field is typically used to contain additional identification information, such as the real name of the user of the account. Some sites put additional information in this field such the user's office phone extension number. Be aware that whatever you put in this field will show up when anyone uses the "finger" command to inquire about the user account.

The Login Shell menu selects the command interpreter or shell that will be started by the login process when the user logs in using this account. The various shells have advantages and disadvantages; some users prefer one shell over another. In our example, this account will be given the default Bourne shell.

> **!** **WARNING:** *Be very careful if you choose to change the shell of the root user. The setting provided with Solaris is chosen to allow for system operation even if problems occur which may make other shells inaccessible, such as disk problems. You can render a system unusable by using other shells without taking precautions to make the shell available under all possible conditions.*

> **✗** **TIP**: *It is often useful to have a root window available while experimenting with changes to the root shell and/or system security. If something goes wrong, you still have root access to the system to carry out repairs.*

Account Security

The Account Security section deals with the account password used by the account user to authenticate him/herself to the system. The password itself can be set in the following four different states by the Add User form.

❑ *Cleared until first log-in.* This is the default setting. An account created in this manner will prompt the user to give a password the first time the user logs in to the account. While this is handy, consider the implications of setting an account's password to this state, especially in an environment where the account may not be used and is likely to be discovered by someone other than its owner. See the discussion of system security in Chapter 10, "Managing System Security."

❑ *Account is locked.* In this state, the account exists but cannot be logged into until and unless a password is set for the account. An account can be put in this state automatically as described below.

❑ *No passwd -- set uid only.* This setting creates an account which cannot be logged into. It is used when an account is needed for a daemon or system program to use. An example of this is the *uucp* account which allows the uucp program to own files and directories needed for that program to function.

❑ *Normal Password.* This selection brings up a small form to which you can enter a password which will be assigned to the account when it is created.

Password Aging

The three date fields that follow the Password menu control a function called "password aging." The aging process allows the system manager to enforce the practice of changing account passwords on a regular basis. Reusable passwords, such as those found in Solaris, are vulnerable to being guessed if they are kept the same for long periods of time. Changing the password periodically helps to reduce this risk.

The downside to password aging is the psychological factor. Some users dislike changing passwords. Being asked to change with no warning may contribute to a user choosing a simpler, easily guessed password, or the user may simply enter a new password and then change back to the old password immediately afterward. Password aging is most effective when the account user understands the reasons for periodically changing a password and the definition of a good password, and is given a chance to choose a good password.

The Solaris password aging system gives you control over three aspects of the process. The Min Change field specifies the minimum time in days between password changes. Setting this to a value other than zero prevents a user from setting a new password and then immediately switching back to the old password until the time specified has passed. The Max Change field specifies the age the password must reach before the password aging system requests that the user change the password. The Warning field sets the number of days that a user will be notified prior to being required to change the password. This period gives the user time to think of a new password before she or he is required to make the change.

For further protection, Solaris adds an inactivity timer and an expiration date. These help to prevent inactive accounts or improper use of accounts owned by people who may no longer use them. The Max Inactive field sets the maximum time in days that an account can be left idle before it is "locked." The expiration date sets a date at which the account is considered expired and is locked. These mechanisms are especially handy for accounts which are transient in nature, such as student accounts in an academic environment and accounts created for temporary employees.

Home Directory

The Home Directory section gives you the ability to have the User Account Manager automatically create and populate the user's home directory automatically as part of the account creation. This is a considerable time savings and is worth examining in detail.

The Path field contains the UNIX directory path to the user's home directory. Typically the path is similar to */export/home/smithb*, as it would be in the case of the user account we are setting up as an example. The Server field specifies the file server or peer workstation on which this path exists. Provided that the Account Manager software package is installed on the server, the User Account Manager will contact that machine and create the needed directory as part of the account creation process.

The Skeleton Path allows you to indicate where the User Account Manager should look for any files you wish to place in the user's account. Typically, you place a common shell initialization file such as *.profile* or *.cshrc* and a *.login* file into the user's home directory.

✔ **NOTE:** *Under Solaris version 2.3, the Skeleton Path feature does not copy files beginning with a period (.) as documented. One way to work around this is to specify two paths in the Skeleton Path field, such as /etc/skel/bourne/.??* /etc/skel/bin. The first path and magic characters will copy the "dot" (.) files in /etc/skel/bourne. The second path is to a directory with a file or directory in it which will get copied to the account's home directory. This file or directory can either be removed afterwards, or you can use it to place something like a "bin" directory in the account.*

✘ **TIP**: *Patch 101159-01 fixes this feature under Solaris 2.3. The skeleton path copies dot files correctly under Solaris 2.4.*

The AutoHome Setup check box tells the User Account Manager to make the proper changes to the NFS automount daemon files to allow this user account's home directory to automatically appear in the */home* directory, no matter which of the workstations on your network the user uses. This has the advantage of hiding the user account's actual home directory path so that the user account can be moved if needed without affecting programs the user may use which depend on a certain path to the user's home directory. How this works and how to set up the automount daemon are covered in Chapter 18, "Automating NFS with Automount."

The final part of this section has a three-by-three grid of check boxes which allow you to set the UNIX protection bits for this account's home directory. The group settings refer to the primary group you have chosen for this user.

Miscellaneous

This section has one field, Mail Server. This field specifies the address to which all this user's mail will be sent. It is typically the user's own workstation, although you might route mail to a central file server or departmental server.

The completed Add User form.

```
┌─────────────────────────────────────────────────┐
│  🔊        User Account Manager: Add User         │
├─────────────────────────────────────────────────┤
│  USER IDENTITY                                    │
│              User Name: smithb                    │
│                User ID: 1001                      │
│          Primary Group: account                   │
│        Secondary Groups:                          │
│               Comment: Bob W. Smith               │
│                                                   │
│            Login Shell: ▽  Bourne  /bin/sh        │
│  ACCOUNT SECURITY                                 │
│               Password: ▽  Normal password...     │
│            Min Change: 0      days                │
│            Max Change:        days                │
│          Max Inactive:        days                │
│        Expiration Date:▽ None ▽ None ▽ None       │
│               Warning:        days                │
│  HOME DIRECTORY                                   │
│         Create Home Dir: ✓  Yes if checked        │
│                   Path: /export/home/smithb       │
│                 Server: glenn                     │
│          Skeleton Path: /etc/skel/bourne          │
│                                                   │
│         AutoHome Setup: ☐  Yes if checked         │
│          Permissions  ReadWrite Execute           │
│                 Owner: ✓   ✓   ✓                  │
│                 Group: ✓   ☐   ✓                  │
│                 World: ✓   ☐   ✓                  │
│  MISCELLANEOUS                                    │
│            Mail Server: smithb@glenn              │
│                                                   │
│                                                   │
│            ( Add )  ( Reset )  ( Help... )        │
└─────────────────────────────────────────────────┘
```

✘   *TIP: If you have a large number of user accounts to install, select an account similar to the next account to be installed and use the Copy User item from the Edit menu in the User Account Manager. This will open the Add User form with many of the fields already filled in using the values of the selected user. You can then enter only the items which change such as the user name and UID.*

Modifying and Deleting Accounts

With the foundation work required to set up accounts behind us, using the **admintool** to modify and delete accounts becomes very easy.

Modifying an account is simply a matter of opening the User Account Manager as before, and double-clicking on a user name in the list or selecting Modify/View User... from the Edit menu.

Selecting an account to be modified.

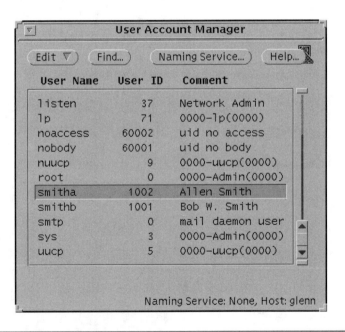

All of the fields you filled in during the account creation can now be edited and changed. A common activity is to lock and unlock accounts or change the account's password using the Password menu. Selecting Normal Password... will bring up a small form in which a new password can be entered.

However, the Modify User form does not completely handle all changes you may wish to make. Watch out for changes to fields listed in the next table.

Passwd Fields to Watch Out For

Field name	Description
User ID	While the Modify User form *will* change the UID number for the user in the /etc/passwd file or in the NIS+ database, it *will not* change the ownership of the files in the account's home directory or elsewhere (e.g., /tmp). You must do this manually as described below.
Primary Group	The same rule applies for the primary group. The /etc/passwd or NIS+ database files will be changed, but not the group ownership assigned to files in the account's home directory or elsewhere (e.g., /tmp).
Path	The user's home directory path will be changed only in the /etc/passwd and NIS+ database files. The directory itself must be moved manually *before* you change the account form, or the account form will report an error as it will not be able to find the new path.
Server	The server on which the user's account resides will likewise change only in the /etc/passwd or NIS+ databases. It must be moved between machines manually.

Changing File Ownership

If you modify the UID or GID numbers assigned to an account, you will need to manually modify the ownership of the files and directories in the account's home directory so that the account will continue to have access to those files and directories. This is easy to do with the **chown** and **chgrp** commands. These two commands work in a similar manner, taking the name or number of the UID or GID you wish to change and the name of a file. The common usage when changing the UID or GID number for an account is to use the **-R** option to **chown** and **chgrp** to recursively change the ownership of all files in a sub-tree.

❏ **Chown** sets the file ownership by changing the UID number the file is tagged with. You can specify the UID as a number or as a user name and chown will look up the number for you. The **-R** option will recursively descend through any directories it finds in the list of files given it, and change the ownership of the directory and the files in them. Examples of typical chown commands appear below, and produce no output unless there is an error.

```
chown dwight file1 file2 file3
chown -R dwight big-directory
```

❑ **Chgrp** sets the file group ownership by changing the GID number the file is tagged with. As with chown, you can specify the GID as a number or as a group name and chgrp will look up the number. Chgrp also has the **-R** option to recursively descend through directories and change the group ownership of all files and directories found. Typical chgrp commands also produce no output unless there is an error. Examples appear below.

```
chgrp 105 file
chgrp system file4 file9
chgrp -R accounting secret-directory
```

✖ TIP: *A common mistake is to specify .* as the list of files to be changed when using chown -R or chgrp -R, as in chown -R dwight .*. Unfortunately, the .* expression will match not only the files you might want to change, such as .cshrc or .login, but also the directory above the current directory as referenced by its nickname, three periods (...). To avoid this, use a more restrictive expression such as .??*, which will match any file that begins with a period (.) and has at least two characters after the period. As always, be very careful using wildcard expressions such as the asterisk (*) while working as the root user.*

For example, if the UID and GID numbers were changed to 1002 and 1000 for the *smitha* account, you might use the following sequence of commands to change the user and group ownerships of the files in the *smitha* account home directory.

Changing user and group ownerships.

```
cmdtool - /bin/csh

glenn% su
Password:
# cd /export/home
# ls
bob      smitha  steve
dwight   smithb
# chown -R 1002 smitha
# chgrp -R 1000 smitha
#
```

The sequence of commands used follows: (1) The **su** command is used to become *root*. The root account has permission to change the ownership of any file. (2) The current directory is changed to the directory *above* the account's home directory. This positions the shell to simplify the next two commands. (3) The **chown** and **chgrp** commands are used to change the UID and then the GID numbers assigned to the files in the *smitha* directory, and any directories contained inside the *smitha* directory by using the **-R** option flag.

> ✔ **NOTE:** *If you have already changed the smitha account's UID and GID using the User Account Manager, you can use the account name, smitha, in place of the UID number, 1002, and the group name, account, in place of the GID number, 1000. Both the chown and chgrp commands will look up the numbers from the group and password databases.*

Moving Account Paths

Moving an account's path from one location to another on the same server or between servers requires a bit more work than setting UID and GID numbers. Using the **tar** command and some shell magic you can move paths around without resorting to tapes or temporary files. The basic idea involved is to create a tar archive of the files and directories in the current location, and by means of a pipe (I) or connection between processes, send that archive to a second invocation of tar which extracts the archive in the new location. The procedure appeared at the end of the previous chapter, but bears repeating here. In the following illustration, the *smitha* directory is moved to another file system on the same server.

> ✗ **TIP**: *While you could use the cp command to move user accounts, using tar provides a major advantage. The tar command follows symbolic links, while cp does not.*

```
                          cmdtool – /bin/csh
# cd /export/home
# tar cf - ./smitha | ( cd /export/home2 ; tar xvBpf - )
x ./smitha/, 0 bytes, 0 tape blocks
x ./smitha/.profile, 511 bytes, 1 tape blocks
x ./smitha/bin/, 0 bytes, 0 tape blocks
#
```

Moving an account's home directory.

After moving to one of the home file systems on this machine, a long command is issued consisting of several parts. The first part has the **tar** command creating an archive file of the *smitha* directory and putting it on the standard output. The *./smitha* path is used because it is a "relative" path which will allow the archive created by **tar** to be extracted in any location. Moving along the line to the right is a pipe (|). This is the shell pipe character; it takes the standard output of the tar command and routes it into the next command to the right along the command line.

The two commands inside the parentheses are executed in a new shell created for them. They act as one command as far as the pipe is concerned and will read from the pipe. The two commands move to the new location for this path (cd) and then carefully extract the archive file coming in from the pipe (tar). The options used with the second tar command cause it to extract the archive, maintain the same file ownership and permission bits, continue to read even if the archive file is slow in coming through the pipe, and produce a verbose list of the files as they are extracted from the archive.

Once this is done, you can modify the account's path using the User Account Manager and then delete the old path. However, it is good practice to check to be sure the account can be logged into and no mistakes have been made before removing the original path. A few minutes of checking can save hours of work recovering files and directories from backup tapes.

Moving a Home Directory Between Servers

Moving an account's home directory between servers uses the same general idea of creating a tar archive file, and using a pipe to send it to another **tar** command to extract the contents. Appearing in the following illustration is an example of moving the *smitha* account from the server named *glenn* to the server named *grissom*.

The change of directory and the first tar command used are the same as in the previous example. On the right side of the pipe, the **rsh** command is used to execute commands on the *grissom* server instead of creating a second shell on the local server. The \; is used to prevent the semicolon from being processed on the local machine. This allows two commands to be passed to the remote machine via rsh—one to change to the appropriate directory, and the other to extract the archive file coming through the pipe using tar.

```
cmdtool - /bin/csh
# cd /export/home2
# tar cf - ./smitha | rsh grissom cd /export/home \; tar xvBpf -
x ./smitha/, 0 bytes, 0 tape blocks
x ./smitha/.profile, 511 bytes, 1 tape blocks
x ./smitha/bin/, 0 bytes, 0 tape blocks
#
```

Moving a home directory between servers.

Compared to creating or modifying an account, deleting an account is simple. Just click the account to be deleted from the User Account Manager window and select Delete User from the Edit menu. The Delete User form which appears gives you the option of having the account manager delete the account's home directory and mailbox for you. Depending on your environment, it is often desirable to make a backup copy of the contents of any account before you delete it, just in case.

Managing Accounts Without the Admintool

On systems where you do not have access to OpenWindows, you cannot use tools like the **admintool**. In these cases, such as file servers without any graphics displays, you must resort to the **useradd**, **usermod** and **userdel** commands for account management; **groupadd**, **groupmod** and **groupdel** for group management; and **passwd** or the **vipw** command provided in the Berkeley UNIX compatibility package to control passwords.

The basic strategy of account management is the same as that presented above for use with the admintool. You should carry out preparatory work to decide on an account naming scheme, UID numbers, required groups, and GID numbers. Then make any local modifications you need to the shell initialization files. With these foundations in place, you are ready to create groups and accounts.

groupadd, groupmod, groupdel

This trio of commands works on the group database. Unlike the admintool, the command line group management commands *do not* update the NIS+ databases. These databases are updated manually as described later in the book.

Adding a group is accomplished by specifying the group's name and GID number as options to the **groupadd** command. The following command line will create the *account* group:

```
# /usr/sbin/groupadd -g 1000 account
```

Group modification is executed by using **groupmod**. Changing the *account* group's GID to 1234 could be done as follows:

```
# /usr/sbin/groupmod -g 1234 account
```

> ✔ *NOTE: The **groupmod** command changes the GID number in the /etc/group file only. File ownership must be changed manually using the **chgrp** command as shown in the examples above.*

Similarly, groups are deleted using the **groupdel** command. Deleting the *account* group would be accomplished as follows:

```
# /usr/sbin/groupdel account
```

Useradd, Usermod and Userdel

This trio of commands handles the same functions as the User Account Manager via a series of command line options similar to the **groupadd** family. In the following string, the *smithb* account is created with the **useradd** command in the same way as an account was created with the User Account Manager.

```
# /usr/sbin/useradd -u 1000 -g account -c "Bob W. Smith" -s
/bin/sh -m -d /export/home/smithb -k /usr/skel/bourne smithb
```

This is a lengthy command, but easy to follow. As described in the table below, the individual option flags parallel the four sections of the Add User form.

Option Flags for the Add User Form

Option	Description
-u 1000	Sets the UID number for account.
-g account	Sets the primary group.
-c "Bob W. Smith"	Sets the comment field.
-s /bin/sh	Sets the account's shell to the Bourne shell.
-m	Creates the home directory.
-d /export/home/smithb	Sets the path to the account's home directory.
-k /usr/skel/bourne	Specifies the directory from which initialization files are to be copied into the account's home directory.
smithb	The account's User Name.

✔ *NOTE: The **useradd** command correctly copies the dot (.) files from the skeleton directory. No work-arounds are needed.*

The **useradd** command also has options to set the account's expiration date (**-e**) and the maximum number of days the account can be idle before being locked (**-f**), but it does not have options for setting the password aging time period. Next, the useradd command does not handle setting the user's password.

The **usermod** command uses the same set of option flags as **useradd**. An example of changing the comment field for *smitha* via **usermod** follows:

```
# /usr/sbin/usermod -c "William W. Smith" smitha
```

Finally, the **userdel** command simply takes the name of the account to be deleted.

passwd

To set a user's password manually, you use the **passwd** command from the root account and give the user account's name as the first argument.

```
# passwd smitha
```

The passwd command is also used to control the password aging time limits. The **-n** option sets the minimum number of days between password changes.

The **-x** option sets the maximum number of days between password changes. The **-w** sets the number of days before the expiration date that the user will be warned about password expiration. The command line to set these values for our example user account follows:

```
# passwd -m 2 -x 180 -w 7 smitha
```

As demonstrated below, the password aging feature can be turned off by using **-1** for the maximum age.

```
# passwd -x -1 smitha
```

The password command also has the ability to give the root user password status information. The **-s** option prints a single line of information on the account listed. The line contains the account name, status (NP = no password, LK = locked, PS = normal), the date of the last password change, and the minimum, maximum and warning password aging values.

```
# passwd -a smitha
smitha PS 7/1/94 2 180 7
```

You can obtain a list of the password status for all accounts on a system by using the **-a** option along with the **-s** option.

```
# passwd -s -a
root PS
daemon LK
dwight PS
smitha PS 7/1/94 180 7
( ... )
```

/etc/shadow

The actual password for an account is not stored in the file */etc/passwd*. This is because the */etc/passwd* fle is typically world readable. A simple method of breaking system security is to obtain a copy of the encrypted passwords, and write a program to "crack" the encryption.

To provide more secure passwords, Solaris stores the encrypted passwords in the */etc/shadow* file. This file is readable by the *root* account only. All log-in functions use password retrieval routines which know to check the */etc/shadow* file for the password. By keeping the passwords in a locked file, system crackers cannot obtain a copy of encrypted passwords, and system security is maintained.

For Experts Only: vipw

If you have the Berkeley UNIX compatibility package installed, you can also use the **vipw** command to add, modify and delete account records from the */etc/passwd* file. This command simply allows you to directly edit this data file using an editor, typically the **vi** editor from which the command gets its name.

Direct editing of the password file is prone to errors. You must meticulously adhere to the file format and be careful not to leave incomplete or malformed entries in the file. The vipw command performs no checking other than to verify that the *root* account is sufficiently correct to allow root to log in. Unless you are accustomed to this sort of file editing from working on other UNIX systems, stay away from vipw and use the other commands described above. These commands are designed to prevent errors that would prohibit users from logging into their accounts due to incorrect entries in the */etc/passwd* file.

Summary

An account is a collection of identification, authentication, and permission information stored in data files or an NIS+ database. By using OpenWindows, the **admintool** provides an easy-to-use graphical series of forms for adding, modifying, and deleting user accounts. However, attention must be devoted to preparing for new accounts and handling situations not covered by the admintool. If OpenWindows is not installed on the system you are managing, you will be using a series of command line tools which cover nearly all functions found in the admintool.

Refining System
Boot Procedures

Unlike starting up a PC or Macintosh, the boot sequence of a Solaris system involves many steps and can be modified in a number of places to suit various needs. In this chapter, we will discuss the terminology used to describe the boot sequence, indicate where changes can be made in the sequence, and show some examples of how to change the boot sequence for purposes such as adding local daemons.

The Boot Sequence

The term "boot" comes from the phrase, "pick yourself up by the bootstraps." To boot a computer is to start it running from a stopped state, usually right after turning it on. It refers to the process of starting from scratch and building backup. The following diagram illustrates the different steps in the boot sequence.

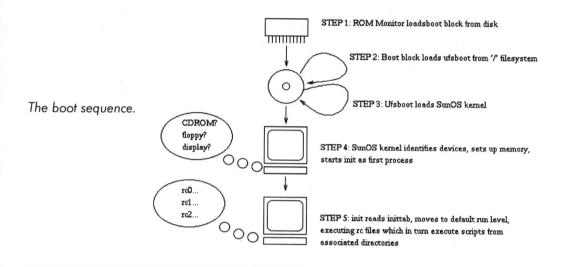

The boot sequence.

STEP 1: ROM Monitor loadsboot block from disk

STEP 2: Boot block loads ufsboot from '/' filesystem

STEP 3: Ufsboot loads SunOS kernel

STEP 4: SunOS kernel identifies devices, sets up memory, starts init as first process

STEP 5: init reads inittab, moves to default run level, executing rc files which in turn execute scripts from associated directories

The first step of this process relies on the physical hardware of the workstation to initialize itself and load a small program from an area of memory which maintains itself even with the power off. This is usually a ROM (Read Only Memory) or PROM (Programmable Read Only Memory) chip. The program loaded is called a "PROM monitor."

Step 1: The PROM Monitor

The PROM monitor has several functions. It can be used to modify some basic hardware parameters, such as the configuration of serial ports used for a console on systems without a graphics display. One such setting is the boot device, which specifies the device on which the PROM monitor should look for the next stage of the boot process. Most importantly, the PROM monitor has routines to load the next stage of the boot process into memory and start it running. The loading can occur from a disk attached to the system, or over the network from a boot server in the case of a diskless workstation, depending on the setting of the boot device parameter.

On a SPARCstation, the PROM monitor initially starts in a restricted state. This state is sometimes referred to as "old command mode" because it was all that was available on some earlier model workstations. The state restricts the operations that can be taken to (1) start the boot process; (2) continue the running program if you accidentally entered the PROM monitor; and (3) switch to the "new command mode." You can continue the boot process by using the **b** command, entering the new command mode through use of the **n** command, or if you have interrupted the operation of the system, return the system to the running state using the **c** (continue) command.

From new command mode you can set two parameters which affect the restricted state. One is a security mode which prevents a user from specifying the boot device to try and avoid a user booting from a removable disk. The other parameter is called *auto-boot?*, and if it is set the workstation will bypass the restricted mode and continue on directly with the boot process.

The b Boot Option

The **b** command accepts an optional argument indicating which device to use in booting and allows you to pass along an option flag to control the boot process. A common usage is to specify the **-s** option to enter run level 1 or single-user mode to perform system maintenance activities such as software installation. The format for the **b** command is *b [device] [file] [options]*. A summary of the **b** command appears below.

Boot Options

Parameter	Description
[device]	Insert cdrom, disk, floppy, net, or tape.
[file]	A bootable file such as stand/diag.
[option]	The option is -a to prompt for additional information, or -s to enter run level 1.

For example, booting a system from the restricted mode of the PROM monitor is done by simply typing "b":

```
b
```

The **-r** option begins a reconfiguration boot, meaning that a flag is passed along to the boot process. The flag indicates that the process needs to check for changes in the available system devices and take actions such as loading device drivers, and creating or deleting entries in the */dev* directory to match the changes. Chapter 11 will discuss device reconfiguration in more detail.

Entering the new command mode is done by typing **n**:

```
n
Type help for more information
ok
```

The new command mode, also known as the Forth Monitor, allows you an extra level of control and customization. You can identify the new command mode by the *ok* prompt instead of the "" prompt used in the restricted mode. The table below presents a list of some of the more common commands available in new command mode.

Forth Monitor Options

Command	Description
boot	Similar to the b command in the restricted mode.
probe-scsi	Tests the internal SCSI bus and lists the devices found. This option is handy when adding new devices to a workstation. The command probe-scsi-all will find all SCSI devices on all SCSI bus adapters.
reset	Causes the PROM monitor to initialize the system and itself as if the power had just been turned on, which is a more desirable way to completely reset the system than switching the power on and off.
printenv	Lists the settable PROM monitor parameters.
setenv	Sets a PROM monitor parameter.

✔ **NOTE:** *Be careful when setting PROM monitor parameters, especially boot-device and boot-file. The PROM monitor makes no checks to see that these parameters are valid; a mistake can prevent your system from automatically booting.*

An example of starting the boot process from the new command mode is shown below.

```
ok boot
```

If the *auto-boot?* parameter is set to true, or if the **b** or **boot** commands are issued, the PROM monitor proceeds to the next stage of the boot process, loading and starting a program known as the "boot block."

Step 2: The Boot Block

The second stage program in the boot process is the **boot block**. As with the PROM monitor, the boot block gets its name from the location in which it is stored. Typically, the boot block is stored in the first few blocks on the hard disk attached to the workstation. The boot block's job is to initialize some of the system's peripherals and memory, and to load the program which will in turn load the SunOS kernel. A boot block is placed on the disk as part of the Solaris installation process, or, in rare circumstances, by the system administrator using the **installboot** program.

Although a diskless machine does not read its boot block from a disk, the term is still used to describe the small program that the PROM monitor loads into the workstation's memory from a boot server over the network. A boot server is simply another system on the network running a set of daemons. Its purpose is to communicate with the PROM monitor and transmit a boot block over the network.

Step 3: The Boot Program

Depending on the location of the **boot block**, its next action is to load a boot program such as **/ufsboot** into memory and execute it. The boot program includes a device driver needed for the device (in other words, the hard drive) on which the SunOS kernel is located. Once started, the boot program loads the SunOS kernel and starts it running. On a diskless workstation the boot program handles setting up NFS access over the network to the workstation's / file system and *swap* area.

Step 4: The SunOS Kernel

The **kernel** is the basis of SunOS and in turn of Solaris. Once loaded into memory by the boot program, the kernel has several tasks to perform before the final stages of the boot process can continue. First, the kernel initializes memory and the hardware associated with memory management. Next, it performs a series of device probes. These are small routines called to check for the presence of various devices such as graphics displays, ethernet controllers, disk controllers, disk drivers, tape devices, and so on. On some systems you may be able to see the status lights blink on some devices such as disk drives as the kernel probes for and locates the devices. This automated search for memory and devices is sometimes referred to as "autoconfiguration."

With memory and devices found and configured, the kernel finishes its start-up routine by creating **init**, the very first system process. The init process is given the process ID number 1 and is the parent of all processes that will be started later. Init is also the process responsible for the remainder of the boot process.

Step 5: init and /etc/inittab

The **init** process, the files it reads and the shell scripts it executes are the most configurable part of the boot process. Management of the process which offers the *login* prompt to terminals, the start-up for daemons, network configuration, disk checking and more occurs during this stage of the boot sequence.

The init process reads in its own configuration file called */etc/inittab*. The */etc/inittab* file contains a series of init directives. The format for these directives follows:

```
id:run level:action:process
```

The directives are described below.

❑ **id**: A one- or four-character label which uniquely identifies the entry. Think of it as the serial number for the process.

❑ **run level**: The system run level at which this process will start running.

❑ **action**: This parameter indicates one of a variety of actions to be taken by init.

❑ **process**: The name of the program which will be acted upon depending on the values of the previous two fields (run level and action).

Solaris Run Levels

The run level is a number specifying the system state. Actions to be taken by **init** are keyed to various run levels. The run levels used in Solaris are described in the following table.

Solaris Run Levels

Run Level	Description
0	Power-down or shutdown state; init stops all system activity and causes the kernel to exit back to the PROM monitor.
1	Single user. Execute only actions to bring the system up for use by the root with only the / and /usr files systems. Used for system maintenance activities such as installing certain software packages.
2	Multi-user. Resources are not exported to other systems.
3	Multi-user. Resources are exported to other systems. This is the state usually entered when the system is booted.
4	An alternative multi-user state. Currently not used.

Run Level	Description
5	This level is used for system shutdown and power-down on Sun4m under Solaris 2.4.
6	Reboot. This level is used for system shutdown.
s or S	Single user. With all file systems, this level is similar to run level 1. All the file systems are left mounted. Terminal log-ins are disabled, but network log-ins are enabled.

More than one run level can be listed, in which case the line is used when init enters any of the listed run levels. An entry with no run level listed is assumed to be valid at all run levels.

init Actions

When an init moves to a given run level, it goes to each line with that run level listed on it and takes a specified action with the process listed on the line. Some processes need to be run once, others need to be run again whenever they stop running, and so on. The actions listed in the table below describe the things init can do with a process. In the next section, we will walk through a sample **inittab** and see how each of these action codes is used.

init Actions

Action Code	Description
respawn	The process is started when entering this run level; init does not wait for the process to finish before moving on to the next entry in inittab, and init will restart the process if it should die.
wait	The process is started and init waits for it to finish before moving on to the next entry in inittab.
once	The process is started, but init does not wait for it to finish and no action is taken if the process dies.
boot	The process is executed only during the first reading of the inittab file when init is first started.
bootwait	The process is executed when init moves from single user (i.e., run level 1) to multi-user (i.e., run level 2); init waits for the process to complete and does not restart it. This code is similar to boot action.

Action Code	Description
powerfail	The process is executed when init receives a power failure signal. This signal is delivered by another process, such as a backup power source monitor.
powerwait	Similar to powerfail, except that init will wait until the process finishes before continuing to read entries in inittab.
off	If the process listed in this entry is running, init will stop it when entering the listed run level.
initdefault	This is a special entry used only to specify the default run level. The run level argument of the line with the init default action is interpreted as the default run level.
sysinit	The process listed in this entry is to be run before init starts processes associated with allowing logins.

A Closer Look at /etc/inittab

The action codes and run levels become easier to understand when you examine an **inittab** file and step through it line by line just as the init process does when a system is being booted. A sample inittab file from a Solaris 2.4 system follows:

```
ap::sysinit:/sbin/autopush -f /etc/iu.ap

fs::sysinit:/sbin/rcS>/dev/console 2>&1 </dev/console

is:3:initdefault:

p3:s1234:powerfail:/sbin/shutdown -y -i5 -g0 >/dev/console 2>&1

s0:0:wait:/sbin/rc0>/dev/console 2&1 </dev/console

s1:1:wait:/sbin/shutdown -y -iS -g0>/dev/console 2>&1 </dev/console

s2:23:wait:/sbin/rc2>/dev/console 2>&1 </dev/console

s3:3:wait:/sbin/rc3/dev/console 2>&1 </dev/console

s5:5:wait:/sbin/rc5>/dev/console 2&1 </dev/console

s6:6:wait:/sbin/rc6>/dev/console 2>&1 /dev/console

of:0:wait:/sbin/uadmin 2 0>/dev/console 2>&1 </dev/console

fw:5:wait:/sbin/uadmin 2 6>/dev/console 2>&1 </dev/console

RB:6:wait:/sbin/sh -c 'echo "\n"The system is being restarted."'
>/dev/console 2>&1

rb:6:wait:/sbin/uadmin 2 1>/dev/console 2>&1 </dev/console

sc:234:respawn:/usr/lib/saf/sac -t 300
```

```
co:234:respawn:/usr/lib/saf/ttymon -g -h -p "'uname -n' console
login: " -T sun -d /dev/console -l console -m ldterm,ttcompat
```

Let's dissect this file to see how the init process works. The file is read by init line by line. The following discussion uses the two-character identifier to indicate the line being discussed.

```
ap::sysinit:/sbin/autopush -f /etc/iu.ap
```

```
fs::sysinit:/sbin/rcS>/dev/console 2>&1 </dev/console
```

Because the first two lines, *ap* and *fs* have no run level and use the action code *sysinit*, the process associated with each line is executed and init waits for it to finish before moving on. The *ap* line initializes the keyboard and mouse drivers for use with the console and other terminal lines. The process on the *fs* line is one of the **rc** or run command shell scripts which will be discussed in detail later. The **rcS** script checks the / and */usr* file systems for consistency.

```
is:3:initdefault:
```

The *is* line sets the default run level to 3 thanks to the **initdefault** action code. The *is* line does not change the run level; it specifies which run level init will move to by default when it is started. By specifying level 3, init will move from level 0 to 1, 1 to 2, and 2 to 3 when the system is booted.

```
p3:s1234:powerfail:/sbin/shutdown -y -i0 -g5 >/dev/console 2>&1
```

Upon booting, init moves from run level 0 to the default run level 3 in the example inittab file. The *p3* line is read. Since the *p3* line lists several run levels, including run level 3, init performs the action. The **powerfail** action causes init to "remember" the process listed on the *p3* line as the process to be run if a power failure signal (sigpwr) is sent to init. This action is used at sites where a backup power supply and special monitoring software are installed to automatically shut the system down in the event of a power failure.

```
s0:0:wait:/sbin/rc0 off>/dev/console 2>&1 </dev/console
```

```
s1:1:wait:/sbin/shutdown -y -iS -g0>/dev/console 2>&1 </dev/console
```

The *s0* line is skipped because it is not for run level 3. The *s1* line is skipped for the same reason.

```
s2:2:wait:/sbin/rc2>/dev/console 2>&1 </dev/console
```

The *s2* line is processed. It runs a run control or **rc** shell script. This script, **rc2**, in turn runs a set of scripts to set the system time zone, and starts a number of system daemons.

```
s3:3:wait:/sbin/rc3>/dev/console 2>&1 </dev/console
```

The *s3* line is processed next. The **rc3** script also runs a series of other scripts to configure the network and starts the additional service daemons.

```
s5:5:wait:/sbin/rc5 ask>/dev/console 2>&1 </dev/console

s6:6:wait:/sbin/rc6 reboot>/dev/console 2>&1 </dev/console

of:0:wait:/sbin/uadmin 2 0>/dev/console 2>&1 </dev/console

fw:5:wait:/sbin/uadmin 2 2>/dev/console 2>&1 </dev/console

RB:6:wait:/sbin/sh -c 'echo "\nThe system is being restarted."'
>/dev/console 2>&1

rb:6:wait:/sbin/uadmin 2 1>/dev/console 2>&1 </dev/console
```

The *s5*, *s6*, *of*, *fw*, *RB*, and *rb* lines are skipped as they do not have the correct run level as noted by the italicized portions.

```
sc:234:respawn:/usr/lib/saf/sac -t 300

co:234:respawn:/usr/lib/saf/ttymon -g -h -p "`uname -n` console
login: " -T sun -d /dev/console -l console -m ldterm,ttcompat
```

The last two lines, *sc* and *co*, are read and the processes listed are run and automatically restarted should they die as a result of the **respawn** action. The *sc* line starts the process which monitors the terminal lines and provides a *login* prompt for users. The *co* line starts the process which monitors the system console and provides a *login* prompt on that device. When init finishes processing the inittab, the system boot is complete.

Modifying /etc/inittab

A common modification is to add entries to the */etc/init.d* script files for processes to be started at specific run levels. Care needs to be taken to place the entry in the correct sequence with respect to the other entries. For example, if you were to add a line for a network license manager daemon, you would want to be sure it is started after things it depends on, such as network configuration or the NIS+ daemons. Most third-party software packages that require modification provide explicit directions on where in the file their entries need to be placed and which run level to use.

Although modifying the inittab can be used to change the final stages of the boot sequence, there are several drawbacks: difficulty in testing your entries, the single-line limit for entries, and difficulty in making entries conditional upon factors other than the run level. For these reasons, the run control or **rc** file system is used, the subject of the next section.

The Run Control Files

The run control or **rc** files and their associated scripts are the most commonly modified component of the boot sequence. You can add or modify many system configuration processes in much the same way as for an inittab entry, but these files are easily tested and have the programming features of the Bourne shell. Run control files give you greater flexibility in configuring the system during the boot process.

Each run level has an associated rc file. Most rc files have a specially designed directory bearing the name of the rc file with a *.d* at the end. The rc file is a short Bourne shell script for scanning its associated directory and running the scripts found there in a certain sequence. The rc files are located in the */sbin* directory, and their directories of scripts are located in the */etc* directory.

In the preceding discussion of the inittab file, you saw lines which contained rc files. The *s3* line follows:

```
s3:3:wait:/sbin/rc3>/dev/console 2>&1 </dev/console
```

The above line is read by init, and when entering run level 3, init will start the */sbin/rc3* script running and wait until it finishes. The *rc3* script will in turn scan the */etc/rc3.d* directory in search of scripts to be run. Each script handles a specific system function, such as the print service or NFS.

For each run level, there is an rc file and usually a directory of scripts to handle the start-up or shutdown of its services. The table below shows the rc file and script directory, and a brief description of the functions the rc file and scripts perform for each run level.

Run Control Script File Relationships

Run Level	RC script	RC directory	Common Functions
0	/sbin/rc0	/etc/rc0.d	Kills all running processes except init and unmounts all file systems.
1	/sbin/rc1	/etc/rc1.d	Kills all non-essential system daemons.
2	/sbin/rc2	/etc/rc2.d	Kills the NFS, volume management and lp services, mounts file systems, and on start-up, starts most system services except NFS server.

Run Level	RC script	RC directory	Common Functions
3	/sbin/rc3	/etc/rc3.d	Starts the NFS server process.
4	none	none	There is no rc4 file under Solaris 2.3.
5	/sbin/rc5	none	In Solaris 2.3, this is the same script as rc0.
6	/sbin/rc6	none	In Solaris 2.3, this is the same script as rc0.
S	/sbin/rcS	/etc/rcS.d	Starts basic network services, mounts /usr and executes reconfiguration needed during a reconfiguration boot when new hardware is added to the system.

The scripts in these directories are run in their ASCII sorting order within two divisions. Files which start with *K* contain commands to kill off processes and are run first when the corresponding run level is entered. The K scripts are given the **stop** argument when run (e.g., **K201p stop**). Files which start with *S* contain commands to start processes and are run next when the corresponding run level is entered. The S scripts are given the **start** argument when run (e.g., **S201p start**). The flow of control from init through an rc file onto a script in an rc directory is shown in the following diagram.

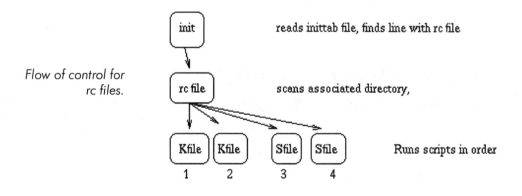

Flow of control for rc files.

While it is sometimes necessary to directly modify one of the rc files, the more common approach is to add, delete, or modify one of the scripts located in the rc directories in */etc*. By convention, the same script is used to start and stop a given service. The script contains a simple *case* statement and takes different actions depending on the argument given to it (*start* or *stop*). The same script may also be used at several run levels. To avoid multiple copies of a script and to ease maintenance, file links are used.

All scripts used by all rc files are located in the */etc/init.d* directory. A link is made from the script into the appropriate rc directory to cause one of these scripts to be run as part of the boot sequence for a certain run level.

File Links

A file link, or simply a *link*, is a term used in UNIX for another directory entry which points to the same file. You can think of a link as an alias because it is another name by which the same information is known. Links are created using the **ln** command shown in the following illustration.

```
┌─────────────────────────────────────────────────────────────────────┐
│ ▽                     cmdtool - /bin/csh                              │
├─────────────────────────────────────────────────────────────────────┤
│ glenn% su                                                          ▲  │
│ Password:                                                             │
│ # cd /etc/rc3.d                                                       │
│ # ln /etc/init.d/cron K12cron                                      ▼  │
│ # ls -l K12cron                                                       │
│ -rwxr--r--   5 root       sys          480 Sep 27  1993 K12cron       │
│ # head -2 K12cron                                                     │
│ #ident   "@(#)cron        1.8     93/07/27 SMI"   /* SVr4.0 1.3.3.1    */ │
│                                                                       │
│ # head -2 /etc/init.d/cron                                            │
│ #ident   "@(#)cron        1.8     93/07/27 SMI"   /* SVr4.0 1.3.3.1    */ │
│                                                                       │
│ # ▲                                                                   │
└─────────────────────────────────────────────────────────────────────┘
```

Creating and examining a file link.

Note that once the link is made, using either the file name or the link name, the contents of the same file are shown. This property allows you to place links to a file where normally you may have put the file itself. Since a link is just another name for the file, any changes you make to the file are seen through all of its links. In the case of the scripts found in the rc directories, this makes maintenance easier as you need only modify the original script to fix problems.

By convention, the files which contain all scripts used by all rc files are located in the */etc/init.d* directory. Their names are given by the function they perform or the system service which they start and stop.

Each rc script file first reads and processes links whose names begin with a *K* to stop processes which should not be running at the run level for this rc file. Next, the rc file reads and processes the links which begin with an *S*, to start processes which should be running at the run level for this rc file. For example, the script which starts the **cron** program, which runs other programs at scheduled times, is found in */etc/init.d/cron*. Because the cron program should not be running at run levels 0 or 1, links are made using the **ln** command in the */etc/rc0.d* and */etc/rc1.d* directories (i.e., */etc/rc0.d/K70cron*, and */etc/rc1.d/ K70cron*).

> ✔ **NOTE:** *Verify that that the editor you use on one of the scripts in an rc directory does not break the link and create a new file as part of the editing process. Text Edit and vi preserve links.*

The cron script and its links in the rc directories.

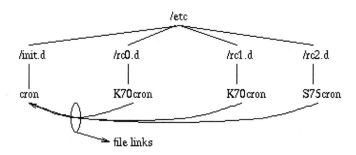

The *70* in the name of the *K70cron* link controls the order in which the links are processed by the rc scripts. For example, when the **rc1** script is run by **init**, it runs the scripts in the */etc/rc1.d* directory in the following order:

1. K00ANNOUNCE
2. K42audit
3. K47asppp
4. K55syslog
5. K57sendmail
6. K65nfs.server
7. K67rpc
8. K68autofs
9. K70cron

10. K80nfs.client

11. S01MOUNTFSYS

The *K* links are read and processed first in numerical order. The rc script runs each K script with a single argument, stop, passed to it. For example, the cron link in */etc/rc1.d* is run as if you had typed */etc/rc1.d/K70cron stop*. Due to its link to */etc/init.d/cron*, this cron link is equivalent to typing */etc/init.d/cron stop*.

The cron process is supposed to be started at run level 2; consequently, a link is made in the */etc/r2.d* directory for */etc/rc2.d/S75cron*. The *S* scripts are read and processed after the K scripts in numerical order based on the two-digit number following the S. Like the K scripts, the S scripts are run as if you had typed */etc/rc2.d/S75cron start*, which is equivalent to */etc/init.d/cron start*, thanks to the file link.

Modifying Run Control Files

Modifications to the run control files are generally made by adding, changing or deleting one of the scripts in */etc/init.d*, and adding or deleting the corresponding links in the **rc** directories as needed. To add a new system daemon, such as a license manager, a new script is created in */etc/init.d*. The script must be able to handle the following two arguments:

❑ **start** This argument is given to the script when it is called as an S script from one of the rc files. When the script sees the start argument it should take whatever start-up action is required, such as starting processes, clearing out directories, testing for the availability of configuration files, and so on.

❑ **stop** This argument is given to the script when it is called as a K script from one of the rc files. When the script sees the stop argument, it should take whatever shutdown and clean-up action is required, such as killing off processes, clearing out temporary files, saving state information, and so on.

As an example, the script used to start up a license manager daemon appears below. The daemon controls how many copies of certain programs are running. The programs contact this daemon over the network for permission to run. This script is placed in the */etc/init.d/lmf* directory. It is written using Bourne shell syntax since the rc files will run these scripts using the Bourne shell.

```
# start and stop the license manager daemon
# save the first argument in the variable "state"
state=$1
# handle each possible value for "state"...
```

```
        1
case $state in

        2
'start')
    # check for the lmf configuration file and if present, start lmfd
        4
    [ -f /usr/lib/lmf.conf ] && /usr/lib/lmfd
        2
    ;;

        3
'stop')
    # find lmfd in the output of ps
        5
    id=`ps -e | grep lmfd | awk '{print $1}'`
    # if a process id was found, then kill it
    if test -n "$id"
    then
            kill $id
    fi
        3
    ;;
        1
esac
```

The heart of the script is the block of lines starting at the *case* and ending at the *esac* (see 1). This block is further divided into two sections: the first one runs from *'start')* to the *;;* (see 2), and the second one runs from *'stop')* to the *;;* (see 3).

The *start* block is executed if the first argument given to the script and saved in the *state* variable is the word "start." The *[-f /usr/lib/lmf.conf] &&* phrase (see 4) is Bourne shell syntax for "check to see if the file /usr/lib/lmf.conf exists and if so do the following." The phrase that follows, */usr/lib/lmfd*, simply starts the license manager daemon. The entire block together checks for the *lmf* configuration file, and if it exists, runs the *lmf* daemon program.

The *stop* block is a bit more involved. The line which begins with *id=* (see 5) executes three commands joined together by pipes and puts the result in the variable *id*. The first command is **ps -e** which lists all the processes that are currently running. The output of this command is passed to **grep lmfd** which filters out the line listing the license manager daemon. That line is then passed along to *awk '{print $1}'*. *Awk* is a programmable filter. The program is the {**print $1**} phrase. Using this program, *awk* prints the first "word," or group of characters separated by spaces in the line passed to it. In this case the output of *awk* is the process ID number. Thus, the entire series of commands finds the process ID number for the license manager daemon and puts that number in the variable *id*.

But what if the license manager daemon was not running? In this case, nothing would be found, and the value of *id* would be empty. This is what the *if* line is testing for. The **kill** command is run only if *id* contains something. The kill command sends the *SIGKILL* signal to the license manager daemon causing it to stop running.

Benefits of Using rc Directory Scripts

One of the benefits of using **rc** directory scripts is that they are easily tested. You can run the script and give it the stop and start arguments and check that it functions correctly before putting in the file links and trying it under actual system boot conditions. This is a good practice and can help you catch mistakes that might interrupt the boot process and leave it incomplete.

The final step in adding this script is to add a link in the appropriate places in the rc directories. Since the daemon in our example needs to communicate over the network, it should be started *after* the network utilities are started. One possible choice is to make the following links:

```
ln /etc/init.d/lmf /etc/rc0.d/K21lmf

ln /etc/init.d/lmf /etc/rc1.d/K21lmf

ln /etc/init.d/lmf /etc/rc3.d/S95lmf
```

This set of links makes sure that the license manager is not running when the system is in run level 1 or single-user mode, and is started after the network services when the system is in run level 3 or multi-user mode.

Changing Run Levels

Up to this point as regards the run level, only the normal boot sequence has been discussed. However, there are several ways in which the run level can be changed. The following commands are usually reserved for system maintenance activities, and leave the system to operate most of the time in the default run level.

❏ **/usr/sbin/shutdown** The is the most frequently used method of changing the run level. It automates the process of run level changes and user notification of impending run level changes. This command is covered in detail in the next chapter.

❏ **/sbin/init** or **/etc/telinit** Directly indicates to the **init** process which run level to move to. No user notification is given, with the exception of init1.

❏ **/usr/sbin/halt** Takes the system directly to run level 0 with no user notification. It is typically used in situations such as system maintenance or when immediate system shutdown is required.

❏ **/usr/sbin/reboot** Takes the system to run level 6, which causes the system to shut down to run level 0, and then execute the boot process as if starting up from power off. It is often used as the final part of the installation of system software packages.

Summary

Modifying the system boot process is an important way that system managers can tailor Solaris to their unique environments. Certain software products and procedures must be started or performed at system boot by adding them to the boot sequence. Through the system of run control files and their associated directories, new boot procedures can be easily added. By using the Bourne scripts as presented here, a new boot procedure can conditionally handle a variety of situations, and is easily developed and tested without the need to repeatedly boot a system.

9

Proper System Shutdowns

In the previous chapter we learned the correct way to boot a system. In this chapter, we will show how to perform a proper system shutdown. In addition, we will look at several ways to bring the system from the current init state to a different init state.

Most of the methods discussed in this chapter will result in the system going through an orderly shutdown process. We will also examine a couple of methods which will not result in an orderly shutdown. While an orderly shutdown is always preferred, there may be times when such a shutdown is not possible.

The shutdown Command

You must have super-user access to use the **shutdown** command. The shutdown command will bring the system down to the init state of your choice in an orderly manner. In order to accomplish this, shutdown will send warning messages to all users warning them of the system shutdown. This command will also notify the system syslog daemon of the shutdown. When the specified time arrives, shutdown will cause the system to sync the memory buffers to disk, and then change the system init state to the desired state.

```
# shutdown

Shutdown started.    Thu Oct 27 07:23:11 EST 1994

Broadcast Message from root (console) on mercury Thu Oct 27 07:23:13...
THE SYSTEM IS BEING SHUT DOWN NOW ! ! !
Log off now or risk your files being damaged.

Do you want to continue? (y or n):    y
The system is coming down.  Please wait.
System services are now being stopped.
Print services stopped.
Stopping the syslog service.
Oct 27 07:24:44 mercury syslogd: going down on signal 15
umount -F cachefs: /usr/local Device busy
The system is down.
Changing to init state s - please wait
#
INIT: New run level: S

INIT: SINGLE USER MODE

Type Ctrl-d to proceed with normal startup,
(or give root password for system maintenance):
Entering System Maintenance Mode

SU 10/27 07:25 + syscon root-root
**
```

Using shutdown with no command line options.

 NOTE : *In order to ensure proper operation of the shutdown command, the user should first exit the OpenWindows environment. The shutdown command will work only if the user is currently in the / (root) directory.*

Three of the most common uses of shutdown are to bring the system to a halt, bring the system down to single-user mode, or reboot the system. All run modes are signified by a numbered init state.

Run Mode init States

init State	State Name	Comment
0	Halted	The operating system is not running.
1	Administration	All file systems are mounted, and all daemons are running, but the console is the only terminal which has access to the operating system. Only root is allowed to log in to the system.

init State	State Name	Comment
2	Multi-user	All file systems are mounted, and all daemons are running.
3	Remote File Sharing	All file systems are mounted, all daemons are running, and the system mounts/allows mounting of remote file systems.
4	Alternative Multi-user	The init state 4 is usually not used.
5	Power-off	Causes the system to shut down to the interactive state. Sun4m systems will power-off automatically.
6	Reboot to inittab	Causes the system to reboot to the init state specified in the /etc/inittab file.
s or S	Single User	The console is the only terminal with access to the Operating System. No interactive file systems are available. No system daemons are present, but remote log-ins are enabled.

```
# shutdown -y -i0 -g60

Shutdown started.    Thu Oct 27 07:30:16 EST 1994

Broadcast Message from root (console) on mercury Thu Oct 27 07:30:18...
THE SYSTEM IS BEING SHUT DOWN NOW ! ! !
Log off now or risk your files being damaged.

Changing to init state 0 - please wait
#
INIT: New run level: 0
The system is coming down.  Please wait.
System services are now being stopped.
Print services stopped.
Stopping the syslog service.
Oct 27 07:31:27 mercury syslogd: going down on signal 15
umount -F cachefs: /usr/local Device busy
umount -F cachefs: /usr/local Device busy
umount: /var/local busy
The system is down.
syncing file systems... [1] done
Halted
>
```

Using shutdown with command line modifiers.

The shutdown command has the following flags:

❑ **-y** tells the system to pre-answer all confirmations with a yes.

❑ **-g N** tells the system to execute the shutdown in *N* seconds. Default is 60 seconds.

❑ **-i N** tells the system to change to the init state specified by *N*.

✔ *NOTE: It is always a good idea to warn users in advance of a shutdown. This allows them to save their files and log off, avoiding the risk of file damage or loss. If you use a grace period of 900 seconds, this will give the users a 15-minute warning of the impending shutdown.*

The Halt Command

Sometimes it is not feasible or necessary to warn the users of an impending shutdown. In this case you may wish to use the **halt** command. While the halt command initiates an orderly shutdown of the operating system, it does not send any warning messages to the users. The halt command will not execute any of the scripts in the */etc/rc?.d*, nor does it allow you to leave the system in **init** state *s* (single-user). This command brings the processor to a halt!

Using halt without flags.

```
# halt
syncing file systems... done
Halted
>
```

You must have super-user access to use the halt command. In most cases, the halt command will bring the system to an orderly halt. The halt command's four flags which control how the system is shut down appear below:

❑ **-l** tells halt not to inform syslog of the system halt.

❑ **-n** tells the halt command not to write (sync) the memory buffers to disk before halting.

❑ **-q** tells the halt command to do a "quick" halt. This will also cause the system not to sync the memory buffers to disk, and may cause some processes to exit less than gracefully.

❑ **-y** tells the halt command to halt the system, even if the terminal issuing the halt command is a dial-up line.

Using halt with command line flags.

```
# halt -l -n
syncing file systems... done
Halted
>
```

!   **WARNING:** *Halting a system without writing the memory buffers to disk can be dangerous to the file system! This method is generally used if it is known that the contents of memory are corrupt. Consequently, you do not want the system to do a **sync** before halting.*

The init 0 Command

Another method for bringing the system to a different init state is through the **init** command. Again, you must have super-user access to use this command. The init command does not send warning messages to the users. Using the init command to change system init states is best reserved for those instances where nothing else has worked.

✔ **NOTE**: *Some system administrators prefer the init0 over the halt command because init0 will execute the scripts in /etc/rc?.d. These scripts will cleanly shut down databases and other systems before the system is halted.*

The program **telinit** is a link to the **/sbin/init** program. Telinit allows a single character argument. This argument is the alpha-numeric identifier of the init state you desire.

In addition to the init state identifiers understood by shutdown, telinit understands the following:

❏ **a,b,c** The a,b,c init states are pseudo run levels. Using one of these states in the */etc/inittab* file or with the telinit command tells the system to run commands which are tagged as level a,b,c but do not change the system run state.

❏ **q,Q** causes the system to immediately re-examine the */etc/inittab* file.

❏ **s,S** causes the system to change state to the single-user mode. The terminal which issues the **telinit s** command becomes the system console.

```
# telinit s
#
INIT: New run level: S

INIT: SINGLE USER MODE

Type Ctrl-d to proceed with normal startup,
(or give root password for system maintenance):
Entering System Maintenance Mode

SU 10/27 07:36 + syscon root-root
#
```

Using telinit to bring the system down.

The reboot Command

The **reboot** command is another method to bring the system down. Reboot causes the system to shut down and reboot to the state specified in the /etc/inittab file. This command does not execute the shutdown scripts in /etc/rc?.d. The reboot command has the following four flags:

❑ **-d** causes the reboot process to generate a core dump. This option is provided for compatibility, but is not supported.

❑ **-l** causes the suppression of notification to the syslog daemon.

❑ **-n** causes the system to halt and then reboot without syncing the memory buffers to disk.

❑ **-q** causes the system to ungracefully halt and reboot without syncing the memory buffers to disk.

!   **WARNING:** *Halting a system without writing the memory buffers to disk can be dangerous to the file system! This method is generally used if it is known that the contents of memory are corrupt. Therefore, you do not want the system to do a **sync** before halting.*

```
 ┌─────────────────────────────────────────────────────────────────────┐
 │ ▽                              xterm                                  │
 ├─────────────────────────────────────────────────────────────────────┤
 │ # reboot                                                              │
 │ Oct 27 07:36:20 mercury reboot: rebooted by root                      │
 │ Oct 27 07:36:21 mercury syslogd: going down on signal 15              │
 │ syncing file systems... done                                          │
 │ rebooting...                                                          │
 │                                                                       │
 │ EEPROM boot device... xd(0,0,0)                                       │
 │ Boot: xd(0,0,0)                                                       │
 │ SunOS Release 5.3 Version Generic [UNIX(R) System V Release 4.0]      │
 │ Copyright (c) 1983-1993, Sun Microsystems, Inc.                       │
 │ configuring network interfaces:ifconfig: ie0: no such interface       │
 │ ifconfig: le0.                                                        │
 │ Hostname: mercury                                                     │
 │ The system is coming up.  Please wait.                                │
 │ checking filesystems                                                  │
 │ /dev/rdsk/c1d0s7: is clean.                                           │
 │ /dev/dsk/c1d0s7 mounted                                               │
 │ starting router discovery.                                            │
 │ starting rpc services: rpcbind keyserv kerbd done.                    │
 │ Setting netmask of le0 to 255.255.255.0                               │
 │ Setting default interface for multicast: add net 224.0.0.0: gateway mercury │
 │ solaris:/opt mounted                                                  │
 │ solaris:/usr/local mounted                                            │
 │ solaris:/usr/openwin mounted                                          │
 │ syslog service starting.                                              │
 │ Print services started.                                               │
 │ volume management starting.                                           │
 │ starting audit daemon                                                 │
 │ Configured 215 kernel events.                                         │
 │ The system is ready.                                                  │
 │                                                                       │
 │ mercury console login:                                                │
 └─────────────────────────────────────────────────────────────────────┘
```

Using reboot to bring the system down and back up.

The Stop-A Command

Sometimes a system will lock up, making the use of the above commands impossible. When all else fails, you can usually stop the system by holding down the <STOP> key (upper left corner of the keyboard), and simultaneously pressing the *A* key. This sequence is known as *Stop-A* (or L1-A). The key sequence stops the system processor, and puts the system under control of the PROM monitor.

```
# STOP-A pressed
Abort at PC 0xF0031870.
>
```

Once you have stopped the system in this manner, it is best to type the **sync** command to the monitor. This will cause the monitor to sync the memory buffers to disk, and then crash the system. This action will force a system crash dump to be saved for post-mortem inspection. You may be able to determine the reason the system was locked up by examining the crash dump information. Consult the manual page for *crash(1M)* for more information on crash dumps.

Using the PROM monitor to cause a crash dump.

```
>sync
panic: zero
syncing file systems... done
  586 static and sysmap kernel pages
   34 dynamic kernel data pages
  179 kernel-pageable pages
    0 segkmap kernel pages
    0 segvn kernel pages
    0 current user process pages
  799 total pages (799 chunks)

dumping to vp ff1b9004, offset 181288
117 pages left        109 pages left        101 pages left
93 pages left          87 pages left         82 pages left
72 pages left          69 pages left         61 pages left
53 pages left          45 pages left         37 pages left
29 pages left          21 pages left         13 pages left
5 pages left
799 total pages, dump succeeded
rebooting...
```

Summary

In this chapter you have learned several ways to shut a system down. The preferred method of system shutdown is to use the **shutdown** command. When this is not possible, there are other commands and methods available which allow you to halt or gain control of the system.

Managing System Security

System security is probably the most talked about topic in the computer industry today. Collections of workstations and servers running Solaris present a variety of security challenges for the system manager. It is essential to understand the level of security your operation requires and what you must do to establish that security. Maintaining the appropriate level of security for your environment requires a balance between technical considerations and the needs of your organization.

For Additional Information

In this chapter, the discussion will be limited to file and directory security, user account security, the ASET tools, and an introductory discussion of remote access security. Readers who now have or plan to have their Solaris systems connected to the Internet, or whose environment requires a more thorough approach, are strongly encouraged to read further on this topic. Books which specifically address UNIX system security should be considered required reading for managers of systems with more advanced security needs.

How Much Security?

When considering system security, the contents of your users' files constitute the most basic item that you are trying to protect. As system manager there are

185

certain questions you should ask yourself. Who must be able to read or modify the file contents? Would knowing the contents of a certain file allow someone to gain access to other files? Would knowing the contents of the file give away information that should not be disseminated?

Think about an ordinary paper file for a moment. If this file is very sensitive you might lock it in a file cabinet or even a safe. The same holds true for the computer equivalent of such files. If the contents of a file on your system are this sensitive, should the file be available at all? Look at the hazards. Workstations and disk drives are relatively easy to carry off. Networked computers allow files to be absconded quickly and invisibly.

How can you protect your most sensitive data? Files which demand the highest security yet still need to be manipulated on a computer should be stored on removable media such as a floppy or tape which can be physically locked up, just as you would do with a paper file of similar importance.

Encrypting Your Sensitive Data

Another approach for securing sensitive files is to encrypt them using the Solaris **crypt** command. The command uses a mathematical function to scramble the file contents in such a way as to make it unreadable until you decrypt the file.

Encryption's Achilles Heel

While encryption may seem to be a less bothersome method of protecting a sensitive file than removing the file from the system, be warned that encryption only protects a file for a limited period of time. Given time, the key or password used to encrypt the file will be guessed. Automated methods to decipher such passwords are available. The length of time to identify the encryption key is a function of the key length, the encryption method used, other information known about the possible contents of the encrypted file, and the computer resources available to the person guessing the key. Strong encryption techniques may require years to circumvent.

If you plan to use encryption for file security, consider getting the strongest encryption tools, that is, tools for setting up the hardest to guess key.

Owners, Groups, and Permissions

Usually, the contents of most files do not require high-level protection. It is sufficient to ensure that they are readable or modifiable only by certain users. Access to the contents of a file on a Solaris system is controlled by a combination of the file's user and group ownership and the protection bits associated with the file. The output of **ls -l** in a typical directory appears below.

```
                              cmdtool - /bin/csh
glenn% ls -l
total 10
-rw-------    1 dwight    nobody     151 Jul  7 19:43 HideMe
-rw-rw-rw-    1 dwight    nobody     652 Jul  7 19:43 ReadMe
drwxr-xr-x    2 dwight    nobody     512 Jul  7 19:45 big-project
drwx------    2 dwight    nobody     512 Jul  7 19:45 secret
drwxr-x---    2 dwight    nobody     512 Jul  7 19:45 small-project
glenn% ls -l big-project
total 0
-rw-rw-rw-    1 dwight    nobody       0 Jul  7 19:45 one
-rw-rw-rw-    1 dwight    nobody       0 Jul  7 19:45 three
-rw-rw-rw-    1 dwight    nobody       0 Jul  7 19:45 two
glenn%
```

The output of ls -l.

The long listing option of the **ls** command produces several columns which contain various pieces of information about the files in the current directory. The columns from left to right are listed below.

1. A symbolic representation of the permission bits, sometimes called the "permission mode."
2. The number of file links made to the file.
3. The file's owner.
4. The file's group ownership.
5. The file size in bytes.
6. The date the file was last modified.
7. The name of the file.

The first, third, and fourth columns from the left to the right contain the security information. The third and fourth columns list the file's user and group ownership, respectively.

File Protection Bits

Each file has three levels of security associated with it which match the three types of users that may access that file. File protection according to the three categories of users is reviewed below.

❏ **owner** The assigned owner of the file.

❏ **group** A logical group the file and user belong to (like a department within a company).

❏ **other** All other users who either do not own the file or are not a member of the file's group.

Upon examining the **ls** listing you will note the letters *rwx*. These are symbolic representations of the individual security bits associated with each file. Each character in the security field represents a significant feature of the file. The first character indicates type information. The possible type codes are listed in the following table.

Protection Type Codes

Type Code	Meaning
-	File.
d	Directory.
b	Block special device entry. A file system entry which SunOS maps to a specific device. Block specials are usually buffered devices such as disks.
c	Character special device entry, or a file system entry which SunOS maps to a specific device. Character specials are "raw" or unbuffered devices such as terminal ports.
p	Named pipe. A special entry used for interprocess communication.
l	Symbolic link. Unlike a file link, a symbolic link contains the path to another file instead of a direct pointer to it. Symbolic links can span file systems and even point to files available via NFS from other machines.

✔ **NOTE:** *In the case of a symbolic link, the permissions of the file referenced apply. The permissions of the link are not used to determine file access.*

Protection Bits:

```
drwxrwxrwx
```
"other"

Group

Owner

special

The permission bits.

The nine remaining characters are treated as three groups of three. The first group indicates permissions for the file owner, the second for the group ownership, and the third for other. Each character triplet denotes the various permissions for each entity. The presence of a character such as *r* indicates that the permission is granted, while a dash (-) in place of the character indicates that the permission is denied. Each triplet is independent; all three permission bits can be set individually for owner, group members, and others. However, the letter spaces in the triple are "overloaded," that is, several less commonly used bits show up as letters other than the common *rwx* to signify special permissions. The permissions and their meanings for files are listed in the following table.

File Permissions

Permission	Meaning
r	Read. Programs can open and read the contents of the file.
w	Write. Programs can store new contents in the file.
x	Execute. Depending on the "magic number" stored in the first two bytes of the file, one of two things happens. If the number indicates that this is a program binary, it is loaded into memory and started running. If the magic number is not present or indicates the file is a shell script, a shell is started and the file is read by the shell.
s	Setuid or setgid.

Permission	Meaning
t	The "sticky" bit. Found in the third position of the third triple. This bit indicates that this file is to be left on the swap device after it finishes execution. It was used to improve performance for frequently executed commands on older versions of UNIX, but has been made obsolete by improved forms of memory management.
l	Mandatory file locking. This letter indicates that the setgid is on and the group execution bit is off. If a program locks this file, the kernel will prevent other programs from accessing it until the lock is cleared.

✔ **NOTE:** *By default, /bin/sh is used to run any files which do not appear to have a magic number. The magic number is a special value at a particular place in the file. This number tells the system of the file modes and execute permissions. To use another shell, place the string #! and the path to the shell as the first line of the file. The string #! is itself a "magic number" and causes the loader to use the remainder of the first line as the path to the command to be run. For example, #!/bin/csh as the first line of a file would cause /bin/csh to be started and the remainder of the file to be read by /bin/csh.*

! **WARNING:** *The setuid and setgid bits are very powerful and easily misused, and can result in security problems. The setuid bit is most often used to allow unprivileged users to execute a command as if they had root privileges. Do not use this facility lightly. Read the detailed description of Set UID problems below.*

As shown in the next table, the protection bits have similar meanings for directories.

Directory Permissions

Function	Meaning
r	Read permission. Files in the directory can be listed.
w	Write permission. Files or links can be added or removed from the directory.
x	Execute permission. Files can be opened in the directory. The shell can change to this directory (cd).

Function	Meaning
s	Setgid. On a directory, setting the setgid bit causes all files created in the directory to be in the same group as the directory itself.
t	The "sticky" bit. Setting the "sticky" bit on a directory means that only the owner of a file in that directory can remove it. The stick bit is most often used for things like /tmp.

Carefully note the difference between *read* and *execute* permissions for a directory. In the following example, notice how a directory with only the *read* permission allows files to be listed but not examined, even though the files have the required permissions.

A directory with the read permission.

```
cmdtool - /bin/csh
glenn% ls -l
total 10
-rw-------   1 dwight   nobody    151 Jul  7 19:43 HideMe
-rwx--x--x   1 dwight   nobody    652 Jul  7 19:43 ReadMe
drwxr-xr-x   2 dwight   nobody    512 Jul  7 19:45 big-project
drw-------   2 dwight   nobody    512 Jul  7 19:45 secret
drwxr-x---   2 dwight   nobody    512 Jul  7 19:45 small-project
glenn% ls secret
one     three   two
glenn% cat secret/one
cat: cannot open secret/one
glenn%
```

✔ **NOTE:** *The accessibility of a given file is a combination of the permissions and ownerships of all directories along the path to the file as well as the permissions and ownerships of the file itself. When planning file protection schemes, consider which files need to be read and which files should to be hidden. Grouping files in directories for security is an approach worth considering.*

The chown and chgrp Commands

Changing file ownerships and groups is easily done using the **chown** and **chgrp** commands.

```
# chown account item
# chgrp group item
```

The *item* listed above is a file or a directory. The *account* and *group* are the user account name and group name as found in */etc/passwd* and */etc/group*, or in the NIS or NIS+ databases, or the numerical UID or GID numbers. To change an entire directory and all its subdirectories, both chown and chgrp accept the **-r** option which will change the entire contents of a directory which is given as the item to be changed.

Setting Protection Using Symbolic Names

Specifying changes to the protection bits is more involved. The **chmod** command makes the changes. It has an -r option like **chown** for handling entire directories and accepts two different methods of specifying the permission bit changes to be made. The first method is symbolic. A set of symbols is used to specify the entity (user, group, other) and the mode (read, write, execute) to be changed. The symbols are listed in the next table.

Chmod Symbols

Entity	Symbol
User	u
Group	g
Everyone (other)	o
All entities	a
Mode	Symbol
Read	r
Write	w
Execute	x
Mandatory locking	l
SetUID or SetGID	s
"Sticky" bit	t

The symbols are combined with the + operator to add the permission, the - operator to remove the permission, and the = operator to assign the permission. For example, you could remove the *read* permission for other from the file named *bob-stuff* with the following command line:

```
# chmod o-r bob-stuff
```

You can specify lists of the symbol, operator, and symbol sets to change multiple permissions at the same time. An example of setting the execute bits for all and restricting the read access on a file named *test99* appears as follows:

```
# chmod a+x,g-r,o-r test99
```

It's a good practice to get into the habit of checking modes and owners on files after you set them. Use **ls -l** and check the symbolic permission bit column to see who can read and execute the file. Check the owner and group. It is very easy to make a typographical error and set the modes in a way you did not intend.

Using Octal Numbers

The second form of specifying the permission bits is to give them as an octal number. This looks confusing at first, but it is not hard to learn and has the advantage of compactly representing all the protection bits in a single easy-to-type form. A simple way to come up with this magic number is to add up the number assigned to each permission bit from a table like the one shown below.

Octal Number Permissions

Number	Bit
4000	SetUID.
400	Read permission for owner.
200	Write permission for owner.
100	Execute permission for owner.
40	Read permission for group.
20	Write permission for group.
10	Execute permission for group.
4	Read permission for other.
2	Write permission for other.
1	Execute permission for other.

✔ **NOTE:** *The SetGID bit can be set or cleared only by using the symbolic form of specifying the permission bits.*

Using this table, you can specify permissions for a file that has read, write, and execute permission for the owner, and read and execute permission for group and other as follows: 400 + 200 + 100 + 40 + 10 + 4 + 1 = 755.

Use the total number with **chmod** as follows:

```
# chmod 755 demofile
```

Setting the Default File Mode

Files created are given a default set of permission bits which is easily customized to suit your environment. The default is set in one of the shell initialization files with the **umask** command. Unmask takes a single argument which is the complement of the mode you wish newly created files to receive. This can easily be calculated by subtracting the desired file mode in octal from the number *777* for directories and *666* for files. This numbering is such that directories will by default have the execute bit set on and files will not.

For example, if you wanted a very secure *600* file mode which would give read and write permission to the file owner only, you would calculate the **umask** as follows: 666 - 600 = 066.

A more friendly or less secure mode of *644* would be set with a value of *022*. To set the value, simply use it as the first argument to **umask** as follows:

```
# umask 022
```

Many locations set their local default value for permission bits by placing a line including the **umask** command in the system-side shell initialization files. On a Solaris system, you can also set **umask** in the */etc/default/login* file. This sets it for all users who log into a system. See the chapter on user accounts for additional information on these files and other initialization files where **umask** might be placed.

In general, think about the contents of a file and who should have access to it when specifying the owner, group, and permission bits. System files which do not need to be read by user programs should be secured from being readable.

Implementing File Security Using Groups and File Protection Modes

Effective file security using UNIX groups and file protection modes requires a little thought and organization. First, consider the structure of information within your organization. Next, consider which users need to share information and which users who, for whatever reason, should not share nor participate in the exchange of information (i.e., guest accounts, remote log-ins, etc.). The people who need to share files should be put in a UNIX group. For example, you might put the members of your accounting department into a group called *account*. See the chapter on user account management for instructions on how to do this.

Continuing with our example, files such as an accounting database or other records can be given the group ownership *account* and have their file modes set to allow members of that group access to them. By selecting a mode which gives read and write permissions to the owner and group, but not to others, you can effectively share files within a selected group but prevent others from having access to the files. Using the combination of a group and the group file protection bits is an often overlooked method of obtaining secure but shared files.

Be Careful with chmod

Like the **rm** command, **chmod** does not check the option flags you have given it to see if they make sense, it just makes the change. Sometimes the changes to the protection bits give unexpected results. Be careful not to fall into the following common traps:

❑ You can remove permissions for the file or directory's owner. If you suddenly find a file which you own but cannot read or write, check that you still have permission to write the file.

❑ Directories require execute permission to access their contents. Removing the execute permission on a directory leaves it in the confusing state of being readable but inaccessible.

❑ Directories require read permission for their contents to be seen by **ls** and other commands. To create a directory that others can read and execute items out of but cannot see the contents, remove the read permission while leaving the execute permission. Be warned that this does *not* prevent others from guessing at the names of other files in the directory nor does it protect them from being read. This procedure only hides them from being listed by commands such as ls.

The Dangers of SetUID and SetGID

Here's a scary scenario. You log in to a workstation as *root*. You need to leave the workstation for a while and you forget to log off or lock your screen. Have you left yourself in peril? Could a user use the unsecured session to gain root access later on without your knowledge?

Sadly, the answer is yes. One approach is to use the *setuid* bit. For example, what if an unscrupulous person were to type the following into your unsecured *root* session:

```
# cp /bin/sh /tmp/gotcha
# chmod 4755 /tmp/gotcha
```

These two commands create a copy of the Bourne shell that when run, will execute with full *root* privileges. The person in this example will not need to get the *root* password, or even to log in as *root.* All the person need do is to run the copy of the shell he or she made which has the *setuid* bit set.

There are many other methods which a determined person could use to exploit the setuid bit. Great care should be exercised in the consideration of which programs are given this ability. For example, suppose you made a setuid *root* copy of the **vi** editor. Did you know that you can start up a shell from within vi? Can you guess what privileges that shell would have?

Taking Precautions

Some general guidelines to avoid *setuid/setgid* problems follow:

❑ Avoid using setuid/setgid whenever possible. If there is another way to implement the function which does not require setuid/setgid, strongly consider using it.

❑ Make the program setuid/setgid to the least privileged user account possible. Avoid setuid root programs unless the program *must* have that privilege to function.

❑ *Never* make a shell script setuid or setgid. Shell scripts are too easily subverted and used to create setuid shells.

❑ If you are developing your own setuid/setgid programs, consider releasing the privilege as soon as you have performed the privileged functions that your program must perform.

❑ Consider having all programs you write which are setuid or setgid write to a log file when they are run. This provides an audit trail allowing you to monitor privileged usage.

Rooting Out Potential Problems

Another precaution worth taking is to scan the files on your systems for setuid and setgid programs. One way to do this is with the **ncheck** command. Ncheck scans on a file system by file system basis. An example of using ncheck follows:

```
# ncheck -F ufs -s /dev/dsk/c0t3d0s6
```

The last argument is the device entry for the file system to be checked. You can identify the device entry for a given file system by typing **df**. The list produced by **ncheck** shows the *inode* or index node number for each file it found and the file name relative to the mount point of the file system. In other words, if you used the device entry of the */usr* file system, the list of file names produced would start at */usr*. A name listed as */lib/acct/accton* would have a full path of */usr/lib/acct/accton*.

Once you have this list, you will want to use **ls** to examine each file to identify its owner, group and permission bits. You can do this all at once by processing the output of ncheck and feeding it directly to ls. An example of this processing as it would be used to check the */usr* file system on a typical system follows:

```
# ls -l 'ncheck -F ufs -s /dev/dsk/c0t3d0s6 | cut -f2 | sed 's:^:/usr:''
```

While appearing complex, this command line elegantly handles the task. The **ls -l** command will produce listings of the owner, group, and permissions for each file name given to it as the output of the phrase between the back quotes. That phrase runs ncheck to produce the list of setuid or setgid files. The second column of that list, the file names, is clipped out by using the **cut** command. Then the list of files is passed through **sed** which uses a regular expression to prepend */usr* to each file name to make them full path names. The result is a list of the setuid and setgid files on the */usr* file system complete with their owners, groups, and permissions.

Account Security

In a previous chapter, we discussed how user accounts were created and managed. One of the features Solaris offers to aid in account management is a variety of controls over the account password. The password is the mechanism by which the system authenticates the user of a given account. The file security mechanisms described above depend on this authentication to ensure that the person who has logged on to a particular account is really the file's owner.

Solaris stores account passwords and most of the other account information in separate places. On a system which is not using NIS or NIS+, these are the */etc/passwd* and */etc/shadow* files. Look at the owners and permissions on these files. The */etc/passwd* file is readable by all. This is because a great number of programs make use of the information in this file. The */etc/shadow* file is protected. This file contains the encrypted version of each user account password along with password aging information. Because the encrypted passwords, like all encrypted text, are susceptible to being guessed, the contents of the */etc/shadow* file must be kept unreadable (except by the root account).

Educate Your Users About Safe Passwords

It is also important to educate your users with regard to the security of the password itself. Writing the password on paper should be discouraged, as should sharing of passwords between users. How important this is depends on your environment. The more secure your environment must be, the more careful user education and password protection you will need.

The next line of defense is to ensure that the password chosen by each user is not easily guessed. Any item of personal information should not be used as a password. Such things as the user's real name, phone number, license plate number, address, spouse's or children's names, office number, and so on should be avoided because these items are too easy for a determined individual to guess.

The use of common words or names is not a good approach either. A determined individual can make use of high speed password guessing software in combination with large dictionaries of words. While this approach is time-consuming, it is getting less so as password guessing tools improve and faster computer hardware becomes available. Be especially careful to avoid famous names such as Superman because these will most certainly be in even the shortest dictionary used to guess passwords.

Better choices for passwords include the following properties: punctuation characters, numbers, and modified words. Some suggestions are word combinations such as *best1boy*; the first letter or number of words in a phrase (e.g., *towamfn* from "There once was a man from Nantucket"); or weird combinations of numbers and letter phrases (e.g., *10%grade*, or *any1410s* from "Anyone for tennis?"). *Do not* use anything suggested here or in other books as you can be sure a determined individual trying to guess at an account password will know of these examples.

Using the Solaris Password Aging Feature

As discussed previously, encrypted text only stays secret for the time period required to guess the encryption key or password. For this reason, user account passwords should be changed on a regular basis. This is the purpose of the Solaris password aging mechanism. The frequency of password changing depends on the security needs of your environment. More frequent changes are better for security but more annoying for the account user and more prone to having the account user select a poor password "just to get back to work." Be sure to spend the time to educate and explain the reasons behind good passwords and changing passwords to all users of your systems. The security of the system as a whole depends in part on each user's choice of a password.

For the system administrator, no password is more important to protect than the password for the *root* account. The root password gives access to *all* data stored on your system and may give access to other systems on your network. The preceding comments about user account passwords go double for the root account. Carefully choose a root password and change it frequently. Make it a habit to frequently check the log files in */var/adm*, especially */var/adm/sulog*, which logs valid and failed uses of the **su** command. The su command is often used to gain root privileges from an ordinary user account.

Tracking Security Using aset

Checking for *setuid* files and monitoring log files can be quite a chore. Fortunately, Solaris provides **aset**, a security tool to help with these chores and optionally act upon problems on your behalf.

The aset tool consists of a set of tasks or separate small programs which check specific areas of system security. The available tasks are *tune, cklist, usrgrp, sysconf, env, eeprom,* and *firewall.* The aset tool is run at a specific security level: low, medium or high. The tasks report and take actions to aid in securing the system based on the security level selected. The following table describes the tasks and their actions at each security level.

Aset Tasks at Each Security Level

Task	Function	Low	Medium	High
tune	Sets system file permissions.	Sets permissions to release values.	Tightens permissions to improve security.	Set permissions to be highly restrictive.
cklist	Checks system files against master list.	Compares some files against previously saved permission settings and reports changes.	Increases the number of areas checked	Checks the most files.

Task	Function	Low	Medium	High
usrgrp	User/Group checks.	Checks for consistency and correctness of passwd and group files; does not fix problems in NIS or NIS+ databases.	Same.	Same.
sysconf	System configuration file checks.	Checks a variety of files in /etc.	Makes changes to restrict access.	Makes the most restrictive set of changes.
env	Root environment check.	Checks PATH and UMASK settings for *root* and default shell initialization files.	Same.	Same.
eeprom	EEPROM security check.	Checks the EEPROM security setting and password; does not make changes, but reports recommendations.	Same.	Same.
firewall	Set system to act as network firewall.	Reports changes needed to convert system into a network firewall.	Same.	Takes actions needed to convert system into a network firewall.

Taking a walk through a typical **aset** run will help you comprehend the items in the table and show how aset is used and can be modified to fit your environment. Starting aset is a matter of becoming *root* and typing the command.

```
# /usr/aset/aset
======= ASET Execution Log =======

ASET running at security level low

Machine = glenn; Current time = 0716_07:47

aset: Using /usr/aset as working directory

Executing task list ...
        firewall
        env
        sysconf
        usrgrp
        tune
        cklist
        eeprom

All tasks executed. Some background tasks may still be running.

Run /usr/aset/util/taskstat to check their status:
        /usr/aset/util/taskstat      [aset_dir]

where aset_dir is ASET's operating directory,currently=/usr/aset.

When the tasks complete, the reports can be found in:
        /usr/aset/reports/latest/*.rpt
You can view them by:
        more /usr/aset/reports/latest/*.rpt
#
```

Starting aset in low security.

To start **aset** at the medium or high security levels, use the **-l** option. An example follows:

```
# /usr/aset/aset -l medium
```

For the */bin/csh* shell, use the following to set the ASETSECLEVEL:

```
# setenv ASETSECLEVEL medium
```

For the */bin/sh* shell, use the following to set the ASETSECLEVEL:

```
# ASETSECLEVEL=medium ; export ASETSECLEVEL
```

While aset is running, you can check on its progress by using the **taskstat** utility.

```
╔══════════════════════════════════════════════════════════════╗
║ ▽                      cmdtool – /bin/csh                       ║
╠════════════════════════════════════════════════════════════════╣
│ # /usr/aset/util/taskstat                                      │
│                                                                │
│ Checking ASET tasks status ...                                │
│ Task firewall is done.                                        │
│ Task env is done.                                             │
│ Task sysconf is done.                                         │
│ Task usrgrp is done.                                          │
│                                                                │
│ The following tasks are done:                                 │
│         firewall                                              │
│         env                                                   │
│         sysconf                                               │
│         usrgrp                                                │
│                                                                │
│ The following tasks are not done:                             │
│         tune                                                  │
│         cklist                                                │
│         eeprom                                                │
│ #  ▲                                                          │
```

Checking aset progress with taskstat.

As aset runs it will generate a large amount of disk activity, so it's a good idea to run it when usage is low on your systems. It is also a good idea to run aset periodically, especially in a networked environment, to check for any changes that may have occurred on your system. As shown below, both of these conditions are met by using the **-p** option to aset.

```
# /usr/aset/aset -p
```

This will put an entry for aset in the *root crontab* file. The **cron** daemon reads each user's *crontab* files and runs programs at the times listed in the crontab file. The **aset -p** command inserts a scheduled run of aset to be performed nightly at midnight. You can check this by typing **crontab -l** and looking for the line which contains aset. To remove this regularly scheduled aset run from the root crontab, type **crontab -e** as root, and delete the line containing aset.

Each aset run creates a set of log files which detail any problems found by aset and all corrective actions taken. The log files are found in directories in */usr/aset/reports*. The directory names correspond to the date and time of the aset run which created the reports. For instance, the directory *0716_07:47* contains the reports for the 7:47 am aset run on July 16. The symbolic link */usr/aset/reports/latest* is set to point to the most recent report directory.

In the report directory are files with the *.rpt* extension. These are the reports generated by the various tasks. At the low security level which was used in the above example, very little is written into most reports. However, even at this level, the system has a few minor problems worth correcting. The contents of *env.rpt*, the root environment report, for the aset in the example follow:

```
# more env.rpt


*** Begin Enviroment Check ***


Warning! umask set to umask 022 in /etc/profile - not
recommended.


*** End Enviroment Check ***
#
```

This indicates a questionable setting for **umask** in */etc/profile*. This setting would create files which were world readable. If this is not what is desired in your environment, a change to the umask line in */etc/profile* is in order. Another error was spotted by the **sysconf** (system file configuration task), and reported as follows in the *sysconf.rpt*:

```
# more sysconf.rpt


*** Begin System Scripts Check ***


Warning! The use of /.rhosts file is not recommended for system
security.


*** End System Scripts Check ***
#
```

Although a */.rhosts* file is a convenience, allowing remote access to root across a network requires that the remote machine be every bit as secure as the local machine. This warning should be carefully considered and the */.rhosts* file removed if it is not needed by your environment.

Reading through all the reports the first time is worthwhile to get a sense of what aset checks for and the problems you may need to correct. For periodic monitoring, reading reports is time-consuming. Another approach is to use the **diff** command to compare reports and see if any significant changes have occurred since the last aset run. This helps to highlight problems which have come up and reduces the repetitive nature of reading the entire report series. A quick shell script which compares the reports in a named directory against the latest reports follows:

```
#!/bin/csh -f
#
# compare files in $1 with latest

cd /usr/aset/reports/$1

foreach i ( *.rpt )
    echo "== $i"
    diff $i ../latest/$i
end
```

Running this script gives the following results on the example system:

```
# /tmp/sample 0716_07:47
== cklist.rpt
4,6c4,7
< No checklist master - comparison not performed.
< ... Checklist master is being created now. Wait ...
< ... Checklist master created.
- - -
> ... Checklist snapshot is being created. Wait ...
> ... Checklist snapshot created.
```

```
>
> No differences in the checklist.
== eeprom.rpt
== env.rpt
== firewall.rpt
== sysconf.rpt
== tune.rpt
== usrgrp.rpt
#
```

Because the July 16th run was the first time aset was run on this system, the **cklist** task had not yet created a master checklist. The **diff** command caught the change and reported the changed lines. No changes were found in the other reports. A short display of differences like this one can be a real time saver, especially if you have numerous systems to manage. With a little work this simple shell script can be extended to mail any changes to a specific user account. This is usually done only if changes are found, further reducing the effort needed for security monitoring in larger collections of workstations.

aset Customization

Of course, the items checked by **aset** may not be appropriate for your location. There are two ways you can control what aset does and which files and directories it checks.

First are the aset environment variables. ASETSECLEVEL was already mentioned, and setting it controls the security level at which aset runs. There is also the ASETDIR variable which allows you to specify an alternative directory for aset to use when looking for files and writing reports.

> ✔ **NOTE:** *The environment variables are typically used for interactive runs of aset. When aset is run by the cron daemon, it uses command line options to select the security level (eg: -l medium) and alternative directory (eg: -d /home/security).*

The second method of customization is to modify the various configuration files for aset. The first of these is **asetenv**. This file is usually found in */usr/aset*. It contains a set of variables near the top which you can customize to suit your environment. The variables are listed in the following table.

asetenv Configuration Variables

Variable	Description
TASKS	Sets the list of tasks to be performed by aset.
PERIODIC_SCHEDULE	Sets the schedule to be entered into the root crontab file when aset -p is run.
UID_ALIASES	Sets the name of the file to consult for a list of UIDs which can be shared by different account names.
YPCHECK	Specifies whether a check of the NIS or NIS+ databases will be made. This check will only report problems, *not* take action to fix them.
CKLISTPATH_LOW	Sets the list of paths used at the *low* security level by the *cklist* task.
CKLISTPATH_MED	Sets the list of paths used at the *medium* security level by the *cklist* task.
CKLISTPATH_HIGH	Sets the list of paths used at the *high* security level by the *cklist* task.

The CKLISTPATH variables contain a set of directories separated by colons. For example, you could set CHKLISTPATH_LOW to check */usr/bin*, */sbin*, and */etc* with the following command line:

```
setenv CHKLISTPATH_LOW /usr/bin:/sbin:/etc
```

The second set of customization files is found in */usr/aset/master* and consists of the *tune* family of files. These files contain the lists of files the *tune* task checks for integrity. The format is described in the top few lines of the file and consists of the path name to the file, its permission bits in octal notation, owner, group, and type. You can add path names of files to be checked by following the format shown. Add files in the *tune* file for the security level at which you are running aset, *tune.low*, *tune.med*, or *tune.high*.

Restoring Permissions to Pre-aset Values

To conclude the discussion of **aset**, there is one more handy aset tool: */usr/aset/aset.restore*. This program restores the system file permissions to the way they were before aset was first run. You might use this tool if you wanted to restore things before removing aset or if you ran aset and found its file permission settings too restrictive for your environment.

Remote Access

For a stand-alone workstation, security is not too difficult to set up and maintain. However, many workstations are connected to modems or networks and these present additional problems.

Modems

There are several ways in which a modem can be configured and used. For our purposes, we will consider PPP and SLIP only insofar as they constitute network connections. UUCP has its own special share of security problems which are better covered elsewhere. That leaves the two most basic modem uses, dial-in and dial-out terminal service.

Dial-out service is secure in the sense that your machine is initiating the connection. You or the user making the dial-out connection should be familiar with the system to which you are connecting. You need to examine any software or data you download (as you would when downloading such items to a PC or Macintosh).

Dial-in service is more of a problem. Your modem will answer the phone for anyone who knows, or accidentally discovers your modem's phone number. Merely making the number unlisted is not always sufficient as a determined individual will use such techniques as automated dialers to find such hidden numbers. The modem connection will give someone connecting to it a login prompt, just like a local terminal. At this point, the security of each account depends upon its password.

Using Dial-in Passwords

Solaris gives you one additional aid in this situation, a dial-in password. The dial-in password is controlled by two files, */etc/dialups* and */etc/d_passwd*. Creating a dial-in password is not as easy as it should be. The steps involved follow:

1. Create */etc/dialups*. This file contains one entry per line with the path of each dial-in modem line (e.g., */dev/term/a*).

2. Create */etc/d_passwd*. This file contains one entry for each possible shell that a dial-in modem user might use. A typical *d_passwd* file might look like the following:

```
/usr/lib/uucp/uucico: passwd-goes-here:
/usr/bin/csh: passwd-goes-here:
/usr/bin/ksh: passwd-goes-here:
/usr/bin/sh: passwd-goes-here:
```

> ✔ *NOTE: The passwd-goes-here components will be filled in during a later step.*

3. Set the owner, group and permission bits for the files:

```
chown root /etc/dialups /etc/d_passwd
chgrp root /etc/dialups /etc/d_passwd
chmod 600 /etc/dialups /etc/d_passwd
```

4. Insert an encrypted password for each shell in the place of the *passwd-goes-here* strings shown above. There are several ways to do this. One way is to set the root password temporarily to each of the shell passwords, save the results, and then set the root password back to what it was when you started. This procedure is inconvenient, but not difficult. An example of the sequence for the *uucico* shell follows:

```
# passwd
New password:
Re-enter new password:
grep root /etc/shadow | awk -F: '{ print $1 }' /tmp/foo
# passwd
New password:
Re-enter new password:
#
```

The */tmp/foo* file now contains the encrypted password string you need to put in the */etc/d_passwd* file. You can now use **vi** or your favorite editor to insert this string in between the colons after the shell you want to protect.

The Network

Setting up the dial-in password files is easy compared to the continual task of securing network connections, especially if your systems are connected to the Internet. A networked Solaris system runs a large suite of network service daemons, and each daemon may need to be individually secured. Add to this the potential for determined individuals to find and exploit bugs which may be present in any of these daemons.

What can you do? To start, you need to have good account security and file security as your base. Next, you need to be careful to grant privileges only to those systems which you can trust. Under no circumstances should privileges be given to all systems. Carefully read the chapters on NIS+ and NFS because they are among the most heavily used network services and need special attention to be used in a secure manner.

Some files to pay careful attention to follow:

❑ **/.rhosts** Do you really need remote access as root? If not, remove this file. If you do, put the minimum number of hosts and accounts into this file.

❑ **/etc/hosts.equiv** This file grants access to remote hosts circumventing password authentication. The */.rhosts* file is more exclusive and should be used instead. Use this only when the remote host is as trusted as your own system in all ways.

❑ **/etc/mail/sendmail.cf** and **sendmail** in general In particular, check the programs the sendmail configuration file lists as being used by sendmail. The mail transport mechanism provided by sendmail has a history of being used to circumvent system security.

Finally, monitor your security status. Tools such as the previously described aset are helpful. You should also familiarize yourself with the information being logged by *syslog* and other daemons in */var/adm*. These logs may not make for interesting reading, but they can point out potential problems or unauthorized access. Again, if you are connected to the Internet, purchase, read, and *heed* a more thorough UNIX- or Solaris-specific security book.

Summary

In this chapter we have discussed the basics of the UNIX file permission scheme, how to view file permissions and how to modify them. The dangers of the setuid and setgid bits have been discussed and should not be overlooked when creating programs which have these attributes. By using the password aging and aset tools found in Solaris, many aspects of system security can be controlled. These tools and techniques are sufficient for many environments. However, if your environment demands more strict security, you would be well advised to read further on this topic and consider employing more advanced tools and techniques.

Working with Solaris 2 Device Names

One of the major functions performed as a system administrator is the installation of and communication with devices on the system. In this chapter, we will examine a few different types of devices and how Solaris accesses them.

Next, we will examine the naming conventions used for system devices under Solaris. We will also learn how to determine which devices are connected to your systems, and how to address those devices.

Before beginning an examination of device naming and addressing, you should become familiar with the devices on your system. For this purpose, you will use the **prtconf** command. This command will give you a list of all of the devices currently connected to your system, as well as a list of all of the device drivers loaded into the operating system kernel.

In this example, the output is from a SPARCServer 1000. This system has two TMS390Z55 processor modules, seven SCSI disk devices, no SCSI tape drives, an le ethernet, and an NVRAM module. The prtconf output also begins to show the hierarchical arrangement of the system devices. Once you become more familiar with device terminology, we will explore the system device hierarchy in more detail.

```
System Configuration:  Sun Microsystems  sun4d
Memory size: 128 Megabytes
System Peripherals (Software Nodes):

SUNW,SPARCserver-1000
    packages (driver not attached)
        disk-label (driver not attached)
        deblocker (driver not attached)
        obp-tftp (driver not attached)
    options, instance #0
    aliases (driver not attached)
    memory (driver not attached)
    virtual-memory (driver not attached)
    openprom (driver not attached)
    boards (driver not attached)
        bif (driver not attached)
        bif (driver not attached)
    cpu-unit, instance #0
        TI,TMS390Z55, instance #0
        bootbus, instance #0
            zs, instance #0
            zs, instance #1
            eeprom (driver not attached)
            sram (driver not attached)
            leds (driver not attached)
        profile, instance #0
    cpu-unit, instance #1
        TI,TMS390Z55, instance #1
        profile, instance #1
    mem-unit, instance #2
    mem-unit, instance #4
    SUNW,nvtwo, instance #0
    io-unit, instance #3
        sbi, instance #0
            dma, instance #0
                esp, instance #0
                    sd (driver not attached)
                    st (driver not attached)
                    sd, instance #0
                    sd, instance #1
                    sd, instance #2
                    sd, instance #3
                    sd, instance #4
                    sd, instance #5
                    sd, instance #6
                    st, instance #0 (driver not attached)
                    st, instance #1 (driver not attached)
                    st, instance #2 (driver not attached)
                    st, instance #3 (driver not attached)
                    st, instance #4 (driver not attached)
                    st, instance #5 (driver not attached)
                    st, instance #6 (driver not attached)
            lebuffer, instance #0
                le, instance #0
            sbusmem, instance #0
            sbusmem, instance #1
            sbusmem, instance #2
            sbusmem, instance #3
    pseudo, instance #0
```

Using prtconf to identify devices connected to the system.

Device Terminology

Understanding device terminology is the first step toward allowing you to troubleshoot problems with devices on your systems. Most devices are named with an acronym which is derived from the device type. For instance, an SCSI disk drive is an *sd* device. But an SCSI disk is also known as a *dsk* device. An

SCSI tape drive is an *st* device. But this same tape drive also has an *rmt* name associated with it.

As you can see, under Solaris a device can have one of a variety of names. The name of the device is also known as the "device identifier." The following list identifies many of the common devices on a SPARC-based system:

Device Names

Device name	Description
cn	System console device.
esp	System SCSI adapter devices.
/dev/fd0a	Solaris 1 compatibility links to Solaris 2 floppy devices.
/dev/fd0b	
/dev/fd0c	
/dev/diskette	Solaris 2.x native mode floppy disk device.
/dev/rdiskette	
le	Lance Ethernet devices.
mbus	System MBus adapter devices.
qe	System Quad Ethernet devices.
sbus	System SBus adapter devices.
sd	Small Computer System Interconnect (SCSI) disk device.
st	SCSI tape devices.
zs	On-board serial port interfaces (typically ttya).
fd/0	stdin file descriptor.
fd/1	stdout file descriptor.
fd/2	stderr file descriptor.

The Device Information Tree

On SPARC-based systems, the devices are attached to a set of interconnected buses. The OpenBoot firmware recognizes these interconnected buses and their respective devices as a tree of nodes. This representation of the device interconnection is called the Device Information Tree. It is possible to get an idea of the structure of this tree by using the prtconf command. The output of prtconf is an ASCII representation of the Device Information Tree. At the root of the tree is a node which describes the entire system. Another view of this device information tree can be provided by using the OpenWindows FileManager and expanding the view of the */devices* directory.

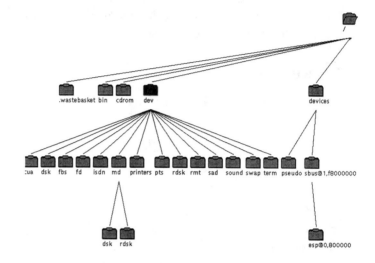

*Typical SPARC
station 2 device
information tree.*

Nodes on the tree which have children generally represent system buses and the associated controllers on the buses. Each of these parent nodes is allocated a physical address space that distinguishes the devices on this node from one another. Each child of a parent node is allocated a physical address within the parent node's address space.

The physical address of the nodes is generally assigned in relation to the device's physical characteristics, or the bus slot in which the controller is installed. This is done in an attempt to keep device addresses from changing as systems are upgraded, and new devices are installed on the system.

Each device node on the Device Information Tree can have the following:

❑ Properties or data structures which describe the node and its associated devices.

❑ Methods or software procedures used to access the devices.

❑ Children, which can be devices, or other nodes attached to the node and which lie directly below it in the tree.

❑ A parent which is the node that lies directly above the current node in the device tree.

Physical Device Names

As mentioned previously, under Solaris there are many names used to reference devices on the system. Most of the names we deal with as system administrators are actually aliases that point you to the physical device names on the system. For instance, you may refer to the *root* file system on a disk as either */dev/dsk/c0t3d0s0* as shown by the **df** command, or *sd3a* as shown by the console information at boot time. As you will see, these are all aliases for the device that the operating system knows as */sbus@1,f8000000/ esp@0,4000/ sd@3,0:a*.

Under the OpenBoot monitor, you have to use either the physical address or one of the aliases provided for these physical addresses to access devices. For instance, the alias for *sd3* might be *disk3*. Under Solaris there are different aliases for each device, and more ways to access the devices! Before you learn to access a device from Solaris, you need to understand the OpenBoot monitor addressing scheme.

The OpenBoot Monitor Address

The physical name of the device is constructed by concatenating the physical names of the nodes above the device in the Device Information Tree with a forward slash (/) character. The generic form of a physical name (*name@address:arguments*) follows:

- ❑ **name** – A name is a text string that generally has a mnemonic value. For example, *sd* represents SCSI disk. Many controller names use some portion of the manufacturer's name or model number.

- ❑ The at sign (@) must precede the address parameter.

- ❑ **address** – The address is a text string representing the physical address of the device on the system. The address is usually in the following form: *hex_number,hex_number*.

- ❑ A colon (:) must precede the arguments parameter.

- ❑ **arguments** – The arguments are a text string whose format depends on the device. The arguments may be used to pass additional information to the device's driver software.

Let's look at the example above and see if you can determine how the *sd3* disk is connected to the system. The physical name of the device follows: */sbus@1,f8000000/esp@0,4000/sd@3,0:a*.

Translations of items in the physical name follow:

/sbus@ means you are looking at an SBus connection of some sort.

1,f80000000 is an address on the main system bus. You know that the SBus in question is directly connected to the main system bus.

esp@ means you are looking at an esp SCSI adapter on the SBus.

0,40000 is an SBus slot number and an offset within that slot. This means that the esp SCSI device is in SBus slot 0 with a hexadecimal address offset of 40000 from the parent node (main system bus) address.

sd@ means that you are looking at a SCSI disk.

3,0 is the SCSI target and logical unit number of the disk you are examining.

Under Solaris the physical device interface to the nodes on the Device Information Tree lies in the */devices* directory. In this directory, you may see subdirectories for audio devices, floppy disk drives, the eeprom, pseudo devices, SBus adapters, and zs (serial port) devices.

```
# ls -lsa /devices
```

```
total 20
   2 drwxrwxr-x   4 root    sys        512 May  7 20:43 .
   2 drwxr-xr-x  23 root    root       512 Oct  5 19:40 ..
   0 crw-------   1 curt    nobody   28,  0 Apr  9  1994 audio@1,f7201000:sound,audio
   0 crw-------   1 curt    nobody   28,128 Apr  9  1994 audio@1,f7201000:sound,audioctl
   0 crw-------   1 root    sys      68, 11 Apr  9  1994 eeprom@1,f2000000:eeprom
   0 brw-rw-rw-   1 root    sys      36,  0 Apr  9  1994 fd@1,f7200000:a
   0 crw-rw-rw-   1 root    sys      36,  0 Apr  9  1994 fd@1,f7200000:a,raw
   0 brw-rw-rw-   1 root    sys      36,  1 Apr  9  1994 fd@1,f7200000:b
   0 crw-rw-rw-   1 root    sys      36,  1 Apr  9  1994 fd@1,f7200000:b,raw
   0 brw-rw-rw-   1 root    sys      36,  2 Apr  9  1994 fd@1,f7200000:c
   0 crw-rw-rw-   1 root    sys      36,  2 Apr  9  1994 fd@1,f7200000:c,raw
   0 crw-------   1 root    sys      74,  0 Apr  9  1994 profile:profile
  14 drwxr-xr-x   2 root    sys       6656 May  7 20:34 pseudo
   2 drwxr-xr-x   3 root    sys        512 Apr  9  1994 sbus@1,f8000000
   0 crw-------   1 lp      sys      29,  0 Apr  9  1994 zs@1,f1000000:a
   0 crw-rw-rw-   1 root    sys      29,131072 Apr  9  1994 zs@1,f1000000:a,cu
   0 crw-rw-rw-   1 root    sys      29,  1 Apr  9  1994 zs@1,f1000000:b
   0 crw-rw-rw-   1 root    sys      29,131073 Apr  9  1994 zs@1,f1000000:b,cu
```

A typical listing of the /devices directory.

Within each subdirectory there are more entries which may be special device files, or directories which contain special device files.

```
# ls -lsa /devices/sbus
```

```
total 8
  2 drwxr-xr-x  3 root    sys      512 Apr  9 1994 .
  2 drwxrwxr-x  4 root    sys      512 May  7 20:43 ..
  0 crw-------  1 curt    nobody   39,  0 Apr  9 1994 cgsix@2,0:cgsix0
  4 drwxr-xr-x  2 root    sys     2048 Apr 10 1994 esp@0,800000
  0 crw-------  1 root    sys      69,  0 Apr  9 1994 sbusmem@0,0:slot0
  0 crw-------  1 root    sys      69,  1 Apr  9 1994 sbusmem@1,0:slot1
  0 crw-------  1 root    sys      69,  2 Apr  9 1994 sbusmem@2,0:slot2
  0 crw-------  1 root    sys      69,  3 Apr  9 1994 sbusmem@3,0:slot3
```

A typical listing of the /devices/sbus directory.

It should be obvious that the */devices* directory under Solaris has a close relationship to the physical addresses used under the OpenBoot monitor. If you key in **ls -lsa** of the */devices* directory and subdirectories, you can see the names, addresses, and arguments used by the OpenBoot monitor to refer to each device.

Logical Device Names

As seen in the previous section, physical device names can be difficult to decipher, and even more difficult to remember! We need an easy-to-use, easy-to-remember way to access devices that does not require you to memorize several eight-digit hex numbers. Fortunately, Solaris provides such a method.

For example, if you look at the */dev/dsk* directory you see entries with names such as */dev/dsk/c0t3d0s0*. This form of device name is often referred to as the "alphabet soup" designator for the device. Disk drives are the only devices which use alphabet soup designators. These logical names for disk devices make it very simple to understand which drive you are referring to.

An alphabet soup name for a device consists of four fields: CN, TN, DN, and SN. A breakdown of these fields follows:

❑ CN stands for controller number *N*. This refers to the logical controller number of the device interface. For instance, a system with one SCSI interface would use *c0*. A system with two SCSI interfaces may have disk devices connected to both the *c0* and the *c1* SCSI interfaces.

❑ TN stands for target number. This is the SCSI Target ID (or SCSI Address) address of a disk connected to the controller.

❏ DN stands for the drive or unit number of the device connected to target controller TN, which is in turn connected to bus controller CN.

❏ SN stands for the slice or partition number of the device you are addressing. See the chapter on managing disks for more information on disk slices and partitions.

You already saw that the device name *sd* refers to a SCSI disk drive. But how does something like *sd3a* get mapped into the physical address and allow you to access the device?

If you look in the */dev* directory under Solaris, you notice that all of the entries are either symbolic links to entries in the */devices* directory, or to subdirectories which contain symbolic links to entries in the */devices* directory.

For our example, look in the */dev* directory for an entry called *sd3a*. In most cases, you will not find a */dev/sd3a* device, but you will find a */dev/rsd3a* device. If you follow the link for this device, you find that it points to an entry in */dev/rdsk/c0t3d0s0*. This file is symbolically linked to an entry in */devices/ sbus@1,f8000000/ esp@0,800000/ sd@3,0:a,raw.*

From this example, you can see that *sd3a* is mapped to */dev/dsk/c0t3d0s0*, and how it is mapped to the physical address */devices/sbus@1,f8000000/ esp@0,800000/sd@3,0:a.* But what is the difference between the *sd3a* and *rsd3a* devices? Both of these logical names refer to the SCSI disk with a target number of 3 and the partition number of 0. The difference between the two entries is that the */dev/rdsk* entry refers to the "raw" or unbuffered device, while the */dev/dsk* entry refers to the "cooked" or buffered device.

A raw device is typically a character mode device capable of transferring one byte of data at a time. Solaris allows unbuffered character mode access to disk drives. The unbuffered, or raw descriptor for the disk devices is used to transfer data in this mode. A cooked device typically transfers large blocks of data on each transfer. Most system activity uses cooked mode transfers to allow for better throughput. The cooked mode descriptors are provided to allow disks to transfer data in block mode.

```
# ls -lsa /dev
```

```
total 716
   2 lrwxrwxrwx  1 root     root           12 Apr  9  1994 audio -> /dev/sound/0
   2 lrwxrwxrwx  1 root     root           15 Apr  9  1994 audioctl -> /dev/sound/0ctl
   2 lrwxrwxrwx  1 root     root           10 May  7 20:43 cgsix0 -> fbs/cgsix0
   2 lrwxrwxrwx  1 root     root           31 Apr  9  1994 conslog -> ../devices/pseudo/log@0:conslog
   2 lrwxrwxrwx  1 root     root           30 Apr  9  1994 console -> ../devices/pseudo/cn@0:console
   2 lrwxrwxrwx  1 root     root           26 Apr  9  1994 diskette -> ../devices/fd@1,f7200000:c
   2 drwxr-xr-x  2 root     root          512 May  7 20:23 dsk
   2 lrwxrwxrwx  1 root     root           35 Apr  9  1994 eeprom -> ../devices/eeprom@1,f2000000:eeprom
   2 lrwxrwxrwx  1 root     root           41 Oct 13 21:26 fb -> /devices/sbus@1,f8000000/cgsix@2,0:cgsix0
   2 lrwxrwxrwx  1 root     root           10 Apr  9  1994 fb0 -> fbs/cgsix0
   2 drwxr-xr-x  2 root     root          512 Apr  9  1994 fbs
   0 dr-xr-xr-x  2 root     root          416 Oct 13 23:16 fd
   2 lrwxrwxrwx  1 root     root           26 May  7 20:43 fd0a -> ../devices/fd@1,f7200000:a
   2 lrwxrwxrwx  1 root     root            8 May  7 20:43 fd0c -> diskette
   2 lrwxrwxrwx  1 root     root           31 Apr  9  1994 kbd -> ../devices/pseudo/conskbd@0:kbd
   2 lrwxrwxrwx  1 root     root           27 Apr  9  1994 kmem -> ../devices/pseudo/mm@0:kmem
   2 lrwxrwxrwx  1 root     root           31 Apr  9  1994 kstat -> ../devices/pseudo/kstat@0:kstat
   2 lrwxrwxrwx  1 root     root           31 Apr  9  1994 ksyms -> ../devices/pseudo/ksyms@0:ksyms
   2 lrwxrwxrwx  1 root     root           28 Apr  9  1994 le -> ../devices/pseudo/clone@0:le
   2 lrwxrwxrwx  1 root     root           27 Apr  9  1994 log -> ../devices/pseudo/log@0:log
   2 drwxr-xr-x  4 root     root          512 Apr  9  1994 md
   2 lrwxrwxrwx  1 root     root           26 Apr  9  1994 mem -> ../devices/pseudo/mm@0:mem
   2 lrwxrwxrwx  1 root     root           32 Apr  9  1994 mouse -> ../devices/pseudo/consms@0:mouse
   2 lrwxrwxrwx  1 root     root            8 May  7 20:43 nrst4 -> rmt/0lbn
   2 lrwxrwxrwx  1 root     root           27 Apr  9  1994 null -> ../devices/pseudo/mm@0:null
   2 lrwxrwxrwx  1 root     root           37 Apr  9  1994 openprom -> ../devices/pseudo/openeepr@0:openprom
   2 drwxr-xr-x  2 root     root          512 Apr  9  1994 printers
   2 lrwxrwxrwx  1 root     root           26 Apr  9  1994 profile -> ../devices/profile:profile
   2 lrwxrwxrwx  1 root     root           31 Apr  9  1994 ptmajor -> ../devices/pseudo/ptm@0:ptmajor
   2 lrwxrwxrwx  1 root     root           30 Apr  9  1994 ptmx -> ../devices/pseudo/clone@0:ptmx
   2 drwxr-xr-x  2 root     root         1024 Apr  9  1994 pts
   2 lrwxrwxrwx  1 root     root           29 Apr  9  1994 ptyp0 -> ../devices/pseudo/ptc@0:ptyp0
   2 lrwxrwxrwx  1 root     root           30 Apr  9  1994 rawip -> ../devices/pseudo/clone@0:icmp
   2 lrwxrwxrwx  1 root     root           30 Apr  9  1994 rdiskette -> ../devices/fd@1,f7200000:c,raw
   2 drwxr-xr-x  2 root     root          512 May  7 20:23 rdsk
   2 lrwxrwxrwx  1 root     root           30 May  7 20:43 rfd0a -> ../devices/fd@1,f7200000:a,raw
   2 lrwxrwxrwx  1 root     root            9 May  7 20:43 rfd0c -> rdiskette
   2 drwxr-xr-x  2 root     root          512 Apr 10  1994 rmt
   2 lrwxrwxrwx  1 root     root           13 May  7 20:43 rsd0a -> rdsk/c0t3d0s0
   2 lrwxrwxrwx  1 root     root            7 May  7 20:43 rst4 -> rmt/0lb
   2 drwxr-xr-x  2 root     root          512 Apr  9  1994 sad
   2 lrwxrwxrwx  1 root     root           12 May  7 20:43 sd0a -> dsk/c0t3d0s0
   2 lrwxrwxrwx  1 root     root           28 Apr  9  1994 sp -> ../devices/pseudo/clone@0:sp
   2 lrwxrwxrwx  1 root     root            6 Apr  9  1994 stderr -> ./fd/2
   2 lrwxrwxrwx  1 root     root            6 Apr  9  1994 stdin -> ./fd/0
   2 lrwxrwxrwx  1 root     root            6 Apr  9  1994 stdout -> ./fd/1
   2 drwxrwxr-x  2 root     sys           512 Apr  9  1994 swap
   2 lrwxrwxrwx  1 root     root           29 Apr  9  1994 syscon -> ../devices/pseudo/cn@0:syscon
   2 lrwxrwxrwx  1 root     root           29 Apr  9  1994 systty -> ../devices/pseudo/cn@0:systty
   2 lrwxrwxrwx  1 root     root           29 Apr  9  1994 tcp -> ../devices/pseudo/clone@0:tcp
   2 drwxrwxr-x  2 root     root          512 Apr  9  1994 term
   2 lrwxrwxrwx  1 root     root           32 Apr  9  1994 ticlts -> ../devices/pseudo/clone@0:ticlts
   2 lrwxrwxrwx  1 root     root           32 Apr  9  1994 ticots -> ../devices/pseudo/clone@0:ticots
   2 lrwxrwxrwx  1 root     root           35 Apr  9  1994 ticotsord -> ../devices/pseudo/clone@0:ticotsord
   2 lrwxrwxrwx  1 root     root           26 Apr  9  1994 tty -> ../devices/pseudo/sy@0:tty
   2 lrwxrwxrwx  1 root     root            6 May  7 20:43 ttya -> term/a
   2 lrwxrwxrwx  1 root     root           30 Apr  9  1994 ttyp0 -> ../devices/pseudo/ptsl@0:ttyp0
   2 lrwxrwxrwx  1 root     root           30 Apr  9  1994 volctl -> ../devices/pseudo/vol@0:volctl
   2 lrwxrwxrwx  1 root     root           25 Apr  9  1994 win0 -> ../devices/pseudo/win@0:0
   2 lrwxrwxrwx  1 root     root           35 Apr  9  1994 winlock -> ../devices/pseudo/winlock@0:winlock
   2 lrwxrwxrwx  1 root     root           29 Apr  9  1994 wscons -> ../devices/pseudo/wc@0:wscons
   2 lrwxrwxrwx  1 root     root           27 Apr  9  1994 zero -> ../devices/pseudo/mm@0:zero
   2 lrwxrwxrwx  1 root     root           29 Apr  9  1994 zsh -> ../devices/pseudo/clone@0:zsh
   2 lrwxrwxrwx  1 root     root           25 Apr  9  1994 zsh0 -> ../devices/pseudo/zsh@0:0
```

The typical contents of the Solaris /dev directory.

If you look in the */devices/sbus@1,f8000000/esp@0,800000* directory, you see that there are two files for each disk partition. One entry for each disk partition has the *:raw* descriptor. You may also notice that there are several entries for each tape drive in this directory. As shown below, instead of using *:raw* as a designator, tape drives use combinations of one to three letters as designators.

- ❑ **b** puts the tape device in Berkeley mode on close.

- ❑ **c** is the data compression tape device. Data written to this device are compressed before written to the tape.

- ❑ **h** is the high density tape device. Data written to this device are stored on the tape in the highest density allowed by this tape device.

- ❑ **l** is the low density tape device. Data written to this device are stored on the tape in the lowest density allowed by this tape device.

- ❑ **m** is the medium density tape device.

- ❑ **n** is the no-rewind device. When this device is used, the tape drive allows the user to write multiple sequential records to the tape.

```
# ls -lsa /dev/sd3a
  2 lrwxrwxrwx  1 root     root        12 Oct  3 08:31 /dev/sd3a -> dsk/c0t0d0s0

# ls -lsa /dev/dsk/c0t0d0s0
  2 lrwxrwxrwx  1 root     root        73 Jul  1 08:48 /dev/dsk/c0t0d0s0 -> ../../devices/io-unit@f,e0200000/sbi@0,0/dma@0,81000/esp@0,80000/sd@0,0:a

# ls -las /devices/io-unit@f,e0200000/sbi@0,0/dma@0,81000/esp@0,80000/sd@0,0:a
  0 brw-r-----  1 root     sys     32,   0 Jul  1 08:15 /devices/io-unit@f,e0200000/sbi@0,0/dma@0,81000/esp@0,80000/sd@0,0:a

# ls -las /devices/io-unit@f,e0200000/sbi@0,0/dma@0,81000/esp@0,80000/sd@0,0:a,raw
  0 crw-r-----  1 root     sys     32,   0 Jul  1 08:16 /devices/io-unit@f,e0200000/sbi@0,0/dma@0,81000/esp@0,80000/sd@0,0:a,raw
```

How does the device name sd3a map to the device name /devices/sbus@1,f8000000/esp@0,800000/sd@3,0:a,raw?

You have seen how to track down a disk device on a Solaris system. What happens if you want to track down a serial port's physical address on a Solaris system? If you know the logical port name, you can track down a serial port just as you did a disk drive. For example, if you want to know how *ttyb* is connected to the system, you can key in **ls -lsa /dev/ttyb**. This shows you that *ttyb* is a symbolic link to */dev/term/b*. If you do an **ls -lsa /dev/term/b**, you find that *ttyb* is a symbolic link to */devices/zs@1,f1000000:b*.

Similarly, when you look up */dev/rst0* you will find a symbolic link to */dev/rmt/0*. This file will point to */devices/sbus@1,f8000000/ esp@0,800000/ st@4,0:*.

Setting SCSI Addresses

Most of the disk and tape devices on current Solaris systems connect to the system via an SCSI interface. Many current serial port adapters, printers, scanners, and other peripherals also use the SCSI interface to connect to the system. Because so many peripherals have SCSI interfaces, it seems logical that you learn how to set the SCSI address of these devices on your systems.

Fortunately, SCSI is a standard bus interconnect. Electrical and mechanical specifications exist which define the SCSI interface. These standards define the use of three address bits on a type 1 SCSI or type 2 SCSI bus. With three bits, you can address eight targets. Each of these targets may further address several devices. In the case of disks, tapes, and most other peripherals, the target number corresponds to the SCSI address of the peripheral.

Some peripherals may allow the connection of several devices to one target number on the SCSI bus. One such example is an ESDI disk controller. A typical ESDI disk controller may connect to the SCSI bus as target 3. The ESDI controller may in turn allow the connection of two disk drives. These disk drives may be referred to as */dev/dsk/c0t3d0s2* and */dev/dsk/c0t3d1s2*. Even though there are two physical disk devices, they require only one SCSI address due to the fact that the ESDI controller is the device which is actually connected to the SCSI bus.

The SCSI standard further states that the device with the largest target address has the most priority. Most systems use SCSI target 7 as the address of the system SCSI adapter. By doing this, the SCSI system always has the highest priority on the bus. In the PC world, many systems use target addresses 4,5,6 as disk drives. This ensures that access to the system disk drives has priority over access to other peripheral devices on the SCSI bus.

In the SPARC world, disk drives are typically set to target addresses 0,1,2,3. The target addresses of 4 and 5 are usually used for tape drives, and address 6 is typically reserved for CD-ROM devices. This addressing scheme was used to allow for backwards compatibility with older hardware. Solaris does not implement the usual device priority scheme associated with SCSI devices.

Displaying System Configurations

Examining the configuration of the devices on your system is frequently necessary. Any time you want to add a new peripheral, you need to know how to address the device and where to install it. One way of displaying the system configuration is to use the OpenBoot monitor **show-devs** command. This command will cause the OpenBoot monitor to display all devices in the device information tree.

Under Solaris there are two commonly used commands for displaying the system configuration:

❑ **prtconf** provides a list of devices and drivers loaded in the system. When used with the **-p** flag, prtconf will display the OpenBoot prom information about the devices. The **-v** flag tells prtconf to display the output in verbose format.

❑ **sysdef** provides a list of devices defined on the system, the driver modules which are loadable, and the state of many tunable kernel variables.

Typical output of the prtconf command.

```
System Configuration:  Sun Microsystems  sun4c
Memory size: 28 Megabytes
System Peripherals (Software Nodes):

4_75
        packages (driver not attached)
            disk-label (driver not attached)
            deblocker (driver not attached)
            obp-tftp (driver not attached)
        options, instance #0
        aliases (driver not attached)
        openprom (driver not attached)
        zs, instance #0
        zs, instance #1
        audio (driver not attached)
        eeprom (driver not attached)
        counter-timer (driver not attached)
        memory-error (driver not attached)
        interrupt-enable (driver not attached)
        auxiliary-io (driver not attached)
        sbus, instance #0
            dma, instance #0
            esp, instance #0
                sd (driver not attached)
                st (driver not attached)
                sd, instance #0
                sd, instance #1 (driver not attached)
                sd, instance #2 (driver not attached)
                sd, instance #3
                sd, instance #4 (driver not attached)
                sd, instance #5 (driver not attached)
                sd, instance #6 (driver not attached)
            le (driver not attached)
            cgsix, instance #0
        memory (driver not attached)
        virtual-memory (driver not attached)
        fd, instance #0
        pseudo, instance #0
```

```
* Hostid 55f20ba4
* sun4c Configuration
packages (driver not attached)
        disk-label (driver not attached)
        obp-tftp (driver not attached)
options, instance #0
aliases (driver not attached)
openprom (driver not attached)
zs, instance #0
audio (driver not attached)
eeprom (driver not attached)
memory-error (driver not attached)
interrupt-enable (driver not attached)
auxiliary-io (driver not attached)
sbus, instance #0
        dma, instance #0
        esp, instance #0
                sd (driver not attached)
                st (driver not attached)
                sd, instance #0
                sd, instance #3
        le (driver not attached)
        cgsix, instance #0
memory (driver not attached)
fd, instance #0
pseudo, instance #0
        arp, instance #0 sad, instance #0 consms, instance #0 conskbd, instance #0 wc, instance #0
        iwscn, instance #0 cn, instance #0 mm, instance #0 openeepr, instance #0 kstat, instance #0
        ksyms, instance #0 tcl, instance #0 tcoo, instance #0 tco, instance #0 log, instance #0
        vol, instance #0 sy, instance #0 ptm, instance #0 pts, instance #0 wabi, instance #0
* Loadable Objects
drv/tco drv/tcoo drv/tcp drv/udp drv/xbox drv/bpp drv/classes drv/dma drv/cgsix drv/bwtwo drv/eeprom drv/fd
drv/lebuffer drv/log drv/mm drv/openeepr drv/profile drv/rootnex drv/sbus drv/sbusmem drv/sd drv/stc drv/wc
drv/zs drv/zsh unix exec/aoutexec fs/procfs strmod/kb exec/elfexec exec/intpexec fs/autofs fs/cachefs fs/fifofs
misc/strplumb misc/swapgeneric sched/TS sched/TS_DPTBL strmod/bufmod strmod/connld strmod/dedump strmod/ldterm
strmod/ms strmod/pckt strmod/pfmod strmod/pipemod strmod/ptem strmod/redirmod strmod/rpcmod strmod/sockmod
strmod/hwc misc/seg_drv drv/arp drv/clone drv/cn drv/conskbd drv/consms drv/esp drv/icmp drv/ip drv/isp
drv/iwscn drv/le drv/options drv/pseudo drv/sad drv/sd drv/sp drv/st drv/sy drv/tcl
* System Configuration swap files
swapfile              dev  swaplo blocks    free
/dev/dsk/c0t3d0s1    32,25      8 164000 147824
* Tunable Parameters
        0       maximum memory allowed in buffer cache (bufhwm)
        0       maximum number of processes (v.v_proc)
        0       maximum processes per user id (v.v_maxup)
        0       page stealing low water mark (GPGSLO)
        0       fsflush run rate (FSFLUSHR)
        0       minimum swapable memory for avoiding deadlock (MINASMEM)
* Utsname Tunables
      5.3   release (REL)
    SunOS   system name (SYS)
  Generic   version (VER)
* Process Resource Limit Tunables (Current:Maximum)
Infinity:Infinity      cpu time
Infinity:Infinity      file size
1fefe000:1fefe000      heap size
  800000: ff00000      stack size
Infinity:Infinity      core file size
      40:     400       file descriptors
Infinity:Infinity      mapped memory
* Streams Tunables
        9   maximum number of pushes allowed (NSTRPUSH)
    65536   maximum stream message size (STRMSGSZ)
     1024   max size of ctl part of message (STRCTLSZ)
SYS         system class name (SYS_NAME)
```

Typical output of the sysdef command.

By examining the output of the prtconf command, you can determine that the system has a single Sbus and one SCSI adapter, with two disk drives at targets 0 and 3. The system also has a cg6 framebuffer on the Sbus, and a floppy drive is available.

Reconfiguring Device Information

Sometimes when a new peripheral is installed in a system, it becomes necessary to reconfigure other peripherals. For instance, you may have to move an Sbus adapter card from one slot to another to allow the installation of a new Sbus adapter card.

Because the device information tree contains information on the slot number of each device on the Sbus, you will need to rebuild the device information tree whenever you move devices around or install new devices in your system. This may be accomplished in the following ways:

❑ **boot -r** This command tells the OpenBoot monitor to reconfigure the device information tree before starting the operating system. Any time you add a new device to or remove a device from a system you should boot the system with the boot -r command so that the system will add/delete the device to/from the device information tree, and load the correct drivers.

❑ **touch /reconfigure** This command tells the system to perform a boot -r next time the system is rebooted.

A more dangerous way to reconfigure the system on the fly is to use commands such as **drvconfig**, **disks**, **tapes**, and **devlinks**. These commands cause the system to probe for new devices, and add them to the device information tree while the system is up and running. While these commands are available and perform the task, it is always best to use the **boot -r** command to let the system find and install the devices at reboot time.

Device Instance Names

In a previous section we examined the output of the **prtconf** and **sysdef** commands. In this output, many of the devices have an instance number associated with them.

```
System Configuration:  Sun Microsystems  sun4c
Memory size: 28 Megabytes
System Peripherals (Software Nodes):

4_75
    packages (driver not attached)
        disk-label (driver not attached)
        deblocker (driver not attached)
        obp-tftp (driver not attached)
    options, instance #0
    aliases (driver not attached)
    openprom (driver not attached)
    zs, instance #0
    zs, instance #1
    audio (driver not attached)
    eeprom (driver not attached)
    counter-timer (driver not attached)
    memory-error (driver not attached)
    interrupt-enable (driver not attached)
    auxiliary-io (driver not attached)
    sbus, instance #0
        dma, instance #0
        esp, instance #0
            sd (driver not attached)
            st (driver not attached)
            sd, instance #0
            sd, instance #1 (driver not attached)
            sd, instance #2 (driver not attached)
            sd, instance #3
            sd, instance #4 (driver not attached)
            sd, instance #5 (driver not attached)
            sd, instance #6 (driver not attached)
        le (driver not attached)
        cgsix, instance #0
    memory (driver not attached)
    virtual-memory (driver not attached)
    fd, instance #0
    pseudo, instance #0
```

Typical output of the prtconf command.

```
* Hostid 55f20ba4
* sun4c Configuration
packages (driver not attached)
        disk-label (driver not attached)
        obp-tftp (driver not attached)
options, instance #0
aliases (driver not attached)
openprom (driver not attached)
zs, instance #0
audio (driver not attached)
eeprom (driver not attached)
memory-error (driver not attached)
interrupt-enable (driver not attached)
auxiliary-io (driver not attached)
sbus, instance #0
        dma, instance #0
        esp, instance #0
                sd (driver not attached)
                st (driver not attached)
                sd, instance #0
                sd, instance #3
        le (driver not attached)
        cgsix, instance #0
memory (driver not attached)
fd, instance #0
pseudo, instance #0
        arp, instance #0 sad, instance #0 consms, instance #0 conskbd, instance #0 wc, instance #0
        iwscn, instance #0 cn, instance #0 mm, instance #0 openeepr, instance #0 kstat, instance #0
        ksyms, instance #0 tcl, instance #0 tcoo, instance #0 tco, instance #0 log, instance #0
        vol, instance #0 sy, instance #0 ptm, instance #0 pts, instance #0 wabi, instance #0
* Loadable Objects
drv/tco drv/tcoo drv/tcp drv/udp drv/xbox drv/bpp drv/classes drv/dma drv/cgsix drv/bwtwo drv/eeprom drv/fd
drv/lebuffer drv/log drv/mm drv/openeepr drv/profile drv/rootnex drv/sbus drv/sbusmem drv/sd drv/stc drv/wc
drv/zs drv/zsh unix exec/aoutexec fs/procfs strmod/kb exec/elfexec exec/intpexec fs/autofs fs/cachefs fs/fifofs
misc/strplumb misc/swapgeneric sched/TS sched/TS_DPTBL strmod/bufmod strmod/connld strmod/dedump strmod/ldterm
strmod/ms strmod/pckt strmod/pfmod strmod/pipemod strmod/ptem strmod/redirmod strmod/rpcmod strmod/sockmod
strmod/hwc misc/seg_drv drv/arp drv/clone drv/cn drv/conskbd drv/consms drv/esp drv/icmp drv/ip drv/isp
drv/iwscn drv/le drv/options drv/pseudo drv/sad drv/sd drv/sp drv/st drv/sy drv/tcl
* System Configuration swap files
swapfile            dev  swaplo blocks    free
/dev/dsk/c0t3d0s1   32,25     8 164000 147824
* Tunable Parameters
        0        maximum memory allowed in buffer cache (bufhwm)
        0        maximum number of processes (v.v_proc)
        0        maximum processes per user id (v.v_maxup)
        0        page stealing low water mark (GPGSLO)
        0        fsflush run rate (FSFLUSHR)
        0        minimum swapable memory for avoiding deadlock (MINASMEM)
* Utsname Tunables
     5.3   release (REL)
   SunOS   system name (SYS)
 Generic   version (VER)
* Process Resource Limit Tunables (Current:Maximum)
Infinity:Infinity       cpu time
Infinity:Infinity       file size
1fefe000:1fefe000       heap size
  800000: ff00000       stack size
Infinity:Infinity       core file size
      40:     400       file descriptors
Infinity:Infinity       mapped memory
* Streams Tunables
     9   maximum number of pushes allowed (NSTRPUSH)
 65536   maximum stream message size (STRMSGSZ)
  1024   max size of ctl part of message (STRCTLSZ)
SYS      system class name (SYS_NAME)
```

Typical output from the sysdef command.

These instance numbers refer to the device address or ID on the system. For example, the disk with instance number 3 is your boot disk */dev/dsk/c0t3d0s0*, or *sd3a*. The esp adapter with an instance number of 0 is the on-board SCSI adapter on this system. Other adapters and devices follow these conventions, thereby allowing you to determine the structure of the device information tree by looking at the instance numbers of the attached devices.

Autoconfiguration

As mentioned in the section on reconfiguring system information, the system will perform an autoconfiguration upon boot if you use the **boot -r** command. You can force the system to autoconfigure upon the next system reboot by using the **touch /reconfigure** command while you are logged in as the super-user.

Summary

This chapter covered how devices on Solaris systems are named, and how they are addressed. You also learned how the logical names, or aliases, point you back to the physical names and addresses of the devices. Several examples showed you how to track down the physical address from typical aliases.

You also saw how to identify the devices and driver modules loaded on your systems, and how to use this information to determine where to install new devices on the system. Once the devices are installed, you learned how to teach the system about the new devices. By using the **boot -r** command after a new device is installed, the system can determine at boot time what devices are connected, and which device drivers to load to allow you access to these devices.

Managing Disks

In the previous chapter, we explored the naming conventions of devices under Solaris 2. The next few chapters focus on specifics of the more typical devices. The devices we discuss are the ones you will be dealing with every day: disks, tapes, terminals, modems, and printers.

One of the most important peripherals on any computer system is the mass storage subsystem. The mass storage subsystem typically consists of disk drives, tape drives, and optical media (e.g., the CD-ROM drive). In order to properly optimize a system, it is important to understand how the mass storage subsystem is organized. In this chapter we will look specifically at the disk subsystem.

Understanding Disk Geometry

In Chapter 2, which covered basics of disk geometry, we stated that a disk drive is divided into many small sections called sectors. Each Solaris data sector is capable of storing 512 bytes of data, and a UNIX file system is comprised of a particular number of sectors bound together by the **newfs** command.

But how are these sectors organized on a disk drive? How do you determine which sectors to bind into a file system? Can you change the size of a file system? To answer these questions, we must examine the organization of the physical disk media.

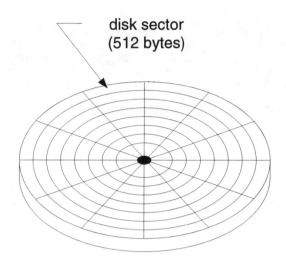

disk sector
(512 bytes)

*A typical internal
disk layout.*

The Physical Disk Media

As you can see from the figure above, a disk drive contains several magnetic surfaces called *platters*. Each of these platters can be thought of as being made up of many concentric cylinders. Each of the cylinders is further divided into sectors. On the smaller inner-most cylinders, the platter may be divided into a small number of sectors. On the outermost cylinders the platter may be divided into a larger number of sectors.

In order to transfer data to and from these sectors, a read/write head is passed over the magnetic surface of the platter. The read/write heads convert electrical impulses into magnetic patterns on the platter surfaces. Depending on the disk drive, there are one or more read/write heads on each platter surface.

The sectors on a drive are numbered sequentially beginning with the first sector on the first head of the first cylinder of the drive. If you have a drive with 55 sectors per track, the first 55 sectors will be numbered zero through 54. The 55th sector will be the first sector on the second platter of the drive. The 110th sector on the drive will be the first sector on the third platter of the drive, and so on. Once you get to the last sector on the last platter, you increment the cylinder number, and go back to the first sector on the first platter to continue numbering the sectors.

 NOTE: *Due to the incorporation of alternate sectors the numbering may not always be as described above. Many factors may affect the sequence of sectors. For instance, a bad sector may be mapped to a spare sector*

such that you would have an out-of-order sector in your counting sequence.

Logical Disks and Partitions

Earlier in this chapter, and in the chapter on installing Solaris, we stated that in order to use a disk drive under Solaris, you must partition the drive, and then bind the sectors in a partition together with **newfs** to form a file system. But why are disks partitioned in the first place? In order to understand the need to partition the disks, we need to take a step back into computer history.

Early system architecture required that large drives be partitioned into smaller logical units.

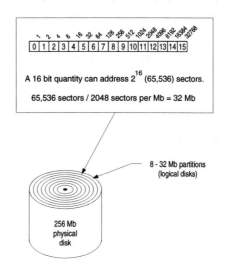

At the time UNIX was first released, most machines that ran UNIX employed 16-bit hardware. As a result a 16-bit unsigned integer number could address 65536 sectors on the disk drive. This meant that the disk drive could be no larger than 65536 sectors * 512 bytes/sector, or roughly 32 megabytes (Mb).

Because large disk drives were available that contained 300 Mb or more, provisions were made to allow the use of these drives on UNIX systems. The solution was to divide these large capacity drives into smaller logical drives. Each logical drive was capable of storing 32 Mb of data. By stacking several of these smaller logical drives together one could use the entire capacity of the 300 Mb disk drive. These logical drives became known as *partitions*.

More recent computer hardware employs 32- or 64-bit processors thereby allowing the system to directly address much larger drives. A 32-bit signed drive related variable can address 2,147,483,648 bytes (2.1 gigabytes or Gb). Under Solaris, you are able to address nearly a terabyte of disk space, with files as large as two gigabytes.

Adding a Disk to a System

The general procedure to add a new SCSI disk to a system is very simple.

1. Determine the address at which you can install the new drive. Use the **prtconf** command as discussed in Chapter 11 to determine which addresses are in use.

2. Use **touch /reconfigure** as shown in Chapter 8 to cause the system to look for new devices upon reboot.

3. Shut the system down using the **shutdown** command as discussed in Chapter 9.

4. Set the drive address jumpers, and install the new drive on the system.

5. Boot the system to the single-user state **boot -s** as discussed in Chapter 8.

6. If required, use the **format** utility to format and partition the new drive.

7. Use **newfs** to bind sectors into the partitions you plan to use.

8. Use **fsck** to check the file system integrity of the partitions you plan to use.

9. Edit the */etc/vfstab* file to add the partitions to the system tables.

10. Use **mkdir** to create the mount point directories for the partitions.

11. Use */etc/halt* as discussed in Chapter 9 to bring the system down.

12. Use **boot -r** to restart the system and cause it to scan for new devices as discussed in Chapter 8.

Once the system is back up and running the new file systems will be available. You will need to edit the system password file by installing user home directories in the new partition. This will allow the users to use this new disk space for home directories. If the new disk is to be used for storage other than home directories, you will need to take other measures to ensure that your users have the read/write permissions they need to complete their work.

Calculating Disk Slice Sizes

What happens if you purchase a disk drive that is not formatted and partitioned for Solaris systems? How do you change the formatting and partitioning such that the drive is useful in your application? The **format** utility gives you the ability to format the drive, and write a Solaris partition map on the drive. These partition maps define how the drive will be sliced into logical units. You may sometimes hear disk partitions referred to as *disk slices*. Let's examine how you would calculate disk slice sizes to develop the partition map.

As we mentioned in Chapter 2, a typical rule of thumb when partitioning disks is to allow for 10% of the sectors in a file system to be consumed by overhead. But just what is this overhead? For our purposes, we will use an everyday command to point out file system overhead. Chapter 13 will focus on the specifics of the Solaris file system structure, the cause of the overhead, and ways to reduce the amount of space lost to the overhead.

Overallocation Overhead

When you look at the output from the **df** command, you will notice that the *used* and *avail* numbers do not add up to the kbytes amount. The difference between these quantities points out the existence of file system overhead. One of the easiest ways to detect uses of the overhead is the overallocation safeguard built into the file system.

The UNIX operating system reserves a certain number of sectors for use as short-term overallocation situations. In some cases you might notice a file system at 110% capacity as you look at the output of df. An example of df on a server might show the following:

```
Filesystem kbytes used avail capacity Mounted on
/dev/dsk/c0t3d0s0 30825 17126 10616 62% /
/dev/dsk/c0t3d0s6 471631 459089 0 108% /export/swap
```

> ✔ **NOTE:** *When a file system reaches the 100% full level, the system will generate a message on the system console. This is a sign that users are not cleaning up after themselves. It is your job as system administrator to perform housecleaning tasks to free up space on that file system.*

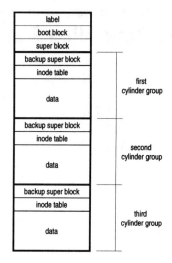

The structure of the Solaris file system.

Super-block Overhead

Another source of file system overhead is the support structure required to keep track of the files in the file system. One of these support structures is called the *super-block*. The super-block can be considered the index of the file system contents. Any references to a file or directory on the partition must first reference the super-block to determine which sectors are part of that file or directory.

The primary super-block is stored in one of the first few sectors of the partition. Backup or alternate copies of the super-block are stored in several places on the partition in case of failure of the primary super-block. On small file systems there are few copies of the alternate super-blocks. On large file systems, there are many copies of the alternate super-blocks. For more information on the super-block and **newfs**, refer to the sections titled, "Tuning Space Usage With The Newfs Command," and "Creating File systems With Newfs."

General Rules to Determine Partition Sizes

A few general rules you may wish to use when trying to determine the appropriate size for a partition are listed below.

1. Determine how much space the application currently occupies.

2. Add 50% to the number from step 1 for growth and expansion of the file system.

3. Add 10% more space for file system overhead.

4. Divide the number from the previous step by the sector size (512).

5. Divide the number from the previous step by (Nheads * Nsects) to determine how many cylinders are required. Round up to the nearest whole number.

For example, an application that requires 100 Mb of storage space, and a new disk drive with a geometry of 20 heads and 97 sectors/track would yield the following calculations:

❑ Original package size N = 100 Mb.

❑ Add space for growth M = N + (N * .5) == 150 Mb.

❑ Add 10% overhead space O = M + (M * .1) == 165 Mb.

❑ Divide by 512 bytes per sector P = 173,015,040 bytes / (512 bytes/sector) == 337920 sectors required.

❑ Ncyl = 337920 sectors / (20 heads * 97 sectors per head per cylinder) == 175 cylinders required for the partition.

✗ *TIP: A quick way to estimate disk space requirements is to use the following formula: 2048 sectors * 512 bytes/sector is equivalent to one (1) Mb of disk space.*

The Volume Table of Contents (VTOC)

Once you determine the size of your partition and format the drive, how does the system recognize this partition? As part of the format process a label is written on the disk. This label contains the Volume Table Of Contents (VTOC). You can view the VTOC by using the **prtvtoc** utility.

The prtvtoc utility lists each partition on the drive, the size of the partition, the mount point for the partition (if known), as well as other information known about the disk drive.

Using prtvtoc to view the volume table of contents (VTOC).

```
# prtvtoc /dev/rdsk/c0t3d0s2
* /dev/rdsk/c0t3d0s2 partition map
*
* Dimensions:
*     512 bytes/sector
*      80 sectors/track
*       9 tracks/cylinder
*     720 sectors/cylinder
*    2500 cylinders
*    1151 accessible cylinders
*
* Flags:
*   1: unmountable
*  10: read-only
*
*                              First    Sector    Last
* Partition  Tag  Flags        Sector   Count     Sector  Mount Directory
          0    2    00              0    66240     66239   /
          1    3    01          66240   248400    314639
          2    5    00              0   828720    828719
          6    4    00         314640   205200    519839   /usr
 _        7    6    00         519840   308880    828719   /var/local
```

Slice Tags and Flags

Part of the information displayed by the **prtvtoc** utility are the *tag* and *flag* fields. These fields identify how the partitions are used, and how they are mounted.

✔ **NOTE**: *The tag and flag fields are optional, and have no impact on system performance.*

The tag field is used to identify how the file system is being used. Valid entries in this field follow:

Tag Field Descriptions

Tag field value	Description
0	Unassigned partition
1	Boot partition
2	Root partition
3	Swap partition
4	Usr partition

Tag field value	Description
5	Backup partition
6	Stand partition
8	Home partition

The flag field is used to determine how the partition is to be mounted. Valid entries in this field include the following:

Flag Field Descriptions

Flag field value	Description
00	Mounted Read/Write
01	Not mountable
10	Mounted Read-only

Repartitioning Disk Drives

As file systems outgrow their current partition or as file systems become unnecessary on your machines, you may have occasion to repartition a disk. It should be apparent from the contents of the VTOC that repartitioning a disk is a destructive process.

> **❗ WARNING:** *Before proceeding with the repartitioning procedure you must save all data contained within the target file system. Failure to do so will result in data loss.*

If it becomes necessary for you to repartition a disk, you must save all of the files from the disk drive by dumping them to tape. Once you have saved all information from the disk, you may use the **format** utility to reformat/repartition the drive. Once you have repartitioned the drive, restore the files you want to keep off of the backup tapes.

Pre-format Considerations

The **format** utility allows you to format, partition, label, and maintain disk drives under Solaris. The format command uses a file containing disk information, */etc/format.dat*, to determine the parameters to be used during the formatting process. Solaris currently allows you to deal with three types of disk drives: SCSI drives, IPI drives, and SMD drives.

These three types of drives have several similarities, but more importantly, they also have several important differences. For instance, the SMD disk drives are hard-sectored storage systems. This means you have to set switches on the disk drive to tell the unit how many sectors are included on each cylinder. You also need to tell format the number of sectors per cylinder, but this number is quite often less than the actual number of data sectors that the drive reports. The discrepancy in these numbers is due to the spare sector allocation scheme used in SMD disk drives. SMD drives require that you follow very strict guidelines in developing format geometry and partition tables.

The IPI and SCSI drives are very similar units. The most notable difference between the units is the cabling required to connect them to the system. The process of determining disk geometry and partition maps for these drives is much more flexible than the process used for SMD disk drives. We will concentrate on SCSI technology because SMD and IPI drives are becoming less popular on current systems.

✔ *NOTE: When formatting SCSI disks, the Solaris format command will determine a default partition map and label for unknown drive types. This is a change from the way the format utility worked under SunOS.*

The following sections cover how to develop a *format.dat* entry for a drive. These methods will work for SCSI and IPI disk drives. The procedure for developing *format.dat* entries for SMD disks is similar to the SCSI and IPI procedure.

Installing Drives Known to format.dat

Solaris provides the **format** utility to format, partition, and label unknown drives for use under Solaris. The format utility reads a table of available drive types from the */etc/format.dat* file. If the unknown drive is described in the *format.dat* file, it is a simple task to format the drive, partition it, and put it into use.

If an exact description of the drive you are installing is not available, it may be possible to use one of the Sun supplied definitions. For instance, if you are attempting to install a 2.4 gigabyte disk drive, you may be able to use the Sun supplied *SUN2.1G* entry to format your disk. This entry may waste a little bit of disk space for your drive, but you will not have to spend the time determining a *format.dat* entry to fit the drive.

✗ **TIP:** *Sun may use several brands and models of disk in their systems. For convenience, several similar capacity drives bear the same disk geometry label. If you purchase a drive model that Sun is known to ship in their systems, you can take advantage of the format.dat entry for the type of drive on your system.*

Understanding format.dat Entries

What happens if a description of the drive is not contained in *format.dat*? You create your own entry, of course. Let's examine the fields of a format.dat entry to determine how you do this. The layout of a typical format.dat file follows.

```
#
# ident    "@(#) format.dat 1.16     93/06/30  SMI"
#
# Copyright (c)  1991 by Sun Microsystems, Inc.
#
# Data file for the 'format' program.   This file defines the known
# disks, disk types, and partition maps.
#
disk_type = "Quantum ProDrive 105S"  \
          : ctlr = SCSI : fmt_time = 1   \
          : cache = 0x07 : trks_zone = 6 : atrks = 0 : asect = 1  \
          : ncyl = 974 : acyl = 2 : pcyl = 1019 : nhead = 6 : nsect = 35  \
          : rpm = 3662 : bpt = 16896

disk type = "SUN0207"  \
          : ctlr = SCRI  \
          : trks_zone = 9 : atrks = 2: asect = 4  \
          : ncyl = 1254 : acyl = 2 : pcyl = 1272 : nhead = 9 : nsect = 36  \
          : rpm = 3600 : bpt = 18432

#
# this is the list of partition tables for embedded SCSI controllers.
#
partition = "Quantum ProDrive 105S"  \
          : disk = "Quantum ProDrive 105S" : ctlr = SCSI  \
          : 0 = 0, 16170 : 1 = 77, 28140 : 2 = 0, 204540 : 6 = 211, 160230

partition = "SUN0207"  \
```

The layout of a typical format.dat file.

The first portion of the *format.dat* file lists each drive type, and format parameters for a particular drive and controller combination. The following fields are mandatory in every format.dat entry, and must contain a value:

❑ **ctlr** is the type of controller the drive emulates. Solaris SCSI drives use the term *SCSI* in this field.

❑ **ncyl** is the number of data cylinders the operating system thinks the drive has.

❑ **acyl** is the number of alternate cylinders to be used for bad block remapping.

❑ **pcyl** is the actual physical number of cylinders on the drive (usually derived from the drive technical manual).

❑ **nhead** is the number of data heads the operating system thinks the drive has, and is sometimes referred to as "tracks."

❑ **nsect** is the number of sectors per track the operating system thinks the drive has. Note that most current SCSI drives provide a variable number of sectors per track. The *nsect* entry is typically an average number derived by dividing the total number of sectors by the total number of tracks.

❑ **rpm** is the rotational speed of the drive.

❑ **bpt** is the number of bytes per track on the drive.

The following format.dat fields are optional:

❑ **cache** is a value used to control the drive cache during the format procedure.

❑ **fmt_time** is a value used to tell the format program how long it will take to format this drive.

❑ **trks_zone** is usually seen on drives which utilize a variable number of sectors per track. The drive is divided into zones and there are *N* tracks per zone.

❑ **atrks** is a number of alternate tracks per zone available for bad block remapping.

❑ **asect** is a number of alternate sectors per zone available for bad block remapping.

The final section of the *format.dat* file contains partition maps for each drive/controller combination. The fields of the partition map section of the *format.dat* file follow:

❑ **partition** is the ASCII label that will be used to identify the partition map.

❑ **disk** is the ASCII label that will be used to identify the type of disk drive.

❑ **ctlr** is the type of controller the drive is connected to.

❑ **0=0,N: 1=X,N2: 2=0,MAX: 6=X3,N3** are patterns that define the slice or partition number {0 through 7}, the starting cylinder of the partition, and the size in sectors of the partition {N1, N2, MAX, N3, ...}.

✔ *NOTE: Slice 2 is always defined as encompassing the entire drive. Hence the partition starts at cylinder zero, and encompasses all sectors between the first sector and the maximum sector on the drive.*

Creating format.dat Entries for SCSI Disks

What do all of those numbers in the *format.dat* entry really mean? As it turns out, an SCSI disk appears to be a block of contiguous sectors to the operating system. The drive controller takes care of mapping the desired block number to the correct cylinder/head/sector address. This means that you can make the numbers in the *format.dat* entry of an SCSI disk be just about anything you like, as long as you do not make an entry that would exceed the formatted capacity of the drive.

What information do you need to be able to derive your own SCSI drive *format.dat* entries? You will need to know at least one of the following:

❑ The number of sectors available on the formatted drive.

❑ The formatted capacity of the drive in megabytes.

✔ *NOTE: For SMD drives you also need to know how many sectors per track, and how many bytes are contained in each sector.*

It is also nice to know the number of bytes per track and the rotational speed of any type of drive, but these can be derived as explained later.

If you know how many sectors exist on the drive, *format.dat* entries may be developed as follows:

❑ Use */usr/games/factor* to factor the number of sectors to prime numbers.

❑ Use these prime factors to develop the *format.dat* entry

❑ */user/games/factor* is a "game" program that ships with Solaris. The factor program will factor the numeric input argument into a series of prime numbers, and print those prime numbers in the output.

For example, assume you have a drive with 10000 sectors:

❑ When you use */usr/games/factor*, it reports that 10000 = 2*2*2*2*5*5*5*5.

❑ By grouping these factors into cylinder/head/sector groupings, you can develop a *format.dat* entry as follows: 5*5*5*2 cylinders, 2*2 heads, 2*5 sectors (250 cylinders * 4 heads * 10 sectors).

If you know the formatted capacity of a drive in megabytes, there are extra steps in the calculations:

❑ Divide the capacity by the sector size (512 bytes/sector).

❑ Feed the resulting number to */usr/games/factor.*

❑ Use the resulting prime factors to develop the *format.dat* entry.

For example, assume you have a drive with formatted capacity of 512 megabytes:

❑ 512,000,000 / 512 = 1,000,000 sectors.

❑ */usr/games/factor* 1,000,000 = 2*2*2*2*2*2*5*5*5*5*5*5.

❑ By grouping these factors into cylinder/head/sector groupings, develop a *format.dat* entry: 5*5*5*5*2 cylinders, 2*2*2 heads, 5*5*2*2 sectors (1250 cylinders * 8 heads * 100 sectors).

Since the number of sectors on real drives never factor so easily, let's try the method for a real drive. One particularly popular drive has 1658 data cylinders, 15 heads, and a formatted capacity of 1,079.1 megabytes. The drive manual tells you that the drive has a capacity of 50910 bytes per track and a rotational speed of 3600 RPM. From this information, you would use the second method to develop a format.dat entry as follows:

❑ 1,079,100,000 bytes / 512 bytes = 2107617 sectors.

❑ */usr/games/factor* 2107617 = 3 * 702539. You appear to be stuck. Subtract a few sectors from the drive, and try again. Suppose you subtract 17 sectors, and try 2107600 sectors. The result is */usr/games/factor* 2107600 = 2*2*2*2*5*5*11*479.

❑ By grouping these factors into cylinder/head/sector groupings, develop a format.dat entry: 479*4 cylinders, 2*2*5 heads, 5*11 sectors (1916 cylinders, 20 heads, 55 sectors).

If you do not know the speed of the drive, you can use 3600 RPM for drives that transfer at 5 Mb/second or less. If the drive transfers at 5 Mb/second or more, you can use 5400 or 7200 rpm. If the drive manual does not specify the number of bytes per track, you could calculate an entry by multiplying the number of bytes/sector * number of sectors/track. Always use the manufacturer's parameters if they are available.

✔ **NOTE:** *Most manufacturers have bulletin boards or technical support phone numbers that users can contact to obtain the manufacturer's format.dat information for most of the popular systems on the market.*

Since the manufacturers know their drives better than anybody else, it is best to follow their recommendations whenever possible.

Using the format Utility

Once you have developed a *format.dat* entry for your drive, you are ready to begin the format process. Invoke the format utility by logging in as the super-user, and type **format** at the prompt as follows:

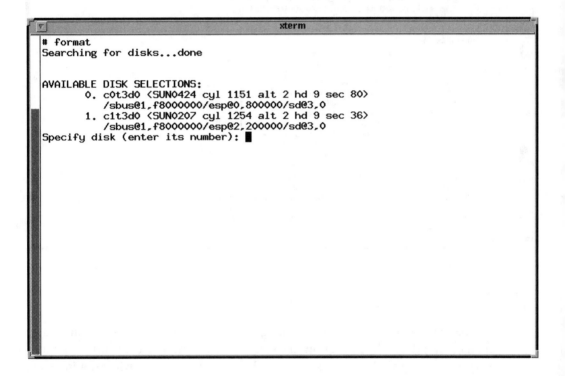

```
                                        xterm
# format
Searching for disks...done


AVAILABLE DISK SELECTIONS:
       0. c0t3d0 <SUN0424 cyl 1151 alt 2 hd 9 sec 80>
          /sbus@1,f8000000/esp@0,800000/sd@3,0
       1. c1t3d0 <SUN0207 cyl 1254 alt 2 hd 9 sec 36>
          /sbus@1,f8000000/esp@2,200000/sd@3,0
Specify disk (enter its number): █
```

Starting the format utility.

The format utility will respond by listing all of the drives it can find attached to this system. You may select the new drive by entering the number for the desired disk drive and pressing <Enter>. If the drive is already formatted, format will inform you, and then display the main format menu. If the drive is not formatted, format will determine a default label for SCSI drives. If you are not working with a SCSI drive, format will inform you that the drive is not formatted, and then display the main format menu.

```
┌─────────────────────────────────────── xterm ───────────────────────────────────┐
│▼                                                                                  │
│ Searching for disks...done                                                        │
│                                                                                   │
│                                                                                   │
│ AVAILABLE DISK SELECTIONS:                                                        │
│         0. c0t3d0 <SUN0424 cyl 1151 alt 2 hd 9 sec 80>                           │
│            /sbus@1,f8000000/esp@0,800000/sd@3,0                                  │
│         1. c1t3d0 <SUN0207 cyl 1254 alt 2 hd 9 sec 36>                           │
│            /sbus@1,f8000000/esp@2,200000/sd@3,0                                  │
│ Specify disk (enter its number): 1                                               │
│ selecting c1t3d0                                                                  │
│ [disk formatted]                                                                  │
│                                                                                   │
│                                                                                   │
│ FORMAT MENU:                                                                      │
│         disk       - select a disk                                                │
│         type       - select (define) a disk type                                  │
│         partition  - select (define) a partition table                            │
│         current    - describe the current disk                                    │
│         format     - format and analyze the disk                                  │
│         repair     - repair a defective sector                                    │
│         label      - write label to the disk                                      │
│         analyze    - surface analysis                                             │
│         defect     - defect list management                                       │
│         backup     - search for backup labels                                     │
│         verify     - read and display labels                                      │
│         save       - save new disk/partition definitions                          │
│         inquiry    - show vendor, product and revision                            │
│         volname    - set 8-character volume name                                  │
│         quit                                                                      │
│ format> █                                                                         │
└───────────────────────────────────────────────────────────────────────────────┘
```

The format utility main menu.

The main menu allows you to configure the operation of format, extract and manage the defect list, partition disks, label disks, and perform surface pattern verification on the disk drives. In the following sections we will examine each of the menu items, and what these items will allow you to do.

> **!** **WARNING:** *When used to format a disk or to perform surface analysis, format is a destructive procedure. Make sure you have performed file system backups before formatting a drive that has been in operation on your system.*

format's disk Command

The **disk** menu is used to select which disk drive you wish to modify. This menu is exactly like the menu first presented by the format command. If you were formatting several disks you could simply select a new disk via the disk menu instead of exiting and restarting format for each drive. The disk menu item displays the current controller and drive geometry information for each drive available on the system.

The format utility disk menu.

```
format> disk

AVAILABLE DISK SELECTIONS:
       0. c0t3d0 <SUN0424 cyl 1151 alt 2 hd 9 sec 80>
          /sbus@1,f8000000/esp@0,800000/sd@3,0
       1. c1t3d0 <SUN0207 cyl 1254 alt 2 hd 9 sec 36>
          /sbus@1,f8000000/esp@2,200000/sd@3,0
Specify disk (enter its number)[1]: █
```

format's type Command

The **type** menu allows you to select the appropriate drive type, and geometry information for the drive you wish to format. The geometry and type information is read in from the entries in the *format.dat* file.

The format utility type menu.

```
format> type

AVAILABLE DRIVE TYPES:
        0. Auto configure
        1. Quantum ProDrive 80S
        2. Quantum ProDrive 105S
        3. CDC Wren IV 94171-344
        4. SUN0104
        5. SUN0207
        6. SUN0327
        7. SUN0340
        8. SUN0424
        9. SUN0535
       10. SUN0669
       11. SUN1.0G
       12. SUN1.05
       13. SUN1.3G
       14. SUN2.1G
       15. Fujitsu M2624FA
       16. Fujitsu M2652SA
       17. Fujitsu M2694ESA
       18. Fujitsu M2654SA
       19. Fujitsu M2654HA
       20. Maxtor 7345
       21. other
Specify disk type (enter its number)[5]: █
```

format's partition Command

The **partition** menu is used to examine and modify the partition information for the drive that you are formatting.

```
format> partition

PARTITION MENU:
        0       - change `0´ partition
        1       - change `1´ partition
        2       - change `2´ partition
        3       - change `3´ partition
        4       - change `4´ partition
        5       - change `5´ partition
        6       - change `6´ partition
        7       - change `7´ partition
        select - select a predefined table
        modify - modify a predefined partition table
        name   - name the current table
        print  - display the current table
        label  - write partition map and label to the disk
        quit
partition> █
```

The format utility partition menu.

The numbered entries in the partition menu refer to the available drive partitions. These partitions are always numbered zero through eight. The remaining entries in the partition menu are submenus which allow you to customize partition tables.

The partition select submenu.

```
partition> select
        0. SUN0207
        1. example
Specify table (enter its number)[1]: 1
```

The **select** menu allows you to select a predefined partition map as supplied in */etc/format.dat*. You are also allowed to "copy" the partition map of another drive of the same type on the system.

```
partition> modify
Select partitioning base:
        0. Current partition table (SUN0207)
        1. All Free Hog
Choose base (enter number) [0]? 1

Part       Tag     Flag   Cylinders        Size        Blocks
  0       root      wm    0                 0          (0/0/0)
  1       swap      wu    0                 0          (0/0/0)
  2     backup      wu    0 - 1253     198.39MB     (1254/0/0)
  3 unassigned      wm    0                 0          (0/0/0)
  4 unassigned      wm    0                 0          (0/0/0)
  5 unassigned      wm    0                 0          (0/0/0)
  6        usr      wm    0                 0          (0/0/0)
  7 unassigned      wm    0                 0          (0/0/0)

Do you wish to continue creating a new partition
table based on above table[yes]? y
Free Hog partition[6]?
Enter size of partition '0' [0b, 0c, 0.00mb]: 0
Enter size of partition '1' [0b, 0c, 0.00mb]: 0
Enter size of partition '3' [0b, 0c, 0.00mb]: 0
Enter size of partition '4' [0b, 0c, 0.00mb]: 0
Enter size of partition '5' [0b, 0c, 0.00mb]: 0
Enter size of partition '7' [0b, 0c, 0.00mb]: 0

Part       Tag     Flag   Cylinders        Size        Blocks
  0       root      wm    0                 0          (0/0/0)
  1       swap      wu    0                 0          (0/0/0)
  2     backup      wu    0 - 1253     198.39MB     (1254/0/0)
  3 unassigned      wm    0                 0          (0/0/0)
  4 unassigned      wm    0                 0          (0/0/0)
  5 unassigned      wm    0                 0          (0/0/0)
  6        usr      wm    0 - 1253     198.39MB     (1254/0/0)
  7 unassigned      wm    0                 0          (0/0/0)

Okay to make this the current partition table[yes]? y
Enter table name (remember quotes): "example"

Ready to label disk, continue? y

partition> ▋
```

*The partition
modify submenu.*

The **modify** menu allows you to modify the current partition map. You can determine the size and name of the file systems on your drive with this menu. Within this menu, commands are provided to allow you to examine, save, and print your modified partition map.

*The partition name
submenu.*

```
partition> name
Enter table name (remember quotes): "example2"
```

The **name** menu allows you to select a partition name for the partition map. This name is saved in the */etc/format.dat* file for future reference.

```
partition> print
Current partition table (SUN0207):
Part      Tag    Flag    Cylinders        Size        Blocks
  0      root     wm      0 -   101      16.14MB      (102/0/0)
  1      swap     wu    102 -   303      31.96MB      (202/0/0)
  2    backup     wu      0 - 1253     198.39MB     (1254/0/0)
  3 unassigned    wm      0                  0        (0/0/0)
  4 unassigned    wm      0                  0        (0/0/0)
  5 unassigned    wm      0                  0        (0/0/0)
  6       usr     wm    304 - 1253     150.29MB      (950/0/0)
  7 unassigned    wm      0                  0        (0/0/0)

partition> █
```

The partition print submenu.

The **print** submenu enables you to view the partition map you are modifying. The information provided in this printout allows you to determine the size, starting cylinder, and other information about the partitions on the disk drive.

The partition label submenu.

```
partition> label
Ready to label disk, continue? y

partition>
```

The **label** menu allows you to write the current partition size, and name information into the volume label. This command operates the same as the label menu item in the **format** utility main menu.

format's current Command

The **current** menu selection displays information about the currently selected drive. The information provided includes the addressing information for the controller for the drive, and the drive geometry information.

The format utility current menu.

```
format> current
Current Disk = c1t3d0
<SUN0207 cyl 1254 alt 2 hd 9 sec 36>
/sbus@1,f8000000/esp@2,200000/sd@3,0

format> █
```

format's repair Command

The **repair** menu selection allows you to add and subtract entries to/from the current drives defect list. You can specify the bad spot location via an absolute block number (for SCSI and IPI disks), or by giving the cylinder/head/sector information for the bad spot (for SMD drives).

<table>
<tr>
<td>The format utility
repair menu.</td>
<td><pre>format> repair
Enter absolute block number of defect: 13303
Ready to repair defect, continue? y
Repairing block 13303 (41/0/19)...ok.</pre></td>
</tr>
</table>

format's label Command

The **label** menu selection writes a label on the current drive. This selection operates the same as the label selection in the partition submenu. The disk label contains information on the disk drive geometry and the size of the partitions, including starting cylinder and number of data sectors.

<table>
<tr>
<td>The format utility
label menu.</td>
<td><pre>format> label
Ready to label disk, continue? y

format> █</pre></td>
</tr>
</table>

format's analyze Menu

The **analyze** menu is used to set the surface analysis parameters for the verification portion of the format utility. This menu also allows you to start one of the various surface analysis programs.

<table>
<tr>
<td></td>
<td><pre>format> analyze</pre></td>
</tr>
<tr>
<td>The format utility
analyze menu.</td>
<td><pre>ANALYZE MENU:
        read   - read only test   (doesn't harm SunOS)
        refresh - read then write   (doesn't harm data)
        test   - pattern testing   (doesn't harm data)
        write   - write then read   (corrupts data)
        compare - write, read, compare (corrupts data)
        purge   - write, read, write   (corrupts data)
        print   - display data buffer
        setup   - set analysis parameters
        config   - show analysis parameters
        quit
analyze> █</pre></td>
</tr>
</table>

The **read**, **refresh**, **test**, **write**, **compare**, and **purge** menu items allow you to start those test sequences. Note that the write, compare, and purge options will destroy any data stored on the disk. The read, refresh, and test items do not destroy data stored on the disk drive.

The **print** item prints out a disk data buffer to the screen. This allows the operator to see the pattern currently being written to the drive. The **setup** option in the **analyze** menu allows you to configure the surface analysis portion of format.

The analyze setup submenu.

```
analyze> setup
Analyze entire disk[yes]?
Loop continuously[no]?
Enter number of passes[2]:
Repair defective blocks[yes]?
Stop after first error[no]?
Use random bit patterns[no]?
Enter number of blocks per transfer[126, 0/3/18]:
Verify media after formatting[yes]?
Enable extended messages[no]?
Restore defect list[yes]?
Restore disk label[yes]?

analyze> 
```

The setup menu allows you to select which portion of the disk to analyze, and which transfer size to use. You also have control over whether bad spots are mapped out or merely reported to you. Once you have made changes in the setup, you can verify the changes with the analyze config menu item.

Using the analyze config command to show current setup.

```
analyze> config
        Analyze entire disk? yes
        Starting block number: 0 (0/0/0)
        Ending block number: 406295 (1253/8/35)
        Loop continuously? no
        Number of passes: 2
        Repair defective blocks? yes
        Stop after first error? no
        Use random bit patterns? no
        Number of blocks per transfer: 126 (0/3/18)
        Verify media after formatting? yes
        Enable extended messages? no
        Restore defect list? yes
        Restore disk label? yes

analyze> 
```

format's defect Menu

The **defect** menu of **format** is used to read and manipulate the manufacturer defect list from a drive. It also allows you to add and subtract defects from this list.

```
format> defect

DEFECT MENU:
        primary   - extract manufacturer's defect list
        grown     - extract manufacturer's and repaired defects lists
        both      - extract both primary and grown defects lists
        print     - display working list
        dump      - dump working list to file
        quit
defect>
```

The format utility defect submenu.

The **primary** menu item allows you to read the vendor defect list off of the disk media. The **grown** and **both** menu items allow you to read the vendor defect list, and the repaired defect list from the disk media.

```
                                  xterm
format> defect

DEFECT MENU:
        primary   - extract manufacturer's defect list
        grown     - extract manufacturer's and repaired defects lists
        both      - extract both primary and grown defects lists
        print     - display working list
        dump      - dump working list to file
        quit
defect>
defect> primary
Extracting primary defect list...Extraction complete.
Current Defect List updated, total of 36 defects.

defect>
```

Using the defect menu primary command to extract the vendor defect list.

Once you have extracted the defect lists from the media, you can save this information in a file with the **dump** menu item. You can also view the defect list information on the screen with the **print** menu item.

```
defect> print
 num       cyl      hd       bfi       len      sec
   1        29       4      19584
   2        35       4      19008
   3        36       4      19008
   4        37       4      19008
   5        38       4      19008
   6        94       2        576
   7       174       4       4608
   8       175       4       4608
   9       176       4       4608
  10       177       4       4608
  11       342       3      29376
  12       358       6       6912
  13       616       4      23040
  14       805       6      18432
  15       881       6       3456
  16       881       6       4032
  17       911       6       2880
  18      1077       6       2304
  19      1078       6       2304
  20      1079       6       2304
  21      1080       6       2304
total of 21 defects.

defect> dump
Enter name of defect file: /tmp/disk.bads
defect file updated, total of 21 defects.

defect> █
```

Viewing and saving the defect list with the print and dump commands.

format's backup Menu

The **backup** menu selection is used to look for backup copies of the disk label. This can be particularly useful on drives on which the primary label has somehow been damaged. If the primary label is intact, **format** will notify you and ask if you still wish to search for backup labels. Once a valid label is found, the backup command will write this label to the disk.

*Using the format
utility backup
command to
restore the drive
label.*

```
format> backup
Disk has a primary label, still continue? y
Searching for backup labels...found.
Restoring primary label.

format> []
```

format's verify Menu

The **verify** menu selection searches the disk for a valid label. Once the label is found, verify displays this information on the screen.

*Using the format
utility to verify the
disk label.*

```
format> verify

Primary label contents:

ascii name  = <SUN0207 cyl 1254 alt 2 hd 9 sec 36>
pcyl        = 1272
ncyl        = 1254
acyl        =    2
nhead       =    9
nsect       =   36
Part       Tag    Flag    Cylinders       Size          Blocks
  0       root     wm      0 -  101      16.14MB       (102/0/0)
  1       swap     wu    102 -  303      31.96MB       (202/0/0)
  2       backup   wu      0 - 1253     198.39MB       (1254/0/0)
  3 unassigned     wm      0               0           (0/0/0)
  4 unassigned     wm      0               0           (0/0/0)
  5 unassigned     wm      0               0           (0/0/0)
  6        usr     wm    304 - 1253     150.29MB       (950/0/0)
  7 unassigned     wm      0               0           (0/0/0)

format> []
```

format's save Menu

The **save** menu selection saves the current setup and partitioning information to the system */etc/format.dat* file. The user is given the choice to select another file to save this information to.

*Using the format
utility to save the
partition
information.*

```
format> save
Saving new partition definition
Enter file name["./format.dat"]: ./format.dat
format> []
```

format's inquiry Menu

The **inquiry** menu selection probes the disk drive and displays the vendor name, product, and firmware revision level of the current disk.

Using the format utility inquiry command.

```
format> inquiry
Vendor:   QUANTUM
Product:  PD210S    SUN0207
Revision: 4925
format> []
```

format's volname Menu

The **volname** menu selection allows you to create a volume name for the drive. Once you have set the volume name, the volname command writes the volume name to the current drive.

```
format> volname
Enter 8-character volume name (remember quotes)["5.3-root"]: "5.3-root"
Ready to label disk, continue? y

format> []
```

Using the format utility volname command.

format's format Command

Once you have performed all of the setup and customization that you desire for the disk, you are ready to format the drive. This is accomplished with the **format** menu selection on the main menu.

The format menu selection is used to start the format process. This will cause the system to issue the **format-unit** command (for IPI and SCSI drives), or to begin writing format information to the disk drive via program control for SMD disk drives. Once the formatting is complete, the format utility will run a few passes of surface analysis on the drive. Once the surface analysis is complete, a geometry label is written to the disk and control is switched back to the format utility main menu.

```
format> format
Ready to format.  Formatting cannot be interrupted.
Continue? y
Beginning format. The current time is Mon Oct 17 10:34:14 1994

Formatting...
done

Verifying media...
        pass 0 - pattern = 0xc6dec6de
    1253/7/0

            pass 1 - pattern = 0x6db6db6d
    1253/7/0

Total of 0 defective blocks repaired.
format> []
```

The format utility format menu.

format's quit Menu

The **quit** menu selection exits the format utility back to the super-user shell prompt.

Using the format utility quit command to return to the shell.

```
format> quit
#
```

Creating File Systems

Now that you have formatted a disk, you need to bind the sectors in each partition into file systems. You can accomplish this with the **newfs** utility.

The **newfs** utility is a front-end program to the **mkfs** program. Newfs allows the system administrator to create file systems with default parameters. Newfs also allows you to customize file system setup parameters if you desire. The newfs command creates the file system super-blocks, divides the file system into several cylinder groups, and takes care of creating all of the file system substructures required by the operating system.

```
# newfs /dev/rdsk/c1t3d0s2
newfs: construct a new file system /dev/rdsk/c1t3d0s2: (y/n)? y
/dev/rdsk/c1t3d0s2:     406296 sectors in 1254 cylinders of 9 tracks, 36 sectors
        198.4MB in 79 cyl groups (16 c/g, 2.53MB/g, 1216 i/g)
super-block backups (for fsck -F ufs -o b=#) at:
 32, 5264, 10496, 15728, 20960, 26192, 31424, 36656, 41888,
 47120, 52352, 57584, 62816, 68048, 73280, 78512, 82976, 88208,
 93440, 98672, 103904, 109136, 114368, 119600, 124832, 130064, 135296,
 140528, 145760, 150992, 156224, 161456, 165920, 171152, 176384, 181616,
 186848, 192080, 197312, 202544, 207776, 213008, 218240, 223472, 228704,
 233936, 239168, 244400, 248864, 254096, 259328, 264560, 269792, 275024,
 280256, 285488, 290720, 295952, 301184, 306416, 311648, 316880, 322112,
 327344, 331808, 337040, 342272, 347504, 352736, 357968, 363200, 368432,
 373664, 378896, 384128, 389360, 394592, 399824, 405056,
#
```

Using newfs to create file systems.

The newfs utility will report several useful facts to you as it operates. The size of the partition is reported along with the file system structure. Newfs will also report the locations of the backup super-blocks for the partition. These backup superblocks are allocated one per cylinder group within the partition. Newfs also reports the file system parameters used for the creation of this partition. For more information on the structure of the file system and the operation of the newfs and mkfs commands, consult the hardcopy Solaris documentation concerning the Berkeley Fast File system.

Once you have created a file system on a disk drive, it is best to use the **fsck** program to check the file system consistency. If errors are encountered by the fsck program, you need to check that you have not inadvertently created overlapping partitions, or incorrectly formatted the disk in some other fashion. If fsck does not find problems with the file system structure, you can proceed on to the next stage of the installation process.

Once you have a clean file system, the next step in the process of making the disk space available to the users is to mount the file system. You can edit the */etc/vfstab* file to add this partition to the system tables. You will need to provide the disk address information, the name of the file system (mount point), the tags and flags information, and the file system type information for each partition you add to the */etc/vfstab* file. The file contents of a typical */etc/vfstab* follow.

```
# cat /etc/vfstab
#device             device    mount     FS     fsck    mount    mount
#to mount           to fsck   point     type   pass    at boot  options
#
#/dev/dsk/c1d0s2  /dev/rdsk/cd1d0s2  /usr  ufs  1       yes      -
/proc                          /proc     proc   -       no       -
fd                   -         /dev/fd   fd     -       no       -
swap                 -         /tmp      tmpfs  -       yes      -
```

Typical /etc/vfstab file contents.

```
/dev/dsk/c0t3d0s0  /dev/rdsk/c0r3d0s0  /      ufs  1    no
-
/dev/dsk/c0t3d0s6  /dev/rdsk/c0t3d0s6  /usr   ufs  2    no
-
/dev/dsk/c0t3d0s3  /dev/rdsk/c0t3dos3  /var   ufs  4    no
-
/dev/dsk/c0t3d0s7  /dev/rdsk/c0t3dos7  /home  ufs  5    yes
-
/dev/dsk/cot3d0s5  /dev/rdsk/c0t3dos5  /opt   ufs  6    yes
-
/dev/dsk/cot3d0s4  /dev/rdsk/c0r3d0s4  /usr/openwin ufs 7
yes
/dev/dsk/c0t3d0s1              swap                  no
#
```

Once you have finished editing the file, you need to make sure that the mount point exists by doing a **mkdir mount_point**. This will make the directory used as the mount point for the file system. When you have completed this task, you need to reboot the system so that the new file system can be checked and mounted by the operating system. Alternately, you could mount the file system manually with the **mount** command.

Tuning Space Usage with the newfs Command

The **newfs** command is used to bind sectors on a drive together into a file system. The newfs utility is a user-friendly front-end program to the **mkfs** utility which does all of the work. Mkfs is a command line driven program which allows you to build partitions of arbitrary size. By selecting the right arguments to the mkfs command, you can tune the drives for optimum performance or optimum space available.

If you use default newfs parameters when creating a new file system, you will typically lose 10% of the usable disk space on the partition. Part of the space loss is due to the amount of over-subscription space which is reserved. The newfs command will allow you to alter the amount of space reserved for over-subscription storage.

The newfs utility also allows you to tune the number of copies of alternate super-blocks, and several other parameters which affect the amount of storage space consumed by the partitioning process.

Refer to Chapter 13 for more information on using newfs to tune file system overhead and performance parameters.

Recognizing Failing Disks

Over time all disk drives will experience a failure of one sort or another. What are the symptoms of a failing disk drive? Is there anything you can do to ward off such failures? Once you see the telltale signs of an impending failure, what can you do to avoid catastrophe?

Most disk drive failures are not characterized by immediate catastrophic failure. A more typical failure will be for bad spots to appear gradually until the system can no longer read/write major portions of the drive. The system will usually print messages on the console terminal informing you of the problem.

In many cases, bad spots on the disk surface can be read without losing data because the disk drive contains logic to detect and correct multi-bit information errors. As the system encounters these spots, you will be informed via console error messages that a retryable error has been encountered. This means that the system had to try several times to read a portion of the disk. These errors are called *retries*. System administrators may not become concerned if they notice retry errors that do not occur frequently. A few soft errors are to be expected from time to time. If the errors become more frequent, the administrator needs to study the problem before it becomes worse.

Sometimes a bad spot appears that cannot be read by the system. The drive logic that detects and corrects these errors also fails to correct the errors on such a bad spot. In this case the system will report that it has encountered fatal disk errors. Whenever a fatal disk error is reported, you should be very concerned about the integrity of the files on the disk drive. Steps must be taken to rectify the problem, or your users' data may be destroyed.

Typical retryable disk error message.

```
                              xterm
WARNING: /sbus@1,f8000000/esp@0,800000/sd@3,0 (sd3):
         Error for command 'read'          Error Level: Retryable

WARNING: /sbus@1,f8000000/esp@0,800000/sd@3,0 (sd3):
         Error for command 'read'          Error Level: Retryable

WARNING: /sbus@1,f8000000/esp@0,800000/sd@3,0 (sd3):
         Error for command 'write'         Error Level: Fatal
```

✘ *TIP: With SCSI disk systems, one common failure mode is due to loose connections or faulty terminators. It often pays to check all cable connections, power supplies, and terminators before you replace a drive.*

Repairing Damaged Disks

You have several courses of action that you can follow when you suspect a disk is failing. The basic procedure for repairing bad disks follows:

- ❏ Reboot the system to determine if the failure is due to corrupted system information.
- ❏ If you know the block number of the bad spot, use the repair portion of the **format** utility to map out a bad spot on the drive.
- ❏ If there are several bad spots on the drive, use the **analyze** portion of the **format** utility to perform non-destructive surface analysis of the drive to search for and optionally repair bad spots.
- ❏ Reformat the defective disk. You must remember to perform a file system backup of all file systems on the drive before you reformat it. Many times a simple reformat will allow you to put the drive back into operation.
- ❏ Replace the drive with a known good drive. Copy all of your data to the new drive. Note that this option can be time-consuming and expensive.

If you notice that a disk drive is generating many error messages on a few disk blocks, you may wish to repair the bad spots with the format utility **repair** command. This will mark the bad spot as unusable so that the system will not attempt to access this sector in the future. The repair facility will also "map" this bad spot to a spare sector on the disk drive, and copy the data from the bad spot to the replacement sector.

Using repair to fix a bad spot on a disk.

```
format> repair
Enter block number of defect: 1479788
Ready to repair defect, continue? y
Repairing block 1479788  (676/16/80)...done
```

In some cases, the system cannot recover the data from a bad spot on the disk. In this case, the system will inform you that it has encountered a fatal error. If you attempt to repair such a sector, quite often the repair facility cannot recover the data from this sector. The bad spot will be mapped out, but the file which contained the bad sector may be destroyed by the mapping process.

```
format> repair
Enter block number of defect: 1488457
Ready to repair defect, continue? y
Block 1488460  (680/16/4), Fatal media error (header not found) during read
Warning: unable to save track data.
Block 1488526  (680/16/70), Fatal media error (header not found) during write
Warning: unable to save track data.
Repairing block 1488457  (680/16/1)...done

format> ▮
```

Repairing a fatal error with the repair command.

If you do not know the block number of the bad spot, or if there appear to be multiple bad spots on the disk, you can use the format utility **analyze** facility to find and repair the errors.

```
analyze> read
Ready to analyze (won't harm SunOS). This takes a long time,
but is interruptable with CTRL-C. Continue? y

      pass 0
Block 1425054  (651/16/21), Fatal media error (header not found) during read
Repairing...succeeded.

Block 1433798  (655/16/17), Fatal media error (header not found) during read
Warning: unable to save track data.
succeeded.

Block 1436028  (656/16/60), Corrected non-media error (soft retry) during read
succeeded.

Block 1435979  (656/16/11), Fatal media error (header not found) during read
Repairing...Warning: unable to save defective data for blkno 1435979.
succeeded.

Total of 4 defective blocks repaired.
analyze>
```

Using analyze to locate and repair bad spots on a disk.

If **analyze** continues to find errors, you may decide to replace the disk drive with a new one. If you have another drive that is the same model and geometry as the failed disk, you can use a simple shell script to copy files from a failing drive to a new drive. A sample of using dd to copy files between disks follows.

```
# cat /home/mercury/curt/tools/diskcopy
# l /bin/csh
# list the partition (slice) numbers to be copied in the parenthesis
# then run this shell file.

foreach i (0 6)
   echo "Copying partition $i from drive 0 to drive 2"
   dd if_/dev/rdsk/c0t0d0s"$i" of_/dev/rdsk/c0t2d0s"$i" bs_1006
   fsck /dev/rdsk/c0t2d0s"$i"
   echo "Partition $i is now copied to the new drive"
   echo ""
end
echo "Copy complete.  Halt the system, remove the bad drive"
echo "change the SCSI ID of the new drive, and reboot the system"
echo "with boot. -r"

# diskcopy
Copying partition 0 from drive 0 to drive 2
** /dev/rdsk/c0t2d0s0
** Last Mounted on /
** Phase 1 - Check Blocks and Sizes
** Phase 2 - Check Pathnames
** Phase 3 - Check Connectivity
** Phase 4 - Check Reference Counts
** Phase 5 - Check Cyl groups
2791 files, 18176 used, 12815 free (343 frags, 1559 blocks, 1.1% fragmentation)
Partition 0 is now copied to the new drive

Copying partition 6 from drive 0 to drive 2
** /dev/rdsk/c0t2d0s0
** Last Mounted on /usr
** Phase 1 - Checks Blocks and Sizes
** Phase 2 - Check Pathnames
** Phase 3 - Check Connectivity
** Phase 4 - Check Reference Counts
** Phase 5 - Check Cyl groups
9812 files, 74988 used, 21259 free (779 frags, 2560 blocks, 0.8% fragmentation)
Partition 6 is now copied to the new drive

Copy complete.  Halt the system, remove the bad drive
change the SCSI ID of the new drive, and reboot the system
with boot. -r
#
```

Using dd to copy files between disks.

If the new disk drive is a different model, or if the geometry of the failing disk differs from that of the new disk, you will need to dump the failing drive to tape. Once you have a current dump of the failing disk you can remove it from the system. You then restore the file system contents to the new drive from your dump tape.

If the **analyze** facility locates a large number of bad spots on the disk, you may decide that it is prudent to reformat the entire disk. If you reformat, you must ensure that you have tapes containing current file system dumps of the failing disk. Once you reformat the drive you will reload the file systems from the dump tapes.

Load Balancing Disk Farms

Some file servers are used to provide large disk storage spaces for other systems on the network. These servers and their disk systems are sometimes referred to as *disk farms*. Such systems typically have several disk interfaces and many disk drives on each interface. In order to provide for maximum performance of these disk farms, a little detective work may be necessary.

In most instances, disk farms are set up to provide for high speed access to important information. Some typical applications may include database systems, medical images, and other space intensive informational services. In these situations, the system administrator may need to tune these file systems for best performance by using **newfs** or **mkfs**.

In a few instances, the disk farm is used for long term archival storage. Because the information on these systems is not accessed very often, high performance is not always the driving criteria in file system tuning. In these cases, the system administrator would use newfs or mkfs to tune the file systems for storage space availability instead of tuning for performance criteria.

If you suspect poor performance of a disk farm, it often pays to monitor the access frequency of each disk on the system. From the data collected, you may be able to determine which disk(s) are being heavily used. In many cases, several heavily used disks may reside on the same disk interface. If you can separate those disks onto separate disk interfaces you may be able to increase system performance.

Disk Mirroring and Striping

If you are providing a disk farm service with your server, you may wish to consider alternate technology for your disk subsystem. One increasingly popular technology is Redundant Array of Inexpensive Disks (RAID). RAID disk arrays consist of an SCSI interface, a specialized controller, and an array of disk drives. RAID systems come with specialized software to control and administer the operation of the disk array. All of the standard Solaris commands work for the RAID disk array, as the driver software takes care of the interface to the RAID subsystem.

RAID disk systems allow you to provide for high-throughput, high-availability disk I/O subsystems. When you use RAID technology, you will have several new options to consider in the I/O subsystem design and implementation. Instead of attempting to implement a RAID subsystem, let's look at the terminology and technology available to you.

RAID I/O subsystems provide you with several "levels" of service. Each RAID level describes a different method of data storage on the disk drive(s). Each level has unique characteristics, and some of these levels are more suitable to certain applications than other I/O implementations.

The most frequently encountered RAID implementations follow:

❑ **RAID LEVEL 0** implements a striped disk array. This array will contain several disk drives. The data is broken down into small segments, and each data segment is written to a separate disk drive. This improves disk I/O performance by spreading the I/O load across many channels and drives. A striped disk does not offer data redundancy, nor does it offer better fault tolerance than a standard I/O subsystem.

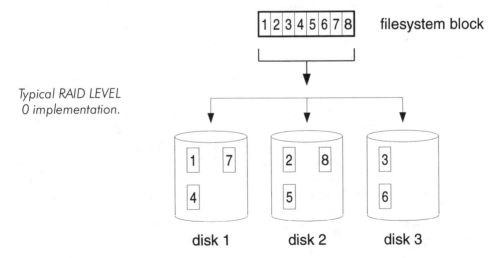

Typical RAID LEVEL 0 implementation.

❑ **RAID LEVEL 1** implements a mirrored disk array. This array will contain two disk modules. The information written to one disk is also written (mirrored) to the other disk. This ensures that the data is available even if one of the disk drives fails. RAID level 1 offers better data availability, but does not offer high-throughput I/O subsystem performance. It is possible to mirror a striped disk array, thereby providing better I/O performance as well as high data availability. The primary disadvantage of using RAID level 1 is the cost of purchasing duplicate disk drives.

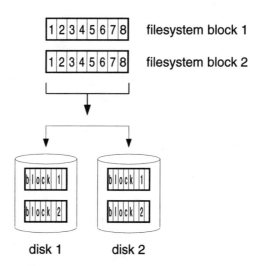

Typical RAID LEVEL 1 implementation.

❑ **RAID LEVEL 2** interleaves data sectors across many disks. The controller breaks up the blocks, and spreads them over a small group of disk drives. An error detection and correction process is built into RAID level 2 systems to provide some measure of fault tolerance. RAID level 2 is not found on many systems, as other RAID levels offer better performance and fault tolerance.

❑ **RAID LEVEL 3** interleaves data sectors across many disks much like RAID level 2. But RAID level 3 uses a single parity disk per group of drives to implement a fault-tolerant disk system. All of the drive spindles are synchronized such that the read/write heads on all drives in the array are active at the same time. This synchronization also ensures that the data is written to the same sector on every drive in the array. If a disk fails, the system continues to operate by recreating the data from the failed disk to the parity disk.

❑ **RAID LEVEL 4** implements striping with the addition of a parity disk. This provides for some of the fault tolerance missing in RAID level 0. RAID level 4 is not found on many systems, as other RAID levels can provide for better throughput and fault tolerance.

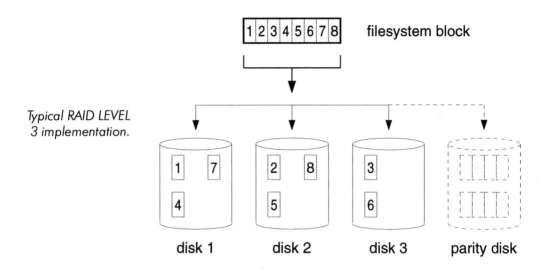

Typical RAID LEVEL 3 implementation.

❑ **RAID LEVEL 5** implements a large disk storage array. Similar to a level 0 RAID array, the disk array uses striping to improve system performance. RAID level 5 also implements a parity protection scheme. This scheme allows the system to continue operation even if one of the disk drives in the array fails. The data that is normally stored on the failed drive is re-created from the parity information stored elsewhere in the array. Once the failed disk drive is replaced, the data is restored automatically by the RAID controller. RAID LEVEL 5 provides improved system availability and I/O subsystem throughput.

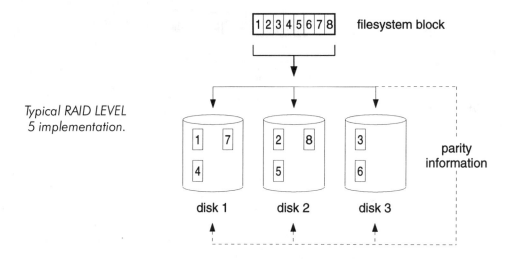

Typical RAID LEVEL 5 implementation.

Hardware solutions are not the only means of implementing disk mirroring and striping. Some software vendors offer applications packages that allow standard SCSI disks connected to standard SCSI controllers to act as a disk array. One such package is Sun Microsystems' *OnLine: Disk Suite.*

Summary

In this chapter we looked at one of the most critical subsystems of a Solaris system. You learned how to install a new disk drive, how to format and partition a disk drive, and how to recognize a failing disk drive. We also examined a few simple methods to repair a failing disk drive, and alternate technologies that allow you to provide faster, more fault-tolerant disk I/O subsystems for your users' data.

In the following chapters, we will revisit some of these topics as you learn more advanced troubleshooting and management techniques.

✗   ***TIP:*** *One of the simplest ways to breathe new life into a sluggish system is to add disk space and disk I/O channels. This allows you to disperse the I/O load of the system across more channels and devices, and to reduce the load on existing devices.*

Working with Local File Systems

Once you have installed and formatted a new disk, the next order of business is to add the disk's storage capacity to your Solaris system by creating one or more file systems on it. In this chapter we will describe a file system and examine the various types of file systems. Next, we will discuss methods for adding file systems to the UNIX file tree for displaying information about file systems, repairing damaged file systems, and tuning file systems to improve performance. It is assumed that you have read Chapters 11 and 12 and are comfortable with Solaris device names. For purposes of review, the steps involved in bringing a drive to life on your system are as follows:

1. Connect the disk, controller, etc. to the system and check for operation.

2. Format the disk to provide mapping of good and bad disk blocks.

3. Partition the disk to allocate collections of disk blocks to different purposes.

4. Create a file system within each disk partition to be used.

5. Arrange for the created file system to be mounted or made part of the UNIX file tree.

The first three steps have already been covered in the previous chapters. We are now ready to focus on the last two steps.

Working with File Systems

As you already know, the UNIX operating system presents a single unified view of the available disk space on your system in the form of the UNIX file tree. This tree is distinguished from a directory tree (a sub-part of the overall tree) in that it always begins at root or / directory and covers the entire collection of files found in all directories below this root directory. The file tree spans multiple file systems of varying types, multiple disks, and multiple partitions on the same disk so that boundaries of file systems, partitions and disks—even remote disks in the case of NFS—are invisible to most programs and users. Appearing in the next illustration is a portion of the UNIX file tree as seen from the File Manager's folder view option. This view shows the portion of the tree leading down into the */dev* directory.

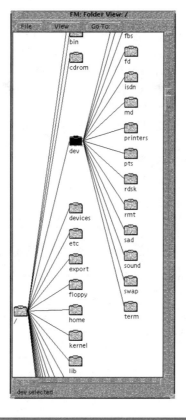

A portion of the UNIX file tree.

Using Mountpoints

At selected spots called "mount points," the file tree spans from one file system to the next. If you were to outline one such division, it may resemble the following illustration.

A file tree spanning four file systems.

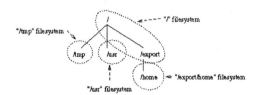

File systems are often referred to by the names of their mount points. One could say the system shown in the above example has a /, a */tmp*, a */usr* and a */export/home* file system. Not all of these file systems are of the same type. Solaris supports a variety of file system types which can be mounted as part of the overall file tree.

File System Types Supported by Solaris

Type	Hardware Medium	Description
ufs	hard disk	Standard UNIX file system, uses BSD UNIX fast file system format.
hsfs	CD-ROM	High Sierra or ISO 9660 file system, the standard file system for CD-ROMs, can only be mounted as read-only.
pcfs	floppy disk	MS-DOS file system, allows direct mounting of DOS disks, and has standard MS-DOS file and directory name length restrictions.
nfs	remote disk via network	Standard for sharing disks via the network between Solaris systems and many other systems including VMS, other UNIX systems, PCs and Macintoshes.

Type	Hardware Medium	Description
tmpfs	memory/swap area	A special purpose, high performance file system designed for temporary data, typically used for /tmp, it is destroyed and recreated each time system is rebooted.
cachefs	hard disk and remote disk via network	A special, performance enhancing file system type which caches files from CD-ROMs or nfs disks on a local disk.
lofs	loopback	A special purpose file system type which allows for a file system to be mounted in several places.
procfs	memory	A special purpose file system type which allows debuggers and other program development tools access to the address space of a process by using file entries.

The first five file system types listed—ufs, hsfs, pcfs, nfs and tmpfs—are the most commonly used. In the example diagram showing the UNIX file tree and file system mount points, the */tmp* file system was of the *tmpfs* type, while the other file systems were of the *ufs* type. This is a fairly common situation for a stand-alone workstation. A workstation on a network may be more complex with many types of file systems.

Procfs is similar in concept to the access to devices provided by the file entries in the */dev* directory. The files found in a *procfs* file system are entries which map the address space of a process into a file. Opening one of these files allows you to read directly from the address space of a running process. This is used by certain debugging tools as a method for observing and changing the behavior of a process while it is running.

Swapfs is a special file system used by the SunOS kernel for paging and swapping. It will be explained in greater detail shortly.

The file tree of a networked workstation.

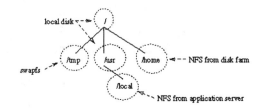

In this example, the workstation shown is "dataless," that is, it has a local disk for programs, but mounts remote disks via NFS to store data. This entire collection of local and remote disks of various types is spanned by the UNIX file tree and appears to a user of this workstation as one seamless tree. You can view the file systems, their mount points and other information by using several different commands. The first is the **mount** command. When run without arguments, this command lists mounted file systems by their mount points, showing the device mounted at each mount point, the mount options used, and the time the file system was mounted. An example follows:

```
glenn% /usr/sbin/mount
/ on /dev/dsk/c0t3d0s0 read/write/setuid on Tue Aug 9 05:58:19
1994
/usr on /dev/dsk/c0t3d0s6 read/write/setuid on Tue Aug 9
05:58:19 1994
/proc on /proc read/write/setuid on Tue Aug 9 05:58:19 1994
/dev/fd on fd read/write/setuid on Tue Aug 9 05:58:19 1994
/tmp on swap read/write on Tue Aug 9 05:58:23 1994
/opt on /dev/dsk/c0t3d0s5 setuid/read/write on Tue Aug 9
05:58:24 1994
glenn%
```

A more common way to look at the file systems mounted on your system is to use the **df** command. This command offers several different ways of displaying information about file systems. You can restrict the information to a single file system by giving a directory in that file system as the last argument to the df command. Running the command with no argument results in the display of information for all mounted file systems.

```
glenn% df
/              (/dev/dsk/c0t3d0s0):11690 blocks9292 files
/usr           (/dev/dsk/c0t3d0s6):786776 blocks322309 files
/proc          (/proc):0 blocks204 files
/dev/fd        (fd):0 blocks0 files
/tmp           (swap):218816 blocks3288 files
/opt           (/dev/dsk/c0t3d0s5):91236 blocks73801 files
glenn%
```

The list produced by df shows the mount point, the device mounted in parentheses, the number of free 512-byte disk blocks, and the number of free files that can be created on the file system. When you give df a directory argument, the output changes as follows:

```
glenn% df /
File system        kbytes    used    ava il capacity    Mounted on
/dev/dsk/c0t3d0s0  20664     14819   3785      80%       /
glenn%
```

This listing shows the device name first, followed by the total, used, and available space in 1024-byte (kbyte) units, the percentage of the file system already in use, and finally, the mount point. To see this listing for all the file systems, use the **-k** option flag with no directory argument. The most complete listing is obtained by using the **-g** option. This option formats and displays the *statvfs* structure, which details some of the parameters used to create the file system and provides a complete description of the space available. This option flag can be used with or without a directory argument to display all file systems or just one file system.

```
glenn% df -g /
/    (/dev/dsk/c0t3d0s0):8192 block size1024 frag size
41328 total blocks11690 free blocks7570 available11520 total
files
9292 free files8388632 filesys id
ufs fstype    0x00000004 flag255 file name length
glenn%
```

> ✔ **NOTE:** *There are three different "block" sizes which will be discussed in this chapter. It is important to keep them straight. A "disk block" is the basic unit of storage on the physical medium. This unit is often 512 bytes long, but not always. An "allocation block" is the basic unit of space in a file system. It is either 8192 or 4096 bytes in size. A "fragment," often 1024 bytes in size, is a portion of an allocation block.*

Swapfs

The *swapfs* type needs a bit more explanation. SunOS, like many modern versions of UNIX, manages memory through a system of fixed-size units called "pages." Program instructions and data are broken up into pages and loaded into memory wherever free pages exist. The operating system, by means of a page table and special memory management hardware, presents a linear memory map to each process even though the instructions and data that make up that process may be scattered throughout memory.

Virtual memory is the process by which physical memory is extended by moving pages which have not be recently referenced out of memory and on to disk. This process of moving program instructions and data in and out of memory is called "paging." The *swapfs* file system is used by SunOS to store pages that are not currently in use. Because of its special usage, a swapfs file system does not appear in the UNIX file tree, and the disk space consumed by swapfs file systems does not appear in the output of commands such as df.

Using the Swap Command

To determine the disk space in use by swapfs file systems, you need to use the **/usr/sbin/swap** command. This command can read and interpret the contents of a swapfs file system and report back on its size and current usage. An example appears in the following illustration.

```
┌─────────────────────── cmdtool – /bin/csh ───────────────────────┐
│ glenn% /usr/sbin/swap -l                                          │
│ swapfile          dev   swaplo blocks   free                      │
│ /dev/dsk/c0t3d0s1     32,25      8 262384 229696                  │
│ glenn% /usr/sbin/swap -s                                          │
│ total: 18304k bytes allocated + 6136k reserved = 24440k used, 113460k available │
│ glenn%                                                            │
└───────────────────────────────────────────────────────────────────┘
```

The two reporting options of the swap command.

The first form of the **swap** command using the **-l** option gives the size of the *swapfs* file system in 512-byte disk blocks along with its current usage, offset, SunOS device name, and major and minor device numbers. The second form is more frequently used. The **-s** option lists current usage by detailing the amount of space allocated, the space claimed for usage by SunOS but not currently being used, the total of those two values, and the amount of unused space. This form of the swap command is often used to help determine how much swapfs space is needed by a system when running certain programs.

How much swap space does your system require? The longstanding "swap space rule of thumb" is two to four times the system memory (RAM). During system installation, Solaris 2 creates a swap area (slice 1 of the system disk) three times the size of memory. This default configuration is considered adequate for Solaris systems running general use applications such as desktop publishing. A host with 32 Mb of memory, therefore, would have a 96 Mb swap area. The host's total virtual memory would be 128 Mb (32 Mb of RAM + 96 Mb of swap).

✔   *NOTE: Solaris 2 requires a minimum 32 Mb of virtual memory.*

More (or less) swap area may be appropriate depending on the applications running on the system. Computer-aided design (CAD) software, for example, is notorious for consuming large quantities of memory. Consult the software installation guide that accompanies third-party software for swap space requirements.

✘   *TIP: If your system requires additional swap space, you can create swap files or swap partitions and direct Solaris to add these to the total system virtual memory using the* **swap** *command with the* **-a** *option.*

Finding the exact amount of swap space for a certain usage mix can only be done by experimenting on a system and using tools such as the **swap** command to examine the swap space consumption.

✘   *TIP: If you are installing a number of workstations for similar tasks, configure one workstation, load the proposed software packages, and measure the swap space used. A little time to experiment can save a lot of time later on by avoiding the need to repartition disks.*

Creating File Systems

Except in special cases, a file system is required before you can use a disk drive with Solaris. The act of creating a file system puts a framework on the disk itself which enables Solaris to store files there. In addition, the new file system is added to the UNIX file tree. The file system framework provides index information for the disk blocks which were initialized and mapped when the disk was formatted.

Working with the Floppy Disk

A good way to experiment with file system creation is to work with a floppy disk. The floppy disk is small enough that file systems can be created quickly, and various commands and options can be tried and tested without the need to have a spare hard disk.

 NOTE: In all examples that follow, another disk device can be substituted for /dev/rdiskette. Typically, this will be the device associated with a particular disk slice or partition such as /dev/rdsk/c2t3d0s4 or /dev/dsk/c2t3d0s4. If you are unfamiliar with the disk device naming scheme, refer to the previous chapter.

Stopping the Volume Manager

The floppy disk drive on a Solaris system is usually under the control of the volume manager which we will address shortly. For the moment, we will disable the volume manager and directly work with the floppy drive. We do this just as the **init** process would, that is, by running the **/etc/init.d/volmgt** script with the **stop** option. When you are finished using the floppy device, volume management can be restarted by running the /etc/init.d/volmgt script with the **start** option.

 *NOTE: For this and most of the operations that follow, you will need root privileges. Either log in as root or use the **su** command to become root.*

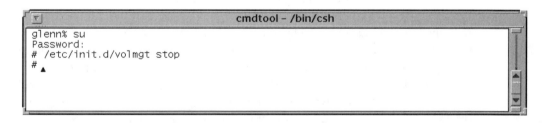

Stopping the volume manager.

Working with the newfs Command

The *ufs* type file systems are most often created using the **newfs** command. This command consults the same */etc/format.dat* file used by the **format** command and the disk's own label to find out the specifications for the disk and builds the appropriate file system. By using the newfs **-N** option we can see the basic parameters of the file system that newfs would build on a floppy disk without actually creating the file system.

```
                          cmdtool - /bin/csh
# newfs -N /dev/rdiskette
/dev/rdiskette: 2880 sectors in 80 cylinders of 2 tracks, 18 sectors
        1.4MB in 5 cyl groups (16 c/g, 0.28MB/g, 128 i/g)
super-block backups (for fsck -F ufs -o b=#) at:
 32, 640, 1184, 1792, 2336,
 #
```

Viewing file system parameters.

The first line printed by newfs describes the basic disk geometry. This floppy disk is two-sided (2 tracks), and has 18 sectors and 80 cylinders for a total of 2880 sectors or blocks. The */dev/rdiskette* entry in the */dev* directory is a link to the raw device entry in the */devices* directory for the *c* slice of the floppy disk. The c slice, by convention, encompasses the entire disk.

What is a c slice? Under Solaris, different regions of the disk are called slices. The slices that a disk is partitioned into can overlap and are not all used at the same time. Slices are numbered for most hard disk devices. However, the floppy device uses an older convention of naming slices with letters. This convention held that the third or c slice would be sized to encompass the entire disk.

A raw device is unbuffered and directly accesses the structure of the device. In this case, the */dev/rdiskette* entry allows direct access to the whole floppy disk. The second line describes the *ufs* file system created in this space. It is 1.4 Mb in size, containing 5 cylinder groups of 16 cylinders per group. Cylinder groups are derived from the Berkeley UNIX fast file system; they are a method by which file blocks are allocated close together on the disk to improve performance. Varying the size of these groups is one way to tune the performance of a *ufs* file system.

The final two lines list the locations of the *super-block* backups. The super-block is the head of the file index node or *inode* information used by the *ufs* file system routines in the Solaris kernel to allocate, read, write, and delete files. Backup copies of these super-blocks are created in case a system crash, power failure, or other problem occurs which leaves the main copy of the super-block damaged. The **fsck** program mentioned here is a file system checking and repair tool which will be discussed in greater detail later.

How newfs Connects to mkfs

When you execute the **newfs** command it invokes the **mkfs** command which does the actual building of the file system on the target device, or the floppy in this case. The mkfs command has a long list of parameters. For most applications a detailed knowledge of the mkfs parameters is unnecessary; newfs makes proper choices for the parameters it passes to mkfs. However, it is useful to know the parameters so that you can modify them to fit special applications which may need specialized adjustments to a file system. For example, you may need a file system tuned to store a large quantity of small, frequently changing files such as those found in the Usenet *net-news* system. Such a file system would require more index nodes or *inodes* than the default options used by newfs. Situations that require manual modification of mkfs parameters are covered in more detail in the section of this chapter on file system optimization. For now, use the **-v** option flag with newfs to see which parameters it passes to mkfs. Here we will use the **-N** option as well to look at the parameters without actually making the file system.

```
                         cmdtool – /bin/csh
# newfs -N -v /dev/rdiskette
mkfs -F ufs -o N /dev/rdiskette 2880 18 2 8192 1024 16 10 5 2048 t 0 -1 8 -1
/dev/rdiskette: 2880 sectors in 80 cylinders of 2 tracks, 18 sectors
        1.4MB in 5 cyl groups (16 c/g, 0.28MB/g, 128 i/g)
super-block backups (for fsck -F ufs -o b=#) at:
 32, 640, 1184, 1792, 2336,
#
```

Viewing the mkfs parameters with the -v and -N options.

Some of the parameters should look familiar. You can change many of these parameters by using an option flag to newfs instead of manually running mkfs. The following table lists each option reading from left to right across the mkfs command line. The first column lists the mkfs parameter, the second column lists the newfs option flag used to modify the parameter, and the third column describes the parameter.

newfs to mkfs Options Cross-reference

mkfs Parameter	newfs Option Flag	Description
-F ufs		Indicates the type of file system to be created.
-o N	-N	The -N option being passed down to mkfs indicating that it should not actually create the file system but only report on what it would do.
/dev/rdiskette		The raw disk device for the slice in which the file system is to be created.
2880	-s	The total size of the file system in disk blocks.
18		The number of sectors per track.
2	-t	The number of tracks per cylinder.
8192	-b	The size of the allocation block. This is a multiple of the size of the disk's physical block. The size shown is matched to the usual size of a single disk read or write operation.
1024	-f	The size of a "fragment." This storage unit allows for very small files to be packed together inside a single allocation block. It is the smallest amount of disk space allocated to a file.
16	-c	The number of cylinders per cylinder group. This can range from 1 to 32, with 16 being the default.
10	-m	The minimum free disk space. The Berkeley UNIX fast file system routines used by the SunOS kernel degrade in performance when a disk fills above 90% of full capacity. Thus, a minimum of 10% free space is usually set aside to ensure good performance.
5	-r	For mkfs this parameter lists the disk's rate of rotation in revolutions per second. However, the -r option to newfs *must* be specified in revolutions per *minute*. The newfs command converts this to revolutions per second when it passes the parameter to the mkfs command.

mkfs Parameter	newfs Option Flag	Description
2048	-i	The number of bytes to allocate per inode. Used when mkfs calculates how many inodes to create.
t	-o	The optimization method. There are two choices: *t* for time or speed with which a file can be written, or *s* for space or the efficiency with which files are placed on the disk to maximize the usage of scattered disk storage blocks.
0	-a	The number of alternate blocks per cylinder. Used with SCSI devices to reserve space to be used in case a disk block becomes unusable due to physical damage.

With these parameters in mind we can now create a file system by running newfs without the -N option. Since creation of a file system will destroy any index information on a disk slice and thereby render any files stored there inaccessible, newfs asks to be sure this is what you really want to do.

```
                         cmdtool - /bin/csh
# newfs -v /dev/rdiskette
newfs: construct a new file system /dev/rdiskette: (y/n)? y
mkfs -F ufs /dev/rdiskette 2880 18 2 8192 1024 16 10 5 2048 t 0 -1 8 -1
/dev/rdiskette: 2880 sectors in 80 cylinders of 2 tracks, 18 sectors
        1.4MB in 5 cyl groups (16 c/g, 0.28MB/g, 128 i/g)
super-block backups (for fsck -F ufs -o b=#) at:
 32, 640, 1184, 1792, 2336,
#
```

Creating a file system.

After asking permission, newfs runs mkfs to create the file system. The mkfs command reports the location of each of the super-block backups as it creates them. It lays down on the disk a set of index nodes (inodes) and the linked data structure used to access them. Typically, about 10% of the total data blocks available are also set aside to avoid the greatly reduced performance a *ufs* file system encounters as the last few data blocks are allocated.

The result of all of this index information and space setting aside is that a file system created with the default newfs parameters will be about 10% smaller than the size of the disk partition it was created in. When you partition a disk in preparation for creating a file system, take care to allow for this extra space. A method for calculating the size of a disk partition for a given file system size appears in the chapter on managing disks.

If mkfs reports an error, it usually means the disk has been improperly partitioned or perhaps it has been formatted incorrectly. The mkfs command expects a disk partition to contain a number of blocks which is an integer multiple of the number of blocks in a single disk cylinder. You may recall from the chapter on managing disks that a cylinder is the circular group of blocks found in a specific track on each of the platters that make up a disk. If your disk appears to be partitioned incorrectly, consult the managing disks chapter for help in correctly formatting and partitioning a disk.

Mounting File Systems

Once a file system has been created, it must be added to the UNIX file tree. To do this manually, you select or create an empty directory to act as a mount point and then use the **mount** command to place the root of the new file system at that mount point.

The mount command has several arguments. Here we will use its most simple form which mounts the file system for read and write access.

```
cmdtool - /bin/csh
# cd /
# mkdir /mnt
# mount /dev/diskette /mnt
#
```

Mounting a file system.

The mount command has several options which control the way in which a file system is mounted. The default action is to mount the file system and base its read and write access on the file permissions of the files in the file system. The mount command options take the following form: *mount -o option,option,...,option <file system>*.

Options are given as a list following the **-o** flag, separated by commas (e.g., mount -o rw,quota). Common options you might wish to use appear below.

Mount Command Options

Option	Description
quota	This option activates the user disk quota system when mounting the file system. Disk quotas allow for tight control over the disk space consumed by each user.
ro	Read only. This overrides the file permissions on any file on the file system and disables all write access.
nosuid	No setUID execution. This overrides the setUID permission on any file on the file system allowing normal execution with only the privileges of the user executing the program.

Unmounting a File System

The complement to mounting a file system is to unmount it. This is done using the **umount** command.

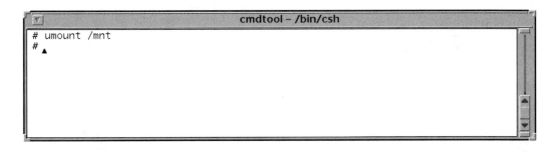

```
                          cmdtool – /bin/csh
# umount /mnt
#
```

Unmounting a file system.

Automatic Mounting

If you needed to type in the **mount** command each time you wanted to mount a disk, it would quickly get tiresome. Solaris has several methods for automating the mounting of disks as well as removing the need to be *root* when mounting removable disks such as floppies and CD-ROMs.

vfstab

One method, usually used with hard disks, is to add the file system to the */etc/vfstab* file. This file is read by the **mountall** command when it is run as part of the system boot sequence. The *vfstab* file lists file systems which are to be mounted when the system is booted. A quick way to add items to *vfstab* is to use the **-p** option to the mount command.

An example using our floppy disk file system follows. First, the file system will be mounted, then the current *vfstab* will be saved, and finally, the **mount** and **grep** commands will be used to append the mount instructions to the */etc/vfstab* file. Saving the current *vfstab* is good practice as it provides an easy way to recover from any mistakes you might make when adding new disks.

Adding a file system to /etc/vfstab.

```
                            cmdtool - /bin/csh
# mount /dev/diskette /mnt
# cp /etc/vfstab /etc/vfstab.old
# mount -p | grep disk
/dev/diskette - /mnt ufs - no suid,rw
# mount -p | grep disk >> /etc/vfstab
#
```

#device	device	mount	FS	fsck	mount	mount
#to mount	to fsck	point	type	pass	at boot	options
#						
#/dev/dsk/c1d0s2	/dev/rdsk/c1d0s2	/usr	ufs	1	yes	-
/proc	-	/proc	proc	-	no	-
fd	-	/dev/fd	fd	-	no	-
swap	-	/tmp	tmpfs	-	yes	-
/dev/dsk/c0t3d0s0	/dev/rdsk/c0t3d0s0	/	ufs	1	no	-
/dev/dsk/c0t3d0s6	/dev/rdsk/c0t3d0s6	/usr	ufs	2	no	-
/dev/dsk/c0t3d0s5	/dev/rdsk/c0t3d0s5	/opt	ufs	5	yes	-
/dev/dsk/c0t3d0s1	-	- swap	-	no	-	

You can also add entries to the *vfstab* file by editing it and entering the needed information by hand. The file format is described in the comment lines at the top of the file. The fields are separated by a tab or spaces. Fields and respective functions appear in the following table.

fstab Fields and Functions

Field name	Description
Device to mount	Lists the name of the device to be mounted. It is the same as the device name you would use in the mount command.
Device to fsck	Lists the name of the "raw" device which is used by the fsck command when checking the integrity of the file system structure. It is the same as the device name used when the file system is created with the newfs command.
Mount point	Directory at which the file system is to be added to the UNIX file tree.
FS type	Type of file system as described in the table near the beginning of this chapter.
fsck pass	Contains a number indicating the ordering method by which the file system will be checked.
Mount at boot	Most file systems are mounted at boot time with the exception of /, /usr, and /proc which are mounted as part of the SunOS initial start-up.
Mount options	Options given to the mount command. Most file systems are mounted with the default options.

The fsck Pass Field

UNIX file systems (ufs) are the only file systems that the File System Checker (fsck) executes on. If the fsck pass field contains a minus sign (-) or a zero (0), no file system integrity checking is performed. A file system with an fsck pass of one (1) indicates that the file system is to be checked sequentially (in the order it is listed in the *vfstab* file). Note that the / file system is always checked first. File systems with a fsck pass number greater than one (1) allow those file systems to be checked in parallel (simultaneously). For systems with a large number of disks spanning multiple disk controllers or disk busses, parallel file system checking is generally faster than sequential checking. For efficiency, use fsck on file systems of similar size on different disks simultaneously.

Volume Manager

Adding entries to the *vfstab* file works well for hard disks but is not suitable for removable media such as floppies and CD-ROMs. These types of devices tend to be mounted and unmounted much more frequently than hard disks. To handle these, Solaris adds a facility called the "volume manager." The volume manager automatically detects the presence of and determines the file system type, and then mounts removable media. Automatic detection of the media is limited to the CD-ROM device. The File Manager does this with a combination of a daemon (*vold*) and a configuration file (*/etc/vold.conf*) which specifies the actions to be taken for various removable devices and file system types. For floppy disks, the volume manager is unable to detect the presence of new disks and must be informed that a new disk is present by typing the **volcheck** command. The way in which the previously created floppy file system would be handled by the volume manager appears in the following illustration.

```
┌─────────────────────────────────────────────────────────────────┐
│ ▼                         cmdtool – /bin/csh                      │
├─────────────────────────────────────────────────────────────────┤
│ glenn% volcheck                                                   │
│ glenn% df                                                         │
│ /              (/dev/dsk/c0t3d0s0):   11726 blocks    9290 files  │
│ /usr           (/dev/dsk/c0t3d0s6):  788064 blocks  322312 files  │
│ /proc          (/proc         ):        0 blocks     201 files    │
│ /dev/fd        (fd            ):        0 blocks       0 files     │
│ /tmp           (swap          ):   218616 blocks    3286 files    │
│ /opt           (/dev/dsk/c0t3d0s5):   91236 blocks   73801 files  │
│ /floppy/unlabeled (/vol/dev/diskette0/unlabeled):   2508 blocks   636 files │
│ glenn% ▲                                                          │
└─────────────────────────────────────────────────────────────────┘
```

Mounting a floppy disk using the volume manager.

The volume manager always mounts floppy disks under the */floppy* directory which it controls. CD-ROMs are likewise mounted under the */cdrom* directory. Note also that the **volcheck** command was issued from an ordinary user account and not the super-user. The volume manager removes the need for users to have root privileges in order to mount removable media. If you had the File Manager running at the time you typed volcheck, you may have noticed another feature of the volume manager which is shown in the next illustration.

The Solaris File Manager communicates with the volume manager and will automatically bring up a new File Manager window when a removable device is mounted. You can also control the volume manager from the File Manager. Under the file menu on the main File Manager window you will find a selection to check for new floppies, which performs the same action as typing the **volcheck** command. The newly created File Manager window also has an eject button which will unmount the file system and eject the disk from the drive.

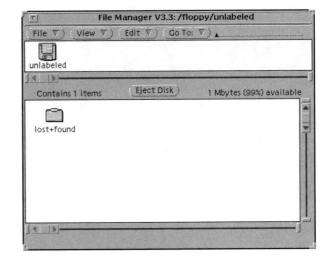

*File manager
detection of
volume manager
mounted disks.*

Mounting Other File System Types

The volume manager is also able to handle file system types other than *ufs*. For instance, inserting an MS-DOS formatted floppy and using the File Manager or the **volcheck** command results in the disk being mounted under the */floppy* directory on a mount point which bears the floppy volume name. Thus, inserting an MS-DOS floppy whose volume name is *transfer* and selecting Check For Floppy from the file menu in the File Manager will cause the window shown in the following illustration to appear. Note the DOS label on the floppy disk icon which indicates the file system type.

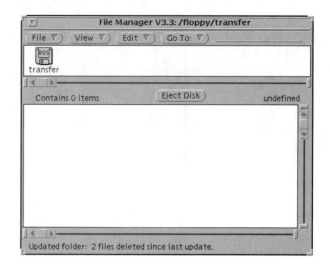

File manager mounting an MS-DOS floppy.

Configuring the Volume Manager

Changing the actions taken and devices under control of the volume manager is a simple matter of modifying the */etc/vold.conf* file. The configuration information in the file is formatted by section. A sample */etc/vold.conf* file follows:

```
#
# @(#)VOLD.CONF = 693/05/17   SMI
#
# Volume Daemon Configuration file
#

# Database to use (must be first)
db db_mem.so

# Labels supported
label dos label_dos.so floppy
label cdrom label_cdrom.so cdrom
label sun label_sun.so floppy
```

```
# Devices to use
use cdrom drive /dev/dsk/c0t6 dev_cdrom.so cdrom0
use floppy drive /dev/diskette dev_floppy.so floppy0


# Actions
insert /vol*/dev/diskette[0-9]/* user=root /usr/sbin/rmmount
insert /vol*/dev/dsk/* user=root /usr/sbin/rmmount
eject /vol*/dev/diskette[0-9]/* user=root /usr/sbin/rmmount
eject /vol*/dev/dsk/* user=root /usr/sbin/rmmount
notify /vol*/rdsk/* group=tty /usr/lib/vold/volmissing -c


# List of file system types unsafe to eject
unsafe ufs hsfs pcfs
```

The lines beginning with a pound sign (#) are considered comments and are used here to help delineate the various sections of the configuration information. The first two sections, beginning with the comments Database and Labels, describe the database routines and disk label types the volume manager recognizes. These two sections should not be modified.

The Devices to Use Section

The third section, marked by the comment, "Devices to use," lists the names and types of the removable media devices the volume manager should monitor. Each line in this section starts with the keyword *use*.

```
use cdrom drive /dev/dsk/c0t6 dev_cdrom.so cdrom0
```

Use is followed by the type of device, either *CD-ROM* or *floppy*, and the keyword *drive*.

```
use cdrom drive /dev/dsk/c0t6 dev_cdrom.so cdrom0
```

Following the device type is the Solaris name for the device. Note how the CD-ROM device name specifies only the first five characters of the full special device name. Because the volume manager will monitor and mount all of the available slices it finds on a CD-ROM disk, the only information needed is the specific controller and target portions of the device name.

```
use cdrom drive /dev/dsk/c0t6 dev_cdrom.so cdrom0
```

Following the special device name is the name of the shared object used to manage the device. This must match up with the device type specified (e.g., if the device type is *cdrom*, the shared object must be *dev_cdrom.so*). Finally, the symbolic name used in the */device* directory is listed. The first device of a given type has a *0* appended to its name, the second, a *1* and so on. For instance, a second CD-ROM drive located at target 5 on the built-in SCSI controller would be placed under volume manager control by adding a line like the following to the *devices* section of the *vold.conf* file:

```
use cdrom drive /dev/dsk/c0t5 dev_cdrom.so cdrom1
```

The Actions Section

The next section, which begins with the comment "Actions," specifies the actions to be taken when certain events happen. The basic events are the insertion of media into a drive (*insert*), removal of media from a drive (*eject*) and notification of problems (*notify*). An example entry in the *actions* section follows:

```
eject /vol*/dev/diskette[0-9]/* user=root /usr/sbin/rmmount
```

Each line lists an event followed by a regular expression. When an event occurs, each line which begins with the name of the event (insert, eject or notify) is checked. If the volume on which the event occurs matches the regular expression, then the remainder of the action line comes into play. The remainder of this line includes the name of the user or group identification to be used to run the listed command with the listed arguments. In the example line above, when the *eject* event occurs and the volume matches the regular expression */vol*/ dev/diskette[0-9]/*, the command */usr/sbin/rmmount* would be run with the user permissions of *root*.

The rmmount.conf Configuration File

The **/usr/sbin/rmmount** command in turn has its own configuration file called */etc/rmmount.conf*. Although not often modified, this file allows you to specify additional actions to occur when a disk is mounted. A common usage for this feature is to allow CD-ROMs which are mounted by the volume manager to be automatically "shared", or made accessible to other workstations on your network via NFS. To do this, a *share* line is added to the bottom of the */etc/rmmount.conf* file as follows:

```
share cdrom*
```

This line would share any CD-ROM mounted by the volume manager without any restrictions. To control access you can add options to the share line in a similar form to the share command. The **share** command is covered in more detail in Chapter 18.

File System Repair

Although UNIX file systems are fairly rugged, problems sometimes occur which damage the index structure of a file system. This happens because Solaris keeps some of the file system structure in memory and periodically updates that structure to disk. This is done to improve file system performance. However, an inadvertent shutdown, such as might occur during a power failure, might result in the index structure on the disk not being completely updated and requiring repair before the file system can be mounted.

Automatic File Checking

As was shown earlier, file systems which are automatically mounted by way of */etc/vfstab* file can be automatically checked using the **fsck** command. The volume manager also will use the fsck command to check any ufs type file systems it mounts. In both of these cases, fsck is run using the **p** or **preen** option. The preen option will automatically fix minor file system problems but will exit if there is any major damage. Here's an example of running fsck's preen option on the floppy file system created earlier.

Using the preen option to fsck to check the floppy file system.

```
                          cmdtool – /bin/csh
# fsck -o p /dev/rdiskette
/dev/rdiskette: is clean.
#
```

If major damage to the index structure of the file system were present, then fsck would need to be run without the preen option, and manual action would need to be taken to repair the damage by answering the questions presented by fsck. Running fsck in this mode provides more detail about the checks fsck performs to ensure the integrity of the file system. The following illustration shows what you would see on an intact file system.

```
                    cmdtool - /bin/csh
# fsck /dev/rdiskette
** /dev/rdiskette
** Last Mounted on /floppy/unlabeled
** Phase 1 - Check Blocks and Sizes
** Phase 2 - Check Pathnames
** Phase 3 - Check Connectivity
** Phase 4 - Check Reference Counts
** Phase 5 - Check Cyl groups
2 files, 9 used, 1254 free (14 frags, 155 blocks, 1.1%
fragmentation)
#
```

An fsck of a clean file system.

Unrecoverable Damage Types

On a damaged file system a number of problems can be present. Some can be repaired, and some not. On a medium-damaged disk (i.e., the platters have been damaged) as in the infamous "head crash," or by exposure to magnetic fields (more often the case of floppies), some data may not be recoverable. The fsck command will inform you of blocks on the disk which are no longer readable. Heavily damaged disks are often beyond repair. Floppies can often be reused once they are reformatted, but hard disks often cannot be saved.

```
                    cmdtool - /bin/csh
# fsck /dev/rdiskette
** /dev/rdiskette

CANNOT READ: BLK 2336
CONTINUE? y

THE FOLLOWING SECTORS COULD NOT BE READ: 2336 2337 2338
2339
#
```

A disk with unrecoverable errors.

Recoverable Damage

A less dramatic problem can occur when the index information on the disk is damaged such as during a power failure while data was being written to the disk. A disk with this type of problem can sometimes be repaired using **fsck**.

Appearing below is an example disk which was damaged by information being written over the primary super-block or base index block. To recover from this problem, fsck's **-o b=#** option is used. This allows fsck to reconstruct the super-block by using the information stored in an alternative super-block. The alternative super-block locations for a given disk are listed by the **newfs** command when the file system is created and can be listed again if you use the -**N** option flag as shown earlier in this chapter.

A disk with a bad super-block.

```
                              cmdtool – /bin/csh
# fsck /dev/rdiskette
** /dev/rdiskette
BAD SUPER BLOCK: MAGIC NUMBER WRONG
USE AN ALTERNATE SUPER-BLOCK TO SUPPLY NEEDED INFORMATION;
eg. fsck [-F ufs] -o b=# [special ...]
where # is the alternate super block. SEE fsck_ufs(1M).
# fsck -o b=640 /dev/rdiskette
Alternate super block location: 640.
** /dev/rdiskette
** Last Mounted on
** Phase 1 - Check Blocks and Sizes
** Phase 2 - Check Pathnames
** Phase 3 - Check Connectivity
** Phase 4 - Check Reference Counts
** Phase 5 - Check Cyl groups
2 files, 9 used, 1254 free (14 frags, 155 blocks, 1.1% fragmentation)
/dev/rdiskette FILE SYSTEM STATE SET TO OKAY

***** FILE SYSTEM WAS MODIFIED *****
#
```

✔   **NOTE:** *The "FILE SYSTEM WAS MODIFIED" warning given by fsck should serve to remind you to run fsck again. By its nature fsck is unable in some situations to correct all the problems present in the index structure of a disk during a single run. Using fsck a second time catches any problems that it was unable to correct on the first run.*

An Example of a Recoverable Disk

Here's another disk with more extensive damage. It appears to be recoverable but will take some work. The first problem is a damaged directory. **Fsck** will reconstruct the directory structure by replacing mandatory parts of the directory file but it may not be able to recover the pointers in the directory file which point to the individual files themselves. The result is files and possibly directories which are no longer in *any* directory. The complete sequence of fsck actions needed to reconstruct the file system to the point it can be mounted is illustrated in the following series.

Using fsck to repair a heavily damaged disk, part 1.

```
                        cmdtool – /bin/csh
 # fsck /dev/rdiskette
 ** /dev/rdiskette
 ** Last Mounted on /mnt
 ** Phase 1 - Check Blocks and Sizes
 ** Phase 2 - Check Pathnames
 DIRECTORY CORRUPTED   I=3   OWNER=root MODE=40700
 SIZE=8192 MTIME=Aug 12 14:51 1994
 DIR=?

 SALVAGE? y

 MISSING '.'  I=3  OWNER=root MODE=40700
 SIZE=8192 MTIME=Aug 12 14:51 1994
 DIR=?

 FIX? y

 DIRECTORY CORRUPTED   I=2   OWNER=root MODE=40755
 SIZE=512 MTIME=Aug 12 14:52 1994
 DIR=

 SALVAGE? y

 MISSING '.'  I=2  OWNER=root MODE=40755
 SIZE=512 MTIME=Aug 12 14:52 1994
 DIR=

 FIX? y
```

Using the Lost+found Directory

Once the directories are repaired, the repair effort moves on to reconnecting those files and directories which no longer belong to any directory. This is where the *lost+found* directory you may have seen comes into play. This directory is used by **fsck** as a place to put files and directories it relinks into the directory tree. In the case of the above disk, the *lost+found* directory itself was damaged and had to be recreated.

The files and directories in the *lost+found* directory are listed by the number of the index node (inode) they inhabit. Because the file name information for a UNIX file is stored in the directory file, directories which are damaged cause the loss of file name information. However, the file's contents, ownership, and permissions are usually left intact. The ownership and permissions are stored in the index node for the file itself and the data are stored in blocks referenced by the index node. Provided the *inode* for the file is intact, **fsck** can save the file's contents even if the name of the file is lost.

✘   *TIP: When fsck asks to reconnect a file, look at the file size. It is often faster and easier to not reconnect files which are zero bytes in size. You may see files like this due to a stock trick some programs use when creating temporary files. The program creates the file, opens it, and then removes it. The result is a file which does not belong to any directory, but can be written and read by the program. Under normal operations the file is cleaned up when the program closes it. However, if your workstation were to be shut down inadvertently, you can end up with an unconnected file which fsck will find.*

```
                    cmdtool - /bin/csh

MISSING '..'  I=2  OWNER=root MODE=40755
SIZE=512 MTIME=Aug 12 14:52 1994
DIR=

FIX? y

** Phase 3 - Check Connectivity
UNREF DIR  I=128  OWNER=bin MODE=40775
SIZE=512 MTIME=Aug 12 14:53 1994
RECONNECT? y

NO lost+found DIRECTORY
CREATE? y

DIR I=128 CONNECTED. PARENT WAS I=2

UNREF DIR  I=3  OWNER=root MODE=40700
SIZE=8192 MTIME=Aug 12 14:51 1994
RECONNECT? y

DIR I=3 CONNECTED. PARENT WAS I=0

** Phase 4 - Check Reference Counts
LINK COUNT DIR I=2  OWNER=root MODE=40755
SIZE=512 MTIME=Aug 12 14:52 1994  COUNT 5 SHOULD BE 3
ADJUST? y

** Phase 5 - Check Cyl groups
```

File system repair efforts, part 2.

With the files and directories reconnected to the file tree in the *lost+found* directory, fsck repairs the reference count information in the directories and updates free block information in the super-block. This corrects the modified directories and super-block with respect to the actions fsck took earlier.

File system repair efforts, part 3.

```
                              cmdtool - /bin/csh
SIZE=8192 MTIME=Aug 12 14:51 1994
RECONNECT? y

DIR I=3 CONNECTED. PARENT WAS I=0

** Phase 4 - Check Reference Counts
LINK COUNT DIR I=2  OWNER=root MODE=40755
SIZE=512 MTIME=Aug 12 14:52 1994  COUNT 5 SHOULD BE 3
ADJUST? y

** Phase 5 - Check Cyl groups
FREE BLK COUNT(S) WRONG IN SUPERBLK
SALVAGE? y

13 files, 49 used, 1214 free (14 frags, 150 blocks, 1.1%
fragmentation)

***** FILE SYSTEM WAS MODIFIED *****
# fsck /dev/rdiskette
** /dev/rdiskette
** Last Mounted on /mnt
** Phase 1 - Check Blocks and Sizes
** Phase 2 - Check Pathnames
** Phase 3 - Check Connectivity
** Phase 4 - Check Reference Counts
** Phase 5 - Check Cyl groups
13 files, 49 used, 1214 free (14 frags, 150 blocks, 1.1%
fragmentation)
# mount /dev/diskette /mnt
```

Finally, fsck is run again to make sure there are no undiscovered problems that the first run of fsck did not find. With the file system structure intact, the file system is mounted. Now comes the tough job of looking through the files in the *lost+found* directory to see if you can decide what they are. This is not easy as the file names are missing. Fortunately, in this case the only items in the *lost+found* directory are directories, and their contents give a good idea of what they originally were. They can be moved back into place and the file system put back into service.

Restoring Files from Backup Versus Repairing a File System

Fortunately, repairing file systems is not a common task for the system manager. When confronted with repairing a file system, keep in mind the balance between restoration of the file system from backups versus the repair effort. If you have a recent backup it may quicker to restore the file system than to attempt repair. Repairing a file system can be very time-consuming, and it is not always easy to determine what fsck leaves behind for you to sort out.

```
┌─────────────────────────────────────────────────────────────────┐
│ ▼                       cmdtool – /bin/csh                        │
├─────────────────────────────────────────────────────────────────┤
│ # ls -lR /mnt                                                     │
│ total 2                                                           │
│ drwx-----T   4 root     root        1024 Aug 12 15:00 lost+found  │
│                                                                   │
│ /mnt/lost+found:                                                  │
│ total 18                                                          │
│ drwx------   2 root     root        8192 Aug 12 14:51 #003        │
│ drwxrwxr-x   2 bin      mail         512 Aug 12 14:53 #128        │
│                                                                   │
│ /mnt/lost+found/#003:                                             │
│ total 0                                                           │
│                                                                   │
│ /mnt/lost+found/#128:                                             │
│ total 76                                                          │
│ -rw-r--r--   1 bin      bin          153 Jun 20 21:26 Mail.rc     │
│ -rw-r--r--   1 root     bin         1221 Jun 30 20:34 aliases     │
│ -rw-r--r--   1 root     root           0 Jun 30 21:26 aliases.dir │
│ -rw-r--r--   1 root     root        1024 Jun 30 21:26 aliases.pag │
│ -rw-r--r--   1 bin      bin         1710 Jun 20 20:35 mailx.rc    │
│ -r--r--r--   1 bin      bin        12118 Sep 27  1993 main.cf     │
│ -r--r--r--   1 bin      bin         9112 Sep 27  1993 sendmail.cf │
│ -rw-r--r--   1 root     bin         1490 Sep 27  1993 sendmail.hf │
│ -r--r--r--   1 bin      bin         9112 Sep 27  1993 subsidiary.cf│
│ #▲                                                                │
│                                                                   │
└─────────────────────────────────────────────────────────────────┘
```

File system repair efforts, part 4.

File System Optimization

For most applications the file system created by **newfs** will provide good performance. However, there are a few situations in which adjusting or tuning the basic file system parameters results in even better performance. One such situation involves applications which have very specific file system needs. For instance, you should consider file system tuning in the following cases: special disks or controllers, applications which write files of a particular size (many small files, few large files), or a desire for more emphasis on storage space efficiency or speed.

The various parameters which affect file system performance can be set using option flags when the file system is created, or can be adjusted later using the **tunefs** command.

The tunefs Command

The **tunefs** command provides a way to adjust a number of file system parameters *after* a file system has been created. You can correct mistakes and adjust for changing disk usage using tunefs. However, some file system parameters cannot be adjusted without recreating the file system. In those cases you will need to dump the file system off to tape or another disk and recreate the file system using different parameters.

As with tuning a musical instrument or a small engine, the best approach is to adopt a cycle of test, adjust, and re-test. The test you use should resemble the application you will be using as closely as possible. The application itself should be used as the test if possible. You will also need a metric for measurement. Usually this is the time it takes for a basic operation. With this in hand, you can evaluate the changes you make in tuning to see if they improve performance in your situation.

> ✔ **NOTE:** *Be aware that a growing number of modern SCSI disks are "smart" in that they have a sophisticated controller and memory buffer attached to them which hide some of the characteristics described here. These disks provide high performance, but are not readily tunable. The internal controller and memory buffer mask the effects of such adjustments as rotational delay factors. The rate at which the disk can transfer data is not affected. If you have already created a file system, you are not necessarily faced with recreating the file system in order to adjust its performance characteristics. The tunefs command allows for several of the file system parameters to be adjusted after the file system has been created. To adjust a parameter using tunefs, the file system must first be unmounted.*

Special Disks or Controllers

By default, **newfs** uses the information in the disk label to calculate several factors related to the ability of the disk, controller, and CPU to read or write information. As the disk rotates, each block in the track moves past the disk heads. If the controller and CPU are fast enough, blocks can be written or read in the order they come under the heads.

Slower controller/CPU combinations, on the other hand, must skip one or more blocks between blocks read or written in order to keep up. The **newfs** and **tunefs** commands allow this aspect of the file system to be adjusted by calculating the required time for a single block read to be processed. The proper ordering of blocks read or written and blocks skipped is calculated from this value and the rotational speed of the disk.

Some disk controllers are capable of writing or reading multiple blocks due to high speed buffer memory located in the controller. The tunefs command allows you to specify the number of such buffers your controller has which improves file system performance by avoiding unnecessary block skipping. The option flags used to adjust these parameters are listed in the following table.

✔ **NOTE:** *The proper values for these parameters require some detailed knowledge of the disk hardware you are working with. Generally, these values are set properly by newfs.*

tunefs Parameters Associated with High Performance Disk Controllers

newfs option	tunefs option	Parameter
-d gap	-d gap	The "gap" is the time in milliseconds for a disk service interrupt to be completed and a new transfer started. This will be used along with the rotational speed of the disk and the number of sectors in a track to determine the number of blocks to skip (if any) between disk transfers.
-C maxcontig	-a maxcontig	The maximum number of blocks that can be written contiguously before a block must be skipped. This number depends on the characteristics of the disk and controller.

Small and Large File Adjustments

Applications which consistently read and write files which are very small or very large can often benefit from a tuned file system. Most tuning parameters can only be changed when the file system is created and cannot be adjusted using **tunefs**.

Large files are often split between cylinder groups across the disk. A cylinder group is a collection of cylinders used by the disk I/O routines in the SunOS kernel to improve disk performance by grouping a file's data blocks close together on the disk. When a large file is split over two or more cylinder groups, the data blocks which make up the file become spread apart across the disk. The result is extra head seek time when reading or writing large files. Adjusting the maximum number of blocks that a file can be allocated per cylinder group may reduce this problem. You can also adjust the basic allocation block and fragment sizes. A larger allocation block size and a larger fragment size favor large files by reducing the time required for file allocation at the expense of reduced space efficiency. If your application exclusively stores small files, a smaller allocation block size will improve speed, and a smaller fragment size will improve the efficiency with which space is used by avoiding allocating blocks much larger than the data to be stored in them.

Adjusting Your File System for Net-news

Applications which use many small files, such as Usenet **net-news**, also require more index nodes (inodes) than are normally created. You can change this by adjusting the number of bytes per *inode*. To find the number of *inodes* created for the file system, divide the size of the file system by the number of bytes per *inode*. The default size is 2048 bytes. This assumes that the average file will be at least 2048 bytes in length. A smaller value may be needed in some cases. When in doubt, err on the side of more *inodes* (a smaller number of bytes per inode). If a file system runs out of *inodes*, no more files can be created even if there are additional storage blocks available.

newfs and tunefs Options for Adjusting Drive Block Sizes

newfs option	tunefs option	Parameter
-b bsize	NA	The basic allocation block size is bytes. Only 4096 or 8192 are accepted. Use 4096 only for file systems which will contain a majority of very small files.
-f frag	NA	The size of a block fragment. Acceptable values are 512, 1024, 2048, 4096, and 8192 (if the basic allocation block is 8192). The small values use the disk space efficiently at the cost of speed. Larger values enhance speed but waste space if they contain small files. The default is 1024.
-i nbpi	N/A	The number of bytes per inode. Lower values result in more inodes, higher values in fewer inodes. The default is 2048 bytes.
N/A	-e maxbpg	The maximum number of blocks a single file can be allocated within a single cylinder group. The default is approximately 25% of the blocks in the cylinder group.

Storage Space Efficiency and Storage Speed

The disk storage routines in the SunOS kernel have two strategies available for disk allocation: *time* or *space*. Time refers to the time required to allocate space and write files. Optimizing time is wasteful of space in that it leaves gaps, trying instead for long continuous disk writes. Space refers to the efficient usage of scattered disk blocks on the disk. Optimizing space wastes time in that a file is allocated to disk blocks which are scattered around the disk and the disk heads must move more frequently to read or write a file. You can set which method is preferred on your file system.

newfs and tunefs Options Related to Space Versus Time Argument

newfs Option	tunefs Option	Parameter
-o strategy	-o strategy	The strategy is either space or time.
-m free	-m free	The minimum free space percentage. A reserve of less than 10% will adversely affect performance.

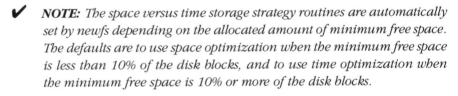

✔   **NOTE:** *The space versus time storage strategy routines are automatically set by newfs depending on the allocated amount of minimum free space. The defaults are to use space optimization when the minimum free space is less than 10% of the disk blocks, and to use time optimization when the minimum free space is 10% or more of the disk blocks.*

You might want to use the *space* strategy on a small disk where efficient utilization of disk space is more important. On a large file system which has a small percentage value for the minimum free space, you may wish to use the *time* strategy to improve performance. Related to the strategy routines is the free space reserve. The SunOS file system routines operate most efficiently when at least 10% of the basic allocation blocks are free. Below that value the routines must do much more work to allocate space for a file. File systems are normally created with a 10% reserve, but you can adjust the reserve.

✔   **NOTE:** *Commands such as df indicate that you are cutting into this reserve by showing a disk as more than 100% full. What has really happened is that 100% as displayed by the df command is really 90% of the total number of disk allocation blocks.*

Summary

Local file systems and their relationships to the UNIX file tree are a basic building block of a Solaris system. Understanding how file systems are created, mounted, checked, and tuned enables you to manage your disk space effectively while meeting the needs of your situation. Thanks to the Solaris volume manager, removable media are now more easily handled and can be mounted and unmounted without need for root privileges.

Managing System Software

In previous chapters you learned about disk geometry and file systems. We discussed how disk drives are divided into file systems, and how these file systems keep track of files and directories. We can now move on to a discussion of how to manage the software that will occupy the file systems on your disks.

This chapter will cover the Solaris concept of software packages, clusters, and configurations. Particular attention will be paid to how packages are installed, removed, and maintained on your file systems.

Understanding Software Packages

Under Solaris 2, software is packaged into small, easy-to-manage portions. These portions were briefly discussed in Chapter 2.

Packages

Bundled and unbundled software for Solaris 2 is distributed in what is commonly referred to as software *packages*. A software package is a collection of files that perform a function, such as the on-line manual pages or the OpenWindows demonstrations. There are over 80 software packages in Solaris 2. Software package names use the SUNWxxx format. For example, the package name for the on-line manual pages is SUNWman, and the package name for the OpenWindows demos is SUNWowdem.

The software packages in Solaris 2 conform to a software standard known as the Applications Binary Interface (ABI). ABI compliant software can be easily managed (i.e., installed and/or removed) with standard systems administration utilities which we will discuss in subsequent sections of this chapter.

Clusters

Related software packages are grouped into software *clusters*. Cluster names do not use the SUNW prefix. Instead they use logical names found in the Sun environment. For example, the OpenWindows Version 3 cluster contains 13 software packages related to OpenWindows version 3.

Configurations

The SunInstall utility further groups software packages and clusters into categories known as software *configurations*. There are four software configurations in Solaris 2. Each configuration supports different levels of system sophistication. The four configurations are core, end user, developer, and entire.

The core software configuration contains the minimum required software to boot and operate a stand-alone host. The core does not include the OpenWindows software nor the on-line manual pages. It does, however, include sufficient networking software and OpenWindows drivers to run OpenWindows from a server sharing the OpenWindows software. A server would not be built from the core configuration. The core software configuration requires approximately 45 Mb of disk space.

The end user software configuration contains the core configuration software and additional software typically used by end users. It includes OpenWindows version 3 and the end user version of AnswerBook. It does not, however, contain the on-line manual pages. The end user software configuration requires approximately 140 Mb of disk space.

The developer software configuration contains the core and end user configuration software and additional software typically used by systems and software developers. It includes the on-line manual pages, the full implementation of OpenWindows and compiler tools, but does not include compilers nor debugging tools. In Solaris 1 and earlier releases of Sun operating systems, compilers were bundled with the release media. Compilers and debuggers are unbundled products in Solaris 2. The developer's software configuration requires approximately 210 Mb of disk space.

The entire software configuration contains the complete Solaris 2 release, and requires approximately 275 Mb of disk space. It is important to note that the software configurations can be modified. For example, the on-line manual pages cluster could be added to the end user configuration. Likewise, the on-line manual pages could be removed from the developer configuration. These modifications can be made when the system is being built or afterwards.

The pkginfo Command

The **pkginfo** command is used if you wish to identify the packages installed on your system.

Using pkginfo to identify the packages installed on a system.

```
                                              local
# pkginfo
application SUNWaws.2      Wabi 2.0 AnswerBook
system      SUNWcar       Core Architecture, (Root)
system      SUNWcar.2     Core Architecture, (Root)
system      SUNWcar.3     Core Architecture, (Root)
system      SUNWcg6       GX (cg6) Device Driver
system      SUNWcg6.2     GX (cg6) Device Driver
system      SUNWcsd       Core Solaris Devices
system      SUNWcsr       Core Solaris, (Root)
system      SUNWcsr.2     Core Solaris, (Root)
system      SUNWcsr.3     Core Solaris, (Root)
system      SUNWcsu       Core Solaris, (Usr)
system      SUNWcsu.2     Core Solaris, (Usr)
system      SUNWdfb       Dumb Frame Buffer Device Drivers
system      SUNWesu       Extended System Utilities
system      SUNWinst      Install Software
system      SUNWvolg      Volume Management Graphical User Interface
system      SUNWvolr      Volume Management, (Root)
system      SUNWvolu      Volume Management, (Usr)
system      SUNWvolu.2    Volume Management, (Usr)
system      SUNWvygmn     SPARCstation Voyager Man Pages
application SUNWwabi       Wabi Application
application SUNWxgldg      XGL Generic Loadable Libraries
application SUNWxgler      XGL English Localization
application SUNWxglft      XGL Stroke Fonts
application SUNWxglrt      XGL Runtime Environment
application SUNWxildg      XIL Loadable Pipeline Libraries
application SUNWxiler      XIL English Localization
application SUNWxilow      XIL Deskset Loadable Pipeline Libraries
application SUNWxilrt      XIL Runtime Environment
system      SUNWxwcft     X Windows common (not required) fonts
system      SUNWxwdv      XWindows Window Drivers
system      SUNWxwmod     OpenWindows kernel modules
system      SUNWxwmod.2   OpenWindows kernel modules
system      SUNWxwopt     nonessential MIT core clients and server extensions
system      SUNWxwplt     X Windows platform software
#
```

The pkginfo command may also be used to display more detailed information on particular packages on your system. Command line options are summarized as follows.

❑ **-q** Do not list any information.

❑ **-x** Designate an extracted listing of package information.

❑ **-l** Specify long format output.

❑ **-p** Display information on partially installed packages.

❑ **-i** Display information for fully installed packages.

❑ **-r** List the installation base for relocatable packages.

❑ **-a arch** Specify the package architecture as arch.

❑ **-v version** Specify the version of the package as version.

❑ **-c category** Display all packages which match category.

❑ **-d device** Specify the device which contains the package to be checked.

❑ **-R root_path** Specify the path to the package to be checked.

For example, to cause pkginfo to display more detailed information on a specific package, use the -l option.

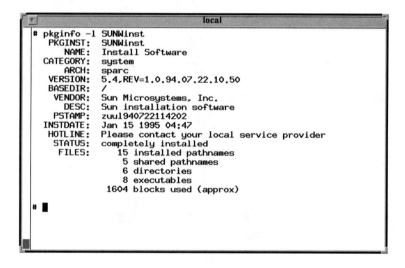

Using pkginfo to display detailed information about packages on a system.

✔ **NOTE:** *The descriptions of command line flags in this (and subsequent) sections are condensed synopses of flag operation. Consult the on-line manual pages for more information on these commands.*

Adding Software

Solaris 2 provides two methods for use during software installation: the command-line oriented **pkg** utilities, and the graphical interface of the Software Manager Tool. We will examine the command line utilities first. Once you understand how the utilities operate, you can explore the uses of the graphical interface utilities.

The pkgadd Command

The **pkgadd** utility allows you to copy a package from the distribution media to a location on one of your system's disks. Command line options for the pkgadd command follow:

❑ **-n** Non-interactive mode.

❑ **-a admin** Use the user-supplied *admin* file in place of the default admin file.

❑ **-d device** Define the device which contains the package to be installed.

❑ **-R root_path** Define the full path to where you want the package installed.

❑ **-r response** Use the *response* file for answers to interactive mode installations.

❑ **-s spool** Install package in the *spool* directory.

❑ **pkginst** The package name and instance which you are installing.

Applications are typically distributed on magnetic or optical media such as cartridge tape, floppy diskette, or CD-ROM. The pkgadd utility copies the package from the media, and installs it in the directory which you specify. A typical invocation of the pkgadd command follows:

```
pkgadd -d device SUNWpkgA
```

The above command tells pkgadd to look on the device specified by the name *device* to locate the SUNWpkgA package.

✔ *NOTE: Under Solaris 2.4, certain unbundled and third-party applications are no longer compatible with the pkgadd utility. These applications require interaction throughout the installation process. To install these packages (released prior to Solaris 2.4), you must set the following environment variable: NONABI_SCRIPTS=TRUE.*

```
                               local
# pkgadd -d /cdrom/cdrom0 -R /home/aman SUNWaman

Processing package instance <SUNWaman> from </cdrom/solaris_2_4_ab>
Solaris 2.4 Reference Manual AnswerBook
(all) 40.2.14
        Copyright 1994 Sun Microsystems, Inc. All Rights Reserved.
              Printed in the United States of America.

The installation options are as follows:
Option: Description:
------------------------------------------------------
1. nil:    less than 1 Megabyte disk space required [slowest performance].
2. heavy:  76.69 Megabytes disk space required [best performance].

Note: If the install option which you choose below fails
      due to lack of space, try another location, or
      choose a lower install option number.

Enter the number of an installation option from the list above (1 or 2).

Select an installation option: 2
Installation option: heavy selected.

The next request for input asks you to specify the parent directory of AnswerBook
Make sure to choose a parent directory on a file system big enough to
accommodate all the files to be moved for the INSTALL OPTION you selected.

Specify the parent of the AnswerBook home directory: /home
 For the heavy option all files will be placed under /home/SUNWaman.
## Software contents file initialized
## Processing package information.
## Processing system information.
## Verifying package dependencies.
## Verifying disk space requirements.
## Checking for conflicts with packages already installed.
## Checking for setuid/setgid programs.

This package contains scripts which will be executed with super-user
permission during the process of installing this package.

Do you want to continue with the installation of this package [y,n,?] y

Installing Solaris 2.4 Reference Manual AnswerBook as <SUNWaman>
## Installing part 1 of 1.
/home/aman/home/SUNWaman/index
/home/aman/home/SUNWaman/index/Keys
/home/aman/home <implied directory>
[ verifying class <Index> ]
/home/aman/home/SUNWaman/toc/OWREFMAN.ind
[ verifying class <ContentsDB> ]
/home/aman/home/SUNWaman/ps/OWREFMAN/0254_audiocontrol.1
[ verifying class <PostScript> ]
## Executing postinstall script.

Installation of <SUNWaman> successful.
#
```

Using pkgadd to install a package under Solaris 2.

Removing Software

The opposite of adding software is removing software. Solaris also provides a command line utility to perform package removal.

The pkgrm Command

The **pkgrm** command is used to undo the **pkgadd** command operation, or to remove a software package from the system. Before removing a package, pkgrm checks the other packages on the system to identify interdependencies. If interdependencies are found, the pkgrm command consults the *admin* file to determine the action to be taken.

Command line options for the pkgrm command follow:

❑ **-n** Non-interactive mode. The command exits if interaction is required.

❑ **-R** Defines the full path name to the package to be removed.

❑ **-a admin** Use the user-supplied *admin* file in place of the default admin file.

❑ **-s spool** Remove the package from the *spool* directory.

❑ **pkginst** Specify the name and instsance of the package to be removed.

Using pkgrm to remove a package under Solaris 2.

```
▽                          local
# pkgrm -R /home/aman SUNWaman

The following package is currently installed:
    SUNWaman        Solaris 2.4 Reference Manual AnswerBook
                    (all) 40.2.14

Do you want to remove this package? y

## Removing installed package instance <SUNWaman>
## Verifying package dependencies.
## Processing package information.
## Removing pathnames in class <PostScript>
/home/aman/home/SUNWaman/ps/OWREFMAN/0254_audiocontrol.1
/home/aman/home/SUNWaman/ps/OWREFMAN
/home/aman/home/SUNWaman/ps
## Removing pathnames in class <ContentsDB>
/home/aman/home/SUNWaman/toc/OWREFMAN.ind
/home/aman/home/SUNWaman/toc
## Removing pathnames in class <Index>
/home/aman/home/SUNWaman/index/index.ref
/home/aman/home/SUNWaman/index/index.log
/home/aman/home/SUNWaman/index/index.dct
/home/aman/home/SUNWaman/index/index.cix
/home/aman/home/SUNWaman/index/index.cfg
/home/aman/home/SUNWaman/index/index.cat
/home/aman/home/SUNWaman/index/Keys
/home/aman/home/SUNWaman/index
## Removing pathnames in class <none>
/home/aman/home/SUNWaman
## Updating system information.

Removal of <SUNWaman> was successful.
#
```

✔ **NOTE:** *Under Solaris 2.4, certain unbundled and third-party applications are no longer compatible with the pkgrm utility. These applications require interaction throughout the process of removal. To remove these packages (released prior to Solaris 2.4), you must set the following environment variable: NONABI_SCRIPTS=TRUE.*

Verifying Software Installation

Once you have installed or removed a package, it is often wise to verify that the package is properly installed (or removed). Solaris provides a command line utility to perform this function.

The pkgchk Command

The **pkgchk** utility checks a package to determine if it is properly installed, or if it has been properly removed. Command line options for this utility follow:

- ❑ **-l** List information on the files which make up the package. This option cannot be used with a, c, f, g, and v options.

- ❑ **-a** Audit the attributes, but do not check the contents of the files.

- ❑ **-c** Audit the contents of the files, but do not check the attributes.

- ❑ **-f** Correct file attributes when possible.

- ❑ **-q** Quiet mode.

- ❑ **-v** Verbose mode.

- ❑ **-x** Search exclusive directories.

- ❑ **-n** Do not check volatile (editable) files.

- ❑ **-p path** Check only the listed path(s) for accuracy.

- ❑ **-i file** Read a list of path names from file.

- ❑ **-d device** Specify the device which contains the *spool* directory.

- ❑ **-R root_dir** Specify the path to the package(s).

- ❑ **-m pkgmap** Check the entire package against the package map.

- ❑ **-e envfile** Use the *envfile* to resolve parameters listed in the *pkgmap* file.

- ❑ **pkginst** Specify the package and instance to be checked.

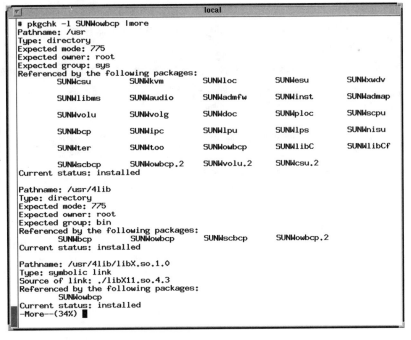

Using pkgchk to check the installation of a package under Solaris 2.

Other pkg Commands

Solaris also provides a series of commands which may be used by applications developers to create package distributions. Several of these commands are briefly described below.

- ❑ **pkgask** Store answers to a request script.
- ❑ **pkgmap** Package contents description file.
- ❑ **pkgmk** Produce an installable package.
- ❑ **pkgparam** Display package parameter values.
- ❑ **pkgproto** Generate prototype file entries for input to pkgmk.
- ❑ **pkgtrans** Translate package formats: (1) file system to data stream; (2) data stream to file system; or (3) file system type 1 to file system type 2.
- ❑ **installf** Add a file to the installed software database.
- ❑ **removef** Remove a file from the installed software database.

For more information on the use of these commands, consult the Solaris 2 AnswerBook, and the on-line manual pages.

Important Files and Directories

The **pkgadd** and **pkgrm** utilities create several files in the */var/sadm* directory to inform you of the success or failure of their respective operations. These files may be browsed with the **more** command to monitor the steps followed during a package installation or removal.

If the installation of a package fails, the reason for the failure will be written to the appropriate package log file in */var/sadm*. In the event that you encounter problems with the installation or removal of a particular package, it may be helpful to peruse the installation log file for the package to determine the source of the problems.

Typical contents of a /var/sadm package installation log file.

```
                                    local
Installation of <SUNWolimt> was successful.
Doing pkgadd of SUNWowbcp to /.
9078 blocks

Installation of <SUNWowbcp> was successful.
Doing pkgadd of SUNWowrqd to /.

Installation of <SUNWowrqd> was successful.
Doing pkgadd of SUNWlibC to /.
384 blocks

Installation of <SUNWlibC> was successful.
Doing pkgadd of SUNWlibCf to /.
198 blocks

Installation of <SUNWlibCf> was successful.
Doing pkgadd of SUNWscbcp to /.
2630 blocks

Installation of <SUNWscbcp> was successful.

Removal of <SUNWowdv> was successful.

The messages printed to the screen by this upgrade have been saved to:

        /a/var/sadm/install_data/upgrade_log

After this system is rebooted, the upgrade log can be found in the file:

        /var/sadm/install_data/upgrade_log


Please examine the file:

        /a/var/sadm/install_data/upgrade_cleanup

It contains a list of actions that may need to be performed to complete
the upgrade.  After this system is rebooted, this file can be found at:

        /var/sadm/install_data/upgrade_cleanup

After performing any necessary cleanup actions, the system should
be rebooted.
#
```

✔ **NOTE:** *While it may appear that log files are superfluous and could be removed, we recommend that you leave them on the system for future reference.*

Using the Software Manager Tool (swmtool)

Now that you have seen how the command line utilities operate, we will explore the use of the graphical interface to the software management process. The *swmtool* may be used to install, remove, and perform an integrity check on the software on your local or remote systems.

The swmtool Interface

To install or remove packages with **swmtool**, you must be operating in a windowing environment, and have super-user permission. If you want to view the installed packages on a system, super-user permission is not required. Once you have opened a window and started a root shell, you can invoke the swmtool with the following command:

```
/usr/sbin/swmtool -d device &
```

Starting swmtool.

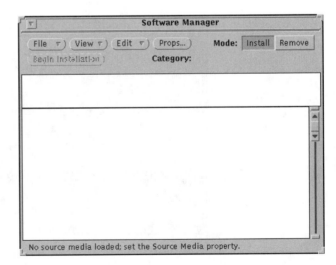

The above command will cause *swmtool* to open a new window on your display. Buttons available within this window will allow you to set the parameters for your package installation or package removal.

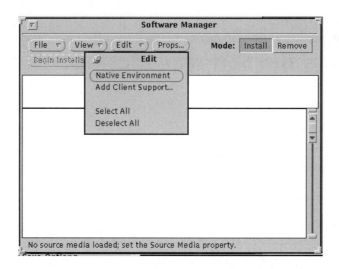

Setting parameters for package installation.

By clicking on the Props button, you can set the source media and the directory on the source media which contains the package to be installed.

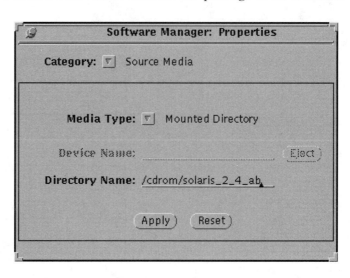

Setting the source media and package directory.

The *swmtool* will read the source volume and display a description of each package available on the media. You may select the package of interest by clicking on the icon to the left of the package description. More information on the package or individual clusters within a package is available by double-clicking on the icon, or by choosing the Expand button on the software menu.

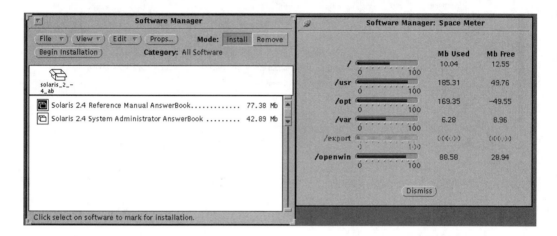

The swmtool command displays the packages available for installation.

Once you have chosen the software to be installed, click on the Begin Installation button to start the installation process. The swmtool command may request input to allow it to properly install the package you have selected.

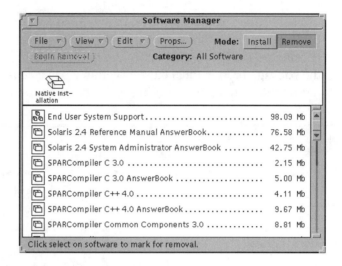

In Remove mode swmtool displays the packages available for removal.

To remove a package with swmtool, you first select the Remove mode of operation. The swmtool command will display a list of packages available on the system. Select the package to be removed by clicking on the icon for the desired package.

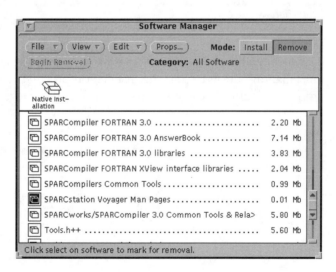

Selecting packages for removal with swmtool.

Once you have selected all packages to be removed, click on the Begin Removal button. The swmtool will ask for confirmation of the removal operation.

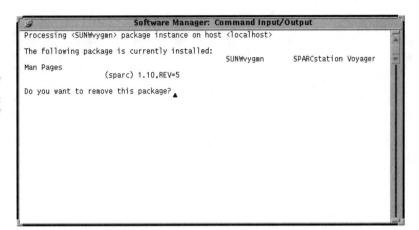

The swmtool command requests removal confirmation.

Upon completion of swmtool tasks, you should exit by selecting the box in the upper left corner of the swmtool window, and moving the pointer to the Exit item on the menu.

Summary

In this chapter we expanded on the Solaris 2 definition of a software package. You learned how to install, remove, and maintain packages with the command line utilities and the graphical user interface utility. The chapter also covered the strengths and weaknesses of each method of software management, and how to determine which method would be most efficient for a particular package.

Now that you have an operating system installed, your mass storage system ready for use, and your end user packages installed, you can turn your attention to preparing the system for your users. The next several chapters discuss topics which will enable you to customize systems to your environment, and tips on how to perform daily system administration functions to keep your systems running smoothly.

Adding Terminals and Modems

Now that you have an understanding of the mass storage subsystem and the management of file systems and software, we can turn our attention to some of the other daily tasks you may face as systems administrators. One of the more common tasks on any computer system is the installation, setup, and policing of the network services and serial lines.

The serial ports on most systems are used for dial-up modem access, tty terminal access, and line printer output. Discussion of line printers on serial ports is found in Chapter 16. In this chapter, we will discuss serial ports when used for dial-up modems and tty terminal access. You will see how to set up ports for particular services, and how to monitor system access through these serial ports.

In many applications, the system administrator will be asked to monitor and control access to the systems via network links. As you may recall, system security was discussed in Chapter 9. In this chapter, you will see how to use the system software to set up and manage the network services to help provide better system security.

Working with Serial Devices

Before we proceed to examine the methods used to add and control serial ports on Solaris systems, we need to define a few basic terms and concepts.

A serial port is an input/output channel between a serial device (terminals, printers, modems, and plotters to name a few) and the operating system. The data is transmitted through a serial port in a bit-by-bit (serial) manner. The speed at which the data are transferred is referred to as the *baud rate*.

The baud rate is a measure of bits per second. For instance, a baud rate of 300 would tell you that the data is being sent at 300 bits per second. There are numerous standard baud rates provided by computer systems. The most common baud rates are 300, 600, 1200, 2400, 4800, 9600, 19,200, and 38,400. Most modern terminals and printers operate at transmission speeds of 9600 baud or faster. Solaris provides the means to set the serial port speed as required by the device, or as desired by the user.

✔ **NOTE:** *Although the terms "baud" and "bits-per-second" do not necessarily equate to the same thing, it is a common practice to refer to them as one and the same. To be more accurate, baud refers to the number of times per second that a signal changes its value. Bits per second refers to the data rate between the computer and the device. For our purposes, we will treat them as interchangeable terms.*

Most of the terminals on the market offer some set of unique features in addition to those found on all similar type units. In order for the operating system to allow the use of different terminal types there must be a table of terminal capabilities available to the operating system. This table is used to determine how to set the serial port appropriately for the connected terminal. Solaris contains such a database of terminal capabilities for many common terminals. In addition, Solaris allows you to add new terminal definitions to this database.

Because serial ports allow access to the operating system, you need to be aware of the use of all such ports on your systems. Unattended terminals are often used by unauthorized users attempting to access your computer systems. You need to be aware of all serial port connections to your systems, and disable any ports which are not currently in use. You should also remind the authorized users of your systems of the dangers of leaving a log-in session unattended.

Using the Service Access Facility

Under Solaris there are two methods available for the system administrator to manage serial port facilities. One method is to use the **admintool** utility to graphically interface to the Service Access Facility (SAF). The second method of serial port administration is to manually invoke the utilities provided by the SAF. Both methods of serial port administration use the same underlying set of utilities.

The SAF is a tool which allows the system administrator to manage serial ports and network devices. The SAF allows the system administrator to carry out the following:

❑ Manage and troubleshoot TTY devices.

❑ Manage and troubleshoot network print service requests.

❑ Manage and troubleshoot the Service Access Controller.

❑ Add and manage listen port monitor services.

❑ Add and manage ttymon port monitor services.

The SAF is not a single program, but rather a series of background processes and commands which control those processes. A few components of the SAF follow:

❑ The top level SAF program is the Service Access Controller (SAC). The SAC controls port monitors which are administered through the **sacadm** command.

❑ The **sacadm** command is used to administer the SAC which controls the ttymon and listen port monitors.

❑ The **pmadm** command administers the ttymon and listen services associated with ports.

❑ The ttymon facility is used to monitor serial line service requests.

❑ The listen facility monitors requests for network services.

We will examine each component of the SAF in detail to see how these facilities interact, and what each facility does for system administrators.

The Service Access Controller (SAC)

The Service Access Controller program manages the operation of all port monitors. These port monitors are actually programs which continuously watch for any request to access devices connected to the serial ports. The SAC process is started automatically when the system is booted to the multi-user *init-state*. When invoked, the SAC initializes the system environment by interpreting the */etc/saf/_safconfig* start-up script. These configuration files allow the system administrator to customize the serial port parameters for their site.

After the SAC has created a custom environment as directed by the startup scripts, it reads the */etc/saf/_sactab* file and starts port monitors as required.

Contents of a
typical
/etc/saf/_sactab
file.

```
# cat /etc/saf/_sactab
# VERSION=1
zsmon:ttymon::0:/usr/lib/saf/ttymon       #
tcp:listen::9999:/usr/lib/saf/listen tcp        #
ttymon0:ttymon::0:/usr/lib/saf/ttymon     #ports00 - 04
modem:ttymon::2:/usr/lib/saf/ttymon       #Serial Ports
#
```

The SAC starts up a new process for each port monitor as directed by the
/etc/saf/_sactab file. The SAC maintains control of these new processes, and can
therefore be considered the *parent* process. The new processes are called *child*
processes.

 TIP: *You can see the process hierarchy and determine which processes
are parents or children by using the ps -ef command. The output column
labeled PID is the process ID. The output column labeled PPID shows the
Parent Process ID.*

Each child process started by the SAC invokes the appropriate /etc/ saf/
port_monitor /_config script to customize its own environment and start the
processes as determined by the configuration file. In most cases, the process
started for the port is the log-in process.

```
# cat /etc/saf/ttymon0/_pmtab
# VERSION=1
00:ux:root:reserved:reserved:reserved:/dev/term/00:::/usr/bin/login::9600::login\:  ::::#/dev/term/00
01:ux:root:reserved:reserved:reserved:/dev/term/01:::/usr/bin/login::9600::login\:  ::::#/dev/term/01
02:ux:root:reserved:reserved:reserved:/dev/term/02:::/usr/bin/login::9600::login\:  ::::#/dev/term/02
03:ux:root:reserved:reserved:reserved:/dev/term/03:::/usr/bin/login::9600::login\:  ::::#/dev/term/03
#
```

Contents of a typical /etc/saf/port_monitor/_pmtab file.

Port Monitors

Solaris 2.3 implements two port monitors: the *ttymon* monitor, and the *listen*
monitor. Each time a user attempts to log in to a system through a directly
connected terminal or modem, the *ttymon* is invoked. Once invoked, ttymon
monitors serial port lines for incoming data. When data is present, ttymon
determines the proper line disciplines and baud rate by consulting the /etc/ttydefs
file.

```
# cat /etc/ttydefs
# VERSION=1
38400:38400 hupcl:38400 hupcl::19200
19200:19200 hupcl:19200 hupcl::9600
9600:9600 hupcl:9600 hupcl::4800
4800:4800 hupcl:4800 hupcl::2400
2400:2400 hupcl:2400 hupcl::1200
1200:1200 hupcl:1200 hupcl::300
300:300 hupcl:300 hupcl::38400

38400E:38400 hupcl evenp:38400 evenp::19200
19200E:19200 hupcl evenp:19200 evenp::9600
9600E:9600 hupcl evenp:9600 evenp::4800
4800E:4800 hupcl evenp:4800 evenp::2400
2400E:2400 hupcl evenp:2400 evenp::1200
1200E:1200 hupcl evenp:1200 evenp::300
300E:300 hupcl evenp:300 evenp::19200
auto:hupcl:sane hupcl:A:9600
console:9600 hupcl opost onlcr:9600::console
console1:1200 hupcl opost onlcr:1200::console2
console2:300 hupcl opost onlcr:300::console3
console3:2400 hupcl opost onlcr:2400::console4
console4:4800 hupcl opost onlcr:4800::console5
console5:19200 hupcl opost onlcr:19200::console
contty:9600 hupcl opost onlcr:9600 sane::contty1
contty1:1200 hupcl opost onlcr:1200 sane::contty2
contty2:300 hupcl opost onlcr:300 sane::contty3
contty3:2400 hupcl opost onlcr:2400 sane::contty4
contty4:4800 hupcl opost onlcr:4800 sane::contty5
contty5:19200 hupcl opost onlcr:19200 sane::contty
4800H:4800:4800 sane hupcl::9600H
9600H:9600:9600 sane hupcl::19200H
19200H:19200:19200 sane hupcl::38400H
38400H:38400:38400 sane hupcl::2400H
2400H:2400:2400 sane hupcl::1200H
1200H:1200:1200 sane hupcl::300H
300H:300:300 sane hupcl::4800H
conttyH:9600 opost onlcr:9600 hupcl sane::contty1H
contty1H:1200 opost onlcr:1200 hupcl sane::contty2H
contty2H:300 opost onlcr:300 hupcl sane::contty3H
contty3H:2400 opost onlcr:2400 hupcl sane::contty4H
contty4H:4800 opost onlcr:4800 hupcl sane::contty5H
contty5H:19200 opost onlcr:19200 hupcl sane::conttyH
#
```

Typical contents of the /etc/ttydefs file.

The ttymon facility uses the information in the */etc/ttydefs* file to determine the default line settings and proceeds to set the line accordingly. Once this is done, ttymon passes control to the *login* process.

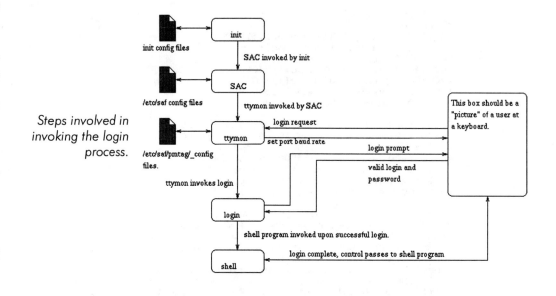

Steps involved in invoking the login process.

The TTY Port Monitor: ttymon

The ttymon facility is a streams-based port monitor. The streams interface is a standardized input/output scheme for use with serial port devices. The streams facility allows the system to communicate with serial port devices through standard system calls and facilities which are used to communicate with other system devices. Streams are defined by the System V Release 4 Interface Description (SVID).

The ttymon facility uses the streams interface to monitor serial ports, and set serial line modes, line disciplines, and baud rates. The ttymon facility also invokes the login process. Ttymon runs under the control of the SAC program and is configured via the **sacadm** command. Each invocation of ttymon can monitor multiple ports. The ports for each ttymon process are specified in the port monitor's administrative file, as created by using the **pmadm** and **ttyadm** commands.

Configuring ttymon: The ttyadm Command

The **ttyadm** command is a ttymon specific administrative command. This command formats ttymon information and writes it to standard output. This provides the ability to present such information to the **sacadm** and **pmadm** commands. The ttyadm command does not administer ttymon, but rather it provides a means for the sacadm and pmadm commands to provide this administration.

The Network Listener Monitor: listen

The listen port monitor monitors the network for service requests. As requests arrive and are accepted, listen invokes the proper server to process the request. The listen monitor is configured via **sacadm**. Each invocation of the listen monitor may provide multiple services. The services provided by listen are specified in the port monitor administrative file which is in turn configured via the **pmadm** and **nlsadmin** commands.

The listen monitor may be used with any connection-oriented provider which conforms to the Transport Layer Interface (TLI) specifications. Under Solaris 2.3, listen monitors provide some services not managed by *inetd*. One example of such a service is the network printing service.

The nlsadmin Command

The **nlsadmin** command is a listen monitor-specific administrative command. This command formats listen information and writes it to standard output. This provides the ability to present such information to the **sacadm** and **pmadm** commands. The nlsadmin command does not administer listen, but rather it provides a means for the sacadm and pmadm commands to provide this administration.

The sacadm Command

The **sacadm** command provides administration of the port monitor for the SAC. By using command line options, the system administrator can use sacadm to accomplish the following tasks:

- ❑ Add or remove port monitors.
- ❑ Start or stop port monitors.
- ❑ Enable or disable port monitors.
- ❑ Install or replace a configuration script.
- ❑ Install or replace a port monitor configuration script.
- ❑ Print port monitor information.

Non-privileged users may request the status of port monitors, and print port and system configuration scripts. All other commands require super-user access.

The pmadm Command

The **pmadm** command provides administration of services for the SAC. By using command line options, the system administrator can use pmadm for the following tasks:

- ❏ Add or remove a network service.
- ❏ Enable or disable a network service.
- ❏ Install or replace a service configuration script.
- ❏ Print service information.

The **pmadm** command may be used by non-privileged users to list the status of the service, or to print out configuration scripts. All other access to the pmadm command require super-user privileges.

The terminfo Database

The *terminfo* is a database built by *tic* that describes the capabilities of terminals and printers. These devices are described in terminfo files by specifying a set of capabilities for the device. The entries in the terminfo database files consist of comma-separated fields. These fields contain capabilities of the device. The capabilities are represented with Boolean, numeric, and string values. The terminfo database is located in */usr/share/lib/terminfo/*.

This database is used by utilities such as the **vi** editor, the **curses** program, **ls**, and **more**. By using the terminfo database these utilities can work with a variety of terminals without the need to modify the programs for each type of terminal on the system.

The information in these database files is compiled from the ASCII definition files in */usr/share/lib/termcap*.

```
w1|wy50|wyse50|Wyse WY-50 in wy50 mode:\
        :is=\E1\E"\E`\072:if=/usr/share/lib/tabset/std:\
        :cd=\EY:ce=\ET:cl=\E+:\
        :up=^K:do=^J:nd=^L:bc=^H:cm=\E=%+ %+ :ho=^^:\
        :al=\EE:dl=\ER:ic=\EQ:dc=\EW:im=:ei=:\
        :co#80:li#24:sg#1:ug#1:am:bs:mi:pt:ta=5^I:sr=\Ej:\
        :so=\EG4:se=\EG0:us=\EG8:ue=\EG0:\
        :is=\Eu\E0:\
        :ku=^K:kd=^J:kr=^L:kl=^H:kh=^^:kb=^H:cr=^M:\
        :NS=\EK:PS=\EJ:\
        :GS=\EH^B:GE=\EH^C\
        :GV=\EH6:GH=\EH\072:GU=\EH=:GD=\EH0:G1=\EH3:G2=\EH2:G3=\EH1:G4=\EH5:\
        :k0=^@@\r:k1=^AA\r:k2=^AB\r:k3=^AC\r:\
        :k4=^AD\r:k5=^AE\r:k6=^AF\r:k7=^AG\r:\
        :k8=^AH\r:k9=^AI\r:kA=^AJ\r:kB=^AK\r:\
        :kC=^AL\r:kD=^AM\r:kE=^AN\r:kF=^AO\r:\
        :c0=^A`\r:c1=^Aa\r:c2=^Ab\r:c3=^Ac\r:\
        :c4=^Ad\r:c5=^Ae\r:c6=^Af\r:c7=^Ag\r:\
        :c8=^Ah\r:c9=^Ai\r:cA=^Aj\r:cB=^Ak\r:\
        :cC=^Al\r:cD=^Am\r:cE=^An\r:cF=^Ao\r:
w2|wy50vb|Wyse WY-50/80vb Wyse WY-50/80 with visible bell:\
        :vb=\EA04\200\200\200\200\200\200\200\200\200\200\200\EA00:\
        :tc=wy50:
w3|wy50w|Wyse WY-50/132    Wyse WY-50 with 132 column screen:\
        :is=\EG0\EC\EX\E`1\E`\073\Er:\
        :vs=\E`\073:co#132:tc=wy50:
wv|wy50vp|wyse-vp|Wyse 50 in ADDS Viewpoint emulation mode with "enhance" on:\
        :am:do=^J:if=/usr/share/lib/tabset/wyse-adds:\
        :le=^H:bs:li#24:co#80:cm=\EY%+ %+ :cd=\Ek:ce=\EK:nd=^F:\
        :up=^Z:cl=^L:ho=^A:ll=^A^Z:kl=^U:kr=^F:kd=^J:ku=^Z:kh=^A:\
        :pt:so=^N:se=^O:us=^N:ue=^O:dl=\El:al=\EM:im=\Eq:ei=\Er:dc=\EW:\
        :is=\E`\072\E`9^O\Er:rs=\E`\072\E`9^O\Er:
wk|wy50vp-nk|wyse-vp-nk|Wyse 50 in ADDS Viewpoint enhanced mode with no cursor keys:\
        :kl@:kr@:kd@:ku@:kh@:tc=wy50vp:
```

Contents of a typical termcap database entry.

 NOTE: *The subject of terminfo entries is more complex than allowed for in the scope of this chapter. For more information on the data contained in the terminfo database, consult the on-line terminfo man page.*

Setting Up Terminals

Now that you have an idea of the function performed by each portion of the SAF, you need to know how to perform simple tasks. As previously mentioned, there are two interfaces to the SAF. The **admintool** program enables you to use a graphical user interface for this interaction. You could also type in the individual SAF facility commands with the proper arguments to accomplish the same functions.

Let's examine a few simple cases of port setup to see how each of these facilities operate, and to point out the strengths and weaknesses of each method of interaction. One of the more common tasks is to add a terminal to a system. This requires you to set up a port via the **sacadm** or the **admintool** command.

The admintool Serial Port Manager.

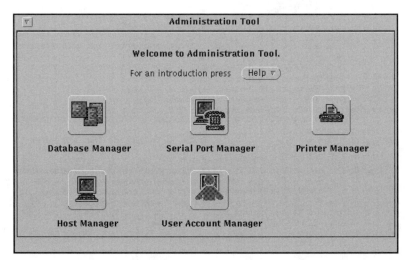

The admintool offers a Serial Port Manager selection which is a screen-oriented process that leads the user through serial port setup. The sacadm command is a program that uses command line options to perform the same tasks. Using the admintool as your interface, you need to select the name of the port that you wish to modify.

Once you have selected the appropriate port, you need to determine exactly what you wish to do with the port. The Modify Service menu of the admintool's Serial Port Manager allows you to set parameters such as the baud rate, terminal type, and port enable or disable, among others. There are standard templates provided under the Use Template icon to allow you to simplify the port setup.

*Selecting the port
to be modified.*

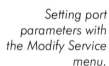

*Setting port
parameters with
the Modify Service
menu.*

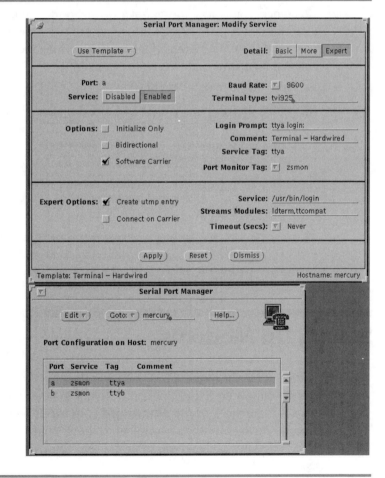

Once you have selected the appropriate parameters for a serial port, you can apply these parameters by clicking the Apply button on this menu. This will cause the proper files to be updated, and the appropriate port monitors will be started.

If you chose to use the **sacadm** command to add a terminal to your system, the basic sequence of steps would be the following:

1. Determine the version number of the port monitor. This is accomplished by using the **ttyadm -v** command. You will need the numeric response in the next step.

```
# ttyadm -v
```

2. Once you know the version of the port monitor program, you need to enable the port. You can use sacadm to enable the port. Substitute the version number from above for the *version*, and substitute the port monitor tag for *pmtag*:

```
# sacadm -a -p pmtag -t ttymon -c /usr/lib/saf/ttymon -v version
```

3. Once the port is enabled, you need to start up a *login* process. You can add a login service for the port you just enabled by using the sacadm command. Substitute the port monitor tag for *pmtag*, the version number for *version*, the device name for *dev_path*, and the tty label for *ttylabel*:

```
# sacadm -a -p pmtag -s svctag -i root -fu -v version -m
"'ttyadmin -S y -d dev_path -l ttylabel -s /usr/bin/login -l
ldterm, ttcompat'"
```

4. As you can see from this example, adding a terminal is much easier to accomplish when you use the Serial Port Manager. Another case where this is true is the process of adding a modem to the system.

Setting Up Modems

Another common request you will encounter as system administrator is to set up and administer dial-up modems. Again, this requires that you use either the **sacadm** command, or the **admintool** command. Using admintool, you follow the same steps for adding a terminal to the system. This time you need to select the appropriate modem type from the Use Template icon in the Modify Service menu.

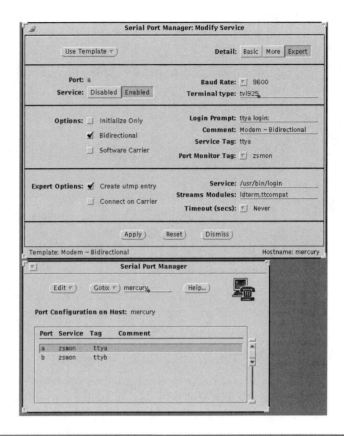

Using admintool to add a modem to the system.

Once you have selected the appropriate parameters for the modem installation, you can cause the changes to be applied by clicking on the Apply icon on this menu.

✔ **NOTE:** *If you wish to use UUCP with the modem you are installing, you need to set the line discipline to use eight data bits, with no parity. This is accomplished by selecting the baud rate menu item, and clicking on the other menu item. You then use the appropriate baud rate (as defined in /etc/ttydefs) that sets the parity and the correct number of data bits. One such entry would be 9600E for a 9600 baud modem.*

If you choose to use the **sacadm** command to add a dial-in or bi-directional modem to your system, the basic sequence of steps would be as follows:

1. Display all port monitors by using the sacadm command.

```
# sacadm -l -t ttymon
```

If the port you plan to use for the modem connection already has a port monitor, skip the next step.

1. If there is no port monitor on the chosen port, use the sacadm command to start one.

```
# sacadm -a -p pmtab -t ttymon -c /usr/lib/saf/ttymon -v 'ttyadm
-V' -y "comment"
```

2. Determine if the chosen port already has a service configured by using the **pmadm** command.

```
# pmadm -l -s svctag
```

If there is no service configured on the port, skip the next step.

1. If there is a service attached to the chosen port, use the pmadm command to delete it.

```
# pmadm -r -p pmtag -s svctag
```

2. Create the desired type of modem service. Use the port service tag listed in the */dev/term* directory for the *svctag* variable.

Modem Services

At this point you need to configure the modems depending on their intended use. If the modem will be used exclusively to allow remote users to log in to the system, it is referred to as a "dial-in" modem. Conversely, if the modem will be used to allow users on this system to contact other computers, the modem is referred to as a "dial-out" modem. Modems which allow incoming or outgoing connections are referred to as "bi-directional" modems.

The port setup for the three types of modems are different. The following commands initialize the serial port for the appropriate type of modem.

Setting Up a Dial-in Modem

A dial-in modem requires that you enable a log-in session manager so that users may log in to the system on this port. The following command provides a typical port setup for a dial-in modem:

```
# pmadm -a -p pmtag -s svctag -i root -v 'ttyadm -V' -fu -m
"'ttyadm -S n -d dev_path -s /usr/bin/login -l ttylabel -m
ldterm,ttcompat'" -y "comment"
```

Setting Up a Dial-out Modem

A dial-out modem has no need for a log-in manager, but it does require a method for the user to "open" the device for communication. If you wish to add a dial-out modem to your system the steps would be the following:

1. Add the modem to */etc/uucp/Devices*. The format of this file is *ACU cua/svctag - speed type*. Use the port service tag listed in the */dev/term* directory for the *svctag* variable:

vi /etc/uucp/Devices

2. Disable log-ins on the chosen port:

pmadm -d -p pmtag -s svctag

Typical contents of the /etc/uucp/Devices file.

```
                              shelltool - /bin/csh
# cat /etc/uucp/Devices
#ident  "@(#)Devices   1.6    92/07/14 SMI"   /* from SVR4 bnu:Devices 2.7 */
# Some sample entries:
# NOTE - all lines must have at least 5 fields use '-' for unused fields
# The Devices file is used in conjunction with the Dialers file. Types that
# appear in the 5th field must be either built-in functions (801, Sytek, TCP,
# Unetserver, DK) or standard functions whose name appears in the first field
# in the Dialers file.
# Two escape characters may appear in this file:
# - \D which means don't translate the phone #/token
# - \T translate the phone #/token using the Dialcodes file
# Both refer to the phone number field in the Systems file (field 5)
# \D should always be used with entries in the Dialers file, since the
# Dialers file can contain a \T to expand the number if necessary.
# \T should only be used with built-in functions that require expansion
# NOTE: - if a phone number is expected and a \D or \T is not present
#         a \T is used for a built-in, and \D is used for an entry
#         referencing the Dialers file. (see examples below)
ACUNORM  cua/a - 9600 tbnorm
ACUPLAIN cua/a - 9600 tbplain
ACUMNP   cua/a - 19200 tbuumnp
ACUPEP   cua/a - 19200 tbuupep
# ---Standard modem line
#ACU cua/b - 2400 hayes
#ACU cua/b - 2400 hayes \D
# ---A direct line so 'cu -lcua/b' will work
# Direct cua/b - 9600 direct
# ---Access a direct connection to a system
# systemx term/00 - Any direct
# where the Systems file looks like
# systemx Any systemx 1200 unused  "" in:-\r\d-in: nuucp word: nuucp
#        (The third field in Systems matches the first field in Devices)

TCP,et - - Any TCP -

# ---To use a STREAMS network that conforms to the AT&T Transport Interface
#        with a direct connection to login service (i.e., without
#        explicitly using the Network Listener Service dial script):
# networkx,eg devicex - - TLIS \D
#        The Systems file entry looks like:
# systemx Any networkx - addressx in:--in: nuucp word: nuucp
#        You must replace systemx, networkx, addressx, and devicex with system
#        name, network name, network address and network device, respectively.
#        For example, entries for machine "sffoo" on a STARLAN NETWORK might
#        look like:
#               sffoo Any STARLAN - sffoo in:--in: nuucp word: nuucp
#        and:
#               STARLAN,eg starlan - - TLIS \D
# ---To use a STREAMS network that conforms to the AT&T Transport Interface
#        and that uses the Network Listener Service dial script to negotiate
#        for a server:
# networkx,eg devicex - - TLIS \D nls
# ---To use a non-STREAMS network that conforms to the AT&T Transport
#        Interface and that uses the Network Listener Service dial script
#        to negotiate for a server:
# networkx,eg devicex - - TLI \D nls
# NOTE: blank lines and lines that begin with a <space>, <tab>, or # are
#               ignored.
#        protocols can be specified as a comma-subfield of the device type
#               either in the Devices file (where device type is field 1)
#               or in the Systems file (where it is field 3).
ACU cua/a - Any hayes
Direct cua/a - Any direct
# █
```

Setting Up a Bi-directional Modem

A bi-directional modem requires the log-in session manager as well as a method for the users to open it for outbound communications. If you wish to add a bi-directional modem to your system the steps would be as follows:

1. Determine if the port already has a port monitor:

```
# sacadm -l -t ttymon
```

2. If no port monitor is present, start one:

```
# sacadm -a -p pmtag -t ttymon -c /usr/lib/saf/ttymon -v 'ttyadm
-V' -y "comment"
```

3. Determine whether the port has any services configured:

```
# pmadm -l -t ttymon
```

4. If there are services associated with this port, delete them:

```
# pmadm -r -p pmtag -s svctag
```

5. Create a bi-directional port service:

```
# pmadm -a -p pmtag -s svctag -i root -v 'ttyadm -V' -fu -m
"'ttyadm -b -S n -d /dev/term/svctag -s /usr/bin/login -l
ttylabel -m ldterm,ttcompat'" -y "comment"
```

6. Add the modem to */etc/uucp/Devices*. The format of this file is *ACU cua/svctag - speed type*. Use the port service tag which is listed in the */dev/term* directory for the *svctag* variable:

```
# vi /etc/uucp/Devices
```

Disabling and Removing Serial Services

There may be instances under which you wish to disable serial port access. Again, you may use the **sacadm** command or the **admintool** to achieve this goal. Using the admintool, you select the Modify Service menu, and click on the Disable port icon. Once you have done this, you need to click on the Apply icon to cause the port to be disabled.

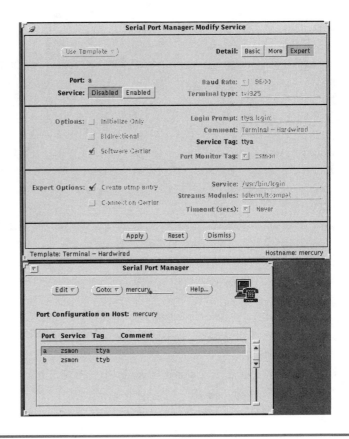

Using the Serial Port Monitor to disable a serial port.

Under most circumstances, you will find that disabling or enabling a port is simpler when you manually invoke the appropriate commands. The basic sequence you need to follow to manually disable a port follows:

1. Determine the port monitor tag for the port which you wish to disable by using the pmadm command.

```
# pmadm -1
```

2. Disable the port by using the pmadm command. Substitute the information provided in step 1 for the *pmtag* field.

```
# pmadm -d -p pmtag -s svctag
```

3. If you wish to remove a serial port service entirely, you could use the Serial Port Manager or the command line interface. To remove a port with the Serial Port Manager, you would activate the Edit menu, and select Delete Service.

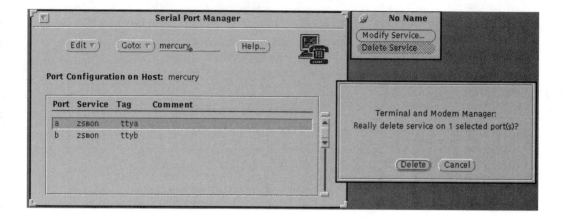

Using the Serial Port Manager to remove a serial port.

4. If you choose to delete the port service with the command line interface, you would start by following steps 1 and 2 above followed by the next step.

5. Delete the port service using the pmadm command.

```
# pmadm -r -p pmtag -s svctag
```

Summary

In this chapter you learned how serial port and network services requests are administered. We examined the role of each utility in the Service Access Facility suite, and how those utilities interact to allow you to administer serial port devices. Once you had an understanding of the SAF utilities, you learned how to use the admintool's Serial Port Monitor to manage serial ports.

You also saw how to use the sacadm and pmadm commands with command line arguments to add, modify, and delete serial port services. You learned that the Serial Port Manager simplifies some operations which normally require that you edit many files and update several databases if attempted via the manual method. Conversely, you saw that some serial port administration issues were simpler to accomplish if you used the command line interfaces.

Managing Printers

The Solaris printing service, **lp**, provides a complete network printing environment that allows sharing of printers across machines, management of special printing situations such as forms, and the filtering of output to match up with special printer types such as those which use the popular PostScript page description language. Managing printers has two sides. On one side is the technical aspect of connecting a printer to a system and configuring the *lp* software to work with the printer. On the other side is printing policy, or who should be allowed to use a particular printer or certain forms, whether a particular printer should be shared among workstations on the network, and so on. The printing service provides tools to make connections to printers and to manage printing policy.

Printing Terminology

Printing services on Solaris use a set of special commands, daemons, filters and directories. Files are not directly sent to the printer, but are spooled and then printed, freeing whatever application submitted the print request to move on to other tasks. The term *spooling* refers to the temporarily storing of a file for later use. It comes from the early history of computing when spooled files were saved on spools of magnetic tape. Here we define spooling as the process of putting a file in a special directory while it waits to be printed. Spooling puts the SunOS multi-tasking capability to good use by allowing printing to go on at the same time as other activities. As you might expect, some disk space should be set aside for a printer spooling area.

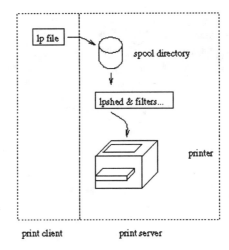

*The printing
service.*

The actual work of printing is done by a printing *daemon*. Daemon is the nickname given to all system processes running on a UNIX system. If you use the *ps -e* to take a look at all the processes on your workstation, you would see a number of daemons. The printing daemon is called *lpsched*.

Most output bound for a printer will require some filtering before it is printed. The term used to describe a program which transforms the contents of one file into another format as the file passes through the program is *filter*. For example, printing an ASCII text file to a PostScript printer will entail filtering the ASCII format into the PostScript format which can then be printed.

When an ASCII file is sent to a printer which accepts the PostScript page description language, the print service first runs the file through a filter to transform from ASCII into PostScript. The resulting PostScript file contains complete instructions in a form the printer can use to print the page and is somewhat larger than the original file due to the addition of this information. After filtering, the PostScript file is sent to the printer which reads the description of the pages to be printed and then prints them.

Printing on the Network

Finally, printing can be set up as a network-wide service. Machines which have printers connected directly to them and which accept print requests from other machines are called *print servers*. Machines which submit print requests over the network to other machines are called *print clients*. A machine can be both a print server and a print client. Printers directly attached to the workstation are known as *local printers*, while printers attached to other workstations reached via the network are known as *remote printers*.

A wide variety of commands are used to set up the printing service, enforce printing policies and handle special devices. Some of these commands, such as **lpadmin**, are used throughout the printing process to manage all aspects of the printing service. Other commands, such as **lpusers**, are used to manage just one aspect of printing. The follow table summarizes printing service commands. These commands will be described in detail later in the chapter as the discussion focuses on printer setup and management situations.

Print-related Commands

Command Name	Description
lpadmin	Printer setup and some management aspects.
Print Manager	Graphical printer setup tool. Part of admintool.
lpusers	Manages printer job priorities.
lpmove	Changes the destination of print jobs in the spool area.
lpforms	Manages forms and their associated parameters.
lpshut	Stops the entire printing service.
lpshed	Starts the printing service.
lp	Submits print jobs.
printtool	Graphical interface for submitting print jobs.
lpstat	Displays printing service and individual jobs and printer status.
cancel	Stops individual print jobs.
enable	Starts a printer printing.
disable	Stops printing on a particular printer.
accept	Starts print jobs accumulating in the print spool for a particular printer.
reject	Stops the print service from accepting jobs to be put in the printer spool area for printing on a particular printer.

Printer Setup

Setting up the printing service involves four phases. First, the printer must be physically connected to a machine which will become known as the *print server*. The print service software on the print server machine is then configured to match the connection parameters, and type and model of the attached printer. Next, other machines which will share this printer need to have their print service configured to act as *print clients*. Finally, special features such as printwheels, forms, and printer access controls will need to be configured to complete the installation.

Setting Up a Local Printer

The most basic printing service configuration is the local printer. Remote printing and print servers are extensions of the local printing process. To configure your system for local printing you need to first attach a printer to a workstation. As there are nearly as many types of printers as there are system types, the details of connecting a printer will not be covered here. In general, you need to connect the printer to the workstation or server and configure the printer as needed to use the connection you have made. Common connection methods include serial connections using the ports available on the rear of many workstations, and parallel connections using special parallel ports or special purpose interface cards such as the S-Bus card used with some SPARC printers. Printers have a variety of configuration methods from small DIP switches to keypads and display panels.

For a common PostScript printer such as an Apple LaserWriter, you will need to purchase or construct a serial cable to connect from the printer to the workstation. The printer manual and the manual for your workstation should provide information on the cable you need. You will also need to make changes to settings on the printer to work with a serial cable. On a printer such as the LaserWriter you will need to set the small DIP switches on the rear of the printer as shown in the printer manual under serial port connections.

To set up the printing service, you will need to know the following information on how your printer is connected.

- ❑ The port to which the printer is connected.
- ❑ If the printer is connected via a serial line, the basic serial parameters such as baud rate, parity, data and stop bits.

❑ The printer type. Solaris supports numerous printers by model name (e.g., HP LaserJet, Apple LaserWriter, NEC Spinwriter).

❑ The input accepted by the printer. Some printers will accept only a certain input language such as PostScript, while others will accept a variety of input languages.

Consider how much disk space is available for the printer spool area. This area is associated with the */var/spool/lp* directory. Depending on how you initially installed Solaris, the spool area may be in a separate disk slice or it may be part of the root directory (/). Sun recommends that at least 8 MB of disk space be reserved to service a single printer for one to three users. The amount needed on a specific system depends on the number and size of the print jobs likely to be run through a particular printer. Factors to consider include the number of users who will submit print jobs, the type of printer, and the speed of the printer. Remember that files with graphical images are bigger than text files which have the same number of pages. If you are setting up a server which will be servicing several printers, consider putting the */var* directory on a separate disk slice with sufficient space for all the printers you plan to service.

✗   *TIP: Allocate more disk space for PostScript printers than for other printer types. PostScript print jobs, especially those containing graphics can be quite large, and are typically much larger than ASCII print jobs. A good rule of thumb is to allow for 1.5 times as much space for a PostScript printer that will be printing mostly text, two to three times as much space for PostScript printers which will be printing large graphical images, and five times as much space for color PostScript images.*

Setting Up an Apple LaserWriter IINT

With these details in hand, let's walk through an example to show the process of printer setup. In our example, the printer is an Apple LaserWriter IINT connected via a serial line on port b of the workstation. The LaserWriter accepts only PostScript data, and expects the serial connection to be 9600 baud, 7 data bits, 1 stop bit, and no parity.

To begin the printer setup process you need to be in OpenWindows with a command window and logged in as the root user. Next, start the **admintool** by typing the following:

```
#admintool &
```

The opening screen of the admintool appears in the next illustration.

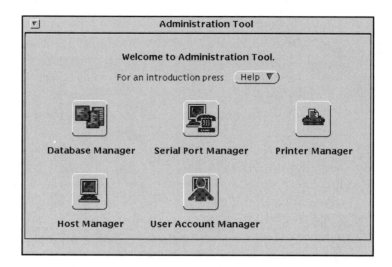

The opening admintool screen.

Clicking on the Printer Manager icon brings up the printer manager screen. Note how the printer manager screen lists the host it is working on. The printer manager can be used to manage printers on machines across your network. We will explore this feature later when we discuss network sharing of printers. For now, select Add Local Printer from Add Printer in the edit menu's pull-right selection.

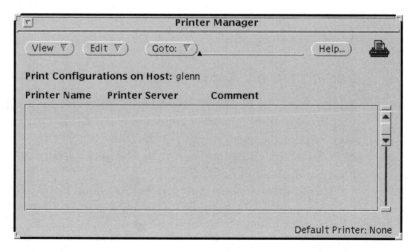

The Printer Manager screen.

The window which appears is a form that you fill in to specify the parameters associated with the printer you are adding. A blank form is shown in the next illustration.

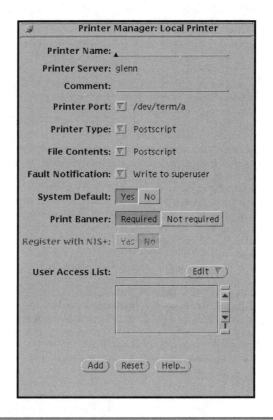

The local printer form.

The first item in the form, Printer Name, can be up to 14 characters long. It is a good practice to make the name descriptive of the printer usage, location, or ownership to aid users in selecting the correct printer for the job. Locations with a large number of printers distributed across their network adopt a uniform naming scheme which encodes the location and type of printer in the name. For example, *Lillyps* might be used to name the PostScript (ps) printer in the Lilly building.

The next field in the form is automatically filled in. It lists the name of the local machine as the printer server. For a local printer, the local machine is both client and server as far as the printing service is concerned.

The third field is for a comment that can be displayed by various printing commands. You might include additional information about the printer such as the room it is located in, and model number or name.

The fourth field asks for the port the printer is connected to. This is one of the items you need to remember when a printer is connected to a workstation. Select from the menu which appears under the little box to the left of the field. Selecting Other gives you a small entry window to enter the SunOS device name for the port the printer is connected to if the printer is not connected to one of the listed ports.

The fifth field for Printer Type refers to the particular manufacturer and model, such as HP Laser or Diablo. Most laser printers which accept the PostScript language can be set to either PostScript or PostScript Reverse. PostScript Reverse causes the printing service to reverse the order of the pages printed when possible. The reversed output order is handy for printers which stack their output face up as it eliminates the need to collate the pages after they are printed.

If your printer is not listed in the pop-up menu near the fifth field, check *terminfo* directories located in */usr/share/lib/terminfo*. In the terminfo directory you will find a series of directories that are single letters and numbers. The terminfo entries are grouped together by the first letter of the entry in these directories. Each entry describes a terminal or printer, and the name of an entry can be used to fill in the printer type field.

If no entry is available for your printer, try an entry for a similar printer. For example, if you have a dot-matrix printer, you might try one of the *epson* entries. If this tactic does not meet with good results, try copying the entry for a similar printer and editing it to describe the features of your printer. The manual page for terminfo lists the format and keywords used in the terminfo entries.

The sixth field, which looks like a duplicate of the fifth field, refers to the type of information that can be sent to the printer rather than the type of printer. Some printers can automatically detect PostScript and ASCII files, others can accept only one type of input or the other. Selecting the type of information your printer accepts causes the print manager to configure the printing service to filter the print job as needed to create the appropriate input type for the printer. For example, if you print an ASCII text file to a printer whose File Contents field is set to PostScript, the printing service will automatically filter the file to be printed with a program which converts the ASCII file to PostScript and then sends the converted file to the printer.

The seventh field, Fault Notification, indicates where problem messages from the printing service are to be sent. *Write to superuser* sends the problem messages directly to the terminal of a user logged in as *root*. Alternatively, you can have problem messages mailed to the root user or simply not sent by using the None option. The importance of printer problems and who needs to be informed depend on the printer, its location, and your local environment.

The eighth field is a two-item choice. If you select Yes, the printer described in this form is where output printed on a particular workstation will go by default. The next item, field nine, asks if a separator page should be printed at the start of each job. This *banner* will include the name of the user who printed the job and is handy at locations with many print jobs being printed by many users.

The tenth field allows for the printer to be registered with NIS+ for easy network-wide access. In this example, NIS+ is not being used so the field is grayed out.

The final field is an access list for this printer. By default any user can print to any local printer. You may wish to limit printer access to the user who owns the printer, or to members of the local work group. A more detailed discussion of printer access is covered below along with the setup of a remote or network accessible printer.

The completed local printer form.

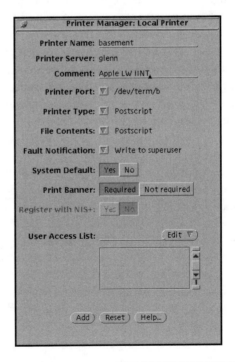

When form is completed, the Add button is clicked on with the mouse and the Printer Manager will install the new printer and make it ready for use.

Printers can also be set up via the command line. The **lpadmin** command covers a super-set of the functions available with the Print Manager. To perform the same printer setup as is shown in the completed local printer form, the following lpadmin commands are used.

```
lpadmin -p basement -D "Apple LW IINT" -v /dev/term/b -T
PostScript -I PostScript -A write -o banner

lpadmin -d basement
```

The first command creates the printer *basement.* The **-p** option specifies the printer name. The **-D** option includes a comment, and the **-v** option specifies the device the printer is attached to. The **-T** and **-I** options specify the printer type and file content, respectively. The **-A** option sets the alert type for announcing printer problems. The **-o** option makes a print banner mandatory. The second command makes *basement* the default printer.

Changing printer parameters is a matter of changing the options in the lpadmin command or selecting the printer from the Printer Manager window by double-clicking on it. A form like the one filled in to create a printer will appear allowing you to edit the fields which need to be changed. To delete a printer, select a printer from the list by single clicking on the printer's entry line and selecting Delete Printer from the Edit menu.

The Modify Printer form contains a different set of fields than the Local Printer form. In particular, several items in the Local Printer form are not listed or not changeable. For example, if you wish to change the printer type, you need to delete and re-create the printer entry.

The new fields that appear in the Modify Printer form refer to remote printers. The Print Server OS field selects the type of printer server operating system to be used. The Enable Print Queue and Accept Print Jobs options control the placement of print jobs in the spool directory for the remote printer and the acceptance of jobs from remote machines.

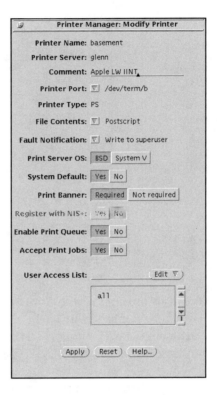

*Selecting a printer
to edit or delete.*

Setting Up Remote Printers

The setup of a local printer configures the local machine as a print server and a print client. The default access list created allows other workstations to send jobs to the printer spool to be printed. The only task remaining for remote printing is to create a printer entry on the remote machine.

In this example, access to the printer named *basement* on the workstation named *glenn* will be set up on the workstation named *grissom*. First, use the Goto field and button in the Printer Manager window to connect to *grissom*. You can now perform printer management functions as if you had walked over to the *grissom* workstation and logged into it. The next step is to select Add Access to Remote Printer from the pull-right item, and Add Printer in the Edit menu of the Printer Manager. A form will appear.

✔ **NOTE:** *For remote printer management to work, the remote system must have the print manager software installed and the user name you are using must be in the sysadmin group.*

Setting up remote printer access.

In the previous illustration, the form was filled in indicating that the printer called *basement* is connected to *glenn*, the printer server, and the printer was described in a comment. The Printer Server OS selection should be set to System V if the printer server is another Solaris workstation. If the printer is located on another manufacturer's workstation this setting will need to be changed to match the printer service provided on that machine. The System Default switch allows the *basement* printer on *glenn* to be set as the default for print jobs submitted from the *grissom* workstation. Clicking on Add will create the needed printer entry to send print jobs over the network from *grissom* to *glenn* and on to the printer.

When using **lpadmin** to set up remote printer access, the **-s** option is used to specify the remote system. On *grissom*, the following lpadmin command line would be used to specify access to the *basement* printer in a similar manner to that shown in the Print Manager example above.

```
lpadmin -p basement -s glenn
```

Access Control

The printing service provides access control for both local and remote printers. This is done through *allow* and *deny* lists, which can be located on either the print client or the print server.

Through the Printer Manager window we can select a printer and edit the access list at the bottom of the Modify Printer form. Take a look at the form pictured in the previous section of this chapter. The list managed by the form is an *allow* list, meaning that users on this list and only users on this list can print on this printer. This technique is handy for situations where the printer is in a particular person's office or is used by a small work group.

However, sometimes what you want is the ability to shut out a certain user or two from using a printer. This is done with a *deny* list. These lists can be created only by using the **lpadmin** command. The following command line denies access to the *basement* printer to user *mary*.

```
lpadmin -p basement -u deny:mary
```

Printing

Solaris provides a number of tools to submit print jobs to the printing service. There are three basic commands: **lp** for submitting jobs, **cancel** for halting print jobs, and **lpstat** for checking on the progress of a submitted job and the general status of the printing system. There is also a nifty OpenWindows interface called **printtool** which combines aspects of both lp and lpstat.

The lp and cancel Commands

The **lp** command allows you to submit print jobs with a wide number of options, change a print job's options while it is in the print spool waiting to be printed, and cancel print jobs. An example of the simplest form of the lp command follows:

```
lp my-stuff
```

This will print the file called *my-stuff* to the default printer. If no file is listed, lp reads from the standard input, making it suitable for sending the output of other commands via a pipe. To better control how *my-stuff* or other print jobs are printed, lp has a variety of option flags. Some of the most frequently used options are listed in the following table.

Frequently Used lp Command Options

Option	Description
-c	Copy before printing. Normally the printing service makes a link to the file to be printed and reads it at the time printing takes place. However, if you plan to remove or overwrite the file before it is printed, using this option forces the printing service to make a copy of the file. The printing service removes this temporary copy at the successful conclusion of the print job.
-d destination	If you want to print on a specific printer or class of printers, give the name of the printer or class as the destination. A destination of any will submit your job to any printer which can satisfy other options you may have set.
-f form	This option specifies the form or paper to be used when printing your job. With a destination of any (see previous option), the form option will route the print job to any printer which has the specified form mounted on it. See the discussion of forms below.
-H handling	This specifies the job handling. By using hold as the handling request, a job can be put in the print spool but not printed. Using resume releases a held job to be printed. Specifying immediate for handling allows users in the lpadmin group to get a print job processed ahead of jobs waiting in the printer spool.
-m	This causes the print service to send the user electronic mail when a print job concludes.
-n copies	This specifies the number of copies of the file to be printed.
-o option	This flag allows a number of printer-specific options. These include options which modify the line and character spacing and even send special control sequences to certain printers. A common usage is to specify the nobanner option to prevent a banner page from being printed. This saves paper for printers which handle few print jobs, and where individual jobs are easily sorted out.
-q priority	This sets the print job's priority in the print queue. The default print priority and the priority limits can be set and controlled on a per user basis as shown later in this chapter.
-S printwheel	This option specifies the printwheel or character set to be used. When used with the -d any flag, the print job is routed to a printer which has the needed printwheel or character set available. See the discussion of printwheels later in this chapter.

Option	Description
-t *title*	Puts the title of the print job on the banner page.
-T *content*	This option specifies the content type of the print job, such as PostScript. Print jobs are routed to printers that can either directly handle the content type, or printers for which a filter is available to convert the content type into a form the printer can handle.
-w	This causes the print service to write a message on the terminal, commandtool or shelltool window when a submitted print job finishes printing.

With such a wide variety of options, a job is occasionally submitted which specifies incorrect options. When this happens, the printing service cannot satisfy the request and the job will be rejected. If the job is accepted, but you want to change the options, you need to know the *request id* of the print job. This is the magic code that **lp** gives you when you submit a print job. The next illustration shows an example of a print job which could not be satisfied, followed by one in which the options were wrong and then corrected by using lp. Note how the request id is used.

```
┌─────────────────── cmdtool – /bin/csh ───────────────────┐
│ ▽                                                          │
│ glenn% lp -S russian /etc/hosts                           │
│ UX:lp: ERROR: The following options can't be handled:     │
│           -S character-set                                 │
│     TO FIX: The printer(s) that otherwise qualify         │
│             for printing your request can't handle        │
│             one or more of these options. Try             │
│             another printer, or change the options.       │
│ glenn% lp -H hold -n 1000 /etc/hosts                      │
│ request id is basement-6 (1 file(s))                      │
│ glenn% lp -i basement-6 -n 1                              │
│ glenn% lp -i basement-6 -H resume                         │
│ glenn% cancel basement-6                                  │
│ request "basement-6" cancelled                           │
│ glenn% ▲                                                   │
└────────────────────────────────────────────────────────────┘
```

Correcting an incorrect print job using the request id.

The cancel Command

The **cancel** command accepts either a request id as shown in the example above, or the name of a printer. Given a request id, cancel removes the print job from the printer spool. Given a printer name, cancel stops the currently printing job. The cancel command can be used only to stop a user's own print jobs. However, the root user can cancel any job submitted by any user. But what if you have forgotten the request id for a print job?

The lpstat Command

The **lpstat** command gives you information on the status of print jobs, printers, and the printing service daemons. Similar to **lp**, lpstat has a number of options. By default, keying in lpstat will list all print jobs submitted to the printing service. Each job is listed along with the request id of the job so that you can cancel or modify the request as needed.

```
                            cmdtool - /bin/csh
glenn% lpstat
basement-7              dwight            969    Aug 30 20:08 on basement
basement-8              dwight             68    Aug 30 20:09 filtered
glenn%
```

Checking on print jobs with lpstat.

More information is available when you include one of the commonly used options listed in the following table.

Frequently Used lpstat Command Options

Option	Description
-a *list*	Check to see if destinations or classes in the *list* are accepting print jobs. If no list is present, all destinations and classes are checked.
-c *list*	List the members of a class. If no *list* is given, all classes and their members are listed.
-d	Report the default print destination.
-f *list* -l	Checks if the form in the *list* is available.
-o *list*	Report on print requests in the *list*.

The printtool Command

OpenWindows provides a handy interface to the printing service called Print Tool. You can start this command by selecting it from the Programs pull-right menu or by typing

```
printtool &
```

in a command tool or shell tool window. The Print Tool will appear as an icon shaped like a laser printer with the name of the default printer. Double-clicking on the Print Tool icon will open it up to reveal the window shown in the following illustration.

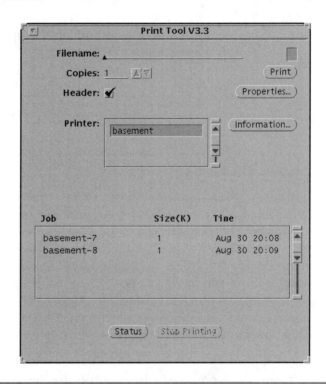

The Print Tool screen.

The print tool window has several areas. The bottom half shows the print jobs currently in the print queue. Selecting a print job by clicking on it activates the Stop Printing button which will stop the selected print job just like the **cancel** command does.

The upper half of the print tool has a field into which you can type the name of a file to be printed, a field to set the number of copies, and a check box to specify a header page. The scrolling list near the center of the screen allows you to select different printers. Clicking on the Print button sends the file listed in the Filename field to the selected printer. The Properties button brings up the dialog box shown below.

The Print Tool properties dialog box.

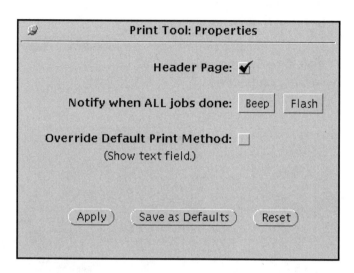

You can select the default for the header page, the type of notification the print tool should provide when your print job finishes printing, and the option of adding a Print Method field to the Print Tool window. The Print Method field allows you to specify your own printing command. You can use the symbolic items $FILES, $PRINTER, $LPDEST, and $COPIES to create a command string which will contain the file names, printer name, lp destination, and number of copies substituted in the appropriate places.

For example, for the *mp* PostScript filter to process a file into a sideways or landscape format and to print the file, you might use the following print method:

```
cat $FILE | mp -l | lp -d $PRINTER -T PostScript
```

When a file is printed via the Print Tool, the symbolic items in the print method are replaced by their values and the command is executed. If you had selected a file named *big-list* and a printer named *secretary*, the substitutions would produce the following command line:

```
cat big-list | mp -l | lp -d secretary -T PostScript
```

The most handy feature of the Print Tool is that it supports "drag and drop." To print a file, you can simply select the file's icon in the OpenWindows File

Manager window and drag and drop it on top of the Print Tool window. This is the same as typing in the file name and clicking on the Print button, or using the **lp** command. The file is submitted as a print job.

Printer and Print Job Management

Sometimes printing problems develop which require printer queues to be managed in more sophisticated ways. In larger organizations with many printers and users there is a constant need to shift printing resources around, and to route print jobs in response to printing demands, hardware failures, and the movement of personnel and equipment. Several commands allow you to deal with these situations.

Print Job Priority

All print jobs are given a priority value from 0 to 39. Jobs print in priority order with lower values printing first. By default, all print jobs are given a priority of 20. You can adjust this default to give individual users a priority limit as well as the hold and immediate handling options previously discussed.

The lpusers Command

The **lpusers** command is used to control the printing priority mechanism. The **-d** option lets you set the default priority for all print jobs. To assign a priority limit for an individual user, the **-q** and **-u** options are used. The -q option is followed by the priority value. The -u option is followed by the user name. You can specify a user on a specific machine by joining the machine name and user name with an exclamation point, such as in *machine!user*. All users of a given machine can be specified as *machine!all*. The same user on all systems can be specified as *all!user*. The -u option used alone removes a priority limit for a given user, while the -q option used alone assigns a priority limit for all users not explicitly listed. The **-l** option lists priority settings. Examples appear in the next illustration.

Using lpusers to set printing priorities.

```
┌─────────────────────── cmdtool – /bin/csh ───────────────────────┐
│▼                                                                  │
│ # lpusers -q 18                                                   │
│ # lpusers -u glenn!dwight -q 15                                   │
│ # lpusers -u all!root -q 0                                        │
│ # lpusers -l                                                      │
│ Default priority: 20                                             │
│ Priority limit for users not listed below: 18                    │
│ Priority  Users                                                  │
│      0       all!root                                             │
│     15       glenn!dwight                                         │
│ #  ▲                                                              │
└──────────────────────────────────────────────────────────────────┘
```

The first command sets the priority limit for all users not explicitly listed. This means that a user not listed cannot specify a priority lower than 18 when using **lp -q** to specify a priority when submitting a print job. If the -q option of lp is not used, the job will be assigned the default priority of 20.

The next two commands give lower priority values to the user account *dwight* on the machine *glenn* and the root account on all machines. These users can submit jobs which will be printed ahead of other jobs.

Finally, the **-l** option to **lpusers** is used to list priority limits. These limits apply for the print service on the machine where the commands were issued. If you have multiple print servers you will need to go to each server in turn and set priority limits.

Disable and Enable, Reject and Accept

Printers can be stopped by using the **disable** command. By default, disable will stop the currently printing job and save it to be reprinted when the printer is returned to service. You can optionally wait for the current job to finish printing and then stop the printer by using the **-W** option, or cancel the current job and not reprint it later by using the **-c** option. You can also leave a message to be displayed when the **lpstat** command is used to explain why the printer is disabled by using the **-r** option flag.

Restarting the printer is a simple matter of using the **enable** command. An example appears in the following illustration.

```
┌─────────────────────────── cmdtool - /bin/csh ───────────────────────────┐
│ ▽                                                                          │
│ glenn% disable -r "Replacing toner cartridge" basement                     │
│ UX:disable: ERROR: You aren't allowed to do that.                          │
│           TO FIX: You must be logged in as "lp" or "root".                 │
│ glenn% su                                                                  │
│ Password:                                                                  │
│ # disable -r "Replacing toner cartridge" basement                          │
│ printer "basement" now disabled                                            │
│ # enable basement                                                          │
│ printer "basement" now enabled                                             │
│ # ▲                                                                        │
└────────────────────────────────────────────────────────────────────────┘
```

Disabling and enabling a printer.

As you can see, the **disable** and enable commands are reserved for use by the root or lp users.

While a printer is disabled, print jobs can still be submitted for printing on that printer. These jobs are held in the printer spool area until printing resumes. You can control the spooling of jobs to be printed by using the **accept** and **reject** commands. These two commands start and stop the acceptance of jobs to be spooled. The only option flag is **-r** which allows you to give a reason when a printer spool is rejecting jobs. An example appears in the next illustration.

```
┌─────────────────────────── cmdtool - /bin/csh ───────────────────────────┐
│ ▽                                                                          │
│ # reject -r "Printer broke" basement                                       │
│ destination "basement" will no longer accept requests                      │
│ # lp -d basement /etc/motd                                                 │
│ UX:lp: ERROR: Requests for destination "basement" aren't                   │
│               being accepted.                                              │
│        TO FIX: Use the "lpstat -a" command to see why                      │
│                this destination is not accepting                           │
│                requests.                                                   │
│ # lpstat -a                                                                │
│ basement not accepting requests since Wed Aug 31 06:18:05 EST 1994 -       │
│         Printer broke                                                      │
│ # accept basement                                                          │
│ destination "basement" now accepting requests                              │
│ # ▲                                                                        │
└────────────────────────────────────────────────────────────────────────┘
```

Rejecting and accepting print jobs.

Once a printer spool has been set to reject, print jobs cannot be sent using **lp**, and the reason you gave for the rejection is printed when the **lpstat** command is used to check on the printer.

Moving Print Jobs

The printer and printer spool control commands are used in concert with other printing system commands to handle various situations. Suppose one of your printers is out of commission or is otherwise going to be unusable for a period of time, and print jobs are pending. Fortunately, the printing service allows you to move print jobs from one printer spool to another.

The basic approach to handling this situation follows: (1) reject print jobs for the unavailable printer to prevent more jobs from accumulating; and (2) move the print jobs to an alternative printer. An example appears in the next illustration.

```
                          cmdtool – /bin/csh
# lpstat -o basement
basement-7              dwight           969    Aug 30 20:08 canceled
basement-10             root              55    Aug 31 06:28 filtered
basement-11             root             969    Aug 31 06:28 filtered
# reject basement
destination "basement" will no longer accept requests
# lpmove basement-7 basement-10 basement-11 main-floor
UX:lpmove: ERROR: Request "basement-7" is done.
        TO FIX: It is too late to do anything with it.
total of 2 requests moved to main-floor
# lpstat -o main-floor
basement-10             root              55    Aug 31 06:28 on main-floor
basement-11             root             969    Aug 31 06:28 filtered
#
```

Moving print jobs to another printer.

Canceled jobs cannot be moved, but any other jobs in a print spool can be directed to another printer.

Removing a Printer

Removing a printer from the print service follows the same general strategy as moving print jobs. First, the printer and spool are stopped and then the printer entry is removed. There are two ways to remove the printer. One is to use the

OpenWindows Printer Manager, select the printer from the listing, and pick Delete Printer from the Edit menu.

You can also use the **lpadmin** command, the command line equivalent to the Print Manager. The command **lpadmin -x printer-name** removes the printer called *printer-name* from the system.

> ✔ **NOTE:** *Neither the Print Manager nor lpadmin will remove a printer which has jobs waiting in its printer spool. Before removing a printer, you need to move or cancel any print jobs in the spool.*

Starting and Stopping the Printing Service

The entire printing service can be stopped and started as needed. With the print service shut off, no jobs are printed or accepted for spooling for any local or remote printer accessible by the workstation. This is done by using the **lpshut** and **lpsched** commands. An example appears in the next illustration.

Stopping and starting the print service.

```
                    cmdtool - /bin/csh
# lpstat -r
scheduler is running
# lpshut
Print services stopped.
# lpstat -r
scheduler is not running
# /usr/lib/lp/lpsched
Print services started.
# lpstat -r
scheduler is running
#
```

The first command shows **-r**, a special option to the **lpstat** command, that indicates whether the print service scheduler is running. The lpshut command stops the scheduler. Starting the scheduler is a matter of running the scheduler by typing the full path to it as shown in the seventh line of the example above.

Forms, Printwheels, and Fonts

Many printers support features such as downloadable fonts, interchangeable printwheels, and font cartridges. In addition, many printers support printing on preprinted forms or paper sources of differing sizes.

Printers with downloadable fonts allow you to change typeface by changing a printwheel or font cartridge, and printing on preprinted forms or differing paper sizes can be handled by the printing service. These special situations are handled by the **lpadmin** command and the special forms handling command, **lpforms**.

The general strategy for forms and different fonts or printwheels depends on where the font or form is located. Fonts or forms resident in the printer, such as fonts loaded in the printer's read-only memory and forms located in additional paper feeders, are handled by informing the print service of their presence. Once informed and with a proper *terminfo* entry for the printer, the print service can automatically switch between printer resident fonts and forms based on the selections made for each print request.

Changing Paper

Many printers do not have additional built-in fonts or printwheels. Changing forms on many printers requires changing and aligning paper or switching paper trays. For these situations you must enter the definitions for the alternative font cartridges and forms into the print service and specify how to announce that a change is needed. The print service will automatically hold print jobs which need a special font or form in the print spool until you inform the print service that the needed form or font is ready.

Printer Resident Fonts

An example of a printer with built-in fonts is Digital Equipment Corporation's LN03 laser printer. The built-in fonts are listed in the *terminfo* entry for the printer and can be listed by using the following three-line C-shell script.

```
                        cmdtool - /bin/csh
glenn% foreach i ( 0 1 2 3 4 5 6 7 8 9 10 11 12 13 14 15 )
? tput -T ln03 csnm $i ; echo " "
? end
usascii
english
finnish
japanese
norwegian
swedish
germanic
french
canadian_french
italian
spanish
line
security
ebcdic
apl
mosaic
glenn%
```

Listing the built-in fonts of an LN03.

This script executes the commands on the second line by repeatedly substituting 0, 1, 2 and so on for *$i* every time. The **tput** command extracts *csnm*, the font name field, from the *terminfo* entry for the LN03 printer. The output is a list of the 16 resident fonts available on the ln03 printer.

Since these fonts are already listed in the terminfo entry, they can be used immediately with the **-S** option to the **lp** command. A command such as **lp -S swedish -d ln03-printer file** would cause the print service to issue commands to the printer to switch to the Swedish font and then print the file.

Using Font Name Aliases

If you find the font names used in the *terminfo* entry for a printer confusing, or want to make the font selection easier, aliases can be specified. A font name alias allows different names to be used for the same font.

```
                        cmdtool - /bin/csh
# lpadmin -p dec -S usascii=text,english=british
# lpstat -p dec -l
printer dec is idle. enabled since Sat Sep  3 07:18:31 EST 1994.
available.
        Form mounted:
        Content types: simple
        Printer types: ln03
        Description: LN03
        Connection: direct
        Interface: /usr/lib/lp/model/standard
        On fault: write to root once
        After fault: continue
        Users allowed:
                (all)
        Forms allowed:
                (none)
        Banner not required
        Character sets:
                text (as usascii)
                british (as english)
                finnish
                japanese
                norwegian
                swedish
                germanic
                french
                canadian_french
                italian
                spanish
                line
                security
                ebcdic
                apl
                mosaic
Default pitch: 10 CPI 6 LPI
Default page size: 132 wide 66 long
Default port settings:
#
```

Defining a font name alias.

The **lpadmin** option **-S** specifies a list of font aliases. Each alias begins with the name given in the *terminfo* entry followed by the alias separated by an equals sign (=). Be careful to avoid spaces in the list of aliases.

You can check to see which fonts and aliases have been defined for a printer by using the **-l** option to **lpstat**. In the above example, settings for the printer (dec) are displayed. The fonts are listed under Character sets about halfway down in the listing.

Non-Resident Fonts

Some printers, such as daisywheels or machines using plug-in font cartridges, require manual intervention to switch fonts. Setting up the printer service to handle these printers is much the same as with printer resident fonts. First, the names of the fonts or printwheels are specified. Next, you can set an alert to warn you when a job requiring a different printwheel is ready to be printed. Finally, you can inform the print service when you intervene to change the font or printwheel so that jobs which are waiting for that font or printwheel can be printed. An example appears in the next illustration.

```
┌─────────────────────────────────────────────────────────────────┐
│ ▽                         cmdtool – /bin/csh                      │
├─────────────────────────────────────────────────────────────────┤
│ # lpadmin -p secretary -S courier,pica                          ▲│
│ # lpadmin -S courier -A write -Q 1 -W 2                          ▓│
│ # lpadmin -S pica -A write -Q 1 -W 2                             ░│
│ # lpadmin -p secretary -M -S courier                            ░│
│ # lp -d secretary -S pica /etc/motd                             ░│
│ request id is secretary-16 (1 file(s))                          ░│
│ # lpstat -d secretary                                           ░│
│ system default destination: basement                            ░│
│ secretary-16           root              55    Sep 05 11:45     ▲│
│ # lpstat -l -d secretary                                        ░│
│ system default destination: basement                            ▼│
│ secretary-16           root              55    Sep 05 11:45     ░│
│       queued for secretary, charset pica                        ░│
└─────────────────────────────────────────────────────────────────┘
```

Configuring the print service for non-resident fonts or printwheels.

The first **lpadmin** command defines two printwheels, courier and pica, for the printer named *secretary*. The next two commands specify the conditions under which a change the printwheel message is given. The **-S** option specifies the printwheel, and the **-A** option selects one of the alert methods. Here you specify *write*, which causes a message to be displayed in the user's window or terminal. You can also specify *mail* to have electronic mail sent, or to run a specific command. The **-Q** option indicates the number of jobs which must accumulate in the printer spool requesting this printwheel before the alert is given. The **-W** option sets the interval in minutes between giving alert messages.

The fourth usage of the lpadmin command is used to indicate to the printing service which printwheel is currently in the printer. The **-M** option stands for mounted or installed and is combined with the **-S** option to specify the printwheel or font cartridge, and the **-p** option to indicate which printer has a particular printwheel installed.

The fifth line shows a request being submitted with the **-S** option to indicate the printwheel needed. Next, the **lpstat** command is used to show the status of the job, including the printwheel information.

The printing service also handles printers for which fonts are downloaded from your Solaris system as needed. This involves installing fonts on your system and editing a table font in one of the print service directories to allow the print service to determine when a font is needed and where the font information is stored. For a SPARC printer, this is covered in the installation instructions. For other printers, refer to the detailed information found in the Solaris administration guide and your printer's manuals.

In general, printers which have additional downloadable fonts will require the following steps:

1. As root, cd to */usr/share/lib*, create the directory *hostfontdir*, and use *chmod* to set file protection bits to mode 775.

2. In the */usr/share/lib/hostfontdir* directory, make directories for each downloadable typeface (e.g., Times, Palatino).

3. Each downloadable font variant is then copied into the directory named for the typeface. For example, the file containing the Times Roman font would be placed in the *Times* directory with *Roman* as file name.

4. In the */usr/share/lib/hostfontdir* directory itself, a file named *map* is created. In the file are lines containing the font name and the path to the downloadable font file (e.g., *Times-Roman /usr/share/lib/hostfontdir/ Times/Roman*).

When a print request specifying a downloadable font is made, the map file is consulted and a listed font file will be attached to the print request and sent to the printer along with the information to be printed.

Forms

The print service's forms support allows for the switching of forms in a fashion similar to printwheel switching. In addition, a user access list can be created to control which users can request and print on a given form such as pre-printed checks.

Defining a form requires a little more work than defining a printwheel. First, the **lpforms** command is used to define the form. You can do this interactively, or by feeding the answers to lpforms from a file. Shown in the following illustration are two form definitions to describe letter- and legal-size paper for a laser printer.

The first form of the lpforms command almost completely describes the form by explicitly giving each option. The only options not used here are **comment**, which allows you to add a description of the form, and an alignment pattern which can be printed to aid in aligning pre-printed forms.

In the second form definition, the only options used are those which differ from the defaults. The result can be viewed by using the **-l** option to lpforms. If an incorrect form was entered, the **-x** option can be used to remove it from the print service. Similar to printwheels, alerts and user lists can be attached to forms.

```
                                    cmdtool - /bin/csh
                         # lpforms -f letter -
                         page length: 60
                         page width: 80
                         number of pages: 1
                         line pitch: 6
                         character pitch: 10
  Defining forms        character set choice: any
using the lpforms       ribbon color: any
     command.           # lpforms -f legal -
                        page length: 84
                        # lpforms -l -f legal
                        page length: 84
                        page width: 80
                        number of pages: 1
                        line pitch: 6
                        character pitch: 10
                        character set choice: any
                        ribbon color: any
                        #
```

Defining forms using the lpforms command.

```
                                    cmdtool - /bin/csh
                         # lpforms -f checks -
                         page length: 30
  Assigning user lists   page width: 80
  and alerts to forms.   number of pages: 1
                         line pitch: 12
                         character pitch: 10
                         character set choice: any
                         ribbon color: any
                         # lpforms -f checks -A mail -Q 2 -W 5 -u allow:accounting!bob
                         #
```

Assigning user lists and alerts to forms.

Here a form is defined for pre-printed checks. The second **lpforms** command assigns an alert message to the form with the **-A, -W**, and **-Q** options. The -A option can be used to send the alert message via mail, writing it on the user's screen (write), running a command you specify, or doing nothing (none). The -W option specifies how often the alert message is to be sent. In the example, it is set to be sent every two minutes. The -Q option specifies how many print jobs must be in the printer spool waiting to be printed before the alert is sent.

The **-u** option specifies a user access list. In this case, an allow list is used. As discussed when setting up a printer, an allow list specifies the user or users who can print on this form. Users not in the allow list cannot print on the form. You can also use a deny list which works the opposite way: the only users denied access to the form are those listed in the deny list. Next, you can use the *machine!user* and *machine!all* notation to specify a user on a specific machine or all users of a machine, respectively.

Printing Problems and Solutions

The two basic printing problems are not producing output or producing incorrect output. In both cases, a good approach toward identifying the problem is to walk backwards along the path the print job takes. Start with the printer itself and go back towards the command used to submit the print request.

At the printer, start with the obvious. Is the printer powered on? Is the machine loaded with paper, ribbon, toner, etc. Laser printers in particular are intelligent devices and can stop for a variety of problems including paper jams and other internal faults. Check the printer to be sure it is ready to accept a print job.

Next, check the connection from the printer to the print server. For intelligent printers you may need to begin by checking the printer's configuration. Some printers have communications settings that are easily changed by mistake. Verify that the printer is using the correct port and that the parameters for the port are accurate, such as baud rate and parity. Determine whether the cable between the printer and computer is plugged in.

At this point, check the print server. A common source of problems is the incorrect definition of the printer when it was set up. Check each field of the local printer form viewed by using the Printer Manager screen accessed from the *admintool.* Determine whether the communications parameters match the settings on the printer. If incorrect output is the problem, check to see that the printer type and file contents fields are correct for your printer. In some cases, you may need to experiment with these settings to find a combination that works with your printer.

If your printing problem occurs on a print client, try sending a print job to the printer directly from the print server. This may help you to determine if the problem is on the client or the server. If the problem is on the client, use the **admintool** and the Printer Manager screen and check the printer configuration as you did for the print server.

Once you have convinced yourself that the printer is properly connected, the printer server is operating, and the print client is correctly configured, move on to check the network. Use a utility such as **ping** to verify whether communications are working between the print client and server. See the "Understanding Basic Local Area Networking" chapter for more information on setting up, monitoring and troubleshooting network problems. Finally, check the network log file, */var/lp/logs/lpNet.* This file lists problems found by the printing service when it sends or receives a print request over the network.

Summary

The Solaris printing service is made up of a broad collection of commands that work together to handle a variety of printing situations. When setting up printing, pay careful attention to the printer's connection to your workstation or server and to the allocation of sufficient printer spool space. Next, employ the printing service's access control mechanisms to implement printer and form access policies.

Understanding Basic Local Area Networking

In the previous chapters you have learned how to manage peripherals and resources directly connected to your systems. It is now time to examine how computer networks allow you to utilize resources indirectly connected to your system. In this chapter you will learn about several of the more common Local Area Network (LAN) technologies used today as well as a few that promise to be the network technologies of the future. In addition, you will learn about important network administration files, basic network security, common network commands, and basic network troubleshooting. The information presented in this chapter will prepare you for using network applications such as Network File Systems (NFS) and Network Information Services (NIS) in the following chapters.

Local Area Network Technologies

Computer networks can be divided into three general categories: Local Area Networks (LANs), Metropolitan Area Networks (MANs) and Wide Area Networks (WANs). LANs are high-speed connections among computers that service a relatively small geographic area. LANs operate at 4Mbps to 2Gbps and do not typically span more than a single office building or small campus.

MANs are slower-speed connections that operate at 9.6Kbps to 64Kbps but provide a larger area of coverage than LANs. As the name implies, MANs typically provide network services for an area the size of a large city.

WANs are generally the most complex network category. Most WANs operate at data rates of 56Kbps to 1.5Mbps, but cover large areas such as a state or the entire United States. WANs are used to interconnect MANs and LANs. This chapter will focus on LANs.

The variety of LAN solutions available today often leaves new (as well as veteran) system administrators in a fog of confusion. Each technology has advantages and disadvantages that must be considered carefully when selecting LANs for use at your site. While several common LAN technologies used on Solaris systems are introduced in this section, the discussion is not an exhaustive study. A few recommended books to help expand the reader's background on the subject of computer networking follow: *Internetworking with TCP/IP* (Prentice Hall, 1991) by Douglas Comer, *Gigabit Networking* (Addison-Wesley, 1994) by Craig Partridge, and *TCP/IP Network Administration* (O'Reilly & Associates, Inc., 1992, 1993) by Craig Hunt.

Ethernet

Ethernet is one of the dominant (if not the most dominant) network technologies in use today. Ethernet is a "bus topology" local area network (LAN) technology developed in the late 1970s by Xerox Corporation. It is based on a network signaling method called Carrier Sense Multiple Access with Collision Detection (CSMA/CD) that was originally designed to run on coaxial cable. Each host connected to an Ether network constantly monitors the network for the presence of the carrier signal (CS). The carrier is a network control signal that lets hosts know that the network is in use. A host may transmit data onto the network only when the network is idle.

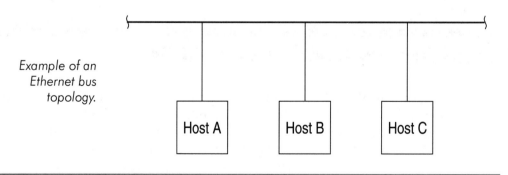

Example of an Ethernet bus topology.

Ethernet has no prearranged order in which hosts transmit data. Any host can transmit onto the network whenever the network is idle. Thus Ethernet is said to be "Multiple Access" (MA). If two hosts transmit simultaneously, however, a data collision occurs. Both hosts will detect the collision (CD) and stop transmitting. Both hosts will then wait a random period of time before attempting to transmit again.

It is important to note that Ethernet is a best-effort delivery LAN. In other words, it does not perform error correction or retransmission of lost data when network errors occur due to events such as collisions. Any datagrams which result in a collision, or which arrive at the destination with errors must be retransmitted. If you consider a highly loaded network, you can see that retransmission could result in a bottleneck.

Ethernet networks typically transmit data at 10 Mbps (megabits per second). This changed in 1993 when Ethernet hardware which operates at 100 Mbps became available. Ethernet is best suited for LANs whose traffic patterns are data bursts. NFS and NIS are examples of network applications that tend to generate "bursty" network traffic.

Integrated Services Digital Network

Through the 1950s, the public telephone network was wholly analog; the switching, and transmission of voice signals were handled by analog circuitry. In the early 1960s the telephone industry began implementation of digital transmission systems. In the 1970s the industry began deploying digital switching systems. The Integrated Services Digital Network (ISDN) is a multiplexed digital networking scheme for use over existing telephone facilities. ISDN is a CCITT (Consultative Committee on International Telephony and Telegraphy) standard.

With the availability of ISDN, the telephone carriers now offer end-to-end digital transmission capabilities. When ISDN is fully deployed, it will provide a universal voice/data network platform. The major advantage of ISDN is that it can be operated over most existing telephone lines. Therefore, it has the potential of providing digital data services to any location on Earth that has telephone service. ISDN is prevalent in Europe and in many U.S. metropolitan areas.

An ISDN connection is typically capable of transmission rates of 64Kbps (kilobits per second) per channel. The 64Kbps circuits are referred to as Basic Rate Interfaces or BRIs. A BRI is comprised of two 64Kbps bearer (B) channels and a single delta (D) channel. The B channels are used for voice and data, while the D channel is used for signaling and X.25 packet networking.

NOTE: *In telephone terminology, 64Kbps refers to 64,000 bits per second. In computer terminology, 64Kbps typically refers to 65,536 bits per second.*

Terminal Adapter (TA) equipment is available to adapt these BRI B channels to existing equipment via standard EIA RS-232 and V.35 connections. More traditional communications devices such as telephones and fax machines may also be attached to the BRI via appropriate interfaces.

Another type of ISDN interface is the Primary Rate Interface (PRI). This is typically an aggregate of 23 B channels and one D channel multiplexed on a single physical interface. These connections are typically used for Private Branch Exchange (PBX) to Central Office (CO) connectivity, and long-distance carrier connectivity.

ISDN transmission rates can be increased to 128 Kbps by *bonding* two ISDN B channels together, which is still considered "slow" for digital data. It is, however, significantly faster than the typical 9600 baud (9.6 Kbps) or the newer 28.8Kbps modems used to connect computer systems via analog telephone lines. The 128Kbps ISDN circuits are referred to as "2B" circuits.

At the *customer* end of an ISDN link, the connection is a single pair of wires. The maximum length of this link is 5,500 meters (18,000 feet). Each ISDN BRI circuit can handle multiple simultaneous voice and data sessions. Up to eight ISDN devices can be connected to each BRI circuit, and each circuit allows X.25 packet multiplexing, or circuit switched modes of operation.

Because ISDN can operate on most existing telephone cabling and electronics, it allows for relatively high-speed, low-cost network connections. Many university campuses and geographically distributed corporations take advantage of ISDN capabilities to provide network connections for their users.

Token Ring

Token ring networks are another widely used network technology. A token ring network utilizes a special data structure called a *token* which circulates around the ring of connected hosts. Unlike the Multiple Access scheme of Ethernet, a host on a token ring can transmit data only when it possesses the token. Token ring networks operate in two modes: receive and transmit.

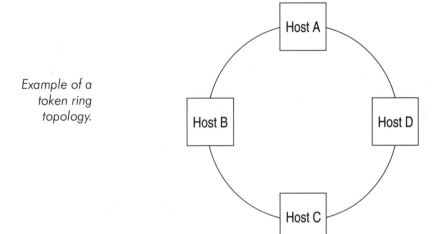

Example of a token ring topology.

In receive mode, a system copies the data from the *input* side of the ring to the *output* side of the ring. If the host is down and unable to forward the information to the next host on the ring, then the network is down. For this reason many token ring interfaces employ a *dropout* mechanism that, when enabled, connects the ring input to the ring output. This dropout mechanism is disabled by the network driver software when the system is up and running. But if the system is not running, the dropout engages and data can get through the interface to the next system on the ring.

In transmit mode, the interface *breaks* the ring open. The host sends its data on the output side of the ring, and then waits until it receives the information back on its input. Once the system receives the information it just transmitted, the token is placed back on the ring to allow other systems permission to transmit information, and the ring is again *closed*.

Fiber Distributed Data Interconnect

Fiber Distributed Data Interconnect (FDDI) is a token ring LAN based on fiber optics. FDDI networks typically operate at 100 Mbps. Unlike Ethernet, FDDI is well-suited for LANs whose traffic patterns include sustained high loads, such as relational database transfers and network tape backups. The FDDI standards define two types of topologies: Single Attachment Stations (SAS) and Dual Attachment Stations (DAS).

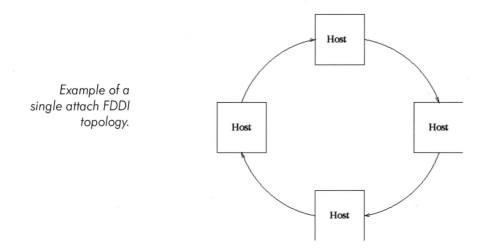

Example of a single attach FDDI topology.

An SAS FDDI ring allows a *star* topology network. A concentrator is placed in the center of the star. A single pair of fibers is connected from the concentrator to each host. If one host needs to send information to another host, the concentrator must forward the information. Single attachment FDDI rings require less fiber than dual attachment FDDI rings, but they contain a serious disadvantage: if a connection between the host and the concentrator is broken, the host is not available to the network. Another disadvantage of a single attachment FDDI ring is the cost of the concentrators.

The DAS FDDI ring employs two counter-rotating fiber rings. In a counter-rotating token ring network, one ring sends information in a clockwise direction, and the other ring sends information in a counter-clockwise direction. But FDDI instills a little twist to this operating pattern.

In normal operation, one FDDI ring is used for all communications, while the second ring sits idle. If the primary data ring is broken, the interface reconfigures itself to use the second ring as a loopback to form a single ring between the remaining hosts. This feature provides some fault tolerance to the network at the cost of extra fiber.

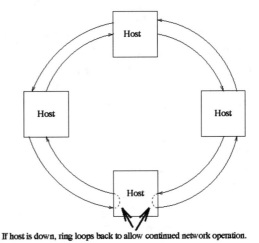

Example of a dual attach FDDI topology.

If host is down, ring loops back to allow continued network operation.

High Performance Parallel Interconnect

High Performance Parallel Interconnect (HIPPI) is a networking standard produced by the ANSI X3T9.3 committee. HIPPI was originally designed to connect two devices (typically a supercomputer and a graphics display device). The current HIPPI standard defines a connection protocol which is sometimes used to provide a point-to-point parallel network topology.

Under the current HIPPI standard, HIPPI switches have been developed which allow the interconnection of multiple hosts. HIPPI connections operate at 800 Mbps or 1600 Mbps. HIPPI metallic cable connections may be up to 25 meters in length. The X3T9.3 standard also defines a *serial* HIPPI using fiber connections which can extend up to ten kilometers in length.

In a HIPPI network, a connection protocol is used to set up connections and allow the transfer of data between the hosts. While many hosts may be connected to the network, only one connection may be established at any given time. If one host needs to send data to another host on the network, a connection negotiation takes place. The sending host must request to be connected to the receiving host. Once the receiving host approves the connection and the connection is set up, the data is sent through the connection.

If the receiving host is busy when the connection is requested, the sender has two options. One option is for the sender to wait for the receiver to become idle (similar to being placed on hold on the telephone). Alternately, if the sender does not wish to wait, it is notified that "all circuits are busy" and that it "may

try its call at a later time." Once the sender has successfully negotiated a
connection and sent all of its data, it must request that the connection be broken.

HIPPI has proven to be a valuable networking technology in the gigabit
network community. Due to its point-to-point nature, the limitation of one active
connection at any time and the expense of the hardware, HIPPI has not been
widely used as a LAN technology.

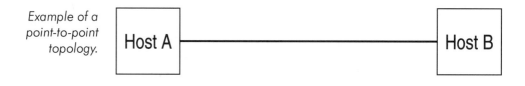

*Example of a
point-to-point
topology.*

Asynchronous Transfer Mode

Asynchronous Transfer Mode (ATM) networks are rapidly becoming a popular
type of networking technology. ATM is the underlying transmission system for
CCITT's next generation of ISDN. ATM networks can operate over fiber optic
cables at speeds up to 622 Mbps. Recent additions to the specifications will allow
ATM networks to operate at rates over 1 Gbps (Gigabit/second), and 2.4Gbps
standards are currently under discussion. Connections over twisted-pair copper
media are currently possible at speeds up to 155Mbps.

ATM, like today's telephone network, is a hierarchical standard which
employs a connection protocol much like the connection protocol that HIPPI
networks use. Most ATM networks are implemented over fiber optic media,
although recent standards also define connections over twisted-pair copper
cable plants. The use of fiber optic connections ensures relatively low-noise,
error-free data transmission. Unlike HIPPI, ATM allows multiple connections
through the network to operate simultaneously.

ATM is based on a cell networking model. While Ethernet allows 1500 byte
data packets, and FDDI allows 4500 byte data packets, ATM operates on 53-byte
data *cells*. A 53-byte cell allows a 5-byte header (which contains control
information), and 48 bytes of data. The control information in the header tells
how this data cell is to be used in relation to the other data cells which are
received. The use of small cells reduces wasted bandwidth on the transmission
media, and reduces transmission delays on the media.

In Ethernet and FDDI networks, the hosts must perform the datagram
disassembly and reassembly when they need to send large amounts of informa-

tion. This causes the host to become a bottleneck on highly loaded networks. In an ATM network, the disassembly and reassembly is performed by the ATM interface. This frees the host to perform other operations. The combination of these factors allows ATM to provide more higher-speed network connections than are available with Ethernet or FDDI.

Most typical fiber-based ATM host connections operate at 100 Mbps (also known as TAXI interfaces), or 155 Mbps (also known as OC-3 connections). The data streams may also be multiplexed together to provide connections at 622 Mbps (OC-12 connections) using existing telephone communications technology. More recent multiplexing equipment allows connections at 1.2Gbps (OC-24) and 2.4Gbps (OC-48) data rates.

Because few computer systems can actually sustain transmission rates above 100 Mbps, the higher speed connections are typically used to provide multiple connections at the lower speeds. The addition of the twisted-pair ATM standards allows the installation of ATM technology in places where twisted-pair cable had previously been used for Ethernet connections.

Working with Ethernet

Before proceeding, we need to define some frequently used terms that describe LAN hardware. To simplify the discussion, we will confine the definitions to those associated with Ethernet, because (1) it is one of the more prevalent network technologies currently deployed, and (2) many of the hardware devices used in an Ether network are similar in function to devices used in other LAN technologies.

A Brief History of Ethernet

Ethernet is actually a network cabling and signaling specification developed by Xerox in the 1970s. The initial implementation of Ethernet was called Experimental Ethernet. In 1980, Digital Equipment Corporation (DEC), Intel, and Xerox jointly published the Department of Defense (DoD) "Blue Book Standard" for Ethernet Version 1 as a second generation standard.

The major difference between Experimental Ethernet and Ethernet Version 1 was the increase in the signaling speed. Experimental Ethernet used 2.94Mbps signaling while Ethernet Version 1 used 10Mbps signaling. This change also required that the length of the coax segment be reduced from 1000 meters to

500 meters. With the change in cable length repeaters were introduced to allow extended length networks. Other minor changes between the Experimental Ethernet and Ethernet Version 1 standards included support for more hosts (1024 for Version 1 versus 256 for Experimental Ethernet), and a change in the coaxial cable impedance from 75 ohm to 50 ohm.

In 1982 an enhanced version of the specification was released as Ethernet Version 2. Ethernet Version 2 is upwardly compatible with Ethernet Version 1. The primary differences between Version 1 and Version 2 specifications were the inclusion of better definitions for the physical channel signaling and the addition of network management functions under Version 2.

Ethernet II versus 802.3

The Ethernet Version 2 specification was used as the basis for the Institute of Electrical and Electronics Engineers (IEEE) Project 802. The superseding IEEE 802.3 standard is generally interchangeable with Ethernet 2, however. Specifications for Ethernet (sometime called 802.3 networks) are contained in the IEEE 802.3 standard.

The major differences between the 802.3 specification and Ethernet Version 2 are minor changes in the data link layer. These differences pertain to the construction of the network packet headers. The 802.3 packets conform to the 802.2 Logical Link Control protocol. Hosts on an 802.3 network use this protocol to distinguish among multiple client protocols. Packets on an 802.3 network also include a header field which contains the packet length. Packets on an Ethernet version 2 network use a *type* field in the header to distinguish between multiple client protocols. There are also small differences in signaling voltages between the two standards.

Basic Ethernet Hardware Components

In general, Ethernet hardware consists of five basic components: the transport medium, transceiver, transceiver cable (AUI), host interface, and terminators. Depending on the type of Ethernet used (Thick-net, Thin-net, Broadband, Fiber optic, or Twisted-Pair), some of these components may not be obvious to the user because they are built into the system hardware. To keep the discussion of Ethernet hardware uncomplicated, we will primarily focus on the components used with Thick-Ethernet. Where possible, differences between the components for each style of Ethernet connection will be noted.

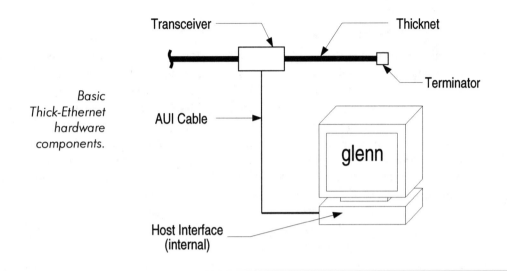

*Basic
Thick-Ethernet
hardware
components.*

The Transport Medium

The transport medium is the backbone of an Ether-network. Since the early 1980s, thick and thin coaxial cable (coax) have been the backbone used in Ether networks. More recently, Twisted-pair cabling and fiber optic backbones have become more popular. A detailed discussion of the different types of transport medium appears later in this chapter.

The Terminators

Terminators are 50 ohm resistors connected to the ends of the coax. One function of the terminators is to "absorb" signals reaching the end of the backbone so that they do not echo back through the coax. Signal echoes are also called *signal reflections*. It is desirable to eliminate the reflections, as they may otherwise collide with active data packets and cause transmission errors.

Terminators are used on Thick-net and Thin-net Ethernets. Twisted-pair Ethernets employ internal hardware devices to properly terminate the signaling lines. Fiber optic Ethernets do not require terminating resistors because separate wires are allocated for transmitting and receiving the data. Broadband Ethernets require termination as specified by the broadband signaling equipment.

The Transceiver

A transceiver is used to "tap" into the transport medium. Transceivers convert the combination of digital and analog signals on the transport medium into signals that hosts can "understand" and vice versa. Transceivers are also known as *Media Access Units* (MAU). In the case of Thick-Ethernet, taps can be installed every 2.5 meters. Transceivers allow the connection of one host to the media. Multi-port transceivers are also available. These units accept the connections from several (usually eight) systems on the *input* ports, and one *output* port is provided to connect the multi-port transceiver to the coaxial cable via a standard (single connection) transceiver unit. Many multi-port transceivers allow a coax-less mode of operation by performing internal termination and signal loopback. It is possible to build a small Ethernet just by connecting eight or fewer systems to a multi-port transceiver.

Thin-net Ethernet typically incorporates the transceiver into the host interface board. The Thin-net interface plugs directly into the thin-net coax via a T connector. Twisted-pair Ethernets also include an integral transceiver in the host interface. At the *media end* of the connection, a concentrator, or hub, may connect several twisted-pair systems to the thick-net coax via a standard transceiver connection. Alternately, the concentrator/hub may connect directly to another concentrator/hub via a twisted-pair connection. In this way it is possible to construct an entire network without using any coaxial cable!

Fiber optic Ethernets use a special transceiver to convert electrical signaling to light pulses (and vice-versa) for transmission over the fiber. Broadband Ethernets use a Radio Frequency (RF) *head-end* unit to multiplex the Ethernet signals onto the broadband coax.

The Attachment Unit Interface (AUI)

The Attachment Unit Interface connects the transceiver to the host interface. The Attachment Unit Interface is also known as *transceiver cable*, or AUI cable, and consists of eight leads with a DB15 connector at each end. The AUI cable can be up to 50 meters in length. AUI cables are used with Thick-net Ethernets, and Fiber optic Ethernets.

Twisted-pair Ethernets use unshielded twisted pair cable to connect the system to the media. These cables employ four pairs of wires with an RJ-45 telephone-style connector at each end.

The Host Interface (HI)

The Host Interface (HI) connects to the host's system bus. To the operating system, the Host Interface looks like an input/output device. The Host Interface connects to the transceiver via the AUI cable. Each Host Interface has a unique hexadecimal serial number (also referred to as the Media Access Controller, or MAC, address) assigned to it at the factory. This MAC address is similar to a social security number in that it uniquely identifies the particular interface board. The Host Interface is configured with a unique network address (usually an Internet Protocol, or IP address) at system boot time. The use of the IP address will be discussed in subsequent sections of this chapter.

Types Of Ethernet Transport Media

There are several types of media used for Ethernet networks. Ethernet is defined in the Institute for Electrical and Electronic Engineers (IEEE) 802.3 specification. The original Ethernet specification defined a base-band coaxial cable network. Coaxial cable (coax) is an electrical cable used for radio frequency (RF) and certain data communications transmission. Base-band networks provide a single channel on the media for all communications, whereas broadband networks multiplex many channels onto the media. The original Ethernet specification defined a connection scheme referred to as a *10base5 network*.

✔ **NOTE:** *The X Base Y numbering system tells you a lot about the network. The X is the signaling speed in megahertz. The word "Base" means it is a base-band network (as opposed to "Broad" for broadband networks). Initially, the Y component of this description referred to the maximum cable segment length in hundreds of meters. Hence a 10Base5 network is 10 megahertz, base-band, with a length limit of 500 meters per cable segment. Recent revisions to the Ethernet specification allow for use of media not allowed in the original specifications. These changes made it possible for the Y component of the naming scheme to be the letter T, or the letter F, referring to Twisted-pair, and Fiber connections. A few of the more popular designators are thick-net (10Base5), thin-net (10Base2), broadband (10Broad36), fiber-optic (10BaseF), and twisted-pair connections (10BaseT).*

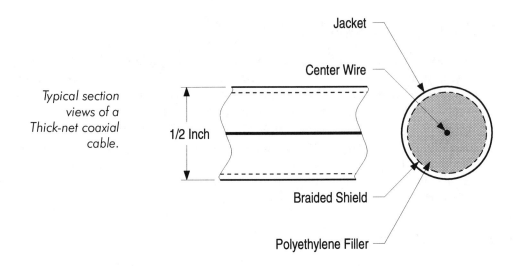

Typical section views of a Thick-net coaxial cable.

Jacket

Center Wire

1/2 Inch

Braided Shield

Polyethylene Filler

Thick-net Ethernet (10Base5)

Thick-net Ethernet is a coaxial cable used for Ethernet networks and is designed to meet stringent electrical specifications. Because the jacket of this coaxial cable is a bright yellow, it sometimes known as *screaming yellow* coax. *Tap* points (i.e., places where transceivers can tap into the main cable) are identified by painted black bands on the cable every 2.5 meters.

Thick-net is typically used on LANs that have many hosts (up to 250) located in one building. Thick-net coaxial segments may be up to 500 meters (1,640 feet) in length. The distance between the two most remote stations on the network may be as much as 1500 meters. The 1500 meter span is made possible by connecting up to three Thick-net segments via repeaters and routers.

Thin-net Ethernet (10Base2)

Thin-net Ethernet (10Base2) is sometimes referred to as *Cheapnet* or *Cheapernet* because it uses industry-standard RG58 A/U coaxial cable which is less expensive than thick-net coaxial cable. Thin-net does not adhere to the stringent specifications of thick coaxial cable. As a result, it can extend to only 185 meters (606 feet) per segment and supports up to 85 hosts. The distance between the two most remote systems may be up to 555 meters. Unlike Thick-net coax, Thin-net coax is not tapped. Instead it must be cut and fitted with BNC-type connectors wherever a network connection is required. Thin-net is typically used in small office LANs with less than 25 hosts.

Broadband Ethernet (10Broad36)

Broadband Ethernet networks are implemented over broadcast media, such as an Ethernet over a television/video cable plant. Broadbanding is achieved by allocating one channel of the broadband media to the Ethernet. Broadband Ethernet is not commonly used.

Fiber Optic Media (10BaseF)

Fiber optic media has become one of the more popular types of computer network media. Fiber optic Ethernets are generally used for networks where long distance connections or high electrical isolation is required. Use of fiber optic media is common in high noise areas such as factory floors, steel plants, and other situations where large amounts of electromagnetic interference is present.

Unlike coaxial cable, fiber cannot be tapped. Instead, it is used in a point-to-point topology such as when two buildings must be linked together. Most fiber-optic Ethernet equipment is capable of operation over distances of up to 2.2 kilometers. Fiber optic connections provide higher bandwidth (capacity), and superior noise immunity. In most cases, the fiber optic cable plant may also be used for other technologies that will one day replace Ethernet.

> ✔ **NOTE:** *A common misconception about fiber optic media is that it is "faster" than metallic media. This is incorrect. Fiber and metallic media carry signals at approximately the same velocity (two-thirds the speed of light). Fiber optic, however, does have a much higher bandwidth (capacity) than copper. Unlike metallic media, fiber optic transmissions are not affected by electromagnetic (EM) disturbances (such as lightning or radio transmissions) because they are optical (laser light pulses) and not electrical in nature.*

Unshielded Twisted-Pair Ethernet (10BaseT)

Unshielded Twisted-pair Ethernet is currently a very popular network scheme. Unshielded Twisted-pair Ethernet (also known as UTPE) uses standardized unshielded cables containing "twisted pairs" of signaling wires. It is the rate of twist of the pairs that produces its unique electrical characteristics.

UTPE networks operate as a bus topology but physically look like a star. Each leg of the star can be up to 100 meters (328 feet) in length. A twisted-pair network may span a distance of 500 meters (1640 feet) between the two most remote systems. At the center of the star is a connection device called a *concentrator* (sometimes called a *hub*).

UTPE cable is rated from category 1 through 5. The higher the wire category number, the higher its bandwidth. Category 4 and Category 5 UTP cabling is capable of supporting data rates of 155 Mbps. UTPE is typically used for small LANs with 16 to 96 hosts per concentrator. Its major advantage over coaxial cable is the use of cheaper wiring which can be used for other types of connections (telephone, ATM, CDDI, among others) in the future.

In addition to the low-cost media, twisted-pair Ethernet electronics offer many ease of use features such as remote configurability via software, advanced security features, and remote network monitoring.

✔ **NOTE:** *In real world applications, most Ethernet communications networks are comprised of several styles of interconnected Ethernet media. It is not unusual to find campus or corporate networks which include Thick-net, Thin-net, Fiber-optic, and Twisted-pair technologies on the same Ethernet.*

A star Ethernet topology.

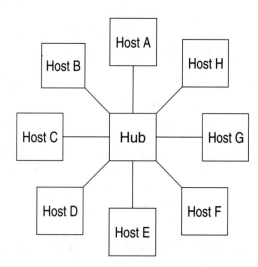

✔ **NOTE:** *Fiber Ethernet and Twisted-pair Ethernet descriptions do not give the length limitations in the specification as is done with the Thick, Thin, and Broadband specifications.*

Working with the Internet Protocol

The process of connecting two computer networks together is called *internetworking*. The networks may or may not be using the same network technology, such as Ethernet or token ring. In order for an Internet connection to function, a transfer device (computer) that forwards datagrams (data) from one network to the other is required. This transfer device is called a *router* or, in some cases, a *gateway*.

In order for internetworked computers to communicate, there must be some way to uniquely identify which computer you wish to communicate with. This identification scheme must be much like a postal mail address; it should give enough information so that you can send information long distances through the network, yet have some assurance that it will be delivered to the desired destination. As with postal addresses, there must be some authority sanctioned to assign addresses and administer the network.

Anyone reading this book has probably heard the term *Internet*. Chances are you have also been on the net exchanging files, passing electronic mail, and general spelunking. So, what is this Internet?

Two networks interconnected via a router.

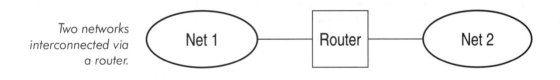

Overview of the Internet

Put simply, the Internet is an interconnection of many dissimilar network technologies around the world. It originated in the mid 1970s as the ARPANET. Primarily funded by the Defense Advanced Research Projects Agency (DARPA), ARPANET pioneered the use of packet-switched networks using Ethernet, and a network protocol (a set of rules) called Transmission Control Protocol/Internet Protocol (TCP/IP). The beauty of TCP/IP is that it "hides" network hardware issues from end users, making it appear as though all connected computers are using the same network hardware. TCP/IP was originally ported to BSD UNIX by Bolt, Beranek, and Newman, Inc (BBN), which is one reason UNIX is prevalent on networks today.

Connecting to the Internet

In the international telephone system, every phone (connection) is assigned a unique phone number. The hierarchical addressing scheme of country code, area code, exchange and line number assures that any phone in the system can establish a connection with any other phone in the system. Telephone numbers are assigned by the telephone companies.

If hosts on a network wish to communicate, there also needs to be an addressing system that identifies the location of each host on that network. In the case of hosts on the Internet, the governing body that grants Internet addresses is the Network Information Center (NIC), affectionately known as "The Nick."

To apply for an Internet address, contact:

> Government Systems, Inc.
> Attn: Network Information Center
> 14200 Park Meadow Drive
> Suite 200
> Chantilly, VA 22021
> 800.365.3642
> 703.802.4535

Technically speaking, sites that do not wish to connect to the Internet need not apply to the NIC for a network address. The network/system administrator may assign network addresses at will. However, if the site decides to connect to the Internet at some point in the future, it will need to re-address all of its hosts to a network address assigned by the NIC. Although reassigning network addresses is not difficult, it is tedious and time-consuming, especially on networks of more than a few dozen hosts. It is therefore recommended that networked sites apply for an Internet address as part of the system's initial setup.

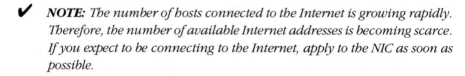

> ✔ **NOTE:** *The number of hosts connected to the Internet is growing rapidly. Therefore, the number of available Internet addresses is becoming scarce. If you expect to be connecting to the Internet, apply to the NIC as soon as possible.*

Classes of Internet Addresses

As previously mentioned, hosts connected to the Internet must have an Internet address, also known as an *IP* (short for Internet Protocol) address. IP addresses are a set of four integers separated by periods. An example of an Internet address is 154.7.3.1. Each integer in the address must be in the range from 0 to 255. IP addresses are also known as "dotted quad" addresses.

There are five classes of Internet addresses: Class A, Class B, Class C, Class D, and Class E. Class A, Class B, and Class C addresses are used for host addressing. Class D addresses are called multi-cast addresses, and will not be discussed in this book. Class E addresses are experimental addresses. It is important to remember that Class A, Class B, and Class C IP addresses consist of a *network number* portion and a *host address* portion.

Class A Addresses

If the number in the first field in an IP address is in the range 1 to 127, then it is a Class A address. There are 127 Class A networks. Each Class A network can have up to 16 million hosts. With Class A networks, the number in the first field identifies the network number, while the remaining three fields identify the host address on that network. Class A addresses are reserved for network organizations such as ARPANET and UUNET, or very large corporations such as General Electric, Inc.

[1-127] . [0-255] . [0-255] . [0-255]

Example of a Class A IP address.

IP =   105   .   186   .   17   .   45

Network Number: 105
Host Address: 186.17.45

! **WARNING:** *127.0.0.1 is a reserved IP address called the loopback address. All hosts on the Internet use this address for their own internal network testing and inter-process communications. Do not make address assignments of the form 127.x.x.x or remove the loopback address unless instructed otherwise.*

Class B Addresses

If the integer in the first field in an IP address is in the range 128 to 191, then it is a Class B address. There are 16,384 Class B networks with up to 65,000 hosts each. With Class B networks, the integers in the first two fields identify the network number, while the remaining two fields identify the host address on that network. Class B addresses are typically assigned to large companies and institutions.

[128-191] . [0-255] . [0-255] . [0-255]

IP =   154 . 7 . 3 . 7

Example of a Class B
IP address.

Network Number: 154.7
Host Address: 3.7

Class C Addresses

If the integer in the first field in an IP address is in the range 192 to 223, then it is a Class C address. There are 2,097,152 Class C networks with up to 254 hosts each. With Class C networks, the integers in the first three fields identify the network address, while the remaining field identifies the host address on that network. Class C addresses are typically assigned to small companies and organizations.

[192-223] . [0-255] . [0-255] . [0-255]

IP =   201 . 23 . 178 . 18

Example of a Class C
IP address.

Network Number: 201.23.178
Host Address: 18

!   **WARNING:** *The numbers 0 and 255 are reserved for special use in an IP address. The number 0 refers to "this network." The number 255, called the broadcast address, refers to all hosts on a network. For example, the address 154.7.0.0 refers to the class B network 154.7. The address 154.7.255.255 is the broadcast address for the 154.7.0.0 network and refers to all hosts on that network.*

The Host's File

One of the most frequently used network administration files is */etc/inet/hosts*. The file is a registry of IP addresses and associated host names known to a system. At a minimum, it must contain the loopback address (127.0.0.1) and the IP address for this host. Many networking commands consult the host file in order to resolve (learn) the IP address of a host name it wants to communicate with. Several of these networking commands will be discussed later in this chapter.

The minimum required entries in the hosts file.

```
                     shelltool - /bin/csh
#
# Internet host table
#
127.0.0.1    localhost    loghost
154.7.3.1    mercury
~
~
~
```

It is generally not required that all hosts connected to your network be listed in the *hosts* file. Typically, only those hosts that are routinely contacted are listed. For security reasons, *root* is the only user who can edit */etc/inet/hosts*. If you routinely communicate with many hosts (more than a dozen or so) on your network, maintaining a large *hosts* file can be cumbersome. If this is the case, using an on-line distributed database system, such as the Domain Name System (DNS) or Network Information Service (NIS+), should be considered. NIS+ is discussed in a later chapter.

A typical host file.

```
                     shelltool - /bin/csh
#
# Internet host table
#
127.0.0.1    localhost    loghost
154.7.3.1    mercury
154.7.3.2    shepard
154.7.3.3    grissom
154.7.3.4    glenn
154.7.3.5    carpenter
154.7.3.6    schirra
154.7.3.7    cooper
```

> **!** **WARNING:** *Trailing blank characters on a line in the hosts file will cause that entry to fail.*

Remote System Access Commands

Once IP addresses are assigned to the hosts on your network, you need a means of using the network. Solaris 2 includes several commands that allow communications between hosts. There are two classes of commands that enable this access: remote log-in protocols, and file transfer protocols.

rlogin

The **rlogin** command is one of several network commands that enables users to establish a login connection to a remote host. In order for rlogin to work correctly, two things must be established:

- ❏ The user must have a log-in account on the remote host, and
- ❏ The remote host must be listed in the local hosts */etc/inet/hosts* file, or the user must know the IP address of the host.

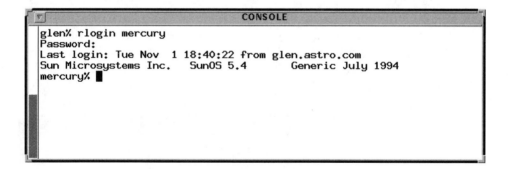

```
                        CONSOLE
glen% rlogin mercury
Password:
Last login: Tue Nov  1 18:40:22 from glen.astro.com
Sun Microsystems Inc.   SunOS 5.4      Generic July 1994
mercury% █
```

A network log-in using rlogin.

telnet

The **telnet** command is another network command which enables users to establish a log-in connection to a remote host. Again, two things must be established for **telnet** to work correctly:

❑ The user must have a log-in account on the remote host, and

❑ The remote host must be listed in the local hosts */etc/inet/hosts* file, or the user must know the IP address of the host.

A network log-in using telnet.

```
                    shelltool - /bin/csh
mercury% telnet 154.7.3.2
Trying 154.7.3.2 ...
Connected to 154.7.3.2.
Escape character is '^]'.

UNIX(r) System V Release 4.0 (shepard)

login: student
Password:
Last login: Wed Nov 23 07:21:18 from 154.7.3.1
Sun Microsystems Inc.   SunOS 5.3       Generic September 1993
shepard% []
```

✔ **NOTE:** *The rlogin command is specific to UNIX systems and may not be supported on other operating systems. The telnet command is one of the TCP/IP protocols and is therefore supported on virtually any machine networking with TCP/IP. For security reasons, many system administrators prefer telnet. Network security is covered later in this chapter.*

rsh

The **rsh** command is the remote shell program. Using rsh to connect to another computer system is sometimes referred to as "using a sneaky shell." Unlike **rlogin** and **telnet**, rsh does not prompt the user for log-in and password. Instead it establishes a connection to the remote system and starts a shell (thus the name remote shell) in which a command can be executed. Before the rsh command starts a shell process on the remote machine, it checks for a valid user account, and whether the user has permission to use this system.

When the command started under rsh exits, the remote shell dies and the connection is broken. The rsh command is generally used to execute commands on a remote host such as automated tape backups and system clock synchronization. Because the rsh command uses a different "entrance" to the remote system, there are times that rlogin and telnet to the remote system will fail, while the rsh command succeeds. Like rlogin, rsh is specific to UNIX systems.

Executing a remote command using rsh.

```
shelltool - /bin/csh
mercury% rsh shepard uname -a
SunOS shepard 5.3 Generic_101674-01 sun4c sparc
mercury% 
```

Using rlogin, telnet and rsh

The rlogin, telnet, and rsh commands not only allow the capability of communication with other computers, but can also be very powerful tools for systems administration. As previously mentioned, because each of these remote access commands use different "entrances" to the remote systems, there are times when one or more of these commands may fail to allow the user access to the remote system. In many cases, one of the three commands will still work, enabling the system administrator to determine the cause of the problem and remotely effect a remedy.

Another advantage to the rlogin, telnet, and rsh commands is the ability to access dissimilar computers from a single point. In a typical environment, it is very unlikely that all computers are the same brand, running the same operating system software. Yet the rlogin, telnet, and rsh commands allow the systems administrator to connect to these dissimilar machines and execute commands native to that system.

The rlogin and telnet commands allow the user to use a terminal emulator of their choosing, and to customize the key mappings to their preferences. Note that both the rlogin and telnet commands (by default) require that the user enter a password on the remote system to gain access. While this feature promotes better system security, it can become a nuisance for a user with accounts on many machines on the network.

✔ *NOTE: In order for the rsh command to operate, the hosts engaged in these operations must be "trusted." Hosts are considered trusted if they are listed in the file /etc/hosts.equiv or in the user's .rhosts file.*

The */etc/hosts.equiv* file allows the system administrator to grant access to this host from any machine listed in the file. While this may be a convenient method to allow easy access to the host, it is also considered a security faux pas.

The rlogin, and rsh commands allow users to create a file in their home directories called *.rhosts* which will disable the password-entry requirement when they are attempting to gain access to this host on their personal account. While this feature can be used to allow convenient access to the systems which the user typically contacts, it is also considered a security problem. The entries in this file consist of the system name, a space character, followed by the name of the user who has permission to access this account via the rsh or rlogin command.

File Transfer Commands

Sometimes a user does not want to log in to a remote system. Many times the user simply needs to transfer data from one computer to another. The following commands do not allow the user to execute commands on the remote machines, but they do allow authorized users to perform file transfers into and out of the system.

ftp

The **ftp** command is one of several network file transfer (copy) commands. Like **telnet**, ftp (File Transfer Protocol) is part of the TCP/IP protocol suite. It allows the transfer of files between networked systems. In most cases, a user wishing to use ftp must have an account on the remote system. However, hosts that are configured as *anonymous ftp servers* do not require an ftp log-in. These hosts are typically located at public institutions and house information (e.g., programs and documents) that is free to the public.

```
                         shelltool - /bin/csh
    ┌─────────────────────────────────────────────────────────────────┐
    │ mercury% ftp 154.7.3.2                                            │
    │ Connected to 154.7.3.2.                                           │
    │ 220 shepard FTP server (UNIX(r) System V Release 4.0) ready.      │
    │ Name (154.7.3.2:kent): student                                    │
    │ 331 Password required for student.                                │
    │ Password:                                                         │
    │ 230 User student logged in.                                       │
    │ ftp> get myfile                                                   │
    │ 200 PORT command successful.                                      │
    │ 150 ASCII data connection for myfile (154.7.3.1,36410) (520 bytes).│
    │ 226 ASCII Transfer complete.                                      │
    │ local: myfile remote: myfile                                      │
    │ 533 bytes received in 0.0077 seconds (68 Kbytes/s)                │
    │ ftp> quit                                                         │
    │ 221 Goodbye.                                                      │
    │ mercury% □                                                        │
    └─────────────────────────────────────────────────────────────────┘
```

A network file transfer (copy) using ftp.

✔ **NOTE:** *Another file program similar to ftp is rcp. It is specific to UNIX systems and may not be supported on other operating systems.*

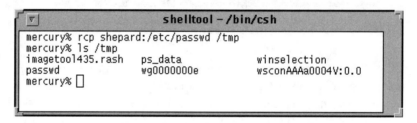

```
                         shelltool - /bin/csh
    ┌─────────────────────────────────────────────────────────────────┐
    │ mercury% rcp shepard:/etc/passwd /tmp                             │
    │ mercury% ls /tmp                                                  │
    │ imagetool435.rash     ps_data              winselection           │
    │ passwd                wg0000000e           wsconAAAa0004V:0.0      │
    │ mercury% □                                                        │
    └─────────────────────────────────────────────────────────────────┘
```

A network file copy using rcp.

✔ **NOTE:** *In order for the rcp command to operate, the hosts engaged in these operations must be "trusted." Hosts are considered trusted if they are listed in the file /etc/hosts.equiv, or in the user's .rhosts file.*

Network Security

Most computer professionals would agree that the term "network security" is an oxymoron. It is almost impossible to stop a motivated intruder from gaining access to systems that are connected to a network. The threats to a system's resources and its data are higher than ever due to the extensive use of computer networking. This is especially true if the systems are connected to the Internet, where millions of connected users have access potential to each system.

Network security is a broad topic. Our goal in this section is to discuss some of the common practices employed by administrators to reduce the likelihood of intrusion. Before we start we'd like to point out that there are a number of books about system security. A few that may be of interest follow: *UNIX System Security* (Addison-Wesley, 1991) by Rik Farrow; *Computer Security Basics* (O'Reilly & Associates, Inc., 1991, 1992) by Deborah Russell and G. T. Gangemi; and *Practical UNIX Security* (O'Reilly & Associates, Inc., 1991) by Eugene Spafford.

> **!** **WARNING:** *A connected system is a vulnerable system.*

There are ten fundamental functions that administrators should consider when dealing with network security:

1. Proper account management.

2. Restrict root access.

3. Log **su** attempts.

4. Restrict */etc/hosts.equiv* and *.rhosts* use.

5. Restrict informational commands.

6. Restrict connectivity commands.

7. Restrict network services.

8. Install a firewall.

9. Use ASET.

10. Be vigilant.

Some of the above functions are not appropriate for certain systems. However, you should be aware of them and review these functions from time to time.

Proper User Account Management

Good network security begins with good system security. Although this alone will not prevent a professional "cracker" from gaining entry, it will stop most amateurs. Be sure that users are using good passwords and changing them often as discussed in the earlier chapter on security. Be certain that everyone is aware that they have a responsibility to protect the system from intruders. It should be a general policy that all information concerning a site's computer operations is confidential. Similar to spies, many crackers often begin their system attacks by gathering information about a site's systems from unsuspecting employees.

✗   *TIP: Good network security begins with good system security.*

Restricting Root Access

If the line *CONSOLE=/dev/console* exists in the */etc/default/login* file, then root cannot gain log-in access to a Solaris 2 system via **rlogin** or **telnet**. This is the default. Do *not* comment out or remove this line. Remember, root has unlimited authority on a system. It cannot be repeated often enough: *do not allow root log-ins from remote systems.*

Part of the /etc/default/login file, showing that no root log-ins are allowed.

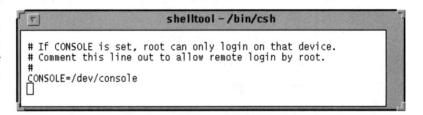

```
                         shelltool - /bin/csh
 ▽
 # If CONSOLE is set, root can only login on that device.
 # Comment this line out to allow remote login by root.
 #
 CONSOLE=/dev/console
 ☐
```

Log su Attempts

As discussed in the security chapter of this book, the **su** command can be used to switch the user-id to root as well as other system users. It is good practice to uncomment the *CONSOLE=/dev/console* and *SULOG=/var/adm/sulog* lines in the */etc/default/su* file. In doing so, su attempts, both failed as well as successful, will be posted to the system console and the *SULOG* file. Check the SULOG file frequently. Repeated failed su attempts could indicate a cracker is attempting to gain root access to your system.

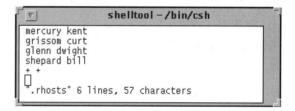

Potential system attack. Note repeated su failures to root (denoted by minus signs) by user student from pts/0.

```
                    shelltool - /bin/csh
  ▽
  SU 10/25 13:48 + pts/2 nick-root
  SU 10/25 18:17 + pts/4 susan-root
  SU 10/25 19:50 - pts/0 student-root
  SU 10/25 19:51 - pts/0 student-root
  SU 10/25 19:51 - pts/0 student-root
  SU 10/25 19:51 - pts/0 student-root
  SU 10/25 19:51 - pts/0 student-root
  SU 10/25 19:52 - pts/0 student-root
  SU 10/25 19:52 - pts/0 student-root
  SU 10/25 19:52 - pts/0 student-root
  SU 10/25 20:54 + console/0 kent-root
  []
```

Restricting /etc/hosts.equiv and .rhosts Usage

The trusted hosts files, */etc/hosts.equiv* and *.rhosts*, are holdovers from BSD UNIX. Their use should be discouraged because of security loopholes. A plus sign character (+), for example, in either of these files means that "all hosts and/or users are trusted." It is good practice to search for these files (using the **find** command for instance) and remove them.

Potential security breach. Do not allow plus sign (+) entries in users' .rhosts file.

```
                    shelltool - /bin/csh
  ▽
  mercury kent
  grissom curt
  glenn dwight
  shepard bill
  + +
  []
  ".rhosts" 6 lines, 57 characters
```

Restricting Informational Commands

Restricting execute permission on informational commands for users can help keep system configuration information and user statistics confidential. Consider using the **chmod** command with mode *750* on informational commands such as the following:

1. **/usr/sbin/dfmounts**
2. **/usr/sbin/dfshares**
3. **/usr/bin/finger**
4. **/usr/sbin/ifconfig**

5. /usr/sbin/mount

6. /usr/bin/netstat

7. /usr/sbin/ping

8. /usr/bin/rpcinfo

9. /usr/bin/rup

10. /usr/bin/rusers

11. /usr/bin/who

Restricting Connectivity Commands

As with the restriction of informational commands, you may want to consider restricting execution permission to connectivity commands, such as **ftp**. In doing so, you prevent internal users from connecting to remote systems. This avoids the possibility of users transferring potentially hazardous files onto your/their system or transferring confidential information out. Consider using the **chmod** command with mode *750* on connectivity commands such as the following:

1. /usr/bin/ftp

2. /usr/bin/rcp

3. /usr/bin/rlogin

4. /usr/bin/rsh

5. /usr/bin/su

6. /usr/bin/telnet

Limiting Network Services

One way to prevent outsiders from obtaining access to your system is to restrict network services. The list of network services provided by your system, such as **telnet**, is located in the file */etc/inet/inetd.conf.* Edit the file and comment-out the services you do not want supported. Do not delete entries, as you may want to add them back later. Consider restricting the following network services:

1. **finger**

2. **ftp**

3. **login (rlogin)**

4. **shell (rsh)**

5. **sprayd**

6. **talk**

7. **telnet**

8. **tftp**

Some administrators will disable file copy services (such as **ftp**) and BSD log-in services (**shell** and **login**) only. In doing so, the BSD log-in security loopholes (i.e., */etc/hosts.equiv* and *.rhosts*) are eliminated. Outside users can still log in to the system via **telnet**, but cannot access the system remotely to transfer files.

Install a Firewall

Networks are typically interconnected using a device called a *gateway* or *router*. Although technically different, gateways and routers perform the same basic function: automatic forwarding of network traffic from one network to another. From a security perspective, this can be a nightmare because hosts connected to your network can be attacked by crackers outside your network.

A firewall is a modified gateway or router that restricts communications between networks. In its basic form, a firewall is created by the following steps:

1. Turning traffic forwarding off (typically known as *ip_forwarding*).

2. Stopping the router from advertising (broadcasting) routing information.

In order to gain access to hosts isolated by a firewall, a user must first remotely log onto the firewall and then log onto an internal host. Needless to say, firewalls must implement strict security rules if the internal network is to remain secure.

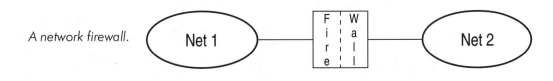

A network firewall.   Net 1   F i r e   W a l l   Net 2

If you are using a Sun system running Solaris 2 as a router, you can turn it into a firewall by editing the following lines in the */etc/inet/inetinit* file:

1. Turn *ip_forwarding* off by changing the line *ndd -set /dev/ip ip_forwarding 1* to *ndd -set /dev/ip ip_forwarding 0*.

2. Turn RIP advertising off by changing the line */usr/sbin/in.routed -s* to */usr/sbin/in.routed -q.*

3. Turn RDISC advertising off by changing the line */usr/sbin/in.rdisc -r* to */usr/sbin/in.rdisc.*

Once changes have been made to */etc/inet/inetinit*, you must reboot the system in order for them to take effect.

Automated Security Enhancement Tool (ASET)

As discussed in the earlier security chapter, ASET is a Solaris 2 utility that performs automatic security sweeps on your system(s). It can be also be used to check the integrity of firewalls. It is good practice to routinely run ASET in order to detect and correct security violations.

Be Vigilant!

It is always good practice to be on "superuser patrol." Much like a police officer pounding the beat, administrators should know their users, note who is logged in to systems, and keep watch for files and permissions that are suspicious. Many intruders have been caught because a diligent system administrator or user noticed that someone was logged in on a valid account but from an suspicious location.

One way to automate this surveillance would be to use the **last** command to determine who has recently logged in to the system. By feeding the output of the last command to the **grep** command, it is very easy to filter out the local log-in sessions. If any of the remaining log-ins look suspicious, it may be wise to monitor certain accounts and/or users to determine if there is indeed a security breach.

Using last to watch for non-local system log-in sessions.

```
                        shelltool - /bin/csh
# last | grep -v astro.com
fred      pts/3      U2.WHOI.EDU          Fri Jan 13 23:16    still logged in
carl      pts/0      cochroch.bus.umi Fri Jan 13 23:05 - 23:16  (00:10)
fred      pts/9      larry.ee.emory.e Fri Jan 13 23:04 - 23:05  (00:01)
fred      pts/2      ftp.hij.ad.jp    Fri Jan 13 23:00 - 23:04  (00:03)
ftp       pts/4      crl.dec.com          Fri Jan 13 22:42 - 23:00  (00:17)
curt      pts/1      localhost            Fri Jan 13 20:21 - 22:19  (01:58)
# 
```

Other methods which have proven useful for automating the security patrol include using the **cron** command to run ASET at regular intervals. The **find** command may also be used to look for *.rhosts* files, or world writeable files and directories. If such files are detected, the system administrator may need to take a closer look to determine if these files contain non-secure entries. The use of the **find** and **cron** commands is covered in more detail in a subsequent chapter.

Network Monitoring

There are several ways to monitor network activity and usage. One basic method is to use the **/usr/sbin/snoop** command. The output from snoop is generally voluminous and somewhat cryptic. However, it is a good command to use when trying to determine whether two hosts on a network are communicating or to identify the type of network traffic generated. Some of the more common uses of snoop include:

❏ Monitoring traffic between two hosts.

❏ Monitoring traffic using a particular protocol.

❏ Monitoring traffic containing specific data.

❏ Monitoring a network to determine which host is creating the most network traffic.

✔ **NOTE:** *By default, snoop is a root restricted command.*

Monitoring network traffic using snoop.

```
                          shelltool - /bin/csh
 # snoop
 Using device le0 (promiscuous mode)
         mercury -> shepard      ICMP Echo request
         shepard -> mercury      ICMP Echo reply
```

A more sophisticated method of monitoring networks is to use a graphical network management tool such as SunNet Manager. Tools like SunNet Manager have the capacity to "discover" systems connected to a network. The discovered systems are then used to construct an interactive schematic of the network.

Alarms (thresholds) on a number of network "health" statistics can be set. If a system on the network fails, an alarm for that condition would be tripped. SunNet Manager would then alert the network manager of the failure by flashing the icon of the failed system on the schematic.

SunNet Manager is not bundled with Solaris 2. It is a separate product marketed by SunConnect, a division of Sun Microsystems.

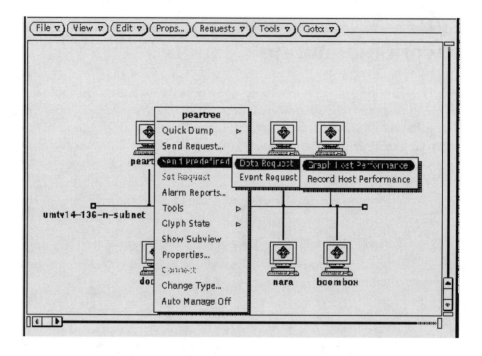

Monitoring network traffic using SunNet Manager.

Basic Network Troubleshooting

As with most computer operations, networks are bound to have problems. Troubleshooting networks can be a tedious process. One method of troubleshooting is to use the monitoring tools described in the previous section. In some cases, it may not be possible to monitor a network because physical connections may be damaged or gateways may be down.

Subnetworks

To reduce the probability of network-wide service interruptions on larger networks, a wise practice is to segment the network into multiple pieces. This is typically accomplished using a technique called "subnetting." While the specifics of subnetting are beyond the scope of this book, it is an important concept for beginning administrators to understand.

In general, the idea behind subnetting is to reduce a large problem into several smaller, more manageable pieces. Three benefits of subnetting are (1) improved network traffic control, (2) isolation of network failures, and (3) isolation from the main network if network security has been breached.

Traffic Control

In the case of network traffic control, many corporate networks place each department on its own subnet. In doing so, traffic generated between hosts on a subnet (department) will be contained within that subnet and not generate network load in other subnets. Hosts on different subnets can still communicate via internetwork connections. Subnets are generally interconnected using devices such as *routers*, which were discussed earlier in this chapter.

Isolation of Network Failures

From a troubleshooting perspective, subnetting allows administrators to isolate (disconnect) pieces (subnets) of a network when trying to resolve network problems. By isolating a subnet, it is often easier to determine the source of a network problem.

Most routers, gateways, hubs, and multi-port transceivers have a *switch* allowing them to operate in stand-alone mode. If the switch is set to *local* mode, the subnet is disconnected from the rest of the network. With the switch set to *remote* mode, the subnet is connected to the rest of the network.

Isolation from Intruders

In much the same way that a ship seals its water-tight doors to contain flooding in the event of a hull breach, subnet isolation is used to contain damage if a network intruder is detected or suspected. Hosts within subnets (departments) can use intra-departmental communication until the security breach has been resolved.

One of the most famous network security breaches occurred in fall 1988, when an experimental *worm* program was accidentally unleashed on the Internet. The worm looked for hosts on the Internet with weak network security. Once the worm gained access to a network host, it would replicate itself and then look for other hosts to continue the process. Many networks connected to the Internet used *network isolation* until a way was found to disarm the worm a few days later.

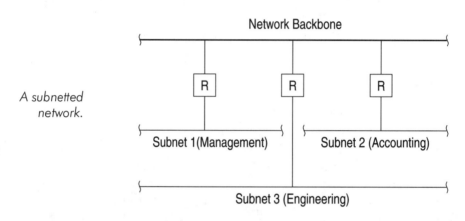

A subnetted network.

When to Subnet

There are no absolute formulas for determining when or how to subnet a network. The network topology, the LAN technology being implemented, network bandwidth, and host applications all affect a network's performance. However, subnetting should be considered if one or more of the following conditions exist:

- ❏ There are more than 20 hosts on the network.
- ❏ Network applications slow down as users begin accessing the network.
- ❏ There is a high percentage of collisions on the network.

Calculating Network Load

Obtaining accurate network load statistics requires sophisticated (and expensive) network analysis equipment. However, network load can be estimated by calculating the network interface collision rate on each host. This can be done by using the **netstat -i** command. Using the command's output, divide the total collisions (Collis) by the output packets (Opkts) multiplied by 100. For example, on *grissom*, the total collisions are 2553 and the total output packets are 242220. The collision rate on *grissom* is 1.05% (2553/242220 * 100 = 1.05%). To obtain the network collision rate, collect **netstat -i** statistics for all hosts on the network and average them.

```
                              shelltool – /bin/csh
grissom% netstat -i
Name  Mtu  Net/Dest     Address      Ipkts   Ierrs Opkts   Oerrs Collis Queue
lo0   8232 127.0.0.0    localhost    11924   0     11924   0     0      0
le0   1500 154.7.3.3    grissom      191120  0     242220  0     2553   0
grissom%
```

Using netstat -i to estimate network load.

Collision rates less than 4% are generally considered acceptable. Rates of 4 to 8% indicate a loaded network. Rates over 8% indicate a heavily loaded network that should be considered for subnetting.

Tracking Down a Network Problem

Tracking down network problems is like detective work. After a while you develop an instinct for where to look for clues. The following discussion is by no means an exhaustive troubleshooting scenario. It will, however, get you started with some basic techniques that all seasoned network detectives use.

If a host cannot be contacted on a network, the first question to answer is whether the problem is specific to the host or the network. A very useful command to make this determination is **ping**. The command name stands for "Packet Internet Groper," and is used to test reachability of hosts by sending an ICMP echo request and waiting for a reply. The command name is often used as a verb, such as in "Ping cooper to see if it's up."

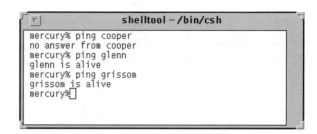

Pinging a host to determine reachability.

By logging onto several hosts on a network, and "pinging" other hosts, it can quickly be determined whether the problem is network or host related. For example, *mercury* is able to "ping" all hosts in its network except *cooper*. It can then be assumed that the network is functioning and the problem centers around *cooper*. The lack of a reply from *cooper* could be due to a variety of difficulties. Some of the more common problems follow:

❏ Faulty physical connection.

❏ Faulty transceiver.

❏ Faulty AUI cable.

❏ Faulty host interface.

❏ Corrupted */etc/inet/hosts file.*

❏ Missing or corrupted */etc/hostname.le0* file.

❏ The interface is turned off.

❏ The host is down.

Rebooting the non-communicating hosts will frequently solve the problem. If rebooting does not work, examination of the files and physical components listed above would be the next step. In the absence of network diagnostic equipment, replacing components may be the only way to track down the failure.

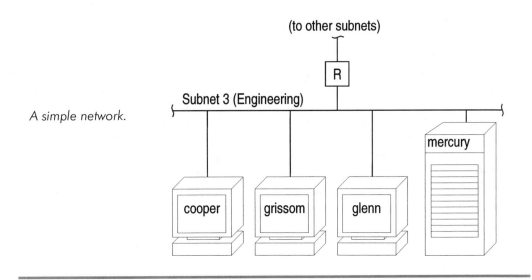

A simple network.

If, on the other hand, no hosts reply to pings, then the problem is specific to the network. Some of the more common network faults follow:

❏ Missing or damaged terminators.

❏ Broken or damaged cable (may not be visible).

❏ Faulty connectors.

❏ Damaged transceiver (may be jamming the network).

Once again, in the absence of network diagnostic equipment, replacing components may be the only way to determine the failure.

If you are unable to contact a host located on a different subnet and you are having no difficulty "pinging" hosts on your subnet, including the *router*, then the problem could be one of items listed below:

❏ Malfunction of the *router* connected to your subnet.

❏ Malfunction of the network on the other side of your *router*.

❏ Malfunction of a distant *router* not directly connected to your subnet.

❏ Malfunction of the remote host.

❏ Failure of a component or connection between the local host and the remote hosts.

To locate the problem, use the techniques discussed earlier in this section for each subnet in question. With subnetted networks, **ping** is often all that is required to locate (or at least narrow down) the source of a network failure.

Summary

In this chapter we discussed the terminology associated with an Ethernet local area network. We also discussed how to obtain an Internet address, and the different classes of Internet addresses. Selected basic remote access commands were discussed, as well as security concerns related to computer networks. Finally, we examined ways to monitor and troubleshoot local area networks. The next few chapters will focus on how the network is used for Network File System (NFS) file sharing, and the Network Information System (NIS).

Accessing Network Resources with NFS

The Network File System (NFS) is an integral component of many Solaris installations. Developed by Sun Microsystems in the mid-1980s, NFS is a published standard, or protocol, which allows file "sharing" among hosts over a network. It is a standard feature on most UNIX systems and is available for most operating systems, including VMS, MS-DOS/Windows, and Macintosh to name a few. Solaris provides a secure version of NFS called Secure NFS. It provides enhanced security features to protect NFS operations from network security breaches. A discussion of secure network communications is covered later in this chapter.

The utility of NFS comes from its ability to transparently access files located on remote hosts via a network connection. For example, NFS allows hosts on a network to access from a central location data or programs, such as the on-line manual pages. This reduces system maintenance requirements by limiting the number of hosts, or locations, where programs and data files must be installed. Furthermore, in environments where users regularly work on different hosts, NFS can automatically mount their centrally located home directories to any host they log on to. To users, it appears as though their home directory follows them from host to host. NFS can also be used to share network devices such as CD-ROMs, or files from different operating systems such as the aforementioned VMS, UNIX, Macintosh or MS-DOS.

NFS Function and Terminology

The most basic NFS configuration consists of one host operating as a server and another operating as a client. The server shares or makes available some or all of its files by running a special set of daemon processes. The **share** command is used to instruct the daemons about what to share with other hosts. By placing configuration information in a special file, */etc/dfs/dfstab*, the share commands can be run automatically when the server is booted. The client attaches or *mounts* one or more of the file system sections made available by the server. The **mounting** command incorporates the identified file system section into the local host's file tree in the same manner local disk-based file systems are mounted. The client also runs a special set of daemon processes and has information concerning which file systems to mount from the server in its own configuration files.

Servers, Clients, and Sharing

A host which is sharing file systems via NFS is called a *server*. A host which is mounting NFS file systems from other hosts is called a *client*. A host can be both client and server. Networks on which there are servers and clients are called *client-server networks*. Networks where hosts are both client and server to each other are often called *peer-to-peer networks*. Most large networks have a mix of clients, servers, and peers.

A file system which is offered for mounting by a server via NFS is said to be *shared*. This term comes from the **share** command used to offer file systems for mounting. A remote file system is mounted on a client using the **mount** command in a similar fashion as is done for other file system types. The portion of the server's file systems that is shared can be mounted in the same or in a different location on the client.

Remote Procedure Call (RPC)

A key to NFS operation is its use of a protocol called *Remote Procedure Call* (RPC). The RPC protocol was developed by Sun Microsystems in the mid-1980s along with NFS. Procedure call is a method by which a program makes use of a subroutine. The RPC mechanism extends the subroutine call to span across the network, allowing the procedure call to be performed on a remote machine.

In NFS, this is used to access files on remote machines by extending basic file operations such as read and write across the network.

To understand the purpose of RPC you must first look at how the computer system interacts with the files stored on its local disk. When a Solaris program is read into memory from disk, or a file is read or written, system calls are made to the read or write procedures in the SunOS kernel. As a result data is read from or written to the file system. When a file is read from or written to an NFS file system on a network, the read or write calls are made over the network via RPC. The RPC mechanism performs the read or write operation needed on the server's file system on behalf of the client. If the NFS client or server is a different type of host or operating system, such as VMS or a PC running Windows, the RPC mechanism also handles any needed data conversion. The result is that the information returned by the read or the write call appears to be the same as if the read or write had occurred on a local disk.

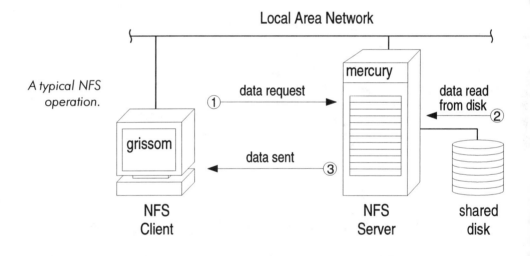

A typical NFS operation.

While this appears complex, it all occurs at the file system level and requires no changes to normal operations on files or internal programs. It is similar to reading and writing a floppy disk versus a hard disk or a CD-ROM. As far as a program is concerned, NFS is just another UNIX file system. The transparent nature of NFS is one of its best features.

NFS File System Differences

The major differences between an NFS file system and other file system types derive from the network connection between NFS clients and servers. NFS file systems can be used by several clients simultaneously. For example, you may wish to share the *usr/share/man* portion of a server's file system among many clients. Since many clients can use a single NFS file system concurrently, you can reduce the amount of disk space required for each system on a network. It also reduces the effort needed to install and maintain software by sharing a single copy of a program among many clients.

While NFS is quite handy and versatile, it does have some drawbacks. On Ethernet it is not as fast as a local disk, especially some of the faster SCSI disks now available. It also can cause problems on clients when the server of a mounted NFS file system becomes unavailable or when network problems occur. NFS is only as good as the underlying network connection. These problems and some preventive measures are discussed later in this chapter and in the chapter on automating NFS with **automount**.

Setting Up an NFS Server

The setup of an NFS server involves dealing with the administrative issue of UID and GID numbering, editing the *dfstab* file, and making sure the needed daemon processes are started. Once an NFS server has been set up, the needed **share** commands and daemons will be automatically started when the server is booted.

Match UID and GID Numbers for All Users

Setting up a host as an NFS server is fairly easy. First, you need to ensure that the clients and servers use identical UIDs and GIDs for all users and groups. In other words, a user must have the same UID number on all hosts on which he or she will be sharing files via NFS. Mismatches can result in files being inadvertently accessible to users who might not normally have access to them. If you are using NIS or NIS+ to handle your */etc/passwd* and */etc/group* files, your UID and GID numbers should already match up across the hosts which share the same NIS or NIS+ server. NFS uses the UID and GID numbers when figuring out file access permissions on remote file systems. See the chapter on NIS or NIS+ if you want to see how to set up those services.

Put share Commands into /etc/dfs/dfstab

With uniform UID and GID numbering in place, the next step is to add lines to the *etc/dfs/dfstab* file. Each line is a **share** command specifying the portion of the server's file tree to be shared, which hosts are allowed to mount it, and how they allowed to mount it. You can also issue the share command on the command line to allow a file system to be shared. Putting the command in */etc/dfs/dfstab* causes the file system to be shared every time the host is booted. A simple example appears in the following illustration.

```
                         cmdtool – /bin/csh
 # more /etc/dfs/dfstab

 #        place share(1M) commands here for automatic execution
 #        on entering init state 3.
 #
 #        share [-F fstype] [ -o options] [-d "<text>"] <pathname> [resource]
 #        .e.g,
 #        share  -F nfs  -o rw=engineering  -d "home dirs"  /export/home2

 share -F nfs -o ro=grissom -d "Manual Pages" /usr/man

 #
```

A simple /etc/dfs/dfstab file.

The final line of the *dfstab* file is the actual share command. The lines preceding it begin with a pound sign (#) and are treated as comments.

The first option to share, **-F nfs**, specifies that the portion of the file system is to be shared via NFS.

The next flag, reading from left to right, is the **-o** flag. This specifies how the portion of the file tree is to be shared and by whom. There are several options that can be used. The **ro=** and **rw=** options specify a list of hosts which are allowed to access the file system on a read-only or read-write basis, respectively. Other options can be used to control secure access to a file system and are discussed later in this chapter.

In the example above, the option **ro=grissom** allows the host named *grissom* to mount the shared resource, */usr/man*, read-only. Additional hosts can be added by separating their names by a colon (e.g., *ro=grissom:glenn*). This can get to be cumbersome for large numbers of hosts. Creating a net group using NIS+ allows you to group collections of hosts together and refer to them by a single name. See the chapter on NIS+ for information on setting up NIS+ and creating a net group.

Moving along the example **share** command past the **-o** option flag and its arguments is the **-d** option. This allows a description of the shared item to be displayed when the server is queried concerning available shared items as shown below. The final item on the line is the path for the portion of the file system to be shared.

Start the Daemons

The next step is to start the required daemon programs. The daemons will start automatically during the boot sequence only if **share** commands are found in */etc/dfs/dfstab*. When setting up an NFS server for the first time, you will need to start them manually after you have prepared the */etc/dfs/dfstab* file. You do this by running the **init** script that would have been run during the boot sequence.

```
┌─────────────────────────────── cmdtool - /bin/csh ───────────────────────────────┐
│ # /etc/init.d/nfs.server start                                                    │
│ # ps -ef | egrep "nfs|mount"                                                      │
│     root   113     1 37    Sep 12 ?          0:00 /usr/lib/autofs/automountd      │
│     root   117     1 58    Sep 12 ?          0:01 /usr/lib/nfs/statd              │
│     root   119     1 80    Sep 12 ?          0:01 /usr/lib/nfs/lockd              │
│     root  3878  3840 14 10:19:38 pts/4       0:00 egrep nfs|mount                 │
│     root  3875     1 51 10:19:19 ?           0:01 /usr/lib/nfs/nfsd -a 16         │
│     root  3877     1 74 10:19:19 ?           0:01 /usr/lib/nfs/mountd             │
│ #                                                                                  │
└───────────────────────────────────────────────────────────────────────────────────┘
```

Starting the nfs server daemons by hand.

A Look at the nfs.server Script

In the example, the **nfs.server** script has been run, the **ps** command was used, and then its output was filtered with the **egrep** command to produce a list of the NFS daemons. The *statd* and *lockd* daemons provide for server crash recovery and file locking across the network. If the host will be running only as an NFS client, then these are the only daemons started.

When a server crashes and comes back into service, the *statd* daemon handles the resolution of any locks that were pending at the time of the crash. Information about file locking and status is not maintained across server crashes.

The *lockd* enforces file locking on the shared file system by communicating with the *lockd* process on clients which mount and use a shared NFS file system.

Next, the *mountd* and *nfsd* daemons are started by the **nfs.server** script. The *mountd* handles requests from clients to mount shared items. It uses the information provided by the **share** command to help it determine permission for mounting and the access allowed to a particular shared item. The *nfsd* daemon sets up the NFS mechanism inside the SunOS kernel and provides its interface to the network.

> ✔ **NOTE:** *The nfsd process does not directly handle RPC requests, but instead passes them on to the SunOS kernel. As a result, the nfsd process may not accumulate CPU time while NFS operations are occurring. Be careful not to use CPU time accumulated by nfsd as a measure of NFS operations.*

The number 16 as given to the *nfsd* is used to allocate threads in the SunOS kernel. Each thread can handle a single RPC operation at a time. A thread is a separate line of execution or control, allowing each request to be handled asynchronously without the overhead of having separate processes handling each request. The number of threads is set depending on the amount of NFS traffic the server is expected to handle. The amount of traffic is a function of the number of clients and how frequently RPC requests will be made. More threads will improve service under heavy loads up to the point at which the server's resources are fully utilized. The proper setting for your environment can be determined only by experimentation, and depends on such factors as the server's CPU and disk system performance, network interconnections, etc. The default of 16 works well for most small to moderately sized situations.

Checking the NFS Server

Besides using the **ps** command, you can also check on an NFS server by using the **showmount** and **share** commands. By using the **-e** option on showmount, you can specify the name of a remote host and see the list of file systems it is currently sharing. Alternatively, the share command, when used without arguments, will list the shared file systems on the local system.

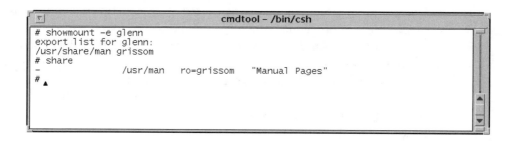

```
                              cmdtool – /bin/csh
# showmount -e glenn
export list for glenn:
/usr/share/man grissom
# share
-                    /usr/man   ro=grissom    "Manual Pages"
#
```

Checking the NFS server with the showmount and share commands.

NFS server setup is a one-time activity. With a server configured, the share commands and daemon processes will automatically be started as part of the system boot procedure. Adding additional shared directories is a matter of adding them to the dfstab file and running the share command.

Setting Up an NFS Client

Configuring an NFS client is even easier. All you need to do is to specify remote file systems you wish to mount in */etc/vfstab* and then issue the mount commands to have those file systems mounted. An NFS file system entry looks just like entries for other file system types and is treated in a similar manner, being mounted automatically at system boot and so on. An example is shown in the next illustration.

The upper part of the window shown above is the */etc/vfstab* file. The last line mounts */usr/share/man* from the host named *glenn*. It is mounted read-only on */mnt/man*. Running the **/etc/init.d/nfs.client** script runs the **mountall** command to mount the remote file systems. The output of the **df** command shows the mounted file system. Note that for NFS file systems the remote host name and shared path is shown in place of the name of the device as is shown for local file systems, and the number of files is shown as -1.

```
┌─────────────────────────────────────────────────────────────────────┐
│ ▼                       cmdtool - /bin/csh                           │
├─────────────────────────────────────────────────────────────────────┤
│ # cat /etc/vfstab                                                     │
│ #device          device         mount       FS     fsck  mount  mount │
│ #to mount        to fsck        point       type   pass  at boot options│
│ #                                                                     │
│ #/dev/dsk/c1d0s2 /dev/rdsk/c1d0s2 /usr       ufs    1     yes    -    │
│ /proc            -              /proc       proc   -     no     -    │
│ fd               -              /dev/fd     fd     -     no     -    │
│ swap             -              /tmp        tmpfs  -     yes    -    │
│                                                                      │
│ /dev/dsk/c0t3d0s0      /dev/rdsk/c0t3d0s0   /      ufs    1     no   │
│                                                                      │
│ /dev/dsk/c0t3d0s6      /dev/rdsk/c0t3d0s6   /usr   ufs    2     no   │
│ -                                                                    │
│ /dev/dsk/c0t3d0s5      /dev/rdsk/c0t3d0s5   /opt   ufs    5     yes  │
│ -                                                                    │
│ /dev/dsk/c0t3d0s1      -         -          swap   -     no     -   │
│ /dev/diskette - /mnt ufs - no suid,rw                                │
│ glenn:/usr/share/man   -         /mnt/man   nfs    -     yes    ro  │
│ # /etc/init.d/nfs.client start                                       │
│ # df                                                                 │
│ /                (/dev/dsk/c0t3d0s0):   10780 blocks    9246 files   │
│ /usr             (/dev/dsk/c0t3d0s6):  775336 blocks  322085 files   │
│ /proc            (/proc         ):       0 blocks     185 files   │
│ /dev/fd          (fd            ):       0 blocks       0 files   │
│ /tmp             (swap          ):  198896 blocks    3092 files   │
│ /opt             (/dev/dsk/c0t3d0s5):   91236 blocks   73801 files   │
│ /mnt/man         (glenn:/usr/share/man):  775336 blocks    -1 files  │
│ #                                                                    │
└─────────────────────────────────────────────────────────────────────┘
```

Adding an NFS file system to /etc/vfstab.

NFS File System Mount Options

Like other special file system types, NFS file systems have a variety of specialized mount options. Most of these options revolve around the networked nature of an NFS file system.

mount Command Options

Option	Description
rw/ro	Read/Write and Read-Only. NFS file systems which are mounted read/write can block activity on the client when the server providing the file system becomes unavailable. See intr and bg below.

Option	Description
hard/soft	The hard option mounts an NFS file system in such a way as to ensure that data is written to the remote file system. If the file server becomes unavailable, a file system mounted with the hard option will stop all remote file operations until the file server becomes available again. All file systems mounted with the read/write option should also use the hard option. The soft option does not provide assurance of data writes to the remote file system, but does not stop remote file operations in the case of a file server becoming unavailable. It is useful for file systems which are mounted read-only.
suid/nosuid	The nosuid option negates the effect of any programs on the remote file system which have their *setuid* bits set. *Setuid* programs run from NFS file systems mounted with the nosuid option are executed with the normal permissions of the user executing the program, *not* those conferred by the *setuid* bit.
bg/fg	These control how a mount of an NFS file system which fails is handled. Mounts with the bg option are retried in the background, freeing the mount command. Use this when mounting file systems in */etc/vfstab* to avoid having a workstation stop during the boot sequence due to a file server being down.
intr/nointr	The nointr option prevents programs from being interrupted when they cause an NFS operation to occur. This can result in programs being uninterruptable when an NFS file server becomes unavailable. The default is to allow interrupts so that programs can be aborted in the event of server failures.
retry=n	The number of times to retry a failed mount. The default of 10,000 is usually sufficient.
timeo=n	The time-out value for retrying NFS operations. Some very slow systems, such as near-line file stores, need to be given more time to complete basic operations by increasing this value.
retrans=n	The number of retransmissions of a given NFS operation. The setting depends on the network and type of server being used.
rsize=n	Read buffer size. Some servers and clients perform better when the buffer used for NFS operations is a different size than the default, in particular, those clients and servers with slower or less reliable network connections.
wsize=n	Write buffer size. Similar to rsize in usage.

Tips on Using mount Command Options

Choosing the correct mix of these options for various circumstances is a bit tricky. General guidelines to help you select the needed options for your particular situation follow.

Use the hard Option

In general, NFS file systems which are mounted **rw** should also use the **hard** option. When a problem occurs in writing to an NFS file system that is mounted **soft**, it is reported when the file is closed. Few programs check the return value from the "close" system call. The hard option handles this at the file system level, forcing the client to retry any failed writes until they succeed (e.g., the server returns to operation). This prevents any possible data loss. However, it has serious ramifications for overall system functioning as discussed toward the end of this chapter.

Use the bg Option

To prevent a client from "hanging" part way through system start-up, use the **bg** option wherever possible. This allows the boot process to complete by putting any NFS file system mounts which are unable to be done at boot time into the "background." The mount will complete automatically once the problem preventing the mount from completing (e.g., network connections, server down, etc.) is fixed.

Use rsize and wsize With Care

Changing the values for **rsize** and **wsize** should be done with great care. NFS puts packets of the largest possible size on a network to improve efficiency. Reducing the size of these by adjusting the rsize and wsize parameters should be done only when some constraint forces you to do so. Older equipment with limited network hardware can cause network problems that can be solved only by changing the NFS buffer sizes.

Use timeo With Equal Care

In a similar vein, the **timeo** value should be adjusted with care. Check to be certain that the underlying network is sound before adjusting this parameter. Flooding a problematic network with extra NFS request retransmissions will only make a bad situation worse. However, slow NFS servers may require increasing the value of **timeo** to avoid sending unnecessary retransmission of NFS requests.

In general, take care to examine your network hardware before making adjustments to the various NFS parameters. NFS is very demanding on a network and can bring to light problems not seen under lesser network loads. Network hardware failures can often result in additional network traffic as a result of NFS request retransmissions. See the section of this chapter on NFS troubleshooting for additional help.

Improving NFS Security

Once you begin using NFS to share files, your network becomes more like a single large computer system than a group of separate machines. The implications of this for system security are important to note. Access to files shared via NFS depends on the security of each machine involved in the sharing. Since the contents of files are transferred over the network, access to the network itself will need to be taken into consideration as well. The ability of other machines on a network to monitor network communications or even alter them is an important and growing security concern as your network grows.

File and Access Security

NFS security is only as good as the security of the individual hosts sharing file systems. There are a few things you can do to "harden" NFS against security problems, but the proper place to begin is by evaluating the security of each client and server. Turn to the chapter on security for a discussion of the basic tools and areas that should be addressed on each host.

Server Sharing Security Options

With the individual hosts secured, move on to evaluate the permissions given by the file server for mounting its file systems. By default, an NFS file server maps access requests made by the root user on a client to a special UID. This UID does not have root file access privileges. This UID is normally set to that of the *nobody* account. You can change it, if necessary, by using the **anon=** option to the **share** command. For example, appearing below is an entry that would be placed in */etc/dfs/dfstab* to share */export/progs* with the root user on remote systems mapped to UID 10.

```
share -F nfs -o anon=10,rw=local -d "local programs" /export/progs
```

In some circumstances you may wish to offer root access to a server's file system, perhaps to facilitate remote software installation. This can be done on a host-by-host basis using the **root=** option. This option accepts a list of hosts in much the same way the **ro=** and **rw=** options do. Hosts listed in the **root=** list will have full root access to the file system.

In situations where you may not have complete control over the security of client workstations, you should try to limit access to file systems offered by the server.

Client Mounting Security Options

On the client's side, you can use the **nosuid** option to improve security. This option disables the effect of the setuid and setgid bits when a program from a remote file system is executed. The programs are run using the normal user's permissions and *not* those conferred by the *setuid* or *setgid* bits. This helps to prevent non-secure programs offered by a server from being used by users on clients to affect the client's security.

Security at the Wire Level

Solaris provides for additional security for NFS operations through a secure version of the base remote procedure call (RPC) mechanism. By default, RPC uses the UNIX UID and GID numbering information as the basis of its authentication method. These numbers can be easily seen by network monitoring tools as they go by on the network and it is impossible for the client and server to determine if the requests they send and receive are genuine.

Secure RPC Uses a Public Key Crypto System

Secure RPC solves the problem of authenticating the client and server by the use of a public key crypto system. A cryptographic system uses a mathematical formula to encrypt or encode information in such a way as to be unreadable except for those who have the needed numerical keys to decrypt or decode the information back into a readable form.

A public key crypto system works like this: For each user, two large numbers are generated. One of the numbers is kept secret, while the other number is published in a public database available to all hosts. The secret number is known as the private key and the published number is known as the public key. The two numbers have the property that something encrypted using one number as the key can be decrypted using the other number as the key. By using a combination of keys from the client and server, information can be exchanged securely with assurance of the sender's and recipient's identity.

The public and private keys are used as follows: The client randomly picks a session key to be used to encrypt data being sent to and from a server. The client encrypts the session key using a combination of the current time, the client's private key and the server's public key, and then sends this encrypted information to the server. The server decrypts the message using the current time, the client's public key, and the server's private key. The server now has the session key and is ready to respond.

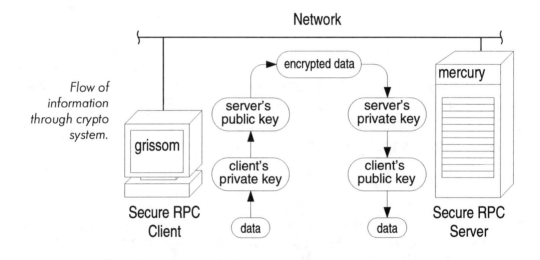

The server and client also have something much more important. Due to the mathematical properties of the keys and the encryption method, the message they exchange can only be decrypted by the specific server whose key was used and could only have come from the specific client whose key was used. This works to ensure that no other host on the network is masquerading as either the client or the server.

The time stamp and session key are used to avoid playback attacks. A playback attack is when a host simply records RPC requests and then reuses the encrypted information later in forged RPC requests. A secure RPC server will reject requests containing invalid time information.

> ✔ **NOTE:** *Time synchronization between your client and server hosts is required for secure RPC to function properly.*

Secure RPC Setup

To set up a secure RPC, you first need to assign a domain name to the collection of hosts that will share public keys. This is covered in the chapter on NIS and NIS+.

Once you have a domain established, the sequence of tasks to perform follows:

1. Generate new public and private keys using **newkey**.

2. Start the keyserver by typing */usr/sbin/keyserv*.

3. Edit */etc/dfs/dfstab* on the servers and clients to add the **secure** option to the **share** commands and NFS file system entries.

Troubleshooting NFS

NFS depends on the underlying network to function. If you are having problems mounting a remote file system, check the network first. Refer to the chapter on networking for some specific items you should check on. For NFS in particular, check to be sure that you can send large data packets reliably between your client and server. On an Ethernet, you can check using the **ping** command. Use the following command on the client:

```
# /usr/sbin/ping -s server 1500 100
```

This will send 100 maximum size packets (1500 bytes) from the client to the server and report statistics for each packet with totals at the end. On a quiet network you should see no lost packets. Even on busy networks, losses of more than one or two packets should be examined. While NFS will continue to function even in the face of severe network problems, performance will suffer greatly. Attempting to adjust NFS mount parameters such as **rsize**, **wsize**, and **retrans** without first checking the network can act to mask problems in your network.

Server Problems

Once you have proven that the network connection is sound, the next items to check are the various NFS daemon processes. These processes, which are run in the background, must be present for NFS to function. Use the **ps** command and look for the following daemons on your NFS server:

❑ **mountd** If this daemon is missing, clients will be unable to mount NFS file systems from this server. You can restart it by becoming *root* and typing */usr/lib/nfs/mountd.* Check for it again using ps. If it fails to start, check your */etc/dfs/dfstab* file for errors.

❑ **nfsd** No nfsd means no NFS service. To restart it, become root and type */usr/lib/nfs/nfsd -a X,* where *X* is the number of threads used by nfsd. The default is 16. If you use another number for your server, use it here when you restart nfsd.

If your clients still do not seem to be able to get NFS services from the server, try killing the nfsd process and restarting it. If that fails, try rebooting your server.

Client Problems

The problems that can occur on clients are usually less a matter of daemons not running and more a matter of errors in configuration. If a client cannot mount NFS file systems that other clients can, carefully check the configuration files. Check for errors in the server's */etc/dfs/dfstab* and the client's */etc/vfstab.* If you are using NIS or NIS+, verify that the client and server are receiving current information from those services. Refer to the chapter on NIS+ for ways to test and verify that your NIS+ service is functioning correctly.

NFS Design Pitfalls

As mentioned earlier, the simple NFS configuration described here has a few drawbacks. To mount a file system read/write and maintain file integrity, file systems need to be mounted using the **hard** option. However, if the file server of such a file system becomes unavailable, processes on the client which refer to the remote file system will stop working, and wait for the server to return to service. This can happen even for file systems which are not directly involved in the processing the client is executing at the time.

As networks grow, maintaining the */etc/vfstab* files on all clients becomes more and more of a chore. The */etc/vfstab* on each client will usually need to be modified as each new file server is added or as file servers are reorganized, renamed, or moved. It becomes more and more likely that a mistake will creep into the file and it becomes more evident that not all clients need to mount all file servers at any given time. If files are shared from a common file server, the */etc/vfstab* method makes no allowance for adding additional file servers to help balance the load or to provide redundancy in the face of failures.

To deal with these problems, Solaris uses a special daemon called an *automounter* and a special file system type known as *autofs*. Most of these problems can be avoided using these tools. The tools are covered in the next chapter.

Summary

Sun's Network File System is a widely available mechanism for sharing files between Solaris systems and a large number of other UNIX, VMS, PC, and Macintosh systems. Through the use of specific options to the share and mount commands, special circumstances which arise from the networked nature of NFS can be handled. However, a simple NFS setup has drawbacks due to problems which occur when file servers are unavailable. These problems can be addressed by using the automount service described in the next chapter.

Automating NFS with automount

As mentioned at the end of the previous chapter on NFS, growing networks present the system manager with many challenges. As new machines are added, correctly maintaining */etc/vfstab* files becomes an increasingly daunting chore. In addition, when a file server becomes unavailable, processes on client workstations may stop even if they do not depend on the unavailable file server. The *automount* service was developed to minimize these problems.

The General Concept of automount

In most cases, an NFS client does not require continuous access to all of the NFS file systems that may be available on a network. Avoiding mounting NFS file systems until needed greatly limits the problems caused by unavailable file servers. By providing mechanisms to identify and use alternative file servers when possible, some of the file server availability problems can be reduced. The combination of the *autofs* file system type and the automount daemon provide an automated NFS file system mounting service that deals with these problems while providing a easier-to-maintain solution for managing the mounting of large numbers of shared file systems.

The automount service works by intercepting file access requests, mounting the needed NFS file system, and then allowing the request to proceed. If, for example, you accessed the directory */usr/man* and it was an unmounted NFS file system under control of the automount service, your request would be caught by the automount daemon, which would mount the needed file system and then allow your request to continue. This mounting process is transparent; the file access occurs as if the file system had been mounted all along. The automount service also cleans up, by unmouting NFS file systems which are no longer being used.

Advantages of automount for the Small Network

While the demands of a large network drove the development of the automount service, it provides benefits for even very small networks. In any case where the unavailability of a file server can cause a problem, the automount service can help avoid the problem. As a small network grows, the automount service makes adding and managing additional shared file systems easy. As additional resources become available, critical programs and data files can be offered on duplicate file servers to further improve reliability and performance. Through the use of the *auto-home* feature, user accounts can appear to have a single home directory while the system manager is freed to move the location of the user's files as needed to adapt to changing configurations and disk usage demands.

autofs and automountd

The autofs is a special file system type which resides in the SunOS kernel. When the automount daemon, automountd, is started, it reads a series of configuration files known as *map files*, and creates autofs file systems associated with each of the mount points listed in the maps. Unlike other mount points, which are attachment points for specific data storage devices in the UNIX file tree, the autofs mount points attach the automountd process to the UNIX file tree. If you imagine the mount point for a local disk as a shelf or cubbyhole, an autofs mount would be person who would direct you to a shelf or cubbyhole based on the rules found in a map file.

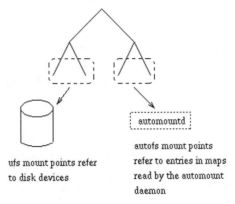

This illustration shows some autofs mount points in a UNIX file tree.

ufs mount points refer
to disk devices

autofs mount points
refer to entries in maps
read by the automount
daemon

When a file or directory access request traverses an autofs mount point, the request is held and a message is sent to the automount daemon. The automount daemon consults the map files for entries pertaining to this mount point and mounts the referenced NFS file system. The access request is then allowed to proceed by being directed to the newly mounted NFS file system.

Steps taken when automount initially mounts an NFS file system.

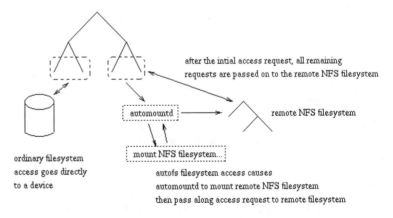

after the intial access request, all remaining
requests are passed on to the remote NFS filesystem

remote NFS filesystem

ordinary filesystem
access goes directly
to a device

autofs filesystem access causes
automountd to mount remote NFS filesystem
then pass along access request to remote filesystem

All subsequent requests for file access which traverse this particular autofs mount point are directed to the mounted NFS file system. The automount daemon monitors the autofs mount point and if it is not traversed for a predefined time period, the referenced NFS file system is automatically un-mounted.

The automatic mounting imposes a brief delay when an unmounted NFS file system is first accessed. Little additional overhead occurs after the initial mount and the automatic unmount occurs in the background, without interfering with ongoing processing on the client. In return for this small additional overhead, a great deal of flexibility and ease of maintenance is gained.

Starting and Stopping the automount Service

Starting the automount service is very simple. It is most easily done by manually running the run control or **rc** shell script used by Solaris to start the automount service during the system boot process. From the root user prompt, type the following:

```
# /etc/init.d/autofs start
```

Conversely, to stop the automount service, key in the following:

```
# /etc/init.d/autofs stop
```

These commands are automatically performed as part of the system boot procedure.

automount Maps

The heart of the **automount** service is its map files. These files specify the autofs mount points, control the mount options used when mounting specific NFS file systems, and allow for automated selection of NFS file systems based on various parameters. The automatic selection of redundant file servers and the general flexibility of the map files allow for a single collection of map files to be used across an entire network. This greatly eases the maintenance chore when shared file systems are added, removed, or moved.

Map files are divided into two types: *direct* and *indirect*. Direct maps list the mount points for remote file systems as their keys. Indirect maps list mount points within a specified directory and use symbolic links which point from the key entry to the remote file system which is mounted elsewhere. Each map file is listed in the master map file. As an additional feature, a separate map file is available for use with the account administration tools to allow user account home directories to be automatically mounted based on the user account name.

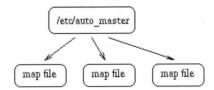

The master automount file and its map files.

The Master Map

The master map forms the basis of the map system, and is the */etc/auto_master* file. The format of lines in the file is simple, consisting of a mount point, the name of a map file which specifies NFS file systems to be mounted at that mount point, and any mount options which are to be applied to the autofs file system at the mount point.

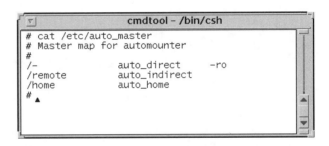

A sample auto_master file.

Each line in the sample *auto_master* file uses a different feature of the master map. The first two lines begin with a pound sign (#) and are treated as comments. You can add comment lines to help document changes you make to the file or to describe what each of the listed map files does. The third line shows a direct map file. The dash (/-) listed for the mount point is a place holder. Direct maps list the path name of each mount point as the key entry in the map file itself. NFS file systems mounted by a direct map are mounted at the mount point listed as the key in the direct map file. This line also specifies the mount point as **-ro** or read-only. A read-only mount point might be used when programs or data such as manual pages are to be mounted.

Direct Maps

Upon reading each line in the master map file, the automount daemon reads the listed map file. Map files are assumed to be in the */etc* directory. You can also include additional entries using the plus sign (+) format as shown below.

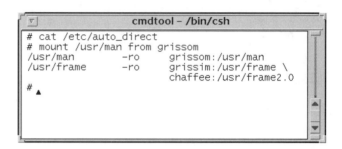

A direct map file.

```
cmdtool - /bin/csh
# cat /etc/auto_direct
# mount /usr/man from grissom
/usr/man        -ro      grissom:/usr/man
/usr/frame      -ro      grissim:/usr/frame \
                         chaffee:/usr/frame2.0
#
```

Each line in the direct map file consists of a key, a list of mount options, and the location of the NFS file system to be mounted. In a direct map the key is the path to the mount point on the client where the NFS file system is to be mounted. The first line of this file shows a simple example where */usr/man* is mounted using the **-ro** or read-only option. The */usr/man* directory is shared by the file server *grissom*.

The second line shows how multiple file servers can be used to redundantly serve applications or data. In this case the directory */usr/frame* contains a popular text processing program. It is available on two different file servers in two different directories. The map file specifies that either of these file servers can be used to obtain */usr/frame*.

To decide which file server to use, the automount daemon consults the client workstation's network address information and tries to use the "closest" file server to reduce network traffic. The closeness measure used is to first try servers on the same network as the client, then those on other networks. This is done to minimize NFS traffic across routers which join networks together. If more than one file server is close, the automount daemon will contact all of the close file servers and use the file server to respond first. If the chosen file server does not respond, the automount daemon will automatically try the other listed file servers. The result is that the nearest available file server will be used.

Notice also that this line has different remote directory names being used to locate */usr/frame* (i.e., */usr/frame and /usr/frame2.0*). When the remote file system is mounted by the automount daemon, the name of the "key" is used regardless of the name of the remote file system. Thus, in this case, if *chaffee* were chosen as the file server, *chaffee:/usr/frame2.0* would be mounted as */usr/frame* on this client. This allows the map file to mask directory naming schemes which might be confusing to users on client workstations. System managers should be aware that this feature can be used to provide easy-to-remember names for users while a different naming scheme can be used on the file server for purposes of labeling the software or data to aid in its management.

> ✖ *TIP:* *When setting up a heterogeneous network of NFS servers and clients from different vendors, consider using the auto_home map. Different vendors have differing conventions for the location of user home directories. With the use of auto_home, these differing locations can be consolidated into a single, easy-to-use scheme.*

> ✔ *NOTE:* *The multiple location feature of the automount service is the key to building highly reliable NFS file sharing. When designing a network where shared collections of programs and data will be used, consider replicating those shared items and using automount to avoid single points of failure.*

Variables Used in Map File Entries

As a further aid to creating maps, the automount daemon understands and can substitute a number of special symbols into map entries. These symbols can be used to create map entries which mount different file systems from the same key depending on the machine type or operating system version in use.

Map File Variable Names

Variable	Meaning	Example
ARCH	CPU architecture type	sun4
CPU	CPU type	SPARC
HOST	Host name	glenn
OSNAME	Operating system name	SunOS
OSREL	Operating system release number	5.4
OSVERS	Operating system version	FCS1.0

For example, you could create a direct map file entry such as the following:

```
/usr/man      chaffee:/export/manuals/$OSREL/man
```

Assuming the file server *chaffee* had several different versions of the manual pages available, this entry would mount the correct version of the manual pages for the client on which it is being used. The ARCH and CPU variables can be used in a similar manner to create maps which can be used on Solaris systems using both SPARC and Intel CPUs without modification. For example, you could mount the correct version (SPARC or Intel) of a local collection of programs with a direct map as follows:

```
/usr/local/bin   grissom:/export/$CPU/local/bin
```

Another map feature is the use of the plus symbol (+). You can include map files inside one another by using the +*mapfile* notation. For example, if you wanted to include a map file named */etc/more_direct_maps* in the direct map file, you would add a line like the following:

```
+more_direct_maps
```

✔ **NOTE:** *Where the automount daemon will look for plus sign (+) entries depends on the automount entry in the /etc/nsswitch file. By default the automount daemon will look in /etc for files first, and then consult the NIS service. See the chapter on NIS for more information.*

The goal in using these map features is to create general purpose maps which can be used anywhere on your network. By carefully crafting a general purpose map, the problem of mounting a large number of NFS file systems on many different clients can be reduced to a single file.

Indirect Maps

A sample
auto_master file.

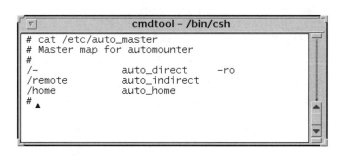

The fourth line of your sample *auto_master* file lists an indirect map. In an indirect map, the NFS file systems referred to by the map are mounted at a different mount point than that listed in the table and a symbolic link is made from that location to the directory listed in the master map. This allows for some more exotic automount tricks. A diagram of an indirect mount which has */home* as its entry in *auto_master* and a key of *frank* in the map file appears in the following illustration.

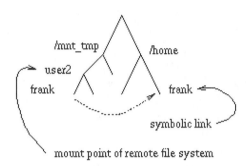

Mount points and symbolic links created by an indirect map.

The auto_home Map

One of the most common indirect maps is the *auto_home* map. The *auto_home* map is an indirect map with keys that are in the */home* directory. It is used to collect users' home directories into a single location, and greatly eases the task of maintaining home directory location information for users.

The next illustration shows a typical *auto_home* map. Indirect maps have the same items in each entry line as found in a direct map: a key, an optional list of mount options, and the location of a remote file system.

An auto_home indirect map.

```
┌──────────────────────────────────────────────┐
│  ▽         cmdtool - /bin/csh                  │
├──────────────────────────────────────────────┤
│ # Home directory map for automounter          │
│ #                                              │
│ dwight   glenn:/export/home/&                  │
│ frank    chaffee:/user2/&                      │
│ tom      grissom:/export/users/&               │
│ steve    glenn:/export/home/█                  │
│ ~                                              │
│ ~                                              │
│ ~                                              │
│ "/etc/auto_home" 3 lines, 64 characters        │
└──────────────────────────────────────────────┘
```

Notice how the line starting with the key *frank* does not contain a full path. The key in an indirect map specifies the name of the symbolic link to be made in the directory specified in the entry for the map in the *auto_master* file. In this case, all the keys in the *auto_home* map will create symbolic links in the */home* directory.

The *&* character stands in place of the key. It is a shorthand notation that can be used in any type of map file. For example, it shortens the entry that begins with the key *tom* to *grissom:/export/home/&* instead of *grissom:/export/home/ tom*.

Indirection by use of symbolic links is useful for several reasons. First, the actual mount point can be placed so as to avoid unnecessary mounting of remote file systems. Consider what could happen if you used the command **ls -F** in a directory that contained numerous autofs mount points controlled by direct maps. All of the remote file systems would be referenced and mounted! The connection used in an indirect map avoid unintended mount point transversal and mounting. The mounting of the remote file system and the creation of the connection occur when the mount point is traversed for access to files or directories beyond the link itself. When a mount occurs, the referenced file system is mounted, and then a connection is made from the *key* to the file system.

Why Use auto_home?

The major administrative reason for using the *auto_home* map is to allow for easier maintenance of users' home directories. Under this system a user can always refer to his or her home directory as being in */home*. From the above example, Tom's home directory could be referred to as */home/tom*, Frank's as */home/frank*, and so on, even though they are located on different file servers or in different directory trees. Since this path is an automatically created symbolic link, the actual location of the directory (e.g., */export/home* on *glenn*) can easily be changed if necessary.

Moving user home directories due to system changes, new disks, disks filling up, and so on is a common occurrence. With the use of *auto_home*, the only change needed when making a move is to adjust the *auto_home* map entry. The user's password file entry and any programs or shell scripts written by the user can remain untouched. This is both easier for the system manager and more convenient for the user.

 NOTE: *Do not use the /home directory for local file systems. The auto-mount service by default will use this directory for the auto_home map. By convention, home directories are placed in the /export file system.*

Map Maintenance

How you maintain maps depends on whether you are using NIS+. When using NIS+, the **nistbladm** command is used to make changes to the map files. The NIS table administration command, nistbladm, updates the NIS+ databases as needed to make the changes made to your automount maps available via NIS+. If changes to the *auto_master* map have been made, you will then need to run the automount command on each client to ensure that new mount points are created. The chapter on NIS+ provides a more detailed description of nistbladm and other commands used to manage NIS+.

Maintaining the auto_home Map File

The *auto_home* map is a special maintenance case. The OpenWindows user account administration tool described in the chapter on creating, deleting and managing user accounts, allows you to easily update the *auto_home* map. If you do not use this tool, you will need to edit this file by hand when you move user home directories around. Be sure to distribute the updated file to all your client workstations as soon as the home directory has been moved to avoid mismatches between the map entry and the actual location of the user's home directory. Mismatches would prevent the user from accessing her/his home directory.

If you are not using NIS+, edit the files first. Then, if changes were made to the *auto_master* map, run the **automount** command. A convenient method for doing this on a large number of clients is to use a tool like **rdist**. As described in the chapter on everyday system administration commands, rdist can use a table of files, commands and host names to automate the distribution of files such as the automount map files. Appearing below is a sample rdist file which will distribute the *auto_master*, *auto_direct* and *auto_home* maps used as examples in this chapter. This rdist file will automatically check each file and update files which are out of date on the listed clients. Whenever the *auto_master* file is updated, rdist will also run the automount command.

```
# Define the clients who will receive the files.
SLAVES = ( grissom shepard )
# Define the files to be distributed
FILES = (
    /etc/auto_master
```

```
        /etc/auto_direct
        /etc/auto_home
        )
# Distribute the files to the clients.
# Specify special handling for the /etc/auto_home file.
${FILES} -> ${SLAVES}
        install;
        special /etc/auto_master /usr/sbin/automount;
```

If these rdist instructions were placed in a file named *auto.dist*, the rdist command could read and use this file with the following command:

```
rdist -f auto.dist
```

Given the above command, rdist would compare the date and size of the files on the host the rdist command was run with the listed clients. Where differences were found, the files on the distribution host would be installed on the clients. If the */etc/auto_master* file were updated on a client, rdist would also run the */usr/sbin/automount* command on that client.

Troubleshooting automount

When trying to locate and fix problems with the **automount** service, bear in mind that automount is built on top of NFS which in turn is built on top of the basic Solaris TCP/IP networking functions. Your first step should be to check that NFS and the network features it depends on are working. Refer to the chapter on NFS and basic networking for additional help. Once you know NFS is working, proceed to check the automount map files.

Disappearing File Systems

A common problem when first beginning to use **automount** is placing **autofs** mount points over the top of existing mount points. This is most commonly seen when you start the automount service and a file system seems to "disappear" beneath the autofs mount point.

If you want to use features such as the *auto_home* map, you must mount the user file systems you have in a location other than */home*. The common convention is to place local file systems in */export* and the *autofs* mount points in the final location. For example, you might mount a user file system such as */export/home* and then use the *auto_home* map to make the user's home directories appear in */home*. This method allows both the file server and clients to use the same automount maps.

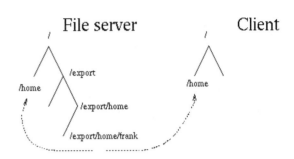

Home directories in /export can be automounted by both clients and servers.

Syntax Errors

Another common problem is syntax mistakes in the map files. If you get error messages or suspect incorrect syntax, try using the **-v** option flag to the **automount** command to obtain additional messages. The next step you could try is using the pound sign comment character (#) to "comment out" lines to help you track down the problem.

```
# bob mercury:/export/home/bob
```

Lines which start with a pound sign are ignored by the automount daemon. By inserting a pound sign on suspect map file lines you can disable them to test whether a problem exists on a particular line.

Summary

The **automount** service allows you to add flexibility and greater reliability to the already useful NFS file service. A single set of map files can be created for use across your entire network. This process greatly reduces the effort required to maintain NFS file access in large networks. By using the *auto_home* map, user home directory maintenance can be simplified.

Network Information Service Fundamentals

Up to this point, we have discussed how to manage system operations information (e.g., host and passwd) on individual hosts. Maintaining system information stored on individual hosts is cumbersome on networks as small as five or six hosts, and becomes unmanageable on larger networks. For example, the */etc/inet/hosts* file is accessed by a variety of network applications in order to establish communications between hosts. If a new host is added to a network of 100 existing hosts, the */etc/inet/hosts* file on each of the existing hosts would need to be updated with the new host's name and IP address. The problem of keeping system information current is especially troublesome with very dynamic information such as passwords.

The NIS+ (Network Information Service Plus) environment addresses this problem by maintaining system information on a central host known as an NIS+ server. The NIS+ server provides its clients with system information (e.g., host and passwd) upon request through the NIS+ look-up service.

This chapter focuses on the supporting concepts needed to configure the NIS+ environment in a local area network.

What is NIS+?

NIS+ is a network look-up service that provides information about users, workstations, and network resources to hosts that reside within a domain. A domain is a collection of NIS+ related hosts. NIS+ is a component of ONC+ (Open Network Computing Plus) in Solaris 2, and *replaces* its predecessor, NIS, which is used in Solaris 1. Like NIS, NIS+ is not proprietary, but is licenseable to any vendor wishing to include the service as part of its operating environment.

✔ **NOTE:** *NIS is also known as YP (Yellow Pages).*

NIS+ Servers and Clients

NIS+ solves the problem of multiple machines sharing the same information by storing the data in databases on NIS+ server hosts. The server hosts make the data available to NIS+ clients on demand. This arrangement is known as the NIS+ Client-Server Model.

Recall from our earlier discussion in the chapter on networking that a *client* is a process running on a host that sends requests for information to a network, and a *server* is a process that responds to client requests. An NIS+ client process uses RPC (Remote Procedure Call) when making information look-up requests. An NIS+ server is a process that services an NIS+ client RPC request, looks up requested information in a database, and returns the information to the client process.

Every NIS+ domain is served by one master server and zero or more replica servers. An NIS+ master server contains the master set of system information in the form of NIS+ tables. If changes are made to the NIS+ tables on the master NIS+ server, they are automatically pushed to the replica servers. An NIS+ replica server maintains copies of the tables in order to distribute the load in answering client requests and to provide backup sources of information in case the master server fails.

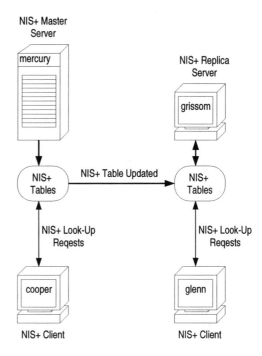

The NIS+ client-server model.

NIS+ Domains

A collection of related hosts and the information managed and utilized among the hosts is called a *domain*. Every NIS+ host must be associated with a specific domain. For example, *ace.com.* might be the domain name issued to a company named Ace Inc. Because Ace is a commercial entity, it would be assigned to the subdomain named *com* (commercial). Similar to IP addresses, domain names are issued by the NIC. Applications to the NIC were discussed in the chapter on networking. The domain name issued by the NIC is often referred to as the *root* domain or *top-level* domain. A root domain must contain two components ending with a dot, such as *ace.com.*

✔ **NOTE:** *NIS+ domain names are not case-sensitive. Thus, Ace.Com. and ace.com. are equivalent.*

The name of the domain that a host is associated with is declared in the */etc/defaultdomain* file. Domains can be divided into subdomains to accurately reflect the hierarchical structure of an organization. For example, a company named Ace Inc. with Hardware, Software, Marketing, and Sales divisions might set up the domain hierarchy shown in the following illustration.

The NIS+ hierarchical structure for ace.com.

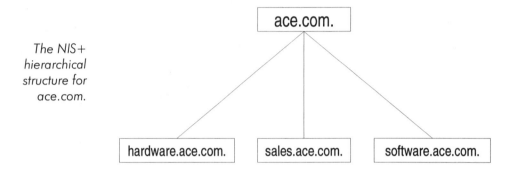

NIS+ Objects

An NIS+ *namespace* is a hierarchical structure in which NIS+ information is stored. The structure includes the root domain and all domains below it. Every namespace has a root master server that serves the root domain at the top of the namespace. An NIS+ namespace is similar in structure to a UNIX file system hierarchy, but is accessed using NIS+ commands (e.g., *nisls, niscat, nismkdir*).

Directory, table, and group objects are the most common types of objects in the NIS+ namespace. Directory objects are similar to UNIX directories in that they can contain other objects such as table and group objects. Table objects store information in the NIS+ namespace and are analogous to a UNIX plain file. The Solaris 2 environment provides 16 default tables, each of which stores information within a domain about hosts, users, networks, services, and so forth. A set of NIS+ tables stores information for that particular domain only. Group objects are used for NIS+ security. Like the group ownership within a UNIX file system, an NIS+ group is a collection of users and hosts identified by a single name and is used to facilitate NIS+ security. The default NIS+ group created in every domain is called *admin*. Although additional NIS+ groups are optional, they are a security convenience allowing an NIS+ administrator to assign access rights to a group of users and hosts.

Directory Objects

Directory objects make up the framework of a namespace and are created with the *nismkdir* command. Each subdomain in an NIS+ hierarchy is analogous to a subdirectory in a UNIX file system. Two default NIS+ directories reside within every domain: the *org_dir* directory stores NIS+ table objects, and the *groups_dir* directory stores NIS+ security group objects. The directory object at the top of a namespace (root domain) is called the *root directory*. A namespace is said to be "flat," if it consists of a root domain only. A flat domain can become hierarchical by creating subdomains

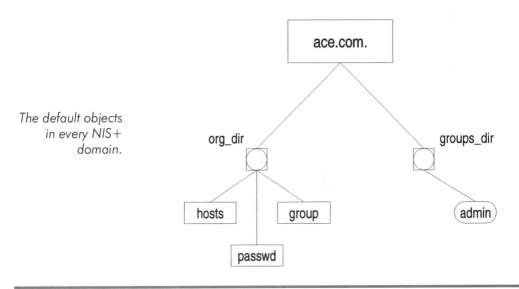

The default objects in every NIS+ domain.

Using NIS+ Object Names

NIS+ object names are formed by appending the root directory name (including the period) to the names. This is called a "fully-qualified name." For example, *sales.ace.com.* and *software.ace.com.* are both fully-qualified names that represent the *sales.ace.com.* and *software.ace.com.* subdomains within the *ace.com.* namespace. Like UNIX files and directories, NIS+ objects can be referred to by partial or full names.

Similar to a relative path name in a UNIX file system hierarchy, a partially-qualified NIS+ name is simply the name of the component. For example, the *hosts* table's partially-qualified name would be *hosts*. A fully-qualified name resembles an absolute UNIX name in that it is the complete name of the component. Such name is formed by starting with the name of the component and appending the names of all involved components up to the root domain, and is delimited by dots (.). For example, the fully-qualified name of the Sales division's *hosts* table at Ace Inc. is *hosts.org_dir.sales.ace.com*. Likewise, the fully qualified name of the Software division's *hosts* table would be *hosts.org_dir.software.ace.com*.

Creating a Flat NIS+ Domain Using NIS+ Scripts

Solaris 2.4 includes three NIS+ administration shell scripts to facilitate the creation of NIS+ servers, tables, and clients. The nisserver, nispopulate, and nisclient scripts are located in the */usr/lib/nis* directory and allow for fast and reliable installation of NIS+ clients and servers.

The nisserver script can be used to set up a root master or its replica NIS+ servers. The nispopulate script can be used to populate NIS+ tables in a specified domain from corresponding files. The nisclient script can be used to initialize NIS+ hosts and users.

Configuring an NIS+ Domain

The purpose of this section is to provide a step-by-step procedure for setting up a flat domain using the NIS+ installation scripts to create the example domain *ace.com*. The first part of the process is to configure the root master server. The second part consists of populating the root master server tables with information. The files in the */etc* directory are frequently used to achieve this step. Finally, clients will be added to the domain.

Configuring a Root Master Server

1. Log in as root on the host that is to become the NIS+ root master for the namespace *ace.com*.

2. Run the nisserver script with the **-r** and **-d** options. The -r option is used to indicate that the server being initialized is a root server, while the -d option specifies the domain name the server is administering.

```
mercury# /usr/lib/nis/nisserver -r -d ace.com.
```

3. The nisserver script will ask for setup verification as follows:

This script sets up the machine "mercury" as a NIS+ Root Master
Server for domain ace.com.

Domainname : ace.com.

NIS+ Group : admin.ace.com.

YP compatibility : OFF

Security level : 2=DES

Is this information correct? (Y or N) **y**

    4. The nisserver script will then run the **nisinit** and **nissetup** commands and
start an NIS server process. You are then prompted to enter an NIS+
network password which is required by NIS+ for security purposes. You
can enter either the master server's root password or another password of
your choice. To keep things simple, most sites use the root password as
the NIS+ password.

adding credential for mercury.ace.com.

Enter login password: **rootpasswd**

Populating a Root Master Server's Tables

    1. On the master server for the domain, run the nispopulate script to populate
the empty tables created by the nisserver script. Typically, the system file
located in the */etc* directory is used as the source for NIS+ table population.

mercury# cd /etc

mercury# /usr/lib/nis/nispopulate -F

    2. The nispopulate script will ask for setup verification as follows:

NIS+ Domainname: ace.com.

Directory Path: (current directory)

Is this information correct? (Y or N) **y**

    3. The source files are listed and you are prompted once more to verify the
creation of the destination NIS+ tables.

This script will populate the following NIS+ tables for domain
your.domain.name. from the files in current directory:

auto_master auto_home ethers group hosts networks passwd
protocols services rpc netmasks bootparams netgroup aliases
shadow

Do you want to continue? (Y or N) **y**

Setting Up the NIS+ Client

1. Use the nisclient script on the root master to create the credentials for the client. In this case *mercury* is the master server for the domain, and *grissom* is the client being initialized.

```
mercury#/usr/lib/nis/nisclient -c grissom
```

2. You are asked to verify the client.

```
You will be adding DES credentials in domain ace.com. for mercury
**nisclient will not overwrite any existing entries ** in the
credential table
Do you want to continue? (Y or N) y
checking ace.com. domain...
checking cred.org_dir.ace.com. permission...
adding DES credential for grissom...
Adding key pair for unix.grissom@ace.com.
Enter grissom.ace.com. root login
password:rootpasswd
Retype password:rootpasswd
```

3. For all new NIS+ clients added, you will need to run the following on the client's machine:

```
nisclient -i -h root_master -a root_master_IP_address -d your.domain name.
```

4. Log on to the designated client as root and execute the nisclient script to initialize the client.

```
grissom# nisclient -i -h mercury -a 154.50.2.2 -d ace.com.
Initializing client "grissom" for domain "ace.com."...
Once initialization is done, you will need to reboot your
machine.
Do you want to continue? (Y or N) y
setting up domain information "ac3e.com."...
setting up the name service switch information...
Please enter the network password that your administrator gave
you.
Please enter the Secure-RPC password for root: rootpasswd
Please enter the login password for root: rootpasswd
```

```
Client initialization completed!!
Please reboot your machine for changes to take effect.
```

Setting Up an NIS+ Replica Server

An NIS+ client can be configured as a replica server. In this case, we will turn the NIS+ client *grissom* created in the previous steps into a replica server.

5. Log in as root and start the NIS+ service daemon, **rpc.nisd**.

```
grissom# rpc.nisd
```

6. Run the nisserver script on the master server to initialize the replica.

```
mercury# /usr/lib./nis/nisserver -R -d ace.com. -h grissom
This script sets up an NIS+ replica server for domain
your.domain.name.
Domainname : ace.com.
NIS+ Server : grissom
```

7. You are prompted to verify the setup.

```
Is this information correct? (Y or N) y
```

This script will set up machine *grissom* as a NIS+ replica server for domain *ace.com.*

In order for *grissom* to serve this domain, you will need to start up the NIS+ server daemon (rpc.nisd) with proper options on *grissom* if they are not already running.

8. Ask once more to verify the setup.

```
Do you want to continue? (Y or N) y
Added "grissom.ace.com." to group "admin.ace.com."
```

Summary

In this chapter we discussed the basic concepts required to configure an NIS+ environment in a local area network. In addition, we provided the basic step-by-step procedures for creating and initializing an NIS+ master server, NIS+ client, NIS+ replica server, and the steps required to populate NIS+ tables.

System Backups and Disaster Recovery

In previous chapters, you have seen how to install Solaris, how to manage users, peripherals, security, and network services. One very important area that we have not explored is how to recover from a disaster. Whether the disaster is caused by a user removing a critical file, or the loss of data due to a disk drive failure, you need to be prepared. One of the simplest ways to protect your data from any form of disaster is to perform system backups at regular intervals.

Importance of System Backups

The most important task of every system administrator is to ensure the availability of the data on the systems you manage. Every file, every database, every byte of information stored on your systems must be available. This requirement dictates that you make backup copies of the data to store away in the event you need to retrieve information at a later date.

But making a copy of the data and storing it in another office in your building may not be a solution to the problem. For instance, in the event of a natural disaster you may need to have copies of the data in remote locations to ensure survivability and accessibility of the backup media.

In the event you suffer a hardware failure or some other form of disaster, you should be able to reload the bulk of your information from the backup media. There will almost always be some loss of information. It is impossible to backup every keystroke as it is made. Therefore, you could lose information that is entered into the system between backups. The goal of a backup procedure is to minimize the loss of such data and allow you to reload quickly and continue with your business.

Which Files Should You Back Up?

One important decision you will need to make is to determine which files you should back up. It is good practice to back up all files on the system at regular intervals. But some of the files rarely change. You need to examine the contents of your system disks to help you determine which files need to be part of your file system backups, and which files you can eliminate from regular backups.

Some of the programs on your systems are part of the operating system. In order to load the operating system you must have some form of distribution media. You could decide that you do not need to back up all of the operating system binaries. But you will need to back up any operating system related files that you created or changed. A few examples might be the NIS database, the password file, the shadow file, the rc files, and any customizations which affect those files.

Another set of files that you may wish to eliminate from regular backups are vendor supplied binaries. If you have the distribution media for commercially purchased software, it is not necessary to regularly back up the files. Again, you need to ensure that you back up any customized files or start-up scripts required for those packages.

Files that you will need to back up regularly include the users' files, any corporate databases or other important data, and any files which have been changed since the time of the last backup. On large systems the amount of data to be backed up may exceed several gigabytes a day. Because of this, you need to decide how and when to perform backups to minimize impact on the system and loss of important data.

How Often Should You Perform Backups?

Another very important factor in successful file system backup strategies is backup frequency. You must determine how much data you can afford to lose before it seriously affects your organization's ability to do business.

In many cases losing the data from a single day is deemed an acceptable loss. This is generally the case for activities such as university teaching laboratories, customer service databases, and Internet service providers.

At the other end of the spectrum, there are situations which do not allow the loss of any data. Corporations which use computers for financial transactions, stock and commodities trading, and insurance activities would be a few examples of this environment.

A reasonable backup schedule for a typical corporation would call for some form of backup to be performed every day. In addition, the backups must be performed at the same time every day. The fact that backups must be maintained on a rigid schedule lends support to the automated backup methods discussed later in this chapter and in Chapter 22.

> ✔ **NOTE:** *The examples in this chapter assume computer system operation seven days a week, and thus, the need for seven backups per week. In some instances, if the corporate computer systems are idle on the weekends, you may be able to use a five day per week backup schedule.*

Backup Strategy and Scheduling

Once you have determined which files you need to back up, and how often you will be performing backups, you need to determine the type of backups you will perform, and the devices you will use to perform these backups. These decisions will play a large part in scheduling backups.

Before you start scheduling the backups, you need to determine the type of backup strategy you will use, the type of backup system you will use, and how much media will be required for the methods you choose. The following sections examine several backup schedules, the media requirements for each schedule, and the strengths and weaknesses of each backup method.

Types of Backups

There are several types of backups that you may elect to perform. The simplest type of dump is a full dump. A full dump is also referred to as a level 0 (level zero) backup. A full dump copies every disk file to the backup media. On systems with large disk storage capacity, it may not be possible to make full dumps very often due to the cost of the tapes, the tape storage space requirements, and the amount of time required to copy the files to the tapes.

Because full dumps are expensive in terms of time and resources, most programs written to perform backups allow for some form of incremental dump.

An incremental dump is one in which files created or modified since the last dump are copied to the backup media. For instance, if you perform a full dump on a Sunday, the Monday incremental dump would contain only the files created or changed since the Sunday dump.

The type of dump to be performed will typically rely on the backup strategy you choose. The strategy includes factors such as how long to keep copies of the dump media on hand, what type of dump to perform on which day of the week, and how easily information can be restored from your backup media.

Backup Strategies

It is vital to perform dumps at regular intervals. This may be accomplished by developing a dump schedule. The dump schedule notes when you should perform full dumps and incremental dumps on the systems. Full dumps allow you to establish a snapshot of the system at a given point in time. All of your data should be contained on a full dump.

Incremental dumps enable you to recover active files with a minimum of media and time. Incremental dumps capture the data which has changed since the last incremental dump of a lower level. Let's look at how the incremental dumps work.

A level 1 dump would back up all files created or changed since the last level 0 dump. A level 2 dump would back up all files since the last level 1 dump, and so on. In general, a level N dump will back up all files which have been altered or created since the last dump at a lower level.

In order to ensure that you capture as much of the system data as possible, the interval between backups should be kept to a minimum. With these constraints in mind, you need to examine a few of the more popular backup strategies.

   NOTE: *In order to ensure successful dumps, it is recommended that you bring the system down to the single-user init state.*

Volume/Calendar Backup

The volume/calendar backup strategy calls for you to perform a full system backup once a month. An incremental backup is performed once a week for files which are changing often. Daily incremental backups catch the files that have changed since the last daily backup.

A typical schedule may be to perform the full (level 0) backup one Sunday a month, and weekly level 3 backups every Sunday of the month. Daily level 5 backups would be performed Monday through Saturday. This would require eight complete sets of media (one monthly tape, one weekly tape, and six daily tapes).

Calendar Manager V3.3: root@grumpy						
View ▽ Edit ▽ Browse ▽ Print ▽					Prev Today Next	

January 1995

Sun	Mon	Tue	Wed	Thu	Fri	Sat
1 9:00a Level 0 Tape A	**2** 9:00a level 5 Tape B	**3** 9:00a level 5 Tape C	**4** 9:00a level 5 Tape D	**5** 9:00a level 5 Tape E	**6** 9:00a level 5 Tape F	**7** 9:00a level 5 Tape G
8 9:00a Level 3 Tape H	**9** 9:00a level 5 Tape B	**10** 9:00a level 5 Tape C	**11** 9:00a level 5 Tape D	**12** 9:00a level 5 Tape E	**13** 9:00a level 3 Tape F	**14** 9:00a level 5 Tape G
15 9:00a Level 3 Tape H	**16** 9:00a level 5 Tape B	**17** 9:00a level 5 Tape C	**18** 9:00a level 5 Tape D	**19** 9:00a level 5 Tape E	**20** 9:00a level 3 Tape F	**21** 9:00a level 5 Tape G
22 9:00a Level 3 Tape H	**23** 9:00a level 5 Tape B	**24** 9:00a level 5 Tape C	**25** 9:00a level 5 Tape D	**26** 9:00a level 5 Tape E	**27** 9:00a level 3 Tape F	**28** 9:00a level 5 Tape G
29 9:00a Level 3 Tape H	**30** 9:00a level 5 Tape B	**31** 9:00a level 5 Tape C				

Typical scheduling for the volume/calendar backup strategy.

In order to recover from complete data loss with the volume/calendar scheme, you would need to restore from the most recent full backup, followed by restoring from the most recent weekly backup, followed by restoring from each daily backup tape written since the weekly backup.

One problem with this backup scheme is that the tapes are immediately reused. For example, every Monday you overwrite last Monday's backup information. Consider what would happen if one of your disk drives failed during the second Monday backup! You would not be able to recover all of the data because you were in the process of overwriting the backup tape when the drive failed. One strength of this backup scheme is that it requires a minimum of media.

Grandfather/Father/Son Backup

The grandfather/father/son backup strategy is similar to the volume/calendar strategy. The major difference between the two schemes is that the grandfather/father/son method incorporates a one-month archive in the backup scheme. This eliminates the problem of overwriting a tape before you make a more recent backup of the file system.

To implement the grandfather/father/son strategy, you would perform a full (level 0) dump once a month to new media. Once a week you would perform an incremental (level 3) backup which would capture all of the files changed since the last weekly backup. This weekly backup would also be saved on new media. Each day you would perform an incremental level 5 backup which captures any files which changed since the last daily backup. The daily backups would reuse tapes which had been written one week earlier.

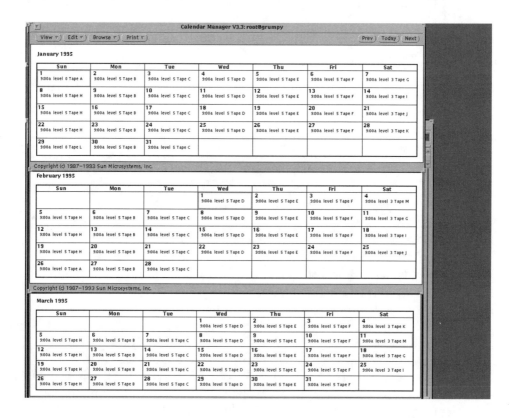

Typical scheduling for the grandfather/father/son backup strategy.

In order to maintain a one-month archive, the monthly full backup tape would be placed in storage. Each weekly full backup would also be placed in storage, When the time came to perform the second monthly full backup, new media would be used. When the third monthly backup was due, you would reuse the tape from the first month's full backup. The weekly backups would be archived in a similar manner.

This scheme would require two sets of monthly backup media (one in storage, one active), five sets of weekly backup media, and six sets of daily backup media. A total of 13 sets of media would be required to implement this strategy with a one-month archive of information.

In order to recover from complete data loss, you would first restore the most recent level 0 backup tape. You would then restore from the most recent of the level 3 backups if that backup was written after the level 0 backup. Once the level 3 backup had been restored you would restore from each of the level 5 backups that were written after the level 3 backup.

This backup strategy requires much more media than the simple volume/calendar strategy. While media cost is increased with this plan, data survivability also increases.

Tower of Hanoi Backup

The Tower of Hanoi backup strategy is a variation of another backup strategy known as the *exponential backup*. These strategies rely on mathematical functions of powers of two. For example, you could use five backup tapes and provide for a 32-day schedule. With six tapes, you could provide for a 64-day schedule.

The Tower of Hanoi backup schedule provides outstanding data survivability, and a minimum of media. Unfortunately, on a seven-day backup system, the scheduling of full backups as opposed to partial backups can become a problem for the operator.

One way to avoid operator confusion would be to perform a special level 0 backup on the first day of each month. This tape would not be one of the five tapes used in the backup cycle. Total media requirements in this scheme would be seven sets of media.

In order to recover from complete data loss, you would first restore from the most recent level 0 backup, and then restore from the level 1 backup if that backup was written after the level 0 backup. You would then restore from the most recent level 3 backup if that backup was written after the level 0 backup, followed by restoring from the most recent level 4 backup if that backup was written after the level 0 backup. Next, you would restore each of the level 5 backups that were written after the level 0 backup.

Calendar Manager V3.3: root@grumpy

View ▾ Edit ▾ Browse ▾ Print ▾   Prev Today Next

January 1995

Sun	Mon	Tue	Wed	Thu	Fri	Sat
1 9:00a level 0 Tape E	2 9:00a level 5 Tape A	3 9:00a level 4 Tape B	4 9:00a level 5 Tape A	5 9:00a level 3 Tape C	6 9:00a level 5 Tape A	7 9:00a level 4 Tape B
8 9:00a level 5 Tape A	9 9:00a level 1 Tape D	10 9:00a level 5 Tape A	11 9:00a level 4 Tape B	12 9:00a level 5 Tape A	13 9:00a level 3 Tape C	14 9:00a level 5 Tape A
15 9:00a level 4 Tape B	16 9:00a level 5 Tape A	17 9:00a level 0 Tape E	18 9:00a level 5 Tape A	19 9:00a level 4 Tape B	20 9:00a level 5 Tape A	21 9:00a level 3 Tape C
22 9:00a level 5 Tape A	23 9:00a level 4 Tape B	24 9:00a level 5 Tape A	25 9:00a level 1 Tape D	26 9:00a level 5 Tape A	27 9:00a level 4 Tape B	28 9:00a level 5 Tape A
29 9:00a level 3 Tape C	30 9:00a level 5 Tape A	31 9:00a level 4 Tape B				

Calendar Manager V3.3: root@grumpy

View ▾ Edit ▾ Browse ▾ Print ▾   Prev Today Next

February 1995

Sun	Mon	Tue	Wed	Thu	Fri	Sat
			1 9:00a level 5 Tape A	2 9:00a level 0 Tape E	3 9:00a level 5 Tape A	4 9:00a level 4 Tape B
5 9:00a level 5 Tape A	6 9:00a level 3 Tape C	7 9:00a level 5 Tape A	8 9:00a level 4 Tape B	9 9:00a level 5 Tape A	10 9:00a level 1 Tape D	11 9:00a level 5 Tape A
12 9:00a level 4 Tape B	13 9:00a level 5 Tape A	14 9:00a level 3 Tape C	15 9:00a level 5 Tape A	16 9:00a level 4 Tape B	17 9:00a level 5 Tape A	18 9:00a level 0 Tape E
19 9:00a level 5 Tape A	20 9:00a level 4 Tape B	21 9:00a level 5 Tape A	22 9:00a level 3 Tape C	23 9:00a level 5 Tape A	24 9:00a level 4 Tape B	25 9:00a level 5 Tape A
26 9:00a level 1 Tape D	27 9:00a level 5 Tape A	28 9:00a level 4 Tape B				

Copyright (c) 1987–1993 Sun Microsystems, Inc.

Typical scheduling for the Tower of Hanoi backup strategy.

A Reasonable Alternative

The following four-week schedule offers a reasonable backup schedule for most sites. By performing a full dump on the first Sunday of the month, you provide a monthly snapshot of your system data. If you use two sets of dump tapes, you can keep this information around for two months.

Note that in the example the Tuesday through Friday incrementals contain extra copies of files from Monday. This schedule ensures that any file modified during the week can be recovered from the previous day's incremental dump.

In order to recover from complete data loss, you would first restore the most recent full (level 0) backup tape. You would then restore from the most recent of the weekly (level 3) backups. Once the weekly backups are restored you would restore from each of the daily (level 5) backups.

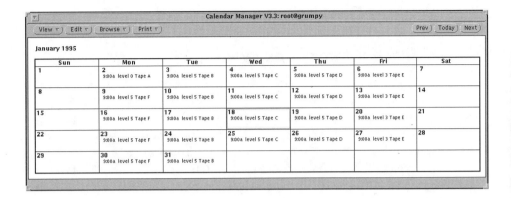

Typical scheduling for a reasonable backup strategy.

Types of Backup Devices

Once you have chosen a backup strategy, you can devote your attention to backup devices. There are several types of backup devices currently available on the market. The primary requirements for a backup device follow:

1. User ability to write data to the device.

2. Media capable of storing the data for long periods of time.

3. Supports standard system interconnects.

4. Supports reasonable input/output throughput.

Most devices used for system backups consist of a magnetic media (tape or disk) and the drive mechanism. The drive mechanism provides the electronics and transport functions to allow you to store digital signals on the magnetic media. Some backup devices use an optical media to store the information as opposed to magnetic media. Still other backup devices use a combination of magnetic and optical storage methods. Let's examine the characteristics of a few of these devices.

Tape Backup Devices

1/2-inch 9-track Tape Drive

Until recently, 1/2-inch tape drives were the mainstay of backup media. The early 1/2-inch tape drives allowed the operator to write information on the tape at 800 bits per inch of tape. Later drives allowed 1600 bits per inch, and the most recent drives allowed 6250 bits per inch. At 6250 bits per inch, a 1/2 inch tape can hold up to 100 megabytes of information.

A typical 1/2-inch tape consists of 2400 feet of 1/2-inch wide tape on a 10-inch plastic reel. The 1/2-inch tape drives are typically large and expensive, but the tape itself is usually very inexpensive. The 1/2-inch format is still a standard media for many industrial operations.

Older 1/2-inch tape drives required special bus interfaces to connect them to a system. Current model drives use the SCSI interface for connection to the system. The availability of current technology bus interconnection helps to ensure that the 1/2-inch tape drives will be around for many years to come.

Due to the vast volume of information stored on 1/2-inch tape, the 1/2-inch tape drive will be required for many years to come. However, with systems containing literally hundreds of gigabytes of disk storage, 1/2-inch tape becomes impractical for data backup.

Cartridge Tape Drive

Cartridge tape drives allow you to store between 10 megabytes and several gigabytes of data on a small tape cartridge. Cartridge tape drives are usually smaller and less expensive than 1/2-inch tape drives. Tape cartridges are typically more expensive than a reel of 1/2-inch tape. Because the data cartridge stores more information, a cartridge tape must be manufactured to tighter tolerances than 1/2-inch tapes.

Because the media is smaller and the drives less expensive, cartridge tape systems became a standard distribution media for many software companies. Many systems still include boot PROM code to boot cartridge distribution tapes. This makes cartridge tapes particularly attractive for disaster recovery situations.

A cartridge tape distribution of the operating system is easily stored in a remote location. In the event of a failure or disaster at the primary computer location, these distribution tapes could be used to reload/rebuild a system to replace the damaged host.

Most cartridge tape systems use SCSI interconnections to the host system. These devices support data transfer rates up to 5Mb per second. This transfer rate may be a little misleading, however, as the information is typically buffered in memory on the tape drive. The actual transfer rate from the tape drive memory to the tape media is typically on the order of 500 kilobytes per second.

8mm Tape Drive

These tape drives are also small and fast, and use relatively inexpensive tape media. The 8mm media can hold between 2 and 10Gb of data. Because of high density storage, 8mm drives have become a standard backup device on many systems. Several companies also use 8mm tape as a distribution media for their software.

The 8mm tape system uses data-grade 8mm tapes. These tapes differ slightly from the consumer video market 8mm tapes. While the manufacturers of 8mm drives strongly suggest that the data grade tapes be purchased for data storage, many users have reported using consumer grade video tapes for many years without problems.

The 8mm drives use the SCSI bus as the system interconnection. Low density 8mm drives can store 2.2Gb of information on tape. These units transfer data to the tape at a rate of 250 kilobytes per second.

High density 8mm drives can store between 5 Gigabytes and 10 Gigabytes of information on a tape. At the "low" end, the 8mm drives do not use data compression techniques to store the information on tape. At the "high" end, the drives incorporate data compression hardware which is used to increase the amount of information that can be stored on the tape.

Regardless of the use of data compression, high density 8mm drives transfer data to tape at a rate of 500 kilobytes per second. High density drives also allow the user to read and write data at the lower densities supported by the low density drives. When using the high density drives in low density mode, storage capacities and throughput numbers are identical to low density drives.

 NOTE: *What would happen if the on-drive compression electronics failed during your backups and did not let you know of this failure? Would the data on the tape be coherent? Would you be able to salvage your files from such a backup tape? Many sites do not enable hardware compression techniques because of possible data loss resulting from compression electronics. These sites choose to use compression software for their backups as an alternative.*

Digital Audio Tape Drive

Digital audio tape (DAT) drives are small, fast, and use relatively inexpensive tape media. Typical DAT media can hold between 2 and 8Gb of data. The DAT media is a relative newcomer to the digital data backup market. The tape drive electronics and media are basically the same as the DAT tapes used in home audio systems.

The various densities available on DAT drives are due to data compression. A standard DAT drive can write 2Gb of data to a tape. By using various data compression algorithms the manufacturers have produced drives which can store between 2 and 8Gb of data on each tape.

DAT drives use SCSI bus interconnections to the host system. Because DAT technology is relatively new, it offers performance and features not available with some of the other tape system technologies. For instance, the DAT drive offers superior file search capabilities as compared to the 8mm helical scan drives on the market.

Jukebox System

Jukebox systems on the market combine a "jukebox" mechanism with one or more tape drives to provide a tape system capable of storing several hundred gigabytes of data. The tape drives in the jukebox systems are typically DAT or 8mm devices. Many of these systems employ multiple tape drives, and special "robotic" hardware to load and unload the tapes.

Jukebox systems require special software to control the robotics. The software keeps track of the contents of each tape, and builds an index to allow the user to quickly load the correct tape on demand. Many commercially available backup packages allow the use of jukebox systems to permit backup automation.

Optical Backup Devices

Magnetic tape has been used as a backup media for many years. Until recently, magnetic tape was the most economical way to back up mass storage devices. Recently, optical storage devices have become another economical means to back up your mass storage systems. A few of the more popular optical backup devices are described as follows.

Compact Disk

Compact Disk Read-Only-Memory devices (CD-ROM) are useful for long term archival of information. Although the name implies that these are read-only devices, recent technology has made it possible to mass market the devices which create the encoded CD-ROM media. These CD-ROM writers (also called CD-recordables) allow you to consider using CD-ROM as a backup device.

One of the major decisions in choosing a backup device is the ability of the media to store the information for long periods of time. CD-ROM media offers excellent data survivability. Another strong point of the CD-ROM as a backup device is the availability of reliable data transportability between systems. This is possible due to CD-ROM's adherence to industry standardized data formats.

Along with these advantages, the CD-ROM offers a few unique disadvantages. The foremost disadvantage to the CD-ROM as a backup device is the setup cost to create a CD. Not only is the CD-ROM writer an expensive device, setting up and creating a CD is a time-intensive operation. Other disadvantages of using the CD-ROM as a backup device include the (relatively) high priced media, and the speed at which the CD-ROM writers operate.

While tape drives can transfer data to the media at typical data rates of 500 kilobytes per second, the CD-ROM writer may take several hours to create a CD-ROM which contains 600Mb of information.

WORM Disk

Write Once Read Many (WORM) storage systems have been around longer than the CD-ROM backup systems, and ways have been found to overcome some of the throughput problems associated with CD-ROM writers. These devices use standard SCSI system interconnects to interface with the system. Most of the WORM devices provide data rates similar to SCSI tape drives (500 kilobits per second).

The media used by WORM devices can often hold several gigabytes of data, and is less expensive than the CD-ROM media. Unfortunately, there are no clear industry standards for recording methods on WORM devices. This has led to a plethora of manufacturers who produce drives with proprietary recording standards. This, in turn, means that the data written on one brand of WORM drive (quite often) cannot be read on another brand of WORM drive.

Because you need to ensure that you can recover from a disastrous failure, you would need to include a spare WORM reader with any backup media that you store in a remote location. This could quickly become an expensive proposition!

Magneto-Optical Backup Devices

Magneto-Optical Disk

A relative newcomer to the optical backup field is the magneto-optical storage system. These systems use a combination of magnetic and optical media to store the data. These two technologies were merged into a single storage system to provide the best features of each, and (hopefully) none of the drawbacks.

Optical storage systems are typically expensive. They are also relatively slow devices, and the media is typically expensive. Consequently, optical storage systems have seen very low usage as backup devices. In contrast, magnetic tape (or disk) storage systems are inexpensive and fast. Unfortunately, the media is bulky, and susceptible to damage and data loss. By combining the two storage systems into one system, manufacturers have been able to provide fast, inexpensive, and reliable backup systems.

Many of the magneto-optical systems are hierarchical storage systems. This means that they keep track of how long a file has been in storage since the last modification. Files which are not accessed or modified are often eligible to be stored on the slower optical storage section of the system. Files which are accessed often are maintained on the magnetic storage section of these systems which allows for faster access to these files.

Most magneto-optical storage systems use standard SCSI bus system interconnections. These systems can typically provide the same (or better) data transfer rates as SCSI tape and disk systems.

Disk Systems as a Backup Device

One problem involved in using tape devices for backups is the (relatively) low data throughput rate. If you had to back up several gigabytes or terabytes of data daily it would not take long to realize that tape drives are not the best backup method. While optical backup devices offer high storage capacity, the optical devices that we discussed are often much slower than tape devices. So how do you back up large-scale systems?

One popular method of backing up large-scale systems is to make backup copies of the data on several disk drives. Disk drives are orders of magnitude faster than tape devices, so they offer a solution to one of the backup problems on large-scale systems. But disk drives are much more expensive than tapes! You would also consume large amounts of system resources to copy 100 1Gb disks to 100 backup 1Gb disks. Fortunately, there are software applications and hardware systems available to transparently perform this function.

Raid Disk Arrays

One operating mode of redundant arrays of inexpensive disks (RAID) enables the system to make mirror image copies of all of your data on backup disk drives. RAID disk arrays also allow for data striping for high speed data access. In Chapter 2 we discussed RAID disk arrays in depth.

Briefly, RAID I/O subsystems provide you with several "levels" of service. Each RAID level describes a different method of storing the data on the disk drive(s). Each level has unique characteristics, and some of these levels are more suitable to certain applications than other I/O implementations would be.

RAID: A Review

The most common RAID implementations are described below.

RAID LEVEL 0 implements a striped disk array. This array will contain several disk drives. The data is broken down into small segments, and each data segment is written to a separate disk drive. This improves disk I/O performance by spreading the I/O load across many channels and drives. A striped disk does not offer data redundancy, nor does it offer better fault tolerance than a standard I/O subsystem.

RAID LEVEL 1 implements a mirrored disk array. This array will contain two disk modules. The information written to one disk is also written (mirrored) to the other disk. This ensures that the data is available even if one of the disk drives fails. RAID level 1 offers better data availability, but does not offer high throughput I/O subsystem performance. It is possible to mirror a striped disk array, therefore providing better I/O performance, as well as high data availability. The primary disadvantage of using RAID level 1 is the cost of purchasing duplicate disk drives.

RAID LEVEL 2 interleaves data sectors across many disks. The controller breaks the blocks up and spreads them over a small group of disk drives. An error detection and correction process is built into RAID level 2 systems to provide some measure of fault tolerance. RAID level 2 is not found on many systems, as other RAID levels offer better performance and fault tolerance.

RAID LEVEL 3 interleaves data sectors across many disks much like RAID level 2. But RAID level 3 uses a single parity disk per group of drives to implement a fault tolerant disk system. All of the drive spindles are synchronized such that the read/write heads on all drives in the array are active at the same time. This synchronization also ensures that the data is written to the same sector on every drive in the array. If a disk fails, the system continues to operate by recreating the data for the failed disk from the parity disk.

RAID LEVEL 4 implements striping with the addition of a parity disk. This provides for some of the fault tolerance missing in RAID level 0. RAID level 4 is not found on many systems, as other RAID levels can provide for better throughput and fault tolerance.

RAID LEVEL 5 implements a large disk storage array. Similar to a level 0 RAID array, the disk array uses striping to improve system performance. RAID level 5 also implements a parity protection scheme. This scheme allows the system to continue operation even if one of the disk drives in the array fails. The data that is normally stored on the failed drive is recreated from the parity information stored elsewhere in the array. Once the failed disk drive is replaced, the data is restored automatically by the RAID controller. RAID level 5 provides improved system availability and I/O subsystem throughput.

Problems with Disks as Backup Devices

While backing up to disk devices is much faster than backing up to other devices, it should be noted that they present a potentially serious problem. One of the important considerations of backup planning is the availability of the data to the users. In the event of a natural disaster, it may be necessary to keep a copy of the corporate data off-site.

When you use tape devices as the backup platform it is a simple matter to keep a copy of the backups off-site. When you use disk drives as a backup media the process of keeping a copy of the backup media off-site becomes a bit more complicated (not to mention much more expensive). In the case of a RAID disk array, the primary copy of the data is stored on one disk, and the backup copy of the data is stored on another disk. But both disks are housed in one box. This makes the task of moving one drive off-site much more complicated!

Recently, RAID disk arrays have been equipped with fiber-channel interfaces. The fiber-channel is a high-speed interconnect that allows you to locate devices several kilometers from the computer. By linking RAID disk arrays to your systems via optical fibers, it is possible to have an exact copy of your data several miles away from your primary computing site at all times.

In applications and businesses where data accessibility is of the utmost importance the use of RAID disk arrays and fiber-channel interconnections could solve the backup and survivability problems!

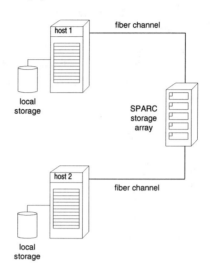

Providing high data accessibility, automatic backups, and survivable systems via RAID and fiber-channel.

Floppy Disk Backups

Another type of system that offers a challenge for backups is the nomadic computer. These are the laptops and other portable computers that are carried by salespersons, executives, and others in the course of their travels. Because space is at a premium on these systems, they often do not contain tape drives for backup purposes. They do, however, usually contain a floppy disk drive.

The floppy disk drive is also a useful backup device on larger desktop systems. Many users may wish to make backup copies of their own files. Some of these users will not have access to system tape drives, optical drives, or other more conventional backup devices. But these users do have access to the floppy disk drives in their desktop workstations.

Floppy disks offer an ideal, low-cost method of backing up files in such instances. While the floppy diskette does not allow storage of very much information, it is an inexpensive and convenient way for users to perform their own backups. And due to the industry standard floppy diskette formats, it also allows users to carry files between systems of different architectures, with different operating systems.

Backup Commands

As you can see, there are several devices available to you to use as backup media. Now you need to look at the various methods of getting your data onto these backup devices. Solaris provides you with several commands to perform this task. The first package we will examine is **ufsdump**, and **ufsrestore**. The ufsdump command is a system level backup utility. It uses a special format when writing information to the tape.

The ufsrestore command understands the special format used by ufsdump, and provides you with the ability to read ufsdump tapes. The ufsdump/ufsrestore utilities are geared toward providing entire file system backups. These utilities are not particularly useful for building distribution media, nor for performing personal file backups.

In contrast, the **tar** utility is more efficient at building distribution tapes or personal archives. The tar command is not very efficient for use as a general backup utility. The tar command is standard across UNIX platforms, so data written under one UNIX variant is usually accessible under another variant. The tar package uses command line flags to control whether it is writing on the tape, or reading from the tape.

The **cpio** command is a longstanding utility in the UNIX arena. It was available in the earliest releases of UNIX software, and therefore has a large base of users which know and trust it. When coupled with commands which can locate files by attributes such as the modify date, cpio can be used as a backup command.

The **dd** command allows you to make high speed copies from one device to another. One caveat must be understood: If you use dd to copy files to tape for backup purposes, you must restore these files to a device which is identical to the original device that you dumped. This is true because of the way that dd operates: dd (in essence) creates a binary image of the data on the new device. Several filters are built into dd to allow you to control this behavior.

The ufsdump Command

One application developed to allow you to back up entire systems at a time is **ufsdump**. The ufsdump program allows you to specify the files to be "dumped" (or backed up to tape), and options to use during the dump. In addition, ufsdump enables you to schedule different levels of dumps on different days. The ufsdump command also allows for dumps which occupy multiple reels of tape. Probably the easiest way to learn about the ufsdump command is to look at a few typical instances of how it is used.

In order to perform a full dump of your system, you must first know which disk devices are present on the system. To obtain this information, you can use the **df** command.

Using df to determine the file systems present on your systems.

```
┌──────────────────── shelltool – /bin/csh ────────────────────┐
│ # df                                                         │
│ /              (/dev/dsk/c0t3d0s0):   27382 blocks  11656 files │
│ /usr           (/dev/dsk/c0t3d0s6):  120062 blocks 112280 files │
│ /proc          (/proc          ):       0 blocks    403 files │
│ /dev/fd        (fd             ):       0 blocks      0 files │
│ /var           (/dev/dsk/c0t3d0s3):   20124 blocks   8159 files │
│ /tmp           (swap           ):  163696 blocks   5877 files │
│ /home          (/dev/dsk/c0t3d0s7):  491922 blocks 193049 files │
│ /opt           (/dev/dsk/c0t3d0s5):  176156 blocks  64629 files │
│ /usr/openwin   (/dev/dsk/c0t3d0s4):   54756 blocks  56015 files │
│ #                                                            │
└──────────────────────────────────────────────────────────────┘
```

✔ **NOTE:** *The ufsdump command requires that you have read access privileges on the system disks.*

Once you have determined which file systems are present on your system, you need to determine the command line options to use for backing up your file systems to tape. The syntax of the ufsdump command follows:

`/usr/sbin/ufsdump [options] [arguments] files_to_dump`

✔ **NOTE:** *Consult the on-line manual page for ufsdump, and Answerbook for more complete descriptions of ufsdump and available options.*

Some of the commonly used command line options to **ufsdump** are listed below:

❑ **0-9** These numeric values specify the dump level. All files listed in the *files_to_dump* list which have been modified since the last ufsdump at a lower dump level are copied to the *dump_file* destination.

❑ **b** Signifies the blocking factor to be used. The default is 20 blocks per write for tape densities of 6250BPI (bytes per inch) or less. The blocking factor of 64 is used for tapes with 6250BPI or greater density. The default blocking factor for cartridge tapes is 126.

✔ **NOTE:** *The blocking factor is specified in 512-byte blocks.*

❑ **c** Signifies that the backup device is a cartridge tape drive. The option sets the density to 1000BPI and the blocking factor to 126.

❏ **d** Signifies the density of the backup media in bits per inch (bpi). The default density is 6250BPI except when the c option is used. When the c option is used, the density is set to 1000BPI per track. Typical values for a few tape devices follow:

- 1/2" tape 6250 BPI

- 1/4" cartridge 1000 BPI

- 2.3-Gb or 5.0-Gb 8mm tape 54,000 BPI

❏ **D** Signifies that the dump device is a floppy diskette.

❏ **f** Signifies the *dump_file*. This option causes ufsdump to use *dump_file* as the file to dump to, instead of */dev/rmt/0*.

❏ **s** Signifies the size of the backup volume. This option is not normally required because ufsdump can detect end-of-media. When the specified size is reached, ufsdump waits for you to change the volume. The size parameter is interpreted as the length in feet for tapes and cartridges, and as the number of 1024-byte blocks for diskettes. Some typical values used with the s option follow:

- 1/2" tape 2300 feet

- 60-Mbyte 1/4" cartridge 425 feet

- 150-Mbyte 1/4" cartridge 700 feet

- 2.3-Gb 8mm 6000 feet

- 5.0-Gb 8mm 13000 feet

- diskette 1422 blocks

❏ **u** This option causes ufsdump to annotate which file systems were dumped, the dump level, and the date in the */etc/dumpdates* file.

❏ **v** This letter signifies that ufsdump should verify the content of the backup media after each tape or diskette is written.

For our purposes, we will assume that you are using an 8mm tape system. Your tape system will be */dev/rmt/0*.

To make a full backup of the entire disk c0t3d0, you would use the following:

```
# ufsdump 0fu /dev/rmt/0 /dev/rdsk/c0t3d0s2
```

```
                    shelltool – /bin/csh
# /usr/lib/fs/ufs/ufsdump 0bdfu 50 54000 /dev/rmt/0bn /dev/rdsk/c0t3d0s0
  DUMP: Date of this level 0 dump: Mon Nov 28 20:40:01 1994
  DUMP: Date of last level 0 dump: the epoch
  DUMP: Dumping /dev/rdsk/c0t3d0s0 (/) to /dev/rmt/0bn
  DUMP: mapping (Pass I) [regular files]
  DUMP: mapping (Pass II) [directories]
  DUMP: estimated 21298 blocks (10.40MB)
  DUMP: Writing 25 Kilobyte records
  DUMP: dumping (Pass III) [directories]
  DUMP: dumping (Pass IV) [regular files]
  DUMP: level 0 dump on Mon Nov 28 20:40:01 1994
  DUMP: 21298 blocks (10.40MB) on 1 volume
  DUMP: DUMP IS DONE
#
```

Using ufsdump to perform a full dump of the system disk.

As shown in the figure, ufsdump sends several messages to the controlling terminal. The messages give you several pieces of information about the status of the dump. Most of the dump information messages are self-explanatory (date of the dump, date of last dump, dump is done). Some of the dump information messages merely echo the command line option settings (files to dump, dump device, block size). Messages from dump that actually provide you with new information about the status of the current dump follow:

❏ *estimated 21298 blocks (10.40MB).* This message tells you the estimated size of the dump.

❏ *XX.XX% done, finished in H:MM.* This message tells you how much of the dump is done, and how long the remainder will take to complete.

❏ *21298 blocks (10.40MB) on 1 volume.* This message tells you how many blocks were dumped, and how many tapes were required.

The ufsrestore Command

Now that you have written your file systems onto a tape, how do you retrieve the information? Solaris provides an application to restore data from the backup media to the system mass storage subsystem. This application is called **ufsrestore**. The syntax of the **ufsrestore** command follows:

```
/usr/sbin/ufsrestore options [ arguments ] [ filename ... ]
```

Note that the *i*, *r*, *R*, *t*, or *x* arguments are mutually exclusive. You may use only one of these arguments at a time!

Some of the most useful options to the **ufsrestore** commands are listed below:

❑ **i** Puts ufsrestore in the interactive mode. Commands available in this mode include:

- **add [filename]** Causes ufsrestore to add the named file or directory to the list of files to extract.

- **cd directory** Causes ufsrestore to change to directory (within the dump file).

- **delete [filename]** Causes ufsrestore to delete the current directory, or file from the list of files to extract.

- **extract** Causes ufsrestore to extract all files on the extraction list from the dump media.

- **help** Causes ufsrestore to display a summary of the available commands.

- **ls [directory]** Causes ufsrestore to list files in directory or the current directory, represented by a period (.).

- **pwd** Causes ufsrestore to print the full path name of the current working directory.

- **quit** Causes ufsrestore to exit immediately.

- **verbose** Causes ufsrestore to toggle its verbose flag.

❑ **r** Tells ufsrestore to restore the entire contents of the media into the current directory.

❑ **x** Tells ufsrestore to extract the named files from the media.

❑ **b** Sets the ufsrestore blocking factor.

❑ **f** Tells ufsrestore to use *dump_file* instead of */dev/rmt/0* as the file to restore from.

❑ **s n** Tells ufsrestore to skip to the nth file when there are multiple dump files on the same tape.

❑ **v** Tells ufsrestore to display the name and inode number of each file it restores.

As with the section on ufsdump, we will assume that you are using an 8mm tape system. Your tape system will be */dev/rmt/0*.

```
┌─────────────────────────────────────────────────────────────────┐
│ ▽                    shelltool - /bin/csh                         │
├─────────────────────────────────────────────────────────────────┤
│ # /usr/lib/fs/ufs/ufsrestore rvf /dev/rmt/0bn                     │
│ Verify volume and initialize maps                                 │
│ Media block size is 126                                           │
│ Dump   date: Tue Nov 29 21:36:09 1994^M                           │
│ Dumped from: the epoch^M                                          │
│ Level 0 dump of a partial file system on glenn:/home/curt/project/snap │
│ Label: none                                                       │
│ Begin level 0 restore                                             │
│ Initialize symbol table.                                          │
│ Extract directories from tape                                     │
│ Calculate extraction list.                                        │
│ Make node ./curt                                                  │
│ Make node ./curt/project                                          │
│ Make node ./curt/project/snap                                     │
│ Extract new leaves.                                               │
│ Check pointing the restore                                        │
│ extract file ./curt/project/snap/a_ws.snp                         │
│ extract file ./curt/project/snap/b_ws.snp                         │
│ extract file ./curt/project/snap/c_ws.snp                         │
│ extract file ./curt/project/snap/d_ws.snp                         │
│ extract file ./curt/project/snap/e_ws.snp                         │
│ extract file ./curt/project/snap/f_ws.snp                         │
│ extract file ./curt/project/snap/g_ws.snp                         │
│ extract file ./curt/project/snap/h_ws.snp                         │
│ extract file ./curt/project/snap/i_ws.snp                         │
│ extract file ./curt/project/snap/j_ws.snp                         │
│ extract file ./curt/project/snap/k_ws.snp                         │
│ extract file ./curt/project/snap/l_ws.snp                         │
│ extract file ./curt/project/snap/ws.snp                           │
│ extract file ./curt/project/snap/m_ws.snp                         │
│ extract file ./curt/project/snap/n_ws.snp                         │
│ extract file ./curt/project/snap/o_ws.snp                         │
│ extract file ./curt/project/snap/p_ws.snp                         │
│ extract file ./curt/project/snap/q_ws.snp                         │
│ extract file ./curt/project/snap/r_ws.snp                         │
│ Add links                                                         │
│ Set directory mode, owner, and times.                             │
│ Check the symbol table.                                           │
│ Check pointing the restore                                        │
│ # ls -las                                                         │
│ total 342                                                         │
│     2 drwxrwxr-x  3 root     sys          512 Nov 18 23:51 .       │
│     2 drwxrwxr-x 12 curt     other       1024 Nov 29 21:37 ..      │
│     2 drwxrwxr-x  3 curt     other        512 Nov 29 21:30 curt    │
│   336 -rw-r--r--  1 root     other     158392 Nov 29 21:40 restoresymtable │
│ # rm restoresymtable                                              │
│ #                                                                 │
└─────────────────────────────────────────────────────────────────┘
```

Using ufsrestore to perform a restore to the system disk.

To completely restore an entire disk (*c0t2d0s2*), you would change directory to the file system you wish to restore (for example, */home*) and then issue a command similar to the following:

```
# ufsrestore rbf 50 /dev/rmt/0 /dev/rdsk/c0t2d0s2
```

```
┌─────────────────────────────────────────────────────────────────┐
│ ▽                    shelltool – /bin/csh                         │
├─────────────────────────────────────────────────────────────────┤
│ # /usr/lib/fs/ufs/ufsrestore ivf /dev/rmt/0bn                     │
│ Verify volume and initialize maps                                 │
│ Media block size is 126                                           │
│ Dump    date: Tue Nov 29 21:36:09 1994                            │
│ Dumped from: the epoch                                            │
│ Level 0 dump of a partial file system on glenn:/home/curt/project/snap │
│ Label: none                                                       │
│ Extract directories from tape                                     │
│ Initialize symbol table.                                          │
│ ufsrestore > ls                                                   │
│ .:                                                                │
│     2 *./        2 *../      4352  curt/                          │
│ ufsrestore > cd curt                                             │
│ ufsrestore > ls                                                   │
│ ./curt:                                                           │
│   4352 ./         2 *../     91395  project/                      │
│ ufsrestore > cd project                                          │
│ ufsrestore > ls                                                   │
│ ./curt/project:                                                   │
│  91395 ./       4352 ../    182786  snap/                         │
│ ufsrestore > cd snap                                             │
│ ufsrestore > ls                                                   │
│ ./curt/project/snap:                                             │
│ 182786 ./       182836 e_ws.snp 182843 k_ws.snp 182864 q_ws.snp  │
│  91395 ../      182837 f_ws.snp 182844 l_ws.snp 182865 r_ws.snp  │
│ 182832 a_ws.snp 182838 g_ws.snp 182860 m_ws.snp 182845 ws.snp    │
│ 182833 b_ws.snp 182839 h_ws.snp 182861 n_ws.snp                  │
│ 182834 c_ws.snp 182841 i_ws.snp 182862 o_ws.snp                  │
│ 182835 d_ws.snp 182842 j_ws.snp 182863 p_ws.snp                  │
│ ufsrestore > add d_ws.snp                                        │
│ ufsrestore > add p_ws.snp                                        │
│ ufsrestore > add f_ws.snp                                        │
│ ufsrestore > extract                                             │
│ Extract requested files                                          │
│ You have not read any volumes yet.                               │
│ Unless you know which volume your file(s) are on you should start│
│ with the last volume and work towards the first.                 │
│ Specify next volume #: 1                                         │
│ extract file ./curt/project/snap/d_ws.snp                        │
│ extract file ./curt/project/snap/f_ws.snp                        │
│ extract file ./curt/project/snap/p_ws.snp                        │
│ Add links                                                        │
│ Set directory mode, owner, and times.                           │
│ set owner/mode for '.'? [yn] y                                   │
│ ufsrestore > quit                                                │
│ # ls -lsa                                                        │
│ total 360                                                        │
│    2 drwxrwxr-x  3 root   sys      512 Nov 18 23:51 .            │
│    2 drwxrwxr-x 12 curt   other   1024 Nov 29 21:37 ..           │
│    2 drwxrwxr-x  3 curt   other    512 Nov 29 21:30 curt         │
│  336 -rw-r--r--  1 root   other 158392 Nov 29 21:40 restoresymtable │
│ # rm restoresymtable                                            │
│ # ▊                                                              │
└─────────────────────────────────────────────────────────────────┘
```

Using ufsrestore in interactive mode.

In order to perform a partial restore to a file system, you would use the interactive mode of ufsrestore. First, you would change directory to a temporary storage space (for example, */tmp/restore*). You would then issue a command similar to the string below:

```
# ufsrestore ibf 50 /dev/rmt/0
```

> ✗ *TIP: One side effect of using ufsrestore is that it creates a "symbol table" file in the file system where you execute the restore. This file is named restoresymtable. It is wise to remove this file because it is usually quite*

*large. Once the restore is complete, you can remove the file by issuing the
following command: rm ./restoresymtable.*

Remote Backup and Restore

How do you perform a file system dump on a system without a backup device?
The **ufsdump** and **ufsrestore** commands allow for their input and output to
be sent to the standard input and output streams. This allows you to perform a
dump on a media-less system much like you would for a system with a local
dump device.

To perform a remote dump using ufsdump, you need to take a closer look
at the -f option.

❑ **f dump_file** This option tells ufsdump to use *dump_file* as the file to dump
to. If *dump_file* is specified as a hyphen (-), ufsdump will dump to standard
output. If the name of the file is of the form *machine:device*, the dump is
carried out from the specified machine over the network using the *rmt*
facility.

✔   **NOTE:** *Since ufsdump is normally run by root, the name of the local
machine must appear in the /.rhosts file of the remote machine.*

To perform a remote restore using the ufsrestore command, you need to take
a closer look at its **-f** option as well:

❑ **f dump_file** This option tells ufsrestore to use *dump_file* as the file to
restore from. If *dump_file* is specified as a dash (-), ufsrestore reads from
the standard input.

✔   **NOTE:** *Since ufsrestore is normally run by root, the name of the local
machine must appear in the /.rhosts file of the remote machine.*

In order to restore your home partition with a remote ufsrestore, you would
issue a command such as the following:

```
# ufsdump 0f - /dev/rdsk/c0t2d0s2 | (cd /home;ufsrestore xf -)
```

The tar Command

What if you do not wish to dump and restore complete file systems? What if
you just want to make a tape of the data associated with one project? Is there a
simpler method than using **ufsdump** and **ufsrestore**? Most UNIX derivatives
provide a standardized utility called **tar**. The tar command creates tape archives,
and provides the ability to add and extract files from these archives.

The syntax for using the tar command follows:

```
# /usr/sbin/tar [key] [flags [ 0-7 ]] [device] [block]
[operations] [-I include-filename] filename ... [-C directory
filename]
```

The tar command's actions are controlled by the **key** argument. This key is a string of characters containing exactly one function letter (c, r, t , u, or x) and one or more function modifiers, depending on the function letter used. Other arguments to the command are file names (or directory names) specifying which files are to be archived or extracted.

Valid tar key arguments include the following:

❑ **c** Create a new tar file. Writing begins at the beginning of the tar file, instead of at the end. This key implies the r key.

❑ **r** Replace files in an existing tar file. The named files are written on the end of the tape. The c and u functions imply this function.

❑ **t** Print a table of contents. The names of the specified files are listed each time they occur on the tar file. If no file name arguments are given, all the names on the tar file are listed.

❑ **u** Update an existing tar file. The named files are added to the tar file if they are not already there, or have been modified since last written on that tar file. This key implies the r key.

❑ **x** Extract or restore files from a tar file. The named files are extracted from the tar file and written to the current directory.

Valid function options for the tar command include the following:

❑ **b** Sets the tar blocking factor. This causes tar to use the block argument as the blocking factor for tape records.

❑ **f File** This causes tar to use the device argument as the name of the tar file. If the name of the tar file is a dash (-), tar writes to the standard output or reads from the standard input, whichever is appropriate. Thus, tar can be used as the head or tail of a pipeline. The tar utility can also be used to move hierarchies with the following command line:

```
% cd fromdir; tar cf - . | (cd todir; tar xfBp -)
```

❑ **h** Follow symbolic links as if they were normal files or directories.

❑ **i** With this option, tar will ignore directory checksum errors.

❑ **l** Tells tar to complain if it cannot resolve all of the links to the files being archived.

❑ **m** Tells tar to not extract the modification times from the tar file. The modification time of the file will be the time of extraction. This option is valid only with the x key.

❑ **v** Causes tar to type the name of each file it treats, preceded by the function letter.

To create an archive of */home/project* and */project/data* on the default tar device, you would issue a command such as the following:

```
% tar c -C /home/project include -C /data/project
```

A user may wish to create an archive of his/her home directory on a tape mounted on drive */dev/rmt/0*. To do so, the user needs to issue a command such as demonstrated below:

```
% cd ; tar cvf /dev/rmt/0
```

To read the table of contents of the tar file, issue a command such as the following:

```
% tar tvf /dev/rmt/0
```

To extract files from the tar file, you would issue a command similar to the one below:

```
% tar xvf /dev/rmt/0
```

It is also possible to get tar to transfer files across the network. To create a tar file on a remote host, you would issue a command such as the following:

```
% tar cvfb 20 filenames | rsh host dd of = /dev/rmt/0 obs = 20b
```

To extract files from a remote tar file into your current local directory, you would issue a command such as the following:

```
% rsh -n host dd if = /dev/rmt/0 bs = 20b | tar xvBfb 20 filenames
```

The cpio Command

Another command that you may use to back up and restore files is **cpio**. The cpio command copies file archives "in and out." The syntax for the cpio command follows:

```
cpio -key [options] filename
```

The key option to cpio determines the actions to be performed. The flags listed below are mutually exclusive.

❑ cpio **-i** (copy in) extracts files from the standard input, which is assumed to be the product of a previous **cpio -o**.

❏ cpio **-o** (copy out) reads the standard input to obtain a list of path names. The cpio command then copies those files to the standard output with path name and status information. Output is padded to a 512-byte boundary by default.

❏ cpio **-p** (pass) reads the standard input to obtain a list of path names of files that are conditionally created and copied into the destination directory tree.

✔ *NOTE: Consult the on-line manual pages for more complete information on the cpio command.*

To make a cpio copy of the files in the current directory in a file called *../newfile*, you would issue the following command:

```
% ls | cpio -oc > ../newfile
```

✔ *NOTE: You could also use find, echo, or cat command as a substitute for the ls command to produce a list of files to be included in the ../newfile.*

To extract the files from *../newfile* you could issue the following command:

```
% cat newfile | cpio -icd
```

To copy the contents of the current directory to a new directory called *newdir*, you could issue the command:

```
% find . -depth -print | cpio -pdlmv newdir
```

✔ *NOTE: When you use cpio in conjunction with find, if you use the L option with cpio then you must use the -follow option with find and vice versa.*

The dd Command

Yet another command available to use as a backup and restore utility is the **dd** utility. The dd command copies the input file to the output with the desired conversions applied to the output. After completing, dd reports the number of whole and partial input and output blocks. The syntax of the dd command follows:

```
dd [ option = value ] ....
```

Valid options to the dd command are listed below.

❏ **if = filename** Use *filename* as the input file. Use *stdin* by default.

❏ **of = filename** Use *filename* as the output file. Use *stdout* by default.

❏ **ibs = n** Use *n* as the input block size. Use 512 by default.

❑ **obs = n** Use *n* as the output block size. Use 512 by default.

❑ **bs = n** Use *n* as the input and output block size This supersedes the *ibn* and *obn* arguments. If no conversion is specified, preserve input block size.

❑ **files = n** Copy and concatenate *n* input files before terminating.

❑ **skip = n** Skip *n* input blocks before performing copy.

❑ **iseek = n** Seek *n* blocks from beginning of the input file before copying.

❑ **oseek = n** Seek *n* blocks from beginning of the output file before copying.

❑ **count = n** Copy *n* input blocks.

❑ **swab** Swap every pair of bytes.

❑ **sync** Pad every input block to *ibs*.

The dd command has a few noteworthy restrictions listed below.

❑ Do not use dd to copy files between file systems with different block sizes.

❑ Using a blocked device to copy a file will result in extra nulls being added to the file to pad the final block to the block boundary.

❑ When dd reads from a pipe, using the *ibs* = *X* and *obs* = *Y* operands, the output will always be blocked in chunks of size *Y*. When *bs* = *Z* is used, the output blocks will be whatever was available to be read from the pipe at the time.

In order to copy the files on device */dev/dsk/c1t3d0s2* to tape drive */dev/rmt/2*, with a 20 block record size, you would issue the command:

```
# dd if=/dev/rdsk/c1t3d0s2 of=/dev/rmt/2 bs=20b
```

To extract this information from the tape to a disk named */dev/dsk/c2t1d0s2*, you would issue the command:

```
# dd if=/dev/rmt/2 of=/dev/rdsk/c2t1d0s2 bs=20b
```

Dealing with Specific Backup Issues

Certain aspects of your backup and restore strategies require special attention. For instance, how would you restore the root file system if your root disk had crashed and you had no way to boot the system? How can you automate your backups to minimize the amount of time you spend performing backups? What happens if a backup requires 2Gb of backup media, and your backup device can write only 1Gb to the media?

These are just a few of the file system backup problems that you should be prepared for as a system administrator. Fortunately, they are also topics that have been encountered and solved by the implementors of Solaris. Now that you understand the basics of performing backups, let's examine these specific topics in more detail.

Restoring the Root File System

It would appear that one of the most difficult problems you will face using ufsrestore is how to restore the *root* file system. If the *root* file system is missing, you cannot boot the damaged system. Further, you would not have a file system tree to restore to!

One way to accomplish a root file system reload is by booting your system to the single-user state from the CD-ROM distribution media. Once the system is running, you could issue the proper commands to reload your root device from your backup media.

As discussed in Chapter 4, the Solaris operating system can be booted from the distribution media. You need to place the Solaris 2.4 distribution CD in the CD-ROM drive and boot Solaris 2.4. The following table gives the system type to boot device mapping for a local CD-ROM drive.

System Type to Solaris Boot Device Correspondence

System Type	Boot Command
4/110	
4/2XX	b sd(0,30,1)
4/3XX	
4/4XX	
SPARCstation 1 (4/60)	
SPARCstation 1+ (4/65)	boot sd(0,6,2)
SPARCstation SLC (4/20)	
SPARCstation IPC (4/40)	
SPARCengine 1E	boot sd(0,6,5)
SPARCstation ELC (4/25)	
SPARCstation IPX (4/50)	
SPARCstation 2 (4/75)	boot cdrom
SPARCstation 10	

System Type	Boot Command
SPARCstation LX (4/30)	
SPARCserver 6XXMP and newer	
SPARCcenter 1000	
SPARCcenter 2000	
SPARCcenter LX	
SPARCclassic	

For example, to boot a SPARCServer 2000 system, the boot command would be the following:

```
ok boot cdrom
```

This will load the SunInstall program from the CD-ROM. At this point, you can follow the instructions in Chapter 4 to load a new copy of the operating system to your new root drive. Alternately, you could select the menu item which allows you to bring up a single-user shell on the system. In this fashion, you could reload your root drive from your backup media instead of loading from the distribution media.

Another method to reload your root file system would be to boot the system to the single-user state as a client of another system on your network. At this point, you could issue the proper commands to reload your root device from your backup media.

Automated Backups

All of the commands mentioned in this chapter may be adapted to provide for automated backups. You simply need to create a shell script file containing the desired commands for your backups. Once you have created the command files, you can submit a job to **cron** to execute these command files at the desired time.

For example, you could place the following commands in a file called */dodump*:

```
# dump /, /usr, /var, /home, /opt, /usr/openwin
#
mt -f /dev/rmt/0b rew
/usr/lib/fs/ufs/ufsdump 0bdfu 50 54000 /dev/rmt/0bn
/dev/rdsk/c0t3d0s0
```

```
/usr/lib/fs/ufs/ufsdump 0bdfu 50 54000 /dev/rmt/0bn
/dev/rdsk/c0t3d0s6

/usr/lib/fs/ufs/ufsdump 0bdfu 50 54000 /dev/rmt/0bn
/dev/rdsk/c0t3d0s3

/usr/lib/fs/ufs/ufsdump 0bdfu 50 54000 /dev/rmt/0bn
/dev/rdsk/c0t3d0s7

/usr/lib/fs/ufs/ufsdump 0bdfu 50 54000 /dev/rmt/0bn
/dev/rdsk/c0t3d0s5

/usr/lib/fs/ufs/ufsdump 0bdfu 50 54000 /dev/rmt/0bn
/dev/rdsk/c0t3d0s4

mt -f /dev/rmt/0b rew

mt -f /dev/rmt/0b offl
```

You could then place a tape in the */dev/rmt/0* tape drive, log in as *root* on the system, and type *# csh -x /dodump*. The system would respond by performing a full backup of all of the file systems that you listed in the *dodump* file. While this is a simplistic method of automating file system backups, it serves to illustrate the point that you can automate the backups. Chapter 22 will discuss more elegant solutions to the backup automation problem using the cron command.

Multi-volume Dumps

Two of the backup commands mentioned in this chapter also allow for multi-volume backups. The **ufsdump** command and the **cpio** command allow a backup to be stored over multiple media sets. The other commands (**tar** and **dd**) will allow you to split the backups onto several sets of media, but they require that you perform much of the work manually.

If you choose cpio as your backup command, you can make it watch for the end of medium event. When cpio detects this event, it stops and prints the following message on the terminal screen:

If you want to go on, type device/file name when ready.

To continue the dump, you must replace the medium and type the character special device name (e.g., */dev/rdiskette*) and press <Enter>. You may choose to have cpio continue the backup to another device by typing its name at the prompt.

✔ **NOTE:** *Simply typing an <Enter> at the prompt will cause cpio to exit!*

```
                              shelltool - /bin/csh
 ▽
# ls -lsa
total 4142
    2 drwxr-xr-x  2 curt      nobody       512 Nov 29 22:44 .
    2 drwxr-xr-x  3 curt      nobody       512 Nov 29 22:40 ..
  784 -rw-r--r--  1 curt      nobody    387407 Nov 29 22:42 fmgcon.snp
  432 -rw-r--r--  1 curt      nobody    209456 Nov 29 22:42 fmgr.snp
  512 -rw-r--r--  1 curt      nobody    247550 Nov 29 22:42 fmrcon.snp
  320 -rw-r--r--  1 curt      nobody    148596 Nov 29 22:42 io.snp
  240 -rw-r--r--  1 curt      nobody    108302 Nov 29 22:42 mtps.snp
  736 -rw-r--r--  1 curt      nobody    364540 Nov 29 22:43 ps.snp
  816 -rw-r--r--  1 curt      nobody    408354 Nov 29 22:44 ted.snp
  240 -rw-r--r--  1 curt      nobody    110650 Nov 29 22:44 vms.snp
   58 -rw-r--r--  1 curt      nobody     28947 Nov 29 22:44 ws.snp
#
# ls |cpio -oc >/vol/dev/aliases/floppy0
End of medium on "output".
To continue, type device/file name when ready.
/vol/dev/aliases/floppy0
3936 blocks
#
# mkdir restoredcpio
# cd restoredcpio
#
# cat /vol/dev/aliases/floppy0 |cpio -icd
End of medium on "input".
To continue, type device/file name when ready.
/vol/dev/aliases/floppy0
3936 blocks
# ls -lsa
total 4142
    2 drwxr-xr-x  2 curt      nobody       512 Nov 29 22:44 .
    2 drwxr-xr-x  3 curt      nobody       512 Nov 29 22:40 ..
  784 -rw-r--r--  1 curt      nobody    387407 Nov 29 22:42 fmgcon.snp
  432 -rw-r--r--  1 curt      nobody    209456 Nov 29 22:42 fmgr.snp
  512 -rw-r--r--  1 curt      nobody    247550 Nov 29 22:42 fmrcon.snp
  320 -rw-r--r--  1 curt      nobody    148596 Nov 29 22:42 io.snp
  240 -rw-r--r--  1 curt      nobody    108302 Nov 29 22:42 mtps.snp
  736 -rw-r--r--  1 curt      nobody    364540 Nov 29 22:43 ps.snp
  816 -rw-r--r--  1 curt      nobody    408354 Nov 29 22:44 ted.snp
  240 -rw-r--r--  1 curt      nobody    110650 Nov 29 22:44 vms.snp
   58 -rw-r--r--  1 curt      nobody     28947 Nov 29 22:44 ws.snp
# ▮
```

Multi-volume dumps using cpio.

If you are using ufsdump as your backup command, things are a little simpler. Like cpio, ufsdump will detect the end of medium event, and stops operation. The ufsdump command will then wait for you to change the media before it continues. Unlike cpio, you do not need to give the name of the backup device for ufsdump to continue. You simply need to confirm that you have changed the media, and that you are ready for it to continue operation.

```
┌──────────────────────────────────────────────────────────────────────────┐
│  ▽                        shelltool – /bin/csh                             │
├──────────────────────────────────────────────────────────────────────────┤
│ # /usr/lib/fs/ufs/ufsdump OoDfu /vol/dev/aliases/floppy0 /home/curt/project/snap │
│   DUMP: Date of this level 0 dump: Tue Nov 29 22:26:50 1994                 │
│   DUMP: Date of last level 0 dump: the epoch                               │
│   DUMP: Dumping /dev/rdsk/c0t3d0s7 (/home) to /vol/dev/aliases/floppy0      │
│   DUMP: mapping (Pass I) [regular files]                                   │
│   DUMP: mapping (Pass II) [directories]                                    │
│   DUMP: estimated 4214 blocks (2.06MB) on 1.51 diskette(s).                │
│   DUMP: Writing 32 Kilobyte records                                        │
│   DUMP: dumping (Pass III) [directories]                                   │
│   DUMP: dumping (Pass IV) [regular files]                                  │
│   DUMP: 66.82% done, finished in 0:00                                      │
│   DUMP: Change Volumes: Mount volume #2                                     │
│   DUMP: NEEDS ATTENTION: Is the new volume (#2) mounted and ready to go?: ("yes" or "no") yes │
│   DUMP: Volume 2 begins with blocks from ino 191561                        │
│   DUMP: 4160 blocks (2.03MB) on 2 volumes                                  │
│   DUMP: DUMP IS DONE                                                       │
│ # ▌                                                                        │
│                                                                            │
│                                                                            │
│                                                                            │
│                                                                            │
└──────────────────────────────────────────────────────────────────────────┘
```

Multi-volume dumps using ufsdump.

Summary

In this chapter you discovered the commands that can be used to make backup copies of your data. In addition, you learned why it is important to make such backup copies of the data, and explored some methods of avoiding data loss due to natural disaster. While we hope you never have to use any of these backup copies to restore the operation of your systems, we realize that eventually your time will come. Good backups take a lot of time and attention to detail. But having a reliable copy of your data is much more acceptable than the time and expense of rebuilding a system without reliable backup copies.

Automating Routine Administration Tasks

As you have seen in previous chapters, administering a Solaris system(s) can be a time-consuming process. Simply keeping track of system files could be a full-time job, let alone managing security and user accounts. In this chapter, we explore ways to automate certain mundane system administration chores. In doing so, you can free up time for more urgent tasks such as helping users.

Finding and Removing Unused Files

An old system administration adage goes something like this: "Disk usage will expand to fill all available disk space."

As a system administrator, what can you do to ensure that enough disk space is available for your users? One way of policing free disk space might be to locate and remove all files that had not been accessed (used) up to some predetermined period of time. Although a valid management trick, this becomes a very time-consuming process if you have to manually examine the time-stamp on every file. Fortunately, Solaris provides a utility called **find** which will allow you to automate this process.

The find Command

The find utility allows you to search for specific information on system disks. You can use find to search for files, directories, or strings of characters on the disks. Once you find what you are looking for, the find command allows you much flexibility in what you do with the information you locate.

You may wish to use find to execute other commands such as using **rm** to remove files, or print the location of the item you searched. You could cascade several functions together and use find to perform other more complex operations. Let's take a look at the find command and a few examples of how it can be used to simplify systems administration.

The syntax for using the find command follows:

```
find pathlist "expression".
```

The **pathlist** argument is a list of files where you want the command to begin searching. The list of files may consist of file names, directory names, or file system names. If you use the root (/) directory as the pathlist, find will traverse *all* of the directories on the system.

The **expression** argument to find is a string of characters that directs what find will search for, and what to do when it finds what it is looking for. A few commonly used expressions for the find utility appear in the following table.

Commonly Used Find Command Expressions

Expression	Action
-name	Search for files which are called *name*.
-atime n	Search for files accessed *n* days ago.
- ls	Prints the current path name and related statistics.
-mtime n	Search for files modified *n* days ago.
-exec command	Execute *command* if file is found.
-print	Causes the current path name to be printed.
-type c	Search for files of *type*. Values for c include: b, c, d, l, p, s, or f for block special, character special, directory, symbolic link, fifo, socket, or plain file.
-fstype type	Search for file systems of *type*.

In the following sections you will see examples of how the find utility is frequently used in daily system administrative activities.

Clearing Out Old Files

As you may recall, in a previous chapter we provided an example of the **find** command in action. It was used to locate and remove all *a.out* and *.o* files in your home directory that were more than seven days old. The find statement to perform this task was as follows:

```
$ find $HOME \(-name a.out -o -name '*.o'\) -atime +7 -exec rm{} ;
```

> ✔ **NOTE:** *The use of parentheses, quotation marks, backslashes, and curly braces is explained in detail later in this chapter. These symbols are required to cause the shell to interpret the command in a particular manner.*

In the above example, the parentheses are used to inform find of multiple file names to search for. The curly braces following the **rm** command tell find to execute the rm command, and remove any files which match the search specifications. The backslashes are used so that the shell does not "interpret" the parentheses and semi-colon characters, but rather passes them to the find command for interpretation.

How might you modify this command to find these same files in all system directories? You simply change the **pathlist** argument from *$HOME* to root (/):

```
# find / \(-name a.out -o -name '*.o'\) -atime +7 -exec rm{} \;
```

> ✔ **NOTE:** *This example should be run as root because root is the only user that can access ALL of the files on the system. Note the root prompt in the example above.*

Other Handy Uses for the find Command

Because **find** can locate so many different things on the disks, there are other uses for this tool. Experienced system administrators use find on a daily basis. The following sections present just a few examples of tasks which you can automate with the find command.

Locating Files

You may need to locate all instances of a particular file so you can update the information in the file. If you were to attempt this manually, you would need to look for the file name in every directory on the system. With the find utility, this process becomes a simple operation.

Using find to locate all instances files named .login.

```
                    shelltool - /bin/csh
# find /home -name .login -print
/home/curt/.login
/home/sally/.login
/home/erin/.login
/home/shaun/.login
/home/varmint/.login
# █
```

Locating Text Strings Using find

You can also use **find** to locate a file that contains a particular string of characters. Why is this useful? One popular method of breaking into systems is to replace system binaries with new versions that contain "back-door" entry points for use by the people who want to break in. Quite often these programs contain a unique string of characters (such as a compiled-in password) that you can look for. If you find such a unique string of characters on your disks, you know that security has been breached, and you can take appropriate steps to repair the damage.

Using find to locate all instances of a particular string.

```
                    shelltool - /bin/csh
# find / -type f -exec grep -l "floobydust" {} \;
/opt/tmp/.xxcsh
/opt/tmp/login
/usr/bin/login
/usr/tmp/.xxcsh
/var/local/tmp/.xxcsh
/var/mail/.xxcsh
#
# █
```

Looking for Permissions

Another common use of the **find** command is to locate files with particular access permissions. For instance, files that are writeable by users other than the file owner could be considered security risks. It would be best to change the access permission of these files so that only the owner has write permission. Instead of spending hours looking for such files manually, you can use find to perform this operation for you!

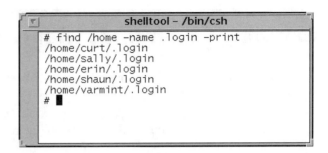

Using find to locate and change permissions on files with mode 777.

In some situations it may be desirable to change the ownership of files owned by a particular user. For instance, you may need to change a user's log-in name or user-id for some reason. In order for the user to be able to access her/his files after you make the *uid/username* change, you would need to **chown** the user's files to the new *uid/username*. You could use find to locate all files owned by that user, and change ownership to the new user name.

```
┌──────────────────────────────────────────┐
│  ▽        shelltool – /bin/csh             │
├──────────────────────────────────────────┤
│ # find / -user 666 -print                 │
│ /home/jimmy                               │
│ /source/jimmy/project                     │
│ /opt/jimmy/project                        │
│ /data/jimmy/proj_data                     │
│ #                                         │
│ # find / -user 666 -exec chown 923 {} \;  │
│ #                                         │
│ # find / -user 666 -print                 │
│ #                                         │
│ # find / -user 923 -print                 │
│ /home/jimmy                               │
│ /source/jimmy/project                     │
│ /opt/jimmy/project                        │
│ /data/jimmy/proj_data                     │
│ #                                         │
│ # ■                                       │
└──────────────────────────────────────────┘
```

Using find to locate and change the ownership of files owned by a user.

A couple of questions that you as system adminstrator should be asking yourself about the use of the find command follow:

❑ How often should these housekeeping functions be performed?

❑ Is there a method that will automatically make the system perform house-keeping functions without my intervention?

Automating Commands with cron

The **cron** command is a chronometer (clock) based function which executes commands at specified dates and times. One of the more common uses of cron is to run *batch* jobs at off-peak hours. Another common use of cron is to run housecleaning and administrative functions at regular intervals. Because cron runs under control of a system daemon program, you need to understand the types of processes available to you under Solaris.

Types of Processes

The Solaris operating system is a multi-user/multi-tasking operating system. This means that many users can be active on the system simultaneously, and many jobs (processes) can be active simultaneously. While only one job is active (per processor) at any given time, many jobs can be in the *run queue*.

The run queue is a list of jobs that are awaiting their slice of run time from the scheduler. Because the slice of run time allotted to each process is so short, many jobs appear to be active simultaneously. In many cases, these jobs are interactive processes started by users sitting at a terminal or using a window on the workstation. These processes are generically referred to as foreground processes.

When you sit at the terminal typing commands to the shell, you are typically executing foreground jobs. These jobs maintain control of the terminal (window) until the execution is complete. Foreground jobs typically read input from the terminal, and write output to the terminal. Some typical foreground jobs include system commands such as **ls**, **cat**, **vi**, and **sh**.

Some of the jobs running on the system are not interactive processes. Solaris also allows you to run jobs in the background. When you run a job in the background, it is disassociated from the terminal. This means that the terminal is free for other uses while your job executes. Because you disassociate the process from the terminal, you must feed the input to background process from another source. You must also feed the output of background processes to a file.

cron Processes

Processes executed by **cron** (*cron jobs*) are background jobs. Many cron jobs are actually a special "flavor" of background processes known as *batch jobs*. A batch job reads its input from one place, processes that input, then writes its output (if it produces any output) to another place.

In order to run a cron job, you must create a **crontab** entry. A crontab entry tells the cron program which command to run, and more importantly, when to run it. The crontab (cron tables) command allows users to create and modify crontab entries. Once the user has created a crontab entry, the crontab program stores that entry in the */var/spool/cron/crontabs* directory. The cron software scans this directory to identify the commands to run at particular times.

By default, the crontab command is not limited to use by the root user. Other users can create their own cron jobs. System administrators using the root user account can control access to cron by editing the following files: */etc/cron.d/cron.allow* and */etc/cron.d/cron.deny*.

As their names imply, *cron.allow* contains a list of all users who are allowed cron access while *cron.deny* contains a list of all users who are denied cron access. By default, both files are empty.

✔ **NOTE:** *Many system administrators limit cron access to system staff members. Otherwise, system users could use cron to hide (i.e., move) "illegal" files prior to security sweeps designed to detect such files.*

crontab Entries

While the **crontab** crontab program is used to create cron table entries, it is the **cron** daemon (program) which examines the entries to determine when cron jobs should be executed. In order for cron to understand the crontab entries, they must conform to a specific template. In particular, each entry in a crontab file consists of the following six fields:

❑ The minute of execution (0-59, asterisk, or list).

❑ The hour of execution (0-23, asterisk, or list).

❑ The day of the month (1-31, asterisk, or list).

❑ The month of the year (1-12, asterisk, or list).

❑ The day of the week (0-6 [Sunday = 0], asterisk, or list).

❑ The command string to be executed.

As noted above, the first five fields may contain a numeric argument. For example, to execute a command on the first day of the month, you would place a one (1) in the third field of the crontab file. This command would be executed on the first day of the month at the time set by the hour, minute, month, and day fields.

Example root crontab file.

```
┌──────────────────────────────────────────────────────────────────────┐
│  ▽                         shelltool – /bin/csh                        │
├──────────────────────────────────────────────────────────────────────┤
│ # cat /var/spool/cron/crontabs/root                                    │
│ #ident   "@(#)root        1.11    93/04/08 SMI"    /* SVr4.0 1.1.3.1      */ │
│ #                                                                      │
│ # The root crontab should be used to perform accounting data collection. │
│ #                                                                      │
│ 0 2 * * 0,4 /etc/cron.d/logchecker                                     │
│ 5 4 * * 6   /usr/lib/newsyslog                                         │
│ 15 3 * * * /usr/lib/fs/nfs/nfsfind                                     │
│ # ▮                                                                    │
└──────────────────────────────────────────────────────────────────────┘
```

Alternately, the first five fields may contain a list of numeric values separated by commas. This allows you to schedule commands to be run multiple times a day with one crontab entry. For example, if you wanted to execute a command on the hour, 15 minutes after the hour, 30 minutes after the hour, and 15 minutes before the hour, you could use the string *0,15,30,45* in the first field of the crontab file. The command would be executed four times an hour as specified by the other four fields.

The asterisk acts as a *wildcard* entry in the crontab file. When cron finds an asterisk in a field, it automatically substitutes every valid value for that field. For example, if you created a crontab entry with an asterisk in the first field cron would execute your command once a minute as long as the conditions set in the other fields were true.

crontab Options

The **crontab** application allows the following three options:

❑ **crontab -e** edits a copy of the current user's crontab file, or creates an empty file to edit if crontab does not exist.

❑ **crontab -l** lists the user's current crontab file.

❑ **crontab -r** removes the user's crontab file from the crontab directory.

Example crontab Entries

You have already seen how to use **find** to locate and remove unused files from your systems. Now that you understand the **cron** utility, let's look at a few ways that you can automate system housecleaning tasks by using the cron command to execute find commands.

The following crontab entries execute find commands to clear out specific files. These files may be system generated temporary files, or files which are otherwise easily recreated.

> ✔ **NOTE:** *Care should be taken when creating such crontab entries, such that you do not remove critical files by accident! It is best to develop and test such entries manually. This gives you the chance to check for unpleasant consequences before you allow the system to perform them automatically.*

The crontab entry below will run at 03:15AM every day of every month. The find command will look through every file system for file names containing the character string *.nfs*. If such files are found, and they are over seven days old, find will remove them.

```
15 03 * * *  find / -name .nfs\* -mtime +7 -exec rm {} \; -o
-fstype nfs -prune >/dev/null 2>&1
```

The next crontab entry will run at 04:15AM every day of every month. The find command will search through the */var/preserve* file system for any files that are over seven days old. If such files are found, they will be removed.

```
15 04 * * *  find /var/preserve/ -mtime +7 -a -exec rm {} \;
>/dev/null 2>&1
```

The crontab entry below will run at 03:05AM every day of every month. The find command will search through the */tmp* file system for any files that have not been accessed in the past 24 hours. If such files are found, and they are not sockets, files with the prefix *saber* or *lock*, they will be removed.

```
05 03 * * *  find /tmp -atime +1 ! -type s ! -name 'saber*' !
-name 'lock*' -exec rm {} \; >/dev/null 2>&1
```

Finally, the next crontab entry will run at 03:10AM every day of every month. The find command will search through the */tmp* file system for directories over one (1) day old. If such directories are found, and they are not the */tmp* directory or the *lost+found* directory, they will be removed.

```
10 03 * * *  cd /tmp ; find . ! -name . ! -name lost+found -type d
-mtime +1 -exec rmdir {} \; /dev/null 2&1
```

> ✘ **TIP:** *The cron command may be used to automate many functions. A few simple examples include automated distribution of new system software, file system backups, performing collection of network usage statistics, and performing system accounting summaries. If you develop a shell script file to perform these tasks, you can also develop a crontab entry which will allow the system to automatically perform the task for you!*

System Automation with Shell Scripts

The UNIX shell is an interactive programming language, as well as a command interpreter. The shell executes commands received directly from the user sitting at the terminal. Alternately, the shell can execute commands received from a file. A file containing shell programming commands is called a *shell file* or *shell script*.

Many of the operations performed by a system administrator are accomplished by typing commands at the terminal. Due to file access permissions, these commands must often be issued by the super-user (root). Under Solaris 2, the standard shell for root is */sbin/sh*. This shell program is a statically linked implementation of the Bourne shell. On the other hand, the program in */usr/bin/sh* is a dynamically linked version of the Bourne shell. You may be asking yourself, "Why are there two versions of the **sh** program?"

Dynamic versus Static Linking: A Review

A statically linked program is one which links (or includes) all library functions at compile time. If changes are made to a library routine due to compiler or other system software upgrades, the program will need to be recompiled to take advantage of those changes. A statically linked program will usually be quite large because it includes all library functions.

A dynamically linked program loads the library functions at run time which allows the program to include the latest version of all library functions upon invocation. No re-compilation is required to enjoy the advantages of updated library routines. Dynamically linked programs are usually smaller than their statically linked counterparts, as the library functions are not included in the on-disk binary image.

> **!** **WARNING:** *Many of the programs in the /sbin directory are statically linked. While it may be tempting to replace these programs with dynamically linked versions to save disk space, this practice is not recommended. The programs in /sbin are statically linked for a very good reason. In the event that the dynamic libraries (typically stored in the /usr file system) are not available due to a partial system failure, the programs in /sbin (such as the root log-in shell) will still function. Consequently, the system administrator can still log in and attempt to recover from the failure.*

The Shell Game

The Bourne shell implements a language commonly referred to as "shell programming language," or shell programming. However, the Bourne shell is just one of many shells available for Solaris. Another popular shell program is */usr/bin/csh*, or the C shell. The C shell offers the user features that are not available in the Bourne shell, such as advanced job control.

Other available shells include the Bourne Again shell (*bash*), the Korn shell (*ksh*), *tcsh* (a variant of csh), and the *zsh* shell. Many of these shells share a common command structure with the Bourne shell and the C shell.

Basic Shell Features

So why the vast selection of shell programs under Solaris? Most shells understand standard Solaris commands. Most shells offer basically the same capabilities to the user. However, the shell programming language recognized by the shell program differs among many of the shell programs. The shell programming language of most shells conforms to either the Bourne shell language or the C shell language. For purposes of illustration, the examples in the following sections will alternate use of the Bourne and C shells.

> ✔ **NOTE:** *Solaris 2 is delivered with the Bourne (sh), C (csh), and Korn (ksh) shells. Because the shell is just another program as far as Solaris is concerned, many users have developed their own shell programs. Several of these other shells can be found as public domain (freeware) on the Internet. Still other shell programs are available as commercial products. We will limit discussion to the shell programs delivered with the Solaris 2 operating system.*

Which Shell Is Right for You?

Due to the fact that the shell is the primary user interface to the system, its selection can be viewed almost as a "religious" issue. Every user selects the shell that s/he is most comfortable with. Each shell has strengths and weaknesses which you can exploit to administer your systems. One of the secrets of system administration is knowing which shell will make a particular task easier to perform. In some cases, a system administrator may choose one shell over another based on familiarity alone.

Even though the Bourne shell and C shell differ, they also share some basic concepts. Both shells allow you to declare local variables. Both shells provide and understand variables which customize the execution environment for the users. Both shells interact with the operating system to provide error handling and other basic features for the user.

✔ *NOTE: In order to create shell scripts to aid in the administration of your systems, you must understand the "language" used by each shell. Unfortunately, this topic is beyond the scope of a single chapter in a system administration book. Entire books have been dedicated to the description of the Bourne shell, C shell, and Korn shell. We will examine a few of the most often used capabilities of the Bourne and C shell programs. The reader is encouraged to seek out more comprehensive coverage of these programs in other publications.*

Environment and Local Variables

One of the similarities between the Bourne and C shell programs is their use of variables. Shell programs support two categories of variables: local and environment.

Local variables consist of variable names chosen by the user. The variables contain data determined by the user. The system binaries have no access to these variables. These variables are much like the local variables that a user would employ when writing a program in a high-level programming language.

Environment variables can be conceived of as a combination of reserved words and global variables in a high-level programming language. The names of these variables cannot be altered by the user. The user can set many of these variables to a value, and the value of these variables may be checked by system binaries. Users can modify some of these variables in order to customize the behavior of the shell to suit their preferences and needs. Some of the environment variables are reserved, and therefore cannot be modified by users.

Environment Variables

Environment variables allow users to customize their operating environment. Some of the more familiar Bourne shell environment variables are shown in the table below.

Popular Bourne Shell Environment Variables

Variable Name	Description
CDPATH	Directory search path for *cd*. Not set by default.
COLUMNS	Width of window. Set by shell.
EDITOR	Command editor. Not set by default.
ENV	Setup script invoked for each command. Set by the user.
ERRNO	Last error code from a system call. Set by shell.
HOME	Default argument for *cd*. Set by the log-in program.
LOGNAME	Your log-in name. Set by login.
LPDEST	Sets the default printer destination. Not set by default.
MAIL	File that contains your new mail. Set by login.
OLDPWD	Previous working directory. Set by shell.
OPTARG	Current argument after *getopts*. Set by shell.
OPTIND	Number of arguments remaining after *getopts*. Set by shell.
PATH	Search path for commands. Set by login.
PPID	Process ID of parent process. Set by shell.
PS1	Primary shell prompt. Set by shell.
PS2	Secondary shell prompt. Set by shell.
PS3	Select shell prompt. Set by shell.
PS4	Debugging prompt. Set by shell.
PWD	Current working directory. Set by shell.
RANDOM	A random number between 0 and 32767. Set by shell.
SECONDS	Number of seconds since log-in. Set by shell.
SHELL	Path to the desired shell. Set by login.
TERM	Sets the terminal type. Not set by default.
TMOUT	Idle time-out delay. Not set by default.
VISUAL	Command exit mode for editors. Not set by default.

These environment variables are available for every log-in session under the shell. For instance, if you open two window sessions on one system, the same list of environment variables is available to you in each window. If you change the value of an environment variable in one window, however, the new value affects only the shell in that window.

Setting an environment variable in one window does not set it for all windows.

The .login File and the Environment Variable

If you want to set an environment variable for all log-in sessions, you need to place the shell commands that perform this operation in the *.login* file in your home directory. This file is executed for each log-in session you initiate. Let's look at an example of using code in the *.login* file to set an environment variable:

Assume you are managing a large network of computers. As system administrator you may have to log in to 25 or more computer systems every day. With the standard shell prompt of *$* under the Bourne shell, or *%* under the C shell, it is very difficult to remember which system you are currently logged in on. Wouldn't it be handy to have the shell's command prompt give you the name of the system that you were logged in on?

By setting an environment variable you can customize your log-in prompt such that it informs you which system you are logged in on. Under the C shell, this variable is called *prompt*. Under the Bourne shell, this variable is called *PS1* (Prompt String 1). If you wish to see what the prompt is currently set to, you can issue the command **echo $prompt** under the C shell, or **echo $PS1** under the Bourne shell.

 NOTE: If you want the shell to print the value of a variable, you must preface the variable name with a dollar sign. Otherwise, the shell will echo the variable name string back to the terminal. For example, if you

had typed echo prompt to the C shell, you would have received the word prompt as the result.

In order to set the *prompt* variable to the system name, you need a way to identify the system name. Solaris provides a utility called **uname** which prints information about the system. If you use the **-n** flag with uname, the output is the host name of the system. Now all you need is a method to capture the output of uname -n and assign it to the correct variable (*prompt*, or *PS1*). The C shell language to perform this follows:

```
set prompt="'uname -n'"
```

To accomplish the same feat with the Bourne shell you would use the following shell command:

```
PS1="'uname -n'$ "
```

If your system uses a name such as *mercury.astro.com*, the output of the uname -n command would be *mercury.astro.com*. If you want to have the prompt tell you the machine name, and not the domain information, you could set the *prompt* variable with the following C shell command:

```
set prompt='uname -n| awk -F\. '{print $1}''
```

The **awk** command is a pattern matching utility which contains its own programming language. In this example, the awk command looks at the output of the uname command. The **-F\.** directive to awk tells it to use the period character as a word separator. The directive **{print $1}** tells awk to print out the first word of the input string (everything up to the first period in this case). This output is used as the "input" for the set directive. Therefore, the *prompt* variable gets set to the value returned by the awk command.

To accomplish the same task under the Bourne shell you could use the following:

```
PS1="'uname -n| awk -F\. '{print $1}''$ "
```

Using an Environment Variable to Reduce Restore Requests

One of the most common mistakes a user makes is accidentally overwriting existing files with inappropriate data. File restoration, in turn, becomes one of the most requested services of the system administrator. To restore the files from backup tapes may require up to several hours of sorting through tapes to find the correct file. At this point you should be asking yourself "Is there a way to minimize these restore requests?"

In many cases, files are overwritten because the user does not realize they already have a file by the same name. One method to avoid loss of files by overwriting is to have the system inform the user of the existing file before the old version is overwritten.

The C shell program provides an environment variable which compels the system to notify the user when s/he is about to "clobber" an existing file. The environment variable which triggers this function is called *NOCLOBBER*. When *NOCLOBBER* is true (set), the shell will inform the user about an attempt to overwrite an existing file with a new copy.

✔   **NOTE:** *NOCLOBBER works only in cases where the file will be overwritten due to redirection.*

Setting
NOCLOBBER
causes the system
to inform the user
of impending file
overwrite
operations.

```
┌──────────────────────── shelltool – /bin/csh ────────────────────────┐
│ ▼ │                                                                   │
│   │ mercury# ls -lsa passwd                                           │
│   │    8 -rw-r--r--    1 root      other         635 Nov 18 22:30 passwd │
│   │ mercury# who >passwd                                              │
│   │ mercury# ls -lsa                                                  │
│   │    8 -rw-r--r--    1 root      other          74 Nov 18 22:31 passwd │
│   │ mercury# set noclobber=1                                          │
│   │ # uptime >passwd                                                  │
│   │ passwd: File exists                                               │
│   │ mercury# ls -lsa passwd                                           │
│   │    8 -rw-r--r--    1 root      other          74 Nov 18 22:31 passwd │
│   │ mercury# logout                                                   │
│   │ # ■                                                               │
└───────────────────────────────────────────────────────────────────────┘
```

✗   **TIP:** *Some sites have resorted to more drastic means to reduce restore requests. These usually include modification of system binaries such that a copy of the file is placed in an on-line storage area for a set period of time. When users notice their mistake, utilities are provided which allow them to copy the original file back to their directories. One such scheme is the entomb mechanism developed at the Purdue University Computing Center (PUCC). Copies of this software are available for anonymous ftp from the machine cc.purdue.edu.*

Local Variables

A local variable is defined for your personal use. You may find that using local variables such as loop counters and character strings is very handy. For example, a shell variable that contains the version of a system's operating system could be helpful. The following code segment sets the *version* variable to tell you which version of the operating system you are using.

```
set version = 'uname -s -r'
```

You can determine the value of the version variable by typing **echo $version**.

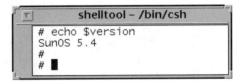

```
shelltool - /bin/csh
# echo $version
SunOS 5.4
#
#
```

As with the environment variable, a local variable is available to you only under the log-in shell in which it was created. In other words, if you have two log-in sessions on one host, and you create a local variable under one of the log-in sessions, this variable will not be available to you under the other log-in session.

```
shelltool - /bin/csh
# date
Fri Nov 18 22:22:10 EST 1994
# echo $i

# i=1024
# echo $i
1024
# date
Fri Nov 18 22:23:34 EST 1994
#
#
```

```
shelltool - /bin/csh
Fri Nov 18 22:22:40 EST 1994
# echo $i

# echo $i

# date
Fri Nov 18 22:24:04 EST 1994
#
#
```

If you want to set a local variable for all log-in sessions, you need to place the shell commands that perform this operation in the *.login* file in your home directory. This file is executed for each log-in session you initiate.

TIP: You may also use local variables in conjunction with other shell programming features. Examples of the use of local variables will be evident in many of the following sections.

Using Quotation Marks in Scripts

You may have noticed the use of quotation marks and backslashes in some of the previous examples. These quotes are required because the shell interprets some characters differently than you might expect. The following characters, known as *metacharacters*, have a special meaning to the shell programs: $, ^, ;, &, { }, [ ], ', ', ", *, ( ), |, ^, <, >, newline space, and <Tab>.

In order to pass these characters on to commands, they must be "quoted" or "escaped" when used as part of a command.

Quoting and Escaping Metacharacters

Quoting or escaping a metacharacter causes the shell to alter its interpretation of the character. There are several ways to quote or escape a metacharacter. Before you learn what the special characters mean, you need to learn how to change their meanings.

The easiest way to tell the shell not to use special interpretations of characters is to precede the character by a backslash (\). This is referred to as *escaping* the character.

Using a backslash to escape a character.

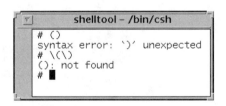

```
           shelltool – /bin/csh
 # ()
 syntax error: ')' unexpected
 # \(\)
 (): not found
 #
```

The single quote (') will protect text from *ANY* substitution. Backslashes, wildcards, double quotes, variables, and command substitution are ignored when enclosed in single quotes. The following rules apply when using single quotations:

❑ Only a single quote can end a single quoted string.

❑ Single quoted strings can span multiple lines.

❑ It is not possible to write a single quote in single-quoted text.

Using single quotes in the shell.

When the shell encounters commands surrounded by back quotes ('), it performs command substitution. The commands inside the back quotes are executed, and the result is substituted in place of the back-quoted command. For example, the command **set prompt="'uname -n'"** causes the shell to execute the **uname -n** command. The result of this command is a string that gives the name of the system. This string is used as the "input" for the **set** command, resulting in the *prompt* variable being set to the string which gives the name of the machine.

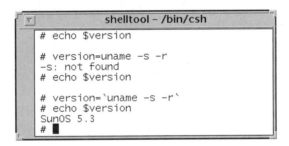

Using back quotes in the shell.

Yet another method of quoting in shell scripts is to use the double quotes ("). The following rules apply to the use of double quotes:

❑ Use the double quotes to protect text from wild card substitution.

❑ The shell removes the quotation marks and passes the string to subsequent commands.

❑ Variable replacement, command substitution, and backslashes are effective inside the double quotes.

❑ To write a double quote (") inside double quotes, it must be escaped by preceding them with a backslash (e.g., "this \ "escapes\ " the double quotes").

❑ Single quotes will be treated as text inside the double quotes.

❑ Quoted text can span multiple lines.

Using double quotes in the shell.

```
                    shelltool - /bin/csh
 # grep this is a test /etc/passwd
 grep: can't open is
 grep: can't open a
 grep: can't open test
 # grep "this is a test" /etc/passwd
 #
```

Redirection Metacharacters

The shell programs allow the user to redirect the input and output streams to programs. The following metacharacters are used to invoke this input/output redirection.

The left angle bracket (<) character causes the shell to take the following word as the name of the input file. This is referred to as input redirection. The following rules apply when using input redirection:

❑ < *file* causes the shell to read its input from *file.*

❑ <&*n* causes the shell to read its input from the file descriptor *n.*

❑ <&- causes the shell to close the standard input file.

❑ <*ag* causes the shell to read up to the line starting with *tag.*

❑ <*ag* causes the shell to read up to the line starting with *tag* while discarding leading white space.

The right angle bracket (>) causes the shell to take the following word as the name of the output file. This is referred to as *output redirection.* The following rules apply when using output redirection:

❑ > *file* causes the shell to write the output to *file.*

❑ >&*n* causes the shell to write the output to the file descriptor *n.*

❑ >&- causes the shell to close the standard output file.

❑ >> *file* causes the shell to append the output to *file.*

❑ | is the pipe character. This character informs the shell to take the output of one command, and "pipe" it into the input of the next command.

```
┌─────────────────────────────────────────────────────────────────────┐
│▽                        shelltool – /bin/csh                          │
├─────────────────────────────────────────────────────────────────────┤
│ # ls -lsa                                                             │
│ total 66                                                              │
│       2 drwxr-xr-x    4 curt      nobody      512 Nov 18 22:58 .      │
│       2 drwxr-xr-x   17 curt      nobody      512 Oct 18 20:25 ..     │
│       2 drwxr-xr-x    2 curt      nobody      512 Nov 18 22:56 figs   │
│       2 drwxr-xr-x    2 curt      nobody      512 Oct  4 20:53 info   │
│      58 -rwxrwxrwx    1 curt      nobody    28917 Nov  7 22:18 sach23.txt │
│ # fmt -s <sach23.txt |spell >spout                                    │
│ # ls -lsa                                                             │
│ total 68                                                              │
│       2 drwxr-xr-x    4 curt      nobody      512 Nov 18 22:59 .      │
│       2 drwxr-xr-x   17 curt      nobody      512 Oct 18 20:25 ..     │
│       2 drwxr-xr-x    2 curt      nobody      512 Nov 18 22:56 figs   │
│       2 drwxr-xr-x    2 curt      nobody      512 Oct  4 20:53 info   │
│      58 -rwxrwxrwx    1 curt      nobody    28917 Nov  7 22:18 sach23.txt │
│       2 -rw-r--r--    1 root      other       529 Nov 18 22:59 spout  │
│ # █                                                                   │
└─────────────────────────────────────────────────────────────────────┘
```

Using input and output redirection in the shell.

Other Metacharacters

The other metacharacters do not fit nicely into a particular group. Nonetheless, they are important characters, and should be examined.

The space character is considered "white space." White space is used as a delimiter for commands and strings in shell programming.

The <Tab> character is another "white space" character.

The newline character signifies the end of a line of input. It is typically used to signify the end of a command.

The tilde (~) is a C shell metacharacter. It refers to the user's home directory. For example, ~ls shaun would list the contents of shaun's home directory.

The caret (^) is used as the delimiter in C shell command substitutions.

The dollar sign ($) is used as a prefix for local and environment variables under the shells.

The ampersand character (&) tells the shell to run this job in the background. Commands are normally run in the foreground. This means that the terminal (or window) is not available for other uses until the command completes its execution. When a job is running in the background, the terminal is free for other activity.

The asterisk (*) is a wildcard character. The asterisk matches any string.

The question mark (?) is another wildcard character. It matches any single character.

The [...] construct is another form of wildcard substitution. The pattern will match one character in the input stream, but the matched character can be any of the characters enclosed in the brackets. For instance, *rm file.[ot]* will remove any *file.o* and *file.t* files in the current directory.

```
                          shelltool - /bin/csh
# ls -lsa
total 472
     2 drwxr-xr-x    4 curt      nobody       512 Nov 18 23:03 .
     2 drwxr-xr-x   17 curt      nobody       512 Oct 18 20:25 ..
     2 drwxr-xr-x    2 curt      nobody       512 Nov 18 22:59 figs
     2 drwxr-xr-x    2 curt      nobody       512 Oct  4 20:53 info
    58 -rwxrwxrwx    1 curt      nobody     28917 Nov 18 23:01 sach23.1xt
    58 -rwxrwxrwx    1 curt      nobody     28917 Nov 18 23:01 sach23.3xt
    58 -rwxrwxrwx    1 curt      nobody     28917 Nov 18 23:01 sach23.axt
    58 -rwxrwxrwx    1 curt      nobody     28917 Nov 18 23:01 sach23.cxt
    58 -rwxrwxrwx    1 curt      nobody     28917 Nov 18 23:01 sach23.ext
    58 -rwxrwxrwx    1 curt      nobody     28917 Nov 18 23:01 sach23.fxt
    58 -rwxrwxrwx    1 curt      nobody     28917 Nov 18 23:01 sach23.gxt
    58 -rwxrwxrwx    1 curt      nobody     28917 Nov  7 22:18 sach23.txt
# ls -lsa sach23.[a-z]xt
    58 -rwxrwxrwx    1 curt      nobody     28917 Nov 18 23:01 sach23.axt
    58 -rwxrwxrwx    1 curt      nobody     28917 Nov 18 23:01 sach23.cxt
    58 -rwxrwxrwx    1 curt      nobody     28917 Nov 18 23:01 sach23.ext
    58 -rwxrwxrwx    1 curt      nobody     28917 Nov 18 23:01 sach23.fxt
    58 -rwxrwxrwx    1 curt      nobody     28917 Nov 18 23:01 sach23.gxt
    58 -rwxrwxrwx    1 curt      nobody     28917 Nov  7 22:18 sach23.txt
# ▮
```

Using wildcard substitution in the shell.

The curly bracket characters ({ }) are operators when appearing by themselves. When embedded in a word, or when used as a command argument, they are treated as text. When used to enclose other text, the brackets are used to preserve operator priority rules.

The parentheses characters, ( ), are used to group commands much like the braces. Differences between the curly brackets and the parentheses follow:

❏ Parentheses do not require leading white space.

❏ Commands enclosed in parentheses are executed by a sub-shell, and hence cannot alter the execution environment of the current shell.

```
                          shelltool - /bin/csh
# find /home -name xxx -o -name spout -print
# find /home \( -name xxx -o -name spout \) -print
/home/curt/book/ch05/fig/xxx
/home/curt/book/fig/ch3/xxx
/home/curt/bin/term/xxx
/home/curt/xxx
/home/shaun/xxx
#
#
# ▮
```

Using grouping metacharacters in the shell.

The semi-colon (;) is a command separator in the shell.

The colon character (:) is a null command to the shell.

The pound sign (#) is recognized as a comment when found at the beginning of a word.

The which Statement

The **which** statement or command is a very useful C shell script program. It determines which program will be executed when you type the name of a program. For instance, if a user has a program named *hello*, and there was a system program named *hello*, which program would be executed when the user types the following?

```
% hello
```

The **which** command consults the user's *.cshrc* file, and searches the *path* environment variable to determine which binary occurs first in the search path. Due to the shell's traversal of the search path, the command that is executed will always be the first occurrence of that command in the search path.

If a user is having problems with a particular utility from her/his account, it is often useful to have the user log in and type the following to determine the path to the binary:

```
% which name_of_utility_here
```

In many cases, you will discover that the user has aliased this utility to some other function, or that the user has a personal program named the same as this utility.

Using which to determine the version of sh that the user is running.

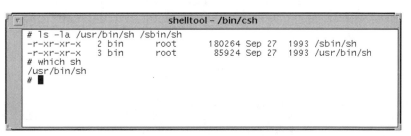

As previously mentioned, statically linked copies of some Solaris utilities are in the */sbin* directory. These commands are provided so that the super-user can log in and perform certain duties even if dynamic libraries are not available. Sometimes it is useful to know which version of a binary you are running. To determine which of the shell programs you are using when logged in as the super-user, issue the following command:

```
# which sh
```

The foreach Directive

Another very useful construct in the C shell is the **foreach** directive. This directive tells the·C-shell to perform a list of instructions for each element in the argument list. The syntax of the **foreach** command follows:

```
foreach local_variable (argument_list)
list of functions to perform
end
```

A roughly similar construct under the Bourne shell uses the **for** statement. The syntax of the **for** statement follows:

```
for local_variable
in argument_list
do
list of functions to perform
done
```

How could you use the **foreach** or **for** statement to simplify systems administration tasks? Let's suppose you have a large network containing many machines under your administration. How would you determine the operation status of each machine on the network? One way would be to make a list of all of the machine names, and then log in to each machine to ensure that it is up and running.

A simpler method to accomplish the same goal would be to use a **foreach** loop to check the machines for you.

Using a foreach loop to determine machine status.

```
shelltool – /bin/csh
mercury# foreach i (glenn gus alan)
? echo -n "$i : "
? rsh $i uptime
? end
glenn : 11:15am  up  2:59,  4 users,  load average: 1.07, 0.64, 0.35
gus : 11:15am  up  3:22,  1 user,  load average: 0.07, 0.04, 0.05
alan : 11:15am  up  3:59,  2 users,  load average: 0.09, 0.03, 0.02
mercury# logout
#
# 
```

Next question: how would you collect all files required for a project so that you could make an archive (or distribution) tape? This becomes a messy proposition if several people have worked on the project, and the source and data files are spread across many file systems and system or user directories.

One way to do this would be to ask the users to copy the files to one central location, and then make an archive tape of all the information. An easier way would be to develop the list of files which require archiving, and then use a **for** loop to archive the files.

Using a for loop to collect and archive a list of files.

```
                         shelltool – /bin/csh
# cat >/tmp/filelist
./home/jimmy/src/project
./var/src/jimmy/project
./opt/jimmy/project
./corp/data/jimmy/proj_data
# for i
> in `cat /tmp/filelist`
do
tar cvf /dev/rmt/0n $i
done
#
a ./home/jimmy/src/project 2 tape blocks
a ./home/jimmy/src/project/proj.c 143 tape blocks
a ./home/jimmy/src/project/proj.h 3 tape blocks
a ./home/jimmy/src/project/utils.c 256 tape blocks
a ./home/jimmy/src/project/menus.c 267 tape blocks
a ./home/jimmy/src/project/Makefile 280 tape blocks
a ./var/jimmy/project 2 tape blocks
a ./var/jimmy/project/audit_trail 268 tape blocks
a ./opt/jimmy/project/project 143 tape blocks
a ./corp/data/jimmy 2 tape blocks
a ./corp/data/jimmy/proj_data 22329 tape blocks
#
# █
```

Using Conditional Statements

The shell programs also allow the use of conditional execution statements. These statements allow you to modify the actions of your shell scripts based on the results of a test on some argument or variable. Conditional statements test the value of some operation, and if the result of the test is true, a particular action is taken. If the result of the test is not true, another action may be taken.

The if Conditional

One of the simple conditional statements available in the shell is the **if** statement. As seen below, this statement operates in the shell much as the if statement in high-level languages such as C or Fortran.

```
If (condition is true)
 Do this
else
 Do that
endif
```

The C-shell if expression uses flags to direct the "test" of the condition. Some of the more useful flags appear in the following table.

Most Frequently Used C-shell Expression Flags

Flag	Result
-r filename	True if user has read permission on file.
-w filename	True if user has write permission on file.
-x filename	True if user has execute permission on file.
-e filename	True if file exists.
-o filename	True if user owns file.
-z filename	True if file is empty.
-f filename	True if file is a plain file.
-d filename	True if file is a directory.

Example of the if Conditional

Let's look at an example of the **if** conditional under Solaris. In the example, you would like to know which version of Solaris you are using. You would like to set up your environment correctly for each version of Solaris available on your network. The **uname** utility can tell you the version of the operating system for your system. Now all you have to do is locate the uname utility, execute uname, and examine the results.

The following code segment tests to determine where an executable version of the uname utility is installed. Once the utility is located, the variable *version* is set to tell you which version of the operating system you are using.

```
if ( -x /usr/5bin/uname ) then
set version = '/usr/5bin/uname -s -r'
else if ( -x /usr/bin/uname) then
set version = '/usr/bin/uname -s -r'
else
set version = '/bin/uname -s -r'
endif
```

In the next section we examine code that uses the *version* variable to perform the environment customization you desire.

The switch Conditional

Another useful conditional statement available in the C-shell is the **switch** statement. The switch statement can be used to replace an if-then-else conditional in a shell script. The switch statement allows you more flexibility in the value matching process than is afforded by the if statement. Therefore, the switch statement is a very popular conditional statement. The syntax of the switch statement follows:

```
switch (variable)
case value
list of actions to perform
breaksw
case value
list of actions to perform
breaksw

. . .

endsw
```

The shell checks the value of *variable*. It compares this value to the value in the first case statement. If the values are equivalent, the list of actions between the words *case* and **breaksw** is performed. Once those statements are completed, the shell exits the switch and resumes execution at the statement following **endsw**.

If the two values were not equivalent, the value of *variable* is compared for equivalence with the value in the next case statement, and so on.

The endsw statement tells the shell that there are no more values to compare which causes the shell to exit the switch statement, and continue execution at the statement following endsw.

An Example of the switch Statement in Action

The following code segment looks at the value of the *version* variable set in the previous section. Depending on the value of the *version* variable, you can have your *.login* file customize the environment for the operating system.

```
switch ( "$version" )
case "SunOS 5.?":
# place code here to customize the Solaris 2 environment
```

```
set path=( /usr/sbin $HOME/bin /usr/local/bin /usr/local/etc
/usr/bin /usr/opt/bin /sbin . )
setenv MANPATH /usr/man:/usr/local/man
setenv LPDEST myprinter
breaksw
case "SunOS 4.1.?":
# place code here to customize the SunOS 4.1.X environment
setenv PATH
:/bin:/usr/local/bin:/usr/opt/bin:/etc:/usr/local:/usr/ucb:/usr/bin:/
usr/new:/usr/etc:/usr/openwin/bin
setenv PS2 ".> "
set prompt="'uname -n'%"
set history=100
umask 0077
set notify
breaksw
case "HP-UX A.09.01"
# place code here to customize the HPUX environment
set cpu = 'hostname | awk '{FS = "."; print $1}''
set prompt="$cpu> "
setenv PAGER /usr/bin/more
breaksw
endsw
```

Summary

In this chapter, we briefly examined a few ways to automate some of the more mundane system administration tasks. We covered the **cron** command, the **find** command, and selected built-in functions of the Bourne and C shells. Examples of ways to cascade these constructs to develop useful administration tools were presented.

We hope that this text becomes a handy reference for beginning and experienced Solaris system administrators. We also hope that the readers enjoyed reading and learning about the topic of Solaris system administration as much as we have enjoyed producing this reference.

Index

More
OnWord Press Titles

Pro/ENGINEER and Pro/JR. Books

INSIDE Pro/ENGINEER
Book $49.95 Includes Disk

**Pro/ENGINEER Quick Reference,
2d ed.**
Book $24.95

Pro/ENGINEER Exercise Book
Book $39.95 Includes Disk

Thinking Pro/ENGINEER
Book $49.95

INSIDE Pro/JR.
Book $49.95

Interleaf Books

INSIDE Interleaf
Book $49.95 Includes Disk

Adventurer's Guide to Interleaf Lisp
Book $49.95 Includes Disk

The Interleaf Exercise Book
Book $39.95 Includes Disk

The Interleaf Quick Reference
Book $24.95

Interleaf Tips and Tricks
Book $49.95 Includes Disk

MicroStation Books

INSIDE MicroStation 5X, 3d ed.
Book $34.95 Includes Disk

MicroStation Reference Guide 5.X
Book $18.95

MicroStation Exercise Book 5.X
Book $34.95
Optional Instructor's Guide $14.95

MicroStation 5.X Delta Book
Book $19.95

**MicroStation for AutoCAD Users , 2d
ed.**
Book $34.95

Adventures in MicroStation 3D
Book 49.95 Includes Disk

MicroStation Productivity Book
Book $39.95
Optional Disk $49.95

MicroStation Bible
Book $49.95
Optional Disks $49.95

Build Cell
Software $69.95

101 MDL Commands
Book $49.95
Optional Executable Disk $101.00
Optional Source Disks (6) $259.95

101 User Commands
Book $49.95
Optional Disk $101.00

Bill Steinbock's Pocket MDL Programmer's Guide
Book $24.95

Managing and Networking MicroStation
Book $29.95
Optional Disk $29.95

The MicroStation Database Book
Book $29.95
Optional Disk $29.95

INSIDE I/RAS B
Book $24.95 Includes Disk

The CLIX Workstation User's Guide
Book $34.95 Includes Disk

Windows NT

Windows NT for the Technical Professional
Book $39.95

SunSoft Solaris Series

The SunSoft Solaris 2.* User's Guide
Book $29.95 Includes Disk

SunSoft Solaris 2.* for Managers and Administrators
Book $34.95

The SunSoft Solaris 2.* Quick Reference
Book $18.95

Five Steps to SunSoft Solaris 2.*
Book $24.95 Includes Disk

One Minute SunSoft Solaris Manager
Book $14.95

SunSoft Solaris 2.* for Windows Users
Book $24.95

The Hewlett Packard HP-UX Series

The HP-UX User's Guide
Book $29.95 Includes Disk

The HP-UX Quick Reference
Book $18.95

Five Steps to HP-UX
Book $24.95 Includes Disk

One Minute HP-UX Manager
Book $14.95

CAD Management

One Minute CAD Manager
Book $14.95

Manager's Guide to Computer-Aided Engineering
Book $49.95

Other CAD

CAD and the Practice of Architecture: ASG Solutions
Book $39.95 Includes Disk

INSIDE CADVANCE
Book $34.95 Includes Disk

Using Drafix Windows CAD
Book $34.95 Includes Disk

Fallingwater in 3D Studio: A Case Study and Tutorial
Book $39.95 Includes Disk

Geographic Information Systems/ESRI

The GIS Book, 3d ed.
Book $34.95

INSIDE ARC/INFO
Book $74.95 Includes CD

ARC/INFO Quick Reference
Book $24.95

ArcView Developer's Guide
Book $49.95

INSIDE ArcView
Book $39.95 Includes CD

DTP/CAD Clip Art

1001 DTP/CAD Symbols Clip Art Library: Architectural
Book $29.95

**DISK FORMATS:
MicroStation**
DGN Disk $175.00
Book/Disk $195.00

AutoCAD
DWG Disk $175.00
Book/Disk $195.00

CAD/DTP
DXF Disk $195.00
Book/Disk $225.00

OnWord Press Distribution

End Users/User Groups/Corporate Sales

OnWord Press books are available worldwide to end users, user groups, and corporate accounts from your local bookseller or computer/software dealer, or from HMP Direct/Softstore: call 1-800-223-6397 or 505-473-5454; fax 505-471-4424; write to High Mountain Press Direct/Softstore, 2530 Camino Entrada, Santa Fe, NM 87505-8435, or e-mail to ORDERS@BOOKSTORE.HMP.COM.

Wholesale, Including Overseas Distribution

High Mountain Press distributes OnWord Press books internationally. For terms call 1-800-4-ONWORD or 505-473-5454; fax to 505-471-4424; e-mail to ORDERS@IPG.HMP.COM; or write to High Mountain Press/IPG, 2530 Camino Entrada, Santa Fe, NM 87505-8435, USA. Outside North America, call 505-471-4243.

Comments and Corrections

Your comments can help us make better products. If you find an error in our products, or have any other comments, positive or negative, we'd like to know! Please write to us at the address below or contact our e-mail address: READERS@HMP.COM.

OnWord Press
2530 Camino Entrada, Santa Fe, NM 87505-8435 USA